February 27 1697

Shelly,

Thank you for your
kindness and understanding —

Beth Bennington

WEBSTER'S CONCISE
WORLD
ATLAS

WEBSTER'S CONCISE

WORLD
ATLAS

**BARNES
&NOBLE**
B O O K S
NEW YORK

This edition published by Barnes & Noble, Inc. by arrangement
with De Agostini Editions Limited, Griffin House,
161 Hammersmith Road, London W6 8SD

1995 Barnes & Noble Books

Printed in the EU, Officine Grafiche De Agostini - Novara 1995

10 9 8 7 6 5 4 3 2

ISBN 1-56619-874-7

CONTENTS

WORLD: Key to map pages

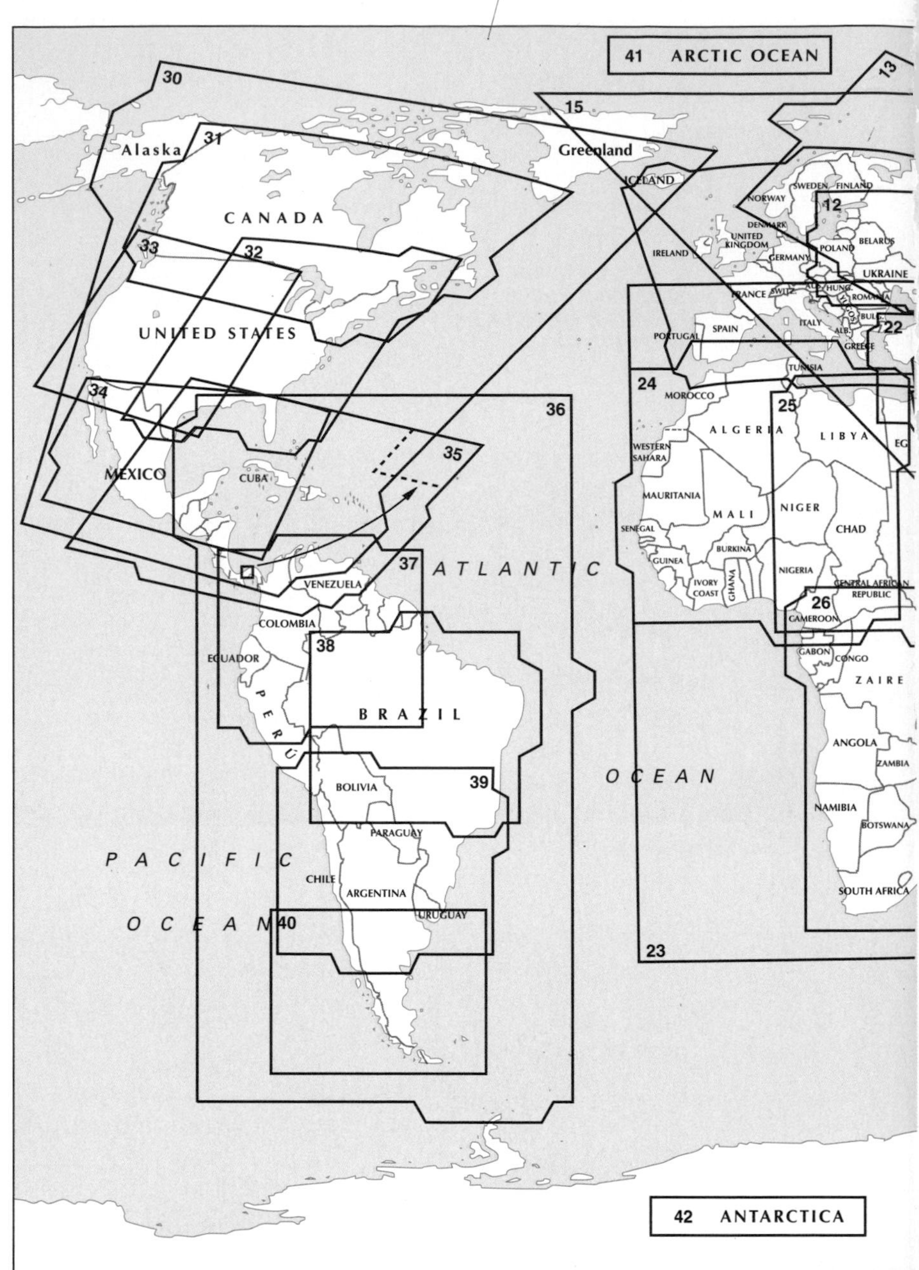

41   ARCTIC OCEAN

30

15

Alaska 31   Greenland

13

ICELAND

C A N A D A

NORWAY   SWEDEN FINLAND

12

33   32

DENMARK
UNITED
KINGDOM   GERMANY POLAND   BELARUS

IRELAND

UKRAINE

FRANCE SWITZ. HUNG. ROMANIA

U N I T E D   S T A T E S

PORTUGAL   SPAIN   ITALY   ALB. BUL.

22

34

GREECE

TUNISIA

36

24   MOROCCO

35   MEXICO   CUBA

25

ALGERIA   LIBYA   EG

WESTERN
SAHARA

MAURITANIA   MALI   NIGER   CHAD

SENEGAL   BURKINA
GUINEA   NIGERIA
IVORY
COAST   GHANA   CENTRAL AFRICAN
                              REPUBLIC
                    CAMEROON

37   A T L A N T I C

VENEZUELA

COLOMBIA

38

26

ECUADOR

GABON   CONGO   Z A I R E

P
E
R
U

B R A Z I L

BOLIVIA   39

ANGOLA   ZAMBIA

O C E A N

PARAGUAY

NAMIBIA   BOTSWANA

P A C I F I C

CHILE   ARGENTINA

SOUTH AFRICA

O C E A N   40   URUGUAY

23

42   ANTARCTICA

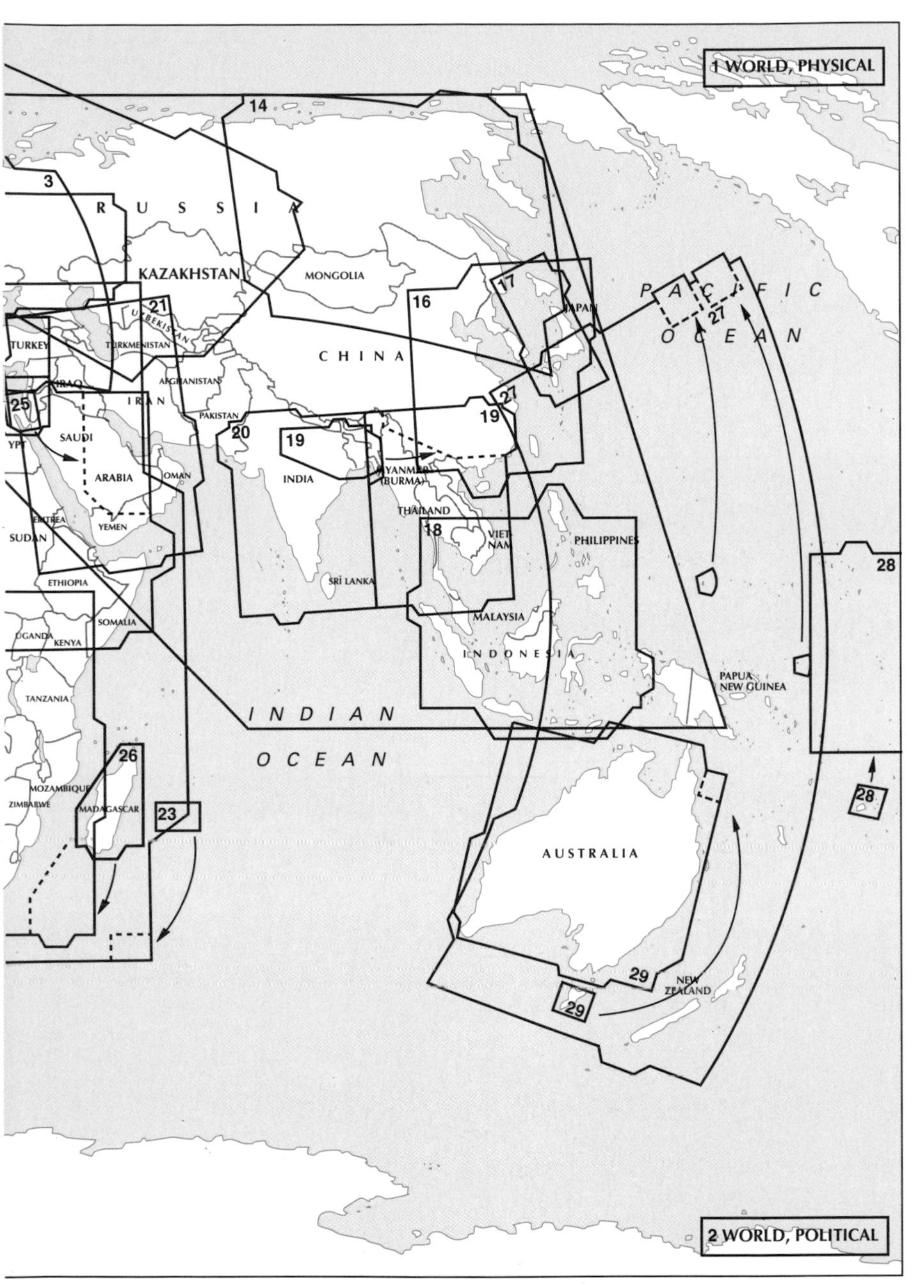

1 WORLD, PHYSICAL

14

3

R U S S I A

KAZAKHSTAN

MONGOLIA

17

16

JAPAN

27

UZBEKISTAN

21

P A C I F I C

O C E A N

TURKEY

TURKMENISTAN

C H I N A

IRAQ

25

IRAN

AFGHANISTAN

YP

SAUDI

PAKISTAN

20

19

27

19

ARABIA

OMAN

INDIA

MYANMAR (BURMA)

ERITREA

YEMEN

SUDAN

THAILAND

18

ETHIOPIA

SRI LANKA

VIET NAM

PHILIPPINES

28

UGANDA

KENYA

SOMALIA

MALAYSIA

TANZANIA

I N D O N E S I A

PAPUA NEW GUINEA

I N D I A N

O C E A N

26

MOZAMBIQUE

ZIMBABWE

MADAGASCAR

23

28

A U S T R A L I A

29

NEW ZEALAND

29

EUROPE: Key to map pages

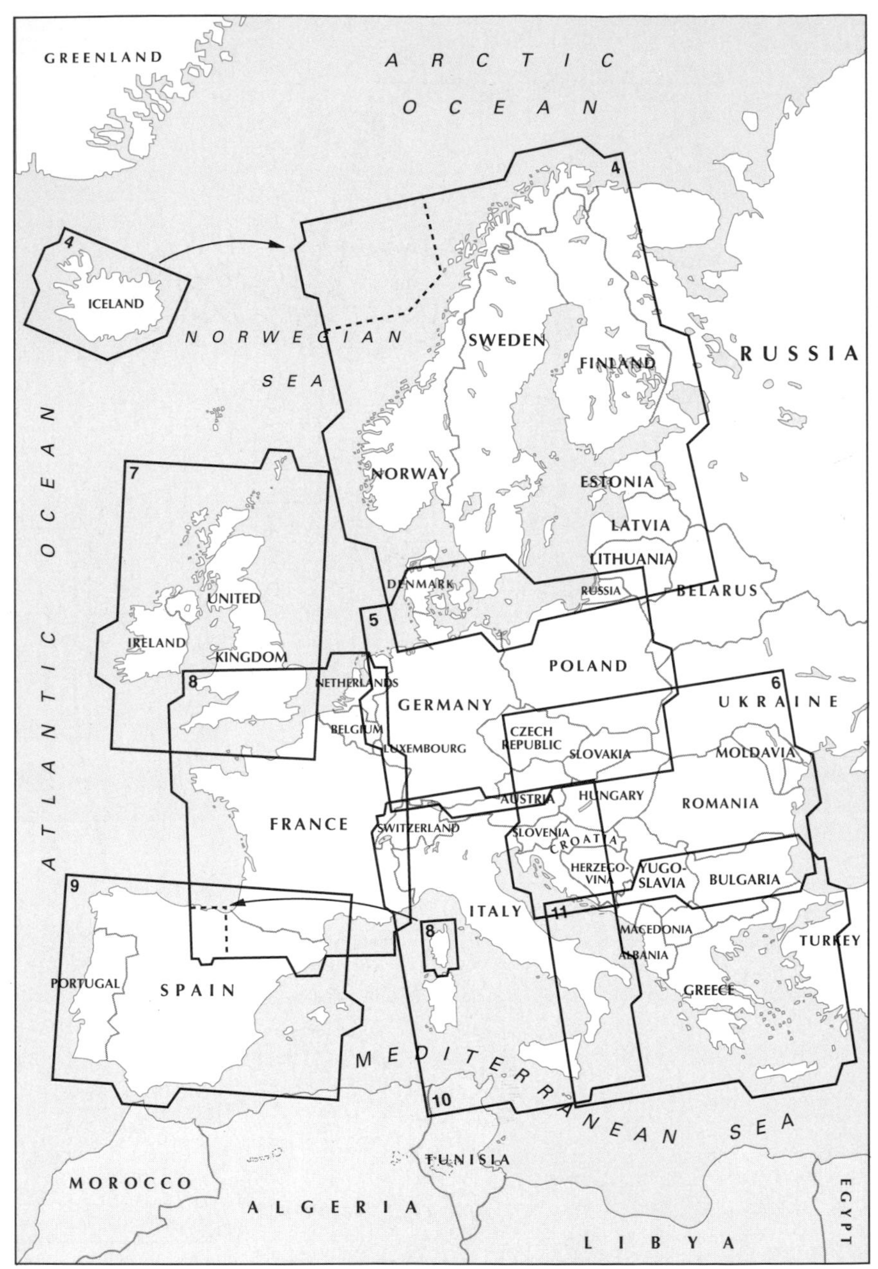

GREENLAND

A R C T I C

O C E A N

4

ICELAND

N O R W E G I A N

S E A

SWEDEN

FINLAND

R U S S I A

7

NORWAY

ESTONIA

LATVIA

LITHUANIA

DENMARK

RUSSIA

BELARUS

UNITED

5

IRELAND

KINGDOM

8

POLAND

6

NETHERLANDS

GERMANY

U K R A I N E

BELGIUM

CZECH
REPUBLIC

SLOVAKIA

MOLDAVIA

LUXEMBOURG

AUSTRIA

HUNGARY

ROMANIA

FRANCE

SWITZERLAND

SLOVENIA

CROATIA

9

HERZEGO-
VINA

YUGO-
SLAVIA

BULGARIA

ITALY

11

MACEDONIA

TURKEY

PORTUGAL

SPAIN

8

ALBANIA

GREECE

M E D I T E R R A N E A N   S E A

10

MOROCCO

TUNISIA

ALGERIA

LIBYA

EGYPT

A T L A N T I C   O C E A N

© ISTITUTO GEOGRAFICO DE AGOSTINI S. p. A. - NOVARA

A GEOGRAPHICAL DICTIONARY OF COUNTRIES, CONTINENT BY CONTINENT

STATE (official name/ English translation)	CAPITAL ① inhabitants	AREA (sq km)	POPULATION	DENSITY (inhab/sq km)	LIFE EXPECT-ANCY (in years) M	F
ALBANIA (Republika e Shqipërisë/ Republic of Albania)	Tirana (Tiranë) 243 000	28 748	3 256 000	113	69.6	75.5
ANDORRA (Principat d'Andorra/ Principauté d'Andorre/ Principality of Andorra)	Andorra la Vella (Andorre-la-Vieille) 15 600	453	52 000	115	74.0	81.0
AUSTRIA (Republik Österreich/ Republic of Austria)	Vienna (Wien) 1 533 000	83 859	7 712 000	92	72.1	78.8
BELGIUM (Koninkrijk België/ Royaume de Belgique/ Kingdom of Belgium)	Brussels (Brussel/Bruxelles) 960 000	30 518	9 950 000	326	70.0	76.8
BOSNIA-HERZEGOVINA (Republika Bosnia i Hercegovina)	Sarajevo 526 000	51 129	4 350 000	85	68.0	73.0
BULGARIA (Republika Bulgarija/ Republic of Bulgaria)	Sofia (Sofiya) 1 221 000	110 994	8 990 000	81	68.3	74.7
CROATIA (Republika Hrvatska/ Republic of Croatia)	Zagreb 763 000	56 538	4 750 000	84	67.0	74.0
CZECH REPUBLIC (Ceská Republika)	Prague (Praha) 1 212 000	78 864	10 365 000	131	68.1	75.4
DENMARK (Kongeriget Danmark/ Kingdom of Denmark)	Copenhagen (København) 467 000	43 093	5 140 000	119	71.9	77.7
ESTONIA (Eesti Vabariik/ Republic of Estonia)	Tallinn 484 000	45 100	1 578 000	35	65.8	75.0
FINLAND (Suomen Tasavalta/ Republiken Finland/ Republic of Finland)	Helsinki (Helsingfors) 491 000	338 145	4 986 000	15	70.7	78.7
FRANCE (République Française/ French Republic)	Paris 2 152 000	543 965	56 600 000	104	72.7	80.9
GERMANY (Bundesrepublik Deutschland/Federal Republic of Germany)	Berlin 3 410 000	356 957	79 479 000	223	72.2	78.7

GROSS NATIONAL PRODUCT ②	LANGUAGES	RELIGIONS	ECONOMY
740	Albanian (Gheg and Tosc [off.])	Muslim 70%; Orthodox 20%	**Economy** Mainly agriculture (cereals, potatoes, sugar beet, olives, fruit), animal farming and industry (food processing, textile and tobacco production, building materials). **Mineral resources** Substantial reserves of chromite and petroleum.
17 600	Catalan (off.); Spanish; French	Catholic	**Economy** As a free-trade (duty-free) zone, considerable income is generated by tourism, trade and banking. **Agriculture** Another main economic activity. Cattle and pigs are the chief livestock, cereals, potatoes and tobacco the principal crops.
17 360	German	Catholic 84%; Protestant 6%	**Industry** Dominates the economy (mechanical, chemical, wood, paper, textile and food production). Tourism is thriving. **Mineral resources** Iron, magnesite, petroleum, lignite, lead. **Agriculture** Almost self-sufficient (cereals, sugar beet).
16 390	Flemish; French	Catholic	**Economy** Relies mainly on manufacturing. Brussels profits from being the HQ of the EC. **Agriculture** Main crops: cereals, potatoes, beet. Dairy farming is thriving. **Industry** Coal mining and the production of machinery, textiles, chemicals, food, diamonds.
1 741	Serbo-Croat	Muslim; Christian	**Economy** Based on agriculture (cereals, tobacco, fruit) and animal farming. **Mineral resources** Copper, lead, zinc, gold and iron. **Industry** Mechanical, electronics, chemical, textile and food industries.
2 320	Bulgarian	Orthodox 80%; Muslim 13%	**Economy** Essentially agricultural (cereals, potatoes, beet, vines, tobacco). Roses are traditionally grown too. **Mineral resources** Coal, iron, copper, lead and zinc. **Industry** The food, mechanical and electronic sectors are well established.
3 226	Croat	Catholic 76%; Orthodox 11%	**Agriculture** Principal crops: cereals, potatoes, beet, vines, olives. Animal farming is productive. **Principal resources** Timber from the large forests, coal, bauxite, hydrocarbons. **Industry** Mechanical, chemical, food, textiles and wood.
7 200	Czech	Catholic	**Economy** Dominated by heavy industry, although the country has profited from its considerable timber and coal reserves. **Agriculture** Cereals, hops and beet are cultivated widely. **Industry** Food, textile, mechanical and chemicals.
20 510	Danish	Protestant	**Agriculture** Animal farming (dairy products, meat) is important to domestic and export markets. Also fishing and arable farming (cereals, potatoes, sugar beet). **Industry** Primarily food, mechanical, chemical and ceramic production.
5 849	Estonian	Lutheran	**Economy** Dominated by agriculture (cereals, potatoes, animal fodder crops), animal farming (pigs, cattle), forestry and mineral resources (bituminous shale, phosphorites, peat). **Industry** Food processing, wood- and metalworking.
22 060	Finnish; Swedish	Protestant	**Economy** Dense forestation provides great quantities of timber, much for export, the rest for wood and paper factories. **Agriculture** Dairy farming and fishing are significant. **Industry** Metalworking, shipbuilding and food processing.
17 830	French	Catholic	**Agriculture** Extensive fishing, arable (cereals, potatoes, beet, grapes for wine) and animal farming. **Principal resources** Coal, petrol, natural gas, timber. **Industry** Food, machinery, vehicles, chemicals, electronics, textiles, fashion, rubber.
20 750	German	Protestant 41%; Catholic 41%	**Economy** Very strong, notably industry (metals, mechanical, chemicals, electronics) and services. **Agriculture** Main crops: potatoes, cereals, beet, hops for brewing. Animal farming. **Mineral resources** Coal, lignite, potassium salts.

STATE (official name/ English translation)	CAPITAL ① inhabitants	AREA (sq km)	POPULATION	DENSITY (inhab/sq km)	LIFE EXPECT-ANCY (in years) M F
GREECE (Ellinikí Dimokratía/ Hellenic Republic)	Athens (Athínai) 885 000	131 957	10 123 000	77	72.2 76.4
HUNGARY (Magyar Köztársaság/ Hungarian Republic)	Budapest 2 016 000	93 033	10 364 000	111	65.4 73.8
ICELAND (Lyðveldið Ísland/ Republic of Iceland)	Reykjavík 96 700	102 819	255 000	2	75.7 80.3
IRELAND (Poblacht na h'Éireann/ Republic of Ireland)	Dublin (Baile Átha Cliath) 503 000	70 283	3 503 000	50	71.0 76.7
ITALY (Repubblica Italiana/ Republic of Italy)	Rome (Roma) 2 693 000	301 302	56 800 000	187	73.2 79.7
LATVIA (Latvija)	Riga 916 000	64 500	2 683 000	41	64.2 74.6
LIECHTENSTEIN (Fürstentum Liechtenstein/ Principality of Liechtenstein)	Vaduz 4 900	160	29 000	181	66.1 72.9
LITHUANIA (Lietuva)	Vilnius 582 000	65 200	3 725 000	57	66.9 76.3
LUXEMBOURG (Grand-Duché de Luxembourg/Grand Duchy of Luxembourg)	Luxembourg 76 000	2 586	381 000	147	70.6 77.9
MACEDONIA (Republika Makedonija)	Skopje 406 000	25 713	2 030 000	79	68.0 72.0
MALTA (Republic of Malta/ Repubblika ta' Malta)	Valletta 9 200	316	354 000	1120	73.8 78.0
MONACO (Principauté de Monaco/ Principality of Monaco)	Monaco 1 234	1.9	30 000	15 789	—
THE NETHERLANDS (Koninkrijk der Nederlanden/Kingdom of the Netherlands)	Amsterdam 695 000	41 574	14 893 000	358	73.7 80.2

GROSS NATIONAL PRODUCT ②	LANGUAGES	RELIGIONS	ECONOMY
5 340	Greek	Orthodox	**Agriculture** Important economically. Main crops: cereals, olives, vines, citrus fruits, cotton, tobacco. Livestock and fishing also important. **Industry** Tourism highly profitable; also food processing, petrochemicals, textiles, metals and chemicals.
2 560	Hungarian	Catholic 64%; Protestant 23%	**Agriculture** Among the major crops are cereals, potatoes, sugar beet and grapes. Animal farming is significant. **Mineral resources** Bauxite, petroleum and coal. **Industry** Machinery, textiles, chemicals and food.
21 240	Icelandic	Protestant	**Economy** Fishing (cod, herrings) is vital. **Agriculture** Small-scale: the inhospitable climate is most suitable for grazing and sheep rearing. **Industry** Mainly fish storage and processing; hydroelectricity fuels the profitable aluminium-smelting plants.
8 500	Irish (off.); English	Catholic 93%; Anglican 3%	**Economy** Essentially agricultural, with livestock (sheep and cattle) of primary importance. Main crops: cereals, potatoes and sugar beet. **Principal resources** Peat, zinc and natural gas. **Industry** Food processing, machinery and brewing.
15 150	Italian	Catholic	**Agriculture** Important to the domestic economy (cereals, olives, vines, citrus fruits, tomatoes, beet). Also animal farming (cattle, pigs) and fishing. **Industry** Cars, machinery, chemicals, food, textiles, clothing and tourism.
6 176	Lettish	Lutheran; Orthodox	**Economy** Heavily industrialized, specializing in metals, food, electronics, textiles, chemicals and wood. **Agriculture** Of secondary importance. Cereals, potatoes, flax, beet and fodder are the main crops. Also dairy farming and fishing.
21 000	German	Catholic	**Economy** Dominated by tourism and industry (particularly precision instruments, chemicals, pharmaceutics, food, textiles, ceramics). **Agriculture** Relatively modest. Main crops: cereals, potatoes, vegetables. Main livestock: cattle, pigs, sheep.
4 796	Lithuanian	Catholic	**Agriculture** Dominates the economy (cereals, potatoes, flax, beet, vegetables). Animal farming and forestry are also important activities. **Industry** Major industries are food, machinery, textiles, wood and chemicals.
24 860	Letzeburgish; French; German	Catholic	**Agriculture** The leading products are cereals, potatoes and grapes. Animal farming is widespread. **Industry** The most developed sector of the economy, particularly iron and steel, machinery, chemicals, rubber and plastics.
1 697	Macedonian	Orthodox	**Economy** Industry and mining (of iron, chromite, copper and lignite) predominate. **Agriculture** Main crops: cereals, tobacco, cotton, fruit. Also sheep breeding and forestry. **Industry** Chiefly food, metals, chemicals and textiles.
5 820	Maltese; English	Catholic	**Agriculture** Cereals, potatoes, vegetables, fruit and flowers. Animal farming and fishing are important. **Industry** Main sectors: clothing, food, electronics, shipbuilding, publishing and tobacco. Tourism is a major source of foreign revenue.
9 636	French; Monegasque	Catholic	**Economy** Light industry, banking, casinos and tourism are the main sources of revenue. **Industry** Textiles, clothing, electronics, chemicals, pharmaceutics and paper are among the chief manufactured goods.
16 010	Dutch	Catholic 36%; Protestant 26%	**Agriculture** Main crops: cereals, potatoes, fruit, beet, flowers (tulips, hyacinths). Animal farming and fishing are important. **Mineral resources** Natural gas, petrol. **Industry** Food, chemicals, electronics and rubber are manufactured.

STATE (official name/ English translation)	CAPITAL ① inhabitants	AREA (sq km) POPULATION		DENSITY (inhab/sq km)	LIFE EXPECT- ANCY (in years) M	F
NORWAY (Kongeriket Norge/ Kingdom of Norway)	Oslo 461 000	323 878	4 242 000	13	73.3	79.8
POLAND (Polska Rzeczpospolita/ Republic of Poland)	Warsaw (Warszawa) 1 656 000	312 683	38 180 000	122	66.8	75.5
PORTUGAL (República Portuguesa/ Portuguese Republic)	Lisbon (Lisboa) 830 000	91 191	10 251 000	112	70.6	77.6
ROMANIA (România)	Bucharest (Bucureşti) 2 127 000	237 500	23 207 000	98	66.5	72.4
SAN MARINO (Serenissima Repubblica di San Marino/Most Serene Republic of San Marino)	San Marino 2 300	60.6	23 000	379	73.2	79.1
SLOVAKIA (Slovenská Republika Republic of Slovakia)	Bratislava 441 000	49 036	5 297 000	108	66.9	75.4
SLOVENIA (Republika Slovenija Republic of Slovenia)	Ljubljana 267 000	20 251	1 950 000	96	67.0	75.0
SPAIN (Reino de España/ Kingdom of Spain)	Madrid 3 121 000	498 507	36 950 000	74	73.6	79.7
SWEDEN (Konungariket Sverige/ Kingdom of Sweden)	Stockholm 674 000	449 964	8 559 000	19	74.2	80.1
SWITZERLAND (Schweizerische Eidgenossenschaft; Confédération Suisse)	Berne (Bern) 134 000	41 285	6 712 000	162	74.0	80.8
UNITED KINGDOM (United Kingdom of Great Britain and Northern Ireland)	London 6 378 000	244 100	55 487 000	227	72.2	77.9
VATICAN CITY (Stato della Città del Vaticano/ State of the Vatican City)		0.44	1 000	—	—	—
YUGOSLAVIA (Federativna Republika Jugoslavija/Federal Republic of Yugoslavia)	Belgrade (Beograd) 1 554 000	102 173	10 300 000	101	68.1	73.6

GROSS NATIONAL PRODUCT ②	LANGUAGES	RELIGIONS	ECONOMY
21 850	Bokmaal; Nynorsk	Protestant	**Agriculture** Main crops: cereals, potatoes. Animals are profitably reared for dairy products (sheep), meat (reindeer), fur. Fishing is a major industry. **Principal resources** Timber, petrol, natural gas. **Industry** Mechanical, chemical and wood-processing.
1 760	Polish	Catholic	**Agriculture** Main crops: cereals, potatoes, beet, tobacco, flax, hops, hemp. Animal farming and fishing are practiced. **Mineral resources** Coal, lignite, copper, silver, sulphur. **Industry** Iron, steel, machinery, food and textiles are important.
4 260	Portuguese	Catholic	**Agriculture** Cereals, potatoes, tomatoes and grapes (for prosperous wine industry) are the chief crops. Fishing (sardines). **Principal resources** Cork, pyrethrum and tungsten. **Industry** Textiles, clothes, chemicals and ceramics.
2 540	Romanian	Orthodox	**Agriculture** Cereals, potatoes, beet, fruit and grapes are the main crops. Animal farming and forestry are important. **Mineral resources** Petroleum, natural gas, lignite, coal, iron. **Industry** Metallurgy, food and chemical production.
8 590	Italian	Catholic	**Economy** Tourism and the sale of postage stamps are the backbone of the economy. **Agriculture** Principal crops: cereals, grapes and olives. **Industry** Principal products: food, textiles, leather goods, ceramics and other local crafts.
5 960	Slovak	Catholic	**Agriculture** An important sector of the economy (cereals, potatoes, sugar beet, vines, tobacco). Cattle, pigs and sheep are reared. **Mineral resources** Copper, iron, lead and zinc. **Industry** Food, textile and metal industries.
6 307	Slovene	Catholic	**Agriculture** Dairy and arable farming (cereals, potatoes, beet, vegetables, fruit). **Principal resources** Timber, iron, lead, zinc, copper, lignite, mercury. **Industry** Iron, steel and textile production, mechanical and chemical engineering.
9 150	Spanish (Castilian); Catalan; Basque; Galician	Catholic	**Agriculture** Dairy farming and fishing are widespread. Main crops: cereals, grapes, citrus fruits, olives. **Principal resources** Cork, coal. **Industry** Main products: consumer goods, chemicals, food, textiles. Tourism is also important.
21 710	Swedish	Protestant	**Agriculture** Limited (cereals, potatoes, beet). Animal farming and fishing at a modest level. **Principal resources** Plentiful timber, iron, lead, zinc, copper and hydroelectricity. **Industry** Motor vehicles, machinery, food, paper and wood.
30 270	German; French; Italian; Romansch	Catholic 48%; Protestant 44%	**Economy** Rich, as a result of its status as an international financial centre and its plentiful hydroelectricity. **Agriculture** Mainly dairy farming. **Industry** Main products: food, textiles, chemicals, pharmaceutics, precision instruments. Tourism.
14 570	English	Protestant; Catholic 9%	**Agriculture** Mainly dairy farming (sheep, cattle) and fishing. **Mineral resources** Rich reserves of petrol, natural gas, coal. **Industry** Services, banking, tourism and manufacturing (metals, chemicals, food, textiles and bricks).
—	Italian and Latin (both off.)	Catholic	**Economy** The City attracts pilgrims and tourists from all over the world. Its revenue derives from charitable donations and income from investments.
2 490	Serbo-Croat	Orthodox	**Economy** Agriculture-based, with cereals, tobacco, fruit and grapes among the main crops. Animal farming and forestry are profitable. **Industry** Major concerns are machinery, textiles, food and paper.

THE COMMONWEALTH OF INDEPENDENT STATES (CIS)

STATE (official name/ English translation)	CAPITAL ① inhabitants	AREA (sq km)	POPULATION	DENSITY (inhab/sq km)	LIFE EXPECT-ANCY (in years) M	F
ARMENIA (Haikakan Hanrapetoutioun)	Yerevan 1 199 000	29 800	3 335 000	112	69.0	74.7
AZERBAIJAN (Republik Azarbaijchan)	Baku 1 150 000	86 600	7 134 000	82	66.6	74.2
BELARUS (BYELORUSSIA) (Respublika Belarus)	Minsk (Mensk) 1 589 000	207 600	10 260 000	49	66.8	76.4
GEORGIA (Sakartvelos Respublika/ Republic of Georgia)	Tbilisi 1 260 000	69 700	5 460 000	78	63.9	73.1
KAZAKHSTAN (Kazak Respublikasy)	Alma-Ata 1 128 000	2 717 300	16 740 000	6	63.9	73.1
KYRGYZSTAN (Kyrgyz Respublikasy)	Bishkek (Biškek) 616 000	198 500	4 394 000	22	64.3	72.4
MOLDOVA (Republika Moldovenească)	Chişinău 665 000	33 700	4 362 000	129	65.5	72.3
RUSSIA (Rossiya/Rossiyskaya Federativnaya Respublika)	Moscow (Moskva) 8 769 000	17 075 400	148 288 000	8	64.2	74.5
TAJIKISTAN (Respublika i Tojikiston)	Dushanbe (Dušanbe) 595 000	143 100	5 303 000	37	66.8	71.7
TURKMENISTAN (Türkmenostan)	Ashkabad 398 000	488 100	3 668 000	7	61.8	68.4
UKRAINE (Ukraïna)	Kiev (Kyiv) 2 587 000	603 700	51 889 000	86	66.1	75.2
UZBEKISTAN (Ozbekiston Respublikasy)	Tashkent 2 073 000	447 400	20 514 000	46	66.0	72.1
CIS (Commonwealth of Independent States)		22 100 900	281 347 000	13		
EUROPE Total ⒶA		10 396 569	709 019 000	68		

GROSS NATIONAL PRODUCT ②	LANGUAGES	RELIGIONS	ECONOMY
4 710	Armenian	Orthodox	**Agriculture** Chief crops are wheat, potatoes, vegetables, fruit, grapes, cotton and tobacco. Livestock includes cattle, sheep and goats. **Industry** Metalwork, machinery, chemicals, food and bricks.
3 750	Azerbaijani	Muslim (Shiite 75%; Sunni 25%)	**Economy** Depends mainly on its reserves of oil (plus natural gas) and manufacturing (machinery, chemicals, petrochemicals). **Agriculture** Arable (cereals, cotton, tobacco, tea, grapes, fruit) and animal farming are significant.
5 960	Belarussian	Orthodox; Catholic	**Economy** Based on agriculture (cereals, potatoes, sugar beet, vegetables, fruit, flax), animal farming (cattle, pigs) and industry (metals, electronics, chemicals, food, textiles).
4 410	Georgian	Orthodox	**Agriculture** Cereals, citrus fruits, grapes, tea, flowers and tobacco. Animals are kept for meat and wool. **Principal resources** Manganese ore, hydroelectricity. **Industry** Developing rapidly. Main products: metals, chemicals and bricks.
3 720	Kazakh	Muslim (Sunni); Orthodox	**Economy** Plentiful resources (coal, petrol, iron, natural gas, tungsten, copper, lead, zinc) aid industrial growth (metals, chemicals, textiles). **Agriculture** Animal farming; much of the population grows crops (cereals, cotton, sugar beet).
3 030	Kyrgyz	Muslim (Sunni); Orthodox	**Agriculture** Cereals, potatoes, sugar beet and fruit are the principal crops, with sheep, goats and cattle the main livestock. **Industry** Textiles, tanning, metallurgy, machinery, electronics, mining (coal, uranium).
3 830	Romanian	Orthodox	**Agriculture** Arable farming – cereals, potatoes, beet, fruit, grapes (for wine), vegetables, sunflower seeds – and animal herding are vital to the economy. **Industry** The major products are machinery, textiles, chemicals and processed food.
5 810	Russian	Orthodox	**Economy** Owing to abundant resources (hydrocarbons, combustibles, timber, minerals) all industrial sectors are highly developed. **Agriculture** Large-scale. Main crops: cereals, potatoes. Animal farming and fishing are also practiced.
2 340	Tajik	Muslim (Sunni)	**Agriculture** The main products are cotton, vegetables, fruit and seeds. Sheep, goats and cattle are raised. **Mineral resources** Uranium, gold, iron and lead. **Industry** Concentrates on food and textiles (carpets).
3 370	Turkmen	Muslim (Sunni)	**Agriculture** Cotton is one of the chief exports; animal breeding (especially karakul sheep) is also important. **Principal resources** Plentiful petroleum and natural gas. **Industry** Machinery, textiles (especially carpets) and petrochemicals.
4 700	Ukrainian	Christian	**Agriculture** Animal and arable farming (cereals, potatoes, sunflower seeds, beet) are widespread. **Economy** Rich deposits of minerals (coal, iron) have helped the development of the iron and steel, mechanical and chemical industries.
2 750	Uzbek	Muslim (Sunni)	**Agriculture** Cotton, cereals, vegetables and fruit are the main crops, sheep and goats the main livestock. **Mineral resources** Large reserves of natural gas, petrol, coal, lead, zinc and gold. **Industry** Machinery-building and chemicals.

Ⓐ Includes the Azores Is (Portugal), Asian Greek Islands, the European parts of Turkey and the CIS; excludes the Canary Is (Spain) and Madeira (Portugal).

① The local form is given in brackets only when it differs from the English form

② Per inhabitant, in US$.

STATE (official name/ English translation)	CAPITAL ① inhabitants	AREA (sq km) POPULATION DENSITY (inhab/sq km)			LIFE EXPECT- ANCY (in years) M F	
AFGHANISTAN (Da Afghānistān Jamhuriat Republic of Afghanistan)	**Kābul** 1 424 000	652 225	16 922 000	26	41.0	42.0
BAHRAIN (Dawlat al-Baḥrain)	**Manama** (Al Manāmah) 151 500	678	516 000	761	71.0	76.0
BANGLADESH (Gana Praja Tantri Bangladesh/People's Republic of Bangladesh)	**Dhaka** 6 105 000	143 998	105 000 000	729	56.9	55.9
BHUTAN (Druk-Yul/ Realm of the Dragon)	**Thimphu** 30 000	47 000	1 476 000	31	49.2	47.8
BRUNEI (Negara Brunei Darussalam/Sultanate of Brunei)	**Bandar Seri Begawan** 55 100	5 765	264 000	46	72.6	76.4
CAMBODIA (Roat Kâmpǔchéa/ State of Cambodia)	**Phnom Penh** 564 000	181 035	8 781 000	48	47.0	49.9
CHINA (Zhonghua Renmin Gongheguo/People's Republic of China)	**Peking** (Beijing) 5 770 000	9 536 499	1155 790 000	121	68.4	71.4
CYPRUS (Kypriakí Dimokratía/ Kibris Cumhuriyeti/ Republic of Cyprus)	**Nicosia** 187 000	9 251	710 000	77	73.9	78.3
INDIA (Bhārat Juktarashtra/ Republic of India)	**Delhi** 294 000	3 287 782	849 638 000	258	58.1	59.1
INDONESIA (Republik Indonesia/ Republic of Indonesia)	**Jakarta** 7 829 000	1 529 072	180 910 000	118	58.5	62.0
IRAN (Jomhurī-e- Islāmī-e-Irān/ Islamic Republic of Iran)	**Tehran** 6 620 000	1 648 196	56 250 000	34	64.0	65.0
IRAQ (Al Jumhūrīya al-'Irāqīya/ Republic of Iraq)	**Baghdād** 3 844 600	434 128	17 903 000	41	63.0	648
ISRAEL (Medinat Yisra'el/ State of Israel)	**Jerusalem** 524 000	20 700	4 975 000	240	74.5	78.1
JAPAN (Nihon or Nippon/ Land of the Rising Sun)	**Tōkyō** 8 163 000	372 819	123 921 000	332	75.9	81.8

GROSS NATIONAL PRODUCT ②	LANGUAGES	RELIGIONS	ECONOMY
160	Dari; Pushto	Muslim (Sunni) 80%	**Economy** Mainly agricultural (cereal crops); cotton is widely cultivated for the textile industry. Animal farming is the basic livelihood of nomads. **Mineral resources** Rich, under-exploited reserves of natural gas and iron ore.
6910	Arabic	Muslim 85%	**Economy** Relies on petroleum, refined locally for export. An important financial centre. **Industry** Booming, particularly food, cement, chemicals, aluminium. **Agriculture** Fishing (fish, pearls) and agriculture are the traditional activities.
220	Bengali (off.); English	Muslim 86.6%; Hindu 12.1%	**Economy** Agriculture-based. Rice is the main crop, followed by jute, tea, sugar-cane, cotton and tobacco. Animal farming is widespread and fishing is important. **Industry** Food processing and textile manufacturing are developing.
180	Dzongkha	Buddhist; Hindu	**Economy** Extremely poor. Agriculture (cereals, potatoes, fruit), stock-raising (mainly cattle, then pigs, sheep and goats) and lumbering (firewood) employ virtually the whole population of this rural country. Local crafts are exported.
27 860	Malay; English; Chinese	Muslim 63%; Buddhist 14%	**Economy** Rich reserves of petroleum and natural gas make Brunei one of the wealthiest countries in Asia. **Agriculture** Rice, bananas and citrus fruits; forestry and fishing. **Industry** Chiefly petrochemicals, food, wood and rubber.
200	Khmer (off.); French	Buddhist	**Agriculture** Dominates the economy, especially rice. Fishing and animal farming are traditional livelihoods. Forests are particularly rich (rubber and timber). **Industry** Primarily food processing, textiles, tobacco and mechanical industries.
370	Chinese; Uighur; Tibetan; Mongol	Confucian 19%; Budd. 14%; Mus. 5%; Christ.	**Economy** Essentially agricultural. The largest rice producer in the world. Pig farming, fishing and silk-worm breeding are important. **Principal resources** China is rich in minerals and fuel. **Industry** All sectors are developing rapidly.
8640	Greek; Turkish	Christian; Cypriot 81%; Mus. 19%	**Economy** Based on agriculture (wine, olives, citrus fruits and potatoes). Sheep and goat farming are practiced on a modest scale, as is fishing. **Industry** Principally mineral extraction (of pyrite, chromite, asbestos) and tourism.
330	Hindi (off.); English; Telugu; Bengali; Marathi; Urdu	Hindu 80%; Muslim 11%	**Economy** Agriculture-based. Cereals and rice are the most profitable crops. Livestock are reared extensively, although mainly to meet subsistence needs. Some income raised through fishing and forestry. **Industry** Growing rapidly.
610	Bahasa Indonesia (off.); Javanese	Muslim 87%; Christian 9.6%	**Economy** Almost half the population is involved in agriculture (rice, tea, coffee, sugar-cane, palm-oil, coconuts, tobacco). Second largest rubber producer. **Principal resources** Rich mineral reserves (oil) contribute to developing industry.
2320	Persian (Farsi)	Muslim (Shia)	**Principal resources** Profits from international sales of oil and natural gas are being used to enhance all sectors of the economy. **Industry** The mining, petrochemical, mechanical and textile (carpet) industries are flourishing.
3650	Arabic; Kurdish	Muslim (Sunni, Shia)	**Economy** Petroleum is a major source of foreign revenue. **Agriculture** Employs a third of the population, thanks to fertile river basins. Cereals grown for domestic market; dates for export. **Industry** Textiles, chemicals, cement, food, paper.
11 330	Hebrew (off.); Arabic	Jewish; Muslim	**Economy** Structurally modern and well organized. All sectors are flourishing, especially agriculture. **Industry** Manufacturing (chemical, mechanical, textiles), mining (diamonds) and tourism are particularly lucrative.
26 920	Japanese	Shintoist; Buddhist	**Economy** Most industrialized in Asia, third world-wide. All manufacturing sectors well developed (mechanics, electronics, chemicals, textiles and paper). **Agriculture** Mainly rice; fishing is important to domestic and export markets.

ASIA

STATE (official name/ English translation)	CAPITAL ① inhabitants	AREA (sq km) POPULATION		DENSITY (inhab/sq km)	LIFE EXPECT-ANCY (in years) M F	
JORDAN (Al Mamlaka al Urdunīyah al Hāshemīyah/Hashemite Kingdom of Jordan)	**Ammān** 936 000	97 740	3 285 000	34	64.2	67.8
KUWAIT (Dawlat al-Kuwait/ State of Kuwait)	**Kuwait City** 44 400	17 818	2 241 000	126	71.2	75.4
LAOS (Satharanarath Pasathipatai Pasason Lao/Lao People's Democratic Republic)	**Vientiane** (Viengchane) 377 400	236 800	4 262 000	18	47.8	50.8
LEBANON (Al-Jumhūrīya al-Lubnānīya)	**Beirut** (Bayrūt) 474 900	10 400	2 965 000	285	65.1	69.0
MALAYSIA (Persekutuan Tanah Malaysia/ Federation of Malaysia)	**Kuala Lumpur** 1 103 000	329 758	18 239 000	55	68.8	73.3
THE MALDIVES (Divehi Jumhuriya/ Republic of Maldives)	**Malé** 55 100	298	222 000	745	62.2	59.5
MONGOLIA (Mongol Uls/ Mongolian Republic)	**Ulan Bator** (Ulaanbaatar) 548 000	1 566 500	2 140 000	1	61.2	63.8
MYANMAR (BURMA) (Pyidaungsu Myanma Naingngandaw/ Union of Myanmar)	**Rangoon** (Yangon) 2 459 000	678 033	42 561 000	63	60.0	63.5
NEPAL (Nepāl Adhirājya/ Kingdom of Nepal)	**Kathmandu** 393 500	147 181	19 379 000	131	55.4	52.6
NORTH KOREA (Chosun Minchu-chui Inmin Konghwa-Guk/Democratic People's Republic of Korea)	**P'yŏngyang** 2 639 000	120 538	22 937 000	190	66.2	72.7
OMAN (Sulṭanat 'Umān/ Sultanate of Oman)	**Muscat** 50 000	212 457	1 559 000	7	62.2	65.8
PAKISTAN (Islāmi Jamhūrīya e-Pakistān/ Islamic Republic of Pakistan)	**Islāmābād** 204 400	796 095	115 520 000	145	59.3	60.7
PHILIPPINES (Republika ñg Pilipinas/ Republic of the Philippines)	**Manila** 1 599 000	300 000	62 000 000	207	62.5	66.1
QATAR (Dawlat al-Qaṭar/ State of Qatar)	**Doha** (Ad Dawhah) 217 000	11 437	455 000	39	66.9	71.8

GROSS NATIONAL PRODUCT ②	LANGUAGES	RELIGIONS	ECONOMY
1120	Arabic	Muslim	**Economy** Quite poor; the arid soil yields only vegetables, citrus fruits and cereals. **Principal resources** Phosphates and potash (the main export). **Industry** Food processing, chemical, cement and tobacco manufacture.
16 160	Arabic	Muslim	**Economy** Rich oil reserves make Kuwait one of the world's wealthiest countries. **Agriculture** Fishing is traditionally strong; irrigation is used to expand arable land. **Industry** Chemical, mechanical and cement plants supplied by natural gas.
230	Lao (off.); French	Buddhist	**Economy** The least developed in Indochina. Agriculture, forestry and fresh-water fishing are almost the only economic activities. **Agriculture** Rice is the principal crop. **Industry** Largely limited to the production of local crafts.
350	Arabic (off.); French	Christian 42%; Muslim 29%	**Agriculture** Olives, citrus fruits, grapes, fruit and vegetables are the main yields. Minimal animal farming and fishing. **Industry** The principal employers in this sector are the oil-refineries, cotton-mills, and cigarette and cement factories.
2490	Malay (off.); English; Chinese	Mus. 53%; Buddhist; Taoist; Christian	**Agriculture** Mainly rice, coconuts, palm-oil, coffee, tea, pineapples and rubber (of which Malaysia is the world's largest exporter). **Mineral resources** Abundant tin, petrol, bauxite, copper. **Industry** Tourism is being promoted.
460	Dhivehi	Muslim	**Agriculture** The majority of the population is involved in fishing or cultivating coconuts (fish and coconut fibre being the principal exports). Most staple foods have to be imported. **Industry** Tourism is growing rapidly.
473	Mongolian	Buddhist	**Economy** Depends mainly on animal herding (sheep, goats, cattle, horses, camels). Some cereals are cultivated. **Industry** Centres on food processing. **Principal resources** The country has deposits of copper and coal.
200	Birmano (off.); English	Buddhist 88%	**Agriculture** Dominates. Teak and forestry products have replaced rice as the principal export. Crops for industrial use include sugar-cane, tobacco, jute and cotton. **Mineral resources** The country has considerable reserves of oil.
180	Nepali (off.); Bihari	Hindu 89%; Buddhist 5%	**Economy** Dominated by cultivation (cereals, potatoes, jute, sugar-cane, tobacco) and animal farming (yak, cattle, buffalo, goats). **Industry** Small-scale, mainly processing industries. Tourism is flourishing and brings in foreign revenue.
1040	Korean	Buddhist; Confucian; Shintoist	**Economy** Dominated by mining (coal, iron, copper, lead). **Industry** Iron and steel production, mechanical and chemical engineering and textile manufacture all well established. **Agriculture** Principal crops are rice, maize and potatoes.
5650	Arabic (off.); English	Muslim (Sunni)	**Economy** Depends on the export of petrol and natural gas. Of lesser importance: agriculture (vegetables, fruit, dates), animal farming (goats, sheep), and fishing. **Industry** Metal-lurgical (copper), petrochemical and cement production.
400	Urdu (nat.); English	Muslim	**Economy** Expanding. **Agriculture** Flourishing, the main crops being cereals, sugar-cane and cotton. Cotton is the principal export, and also supplies a productive textile in-dustry. **Mineral resources** Petroleum, natural gas and coal.
740	Tagalog (Filipino); English	Catholic 84%	**Agriculture** Fundamental to the economy (rice, maize, coconuts, sugar-cane, bananas). Fishing is also important. **Industry** Mining growing rapidly (gold, copper) along with food processing, electronics, chemicals and textiles.
15 870	Arabic	Muslim (Sunni)	**Economy** Relies on its plentiful reserves of petroleum and natural gas. **Industry** Petrochemicals and cement are the chief industrial products. **Agriculture** Fishing and nomadic animal herding are traditional livelihoods.

STATE (official name/ English translation)	CAPITAL ① inhabitants	AREA (sq km)	POPULATION	DENSITY (inhab/sq km)	LIFE EXPECT-ANCY (in years) M	F
SAUDI ARABIA (Al Mamlaka al'Arabīya as-Sa'ūdīya/Kingdom of Saudi Arabia)	**Riyadh** (Ar Riyād) 1 308 000	2 153 168	15 267 000	7	61.7	65.2
SINGAPORE (Republik Singapura/ Republic of Singapore)	**Singapore**	639	2 763 000	4324	70.3	75.8
SOUTH KOREA (Daehan-Minkuk/ Republic of South Korea)	**Seoul** (Sŏul) 10 628 000	99 237	43 530 000	438	66.9	74.9
SRĪ LANKA (Srī Lanka Prajatantrika Samajawadi Janarajaya)	**Colombo** 615 000	65 610	17 247 000	263	69.1	73.4
SYRIA (Al Jumhūrīya al 'Arabīya as Sūrīya)	**Damascus** (Dimashq) 1 326 000	185 180	12 524 000	67	65.2	69.2
TAIWAN (REPUBLIC OF CHINA) (Chung-hua Min Kuo)	**Taipei** 2 718 000	36 202	20 489 000	566	71.3	76.8
THAILAND (Prathet Thai/ Kingdom of Thailand)	**Bangkok** 5 876 000	513 115	55 884 000	109	63.8	68.8
TURKEY (Türkiye Cumhuriyeti/ Republic of Turkey)	**Ankara** 2 553 000	755 688	51 277 000	69	68.0	72.0
UNITED ARAB EMIRATES (Al Imārāt al 'Arabīya al-Muttahida)	**Abu Dhabi** 243 000	83 600	1 945 000	23	68.6	72.9
VIETNAM (Công Hòa Xã Hôi Chu' Nghiã Viêt Nam/Socialist Republic of Vietnam)	**Hanoi** 1 089 000	329 566	67 589 000	205	63.7	67.9
YEMEN (Al-Jumhūrīya al-Yamanīyah/ Republic of Yemen)	**Sana'ā** 427 000	524 342	11 843 000	22	49.0	51.0

ASIA		27 140 550	3 121 179 000	115
ASIA Total Ⓐ		44 032 038	3 210 194 000	73

GROSS NATIONAL PRODUCT ②	LANGUAGES	RELIGIONS	ECONOMY
7070	Arabic	Muslim (Sunni)	**Economy** Petroleum is the most valuable resource (Saudi Arabia is the world's third biggest producer of crude oil). **Industry** Mainly petrochemical. Tourism is also flourishing (many pilgrims visit the sacred cities of Mecca and Medina).
12 890	Chinese; Malay; Tamil; English	Tao. 29%; Bud. 27%; Mus. 16%; Christ. 10%	**Economy** Dominated by industrial sector (electronics, shipyards, textiles, chemicals, rubber, metallurgical and petrochemical plants). A major international financial and commercial centre, the island also has a thriving fishing industry.
6340	Korean (off.)	Budd.40%; Christ. 28%; Conf. 17%	**Agriculture** Mainly rice, potatoes, cotton and tobacco. Also fishing. **Mineral resources** Rich in coal, iron, gold and tungsten. **Industry** Well developed mechanical, electronic, textile and petrochemical sectors .
500	Sinhalese; Tamil (off.); English	Bud. 69%; Hindu 15%; Christ. 7%; Mus. 8%	**Economy** Essentially agricultural (rice, coconuts, tea, cinnamon, coffee). The forests yield caoutchouc. **Industry** Precious stones are mined; textiles, cement, rubber and chemicals are manufactured. Tourism is increasing.
1110	Arabic	Muslim (Sunni) 75%; Christ. 10%	**Economy** Based on agriculture (wheat, cotton, grapes, olives, vegetables and fruit). Sheep farming is widespread. **Industry** Mining (petroleum, phosphates), textiles, food, leather, cement and glass industries are all developing.
8810	Chinese	Confucian; Buddist	**Agriculture** Well-organized; rice, sugar-cane, tea and sweet potatoes are the main crops. Little animal farming, but fishing is profitable. **Industry** Textiles are the primary product, plus electronics, machinery, petrochemicals and toys.
1580	Thai	Buddist	**Economy** Still fundamentally agricultural: rice, maize, cassava and sugar-cane are the chief products. Fishing, forestry (timber, caoutchouc) and mining (tin) are important. Tourism is now the primary foreign exchange earner.
1820	Turkish (off.); Kurdish	Muslim	**Agriculture** Employs almost half the population (cereals, cotton, vine, olive, fruit, sugar beet, tobacco). Animal farming is widespread. **Industry** The food, textile, chemical and machinery sectors are expanding; tourism is flourishing.
19 870	Arabic (off.); English	Muslim 95%	**Economy** One of the wealthiest countries in the world due to extensive on- and off-shore reserves of petroleum and natural gas. Fishing and pearl cultivation are traditional livelihoods. **Industry** Petrochemical, metallurgical and cement.
110	Vietnamese	Buddist; Taoist	**Economy** Much of the work force is employed in cultivating rice. Cassava, sweet potatoes, coconuts, tea and tobacco are also grown. Fishing is important. **Industry** Mining (coal, petrol), metal, food and chemical sectors are well developed.
540	Arabic	Muslim	**Economy** Agriculture (cereals, dates, vegetables, fruit, cotton, coffee) and fishing employ most of the population, while sheep, goats and cattle are herded. **Industry** Oil is mined; chemical, textile,and cement production is increasing.

Ⓐ Includes Christmas and Cocos Is, Hong Kong, Macao, Sinai Peninsula, Gaza Strip and the Asian parts of the CIS, but excludes Irian Jaya and Socotra.

① The local form is given in brackets only when it differs from the English form

② Per inhabitant, in US$

STATE (official name/ English translation)	CAPITAL ① inhabitants	AREA (sq km)	POPULATION	DENSITY (inhab/sq km)	LIFE EXPECTANCY (in years) M	F
ALGERIA (Al Jumhūrīya al Jazā'iriya ad Dīmūqrātīya ash-Sha'bīya)	**Algiers** (Al Jazair) 1 687 600	2 381 741	25 660 000	11	65.0	67.3
ANGOLA (República de Angola/ Republic of Angola)	**Luanda** 1 136 000	1 246 700	10 303 000	8	44.9	48.1
BENIN (République du Bénin/ Republic of Benin)	**Porto-Novo** 164 000	112 622	4 889 000	43	49.0	52.0
BOTSWANA (Republic of Botswana)	**Gaborone** 134 000	600 372	1 320 000	2	52.7	59.3
BURKINA FASO (République de Burkina Faso/ Republic of Burkina Faso)	**Ouagadougou** 442 200	274 200	9 242 000	34	47.6	50.9
BURUNDI (République du Burundi/ Republika y'Uburundi/ Republic of Burundi)	**Bujumbura** 235 400	27 834	5 600 000	201	50.0	54.0
CAMEROON (République du Cameroun/ Republic of Cameroon)	**Yaoundé** 653 700	475 442	11 932 000	25	53.5	56.5
CAPE VERDE (República de Cabo Verde/ Republic of Cape Verde)	**Praia** 61 700	4 033	341 000	84	63.0	67.0
CENTRAL AFRICAN REPUBLIC (République Centrafricaine)	**Bangui** 597 000	622 436	3 015 000	5	48.0	53.0
CHAD (République du Tchad/ Republic of Chad)	**N'djamena** 594 000	1 284 000	5 819 000	4	45.9	49.1
COMOROS (République Fédérale Islamique des Comores)	**Moroni** 22 000	1 862	481 000	258	54.0	59.0
CONGO (République Populaire du Congo/People's Republic of the Congo)	**Brazzaville** 760 000	342 000	2 346 000	7	52.1	57.3
DJIBOUTI (République de Djibouti/ Jumhūrīya Jībutī/ Republic of Djibouti)	**Djibouti** 220 000	23 200	541 000	23	47.4	50.7
EGYPT (Jumhūrīyat Mişr al 'Arabīya/ Arab Republic of Egypt)	**Cairo** (Al Qāhirah) 6 069 000	942 247	54 688 000	58	59.0	60.3

GROSS NATIONAL PRODUCT ②	LANGUAGES	RELIGIONS	ECONOMY
2020	Arabic (off.); French; Berber	Muslim	**Agriculture** Supplies processing industry (vines, vegetables, olives, citrus fruit) and satisfies subsistence needs. **Mineral resources** Hydrocarbons. **Industry** Developing gradually; traditional crafts bring in foreign revenue.
620	Portuguese (off.); Bantu languages	Cath. 65%; Animist; Protestant	**Agriculture** One of the country's main economic activities; coffee, cotton, tobacco, palm-oil, sugar-cane and sisal are the principal crops. **Mineral resources** Mining (petroleum, diamonds and iron) generates considerable income.
380	French (off.); Fon; Yoruba; Adja	Animist 63%; Cath. 18%; Mus. 15%	**Agriculture** Dominates the economy. Cereals, cassava, cotton and palm-oil are the main products. Animal farming and fishing are widely practiced. **Industry** Limited to the processing of agricultural goods.
2590	English (off.); Setswana	Animist; Christian 30%	**Economy** Traditionally based on animal farming (especially cattle) and subsistence agriculture (cereals, legumes, groundnuts, citrus fruit). **Principal resources** Diamonds, coal, copper and nickel are the main mineral exports.
350	French (off.); Mossi; Fulani	Animist; Mus. 30%; Christ. 10%	**Economy** Very poor and with few natural resources. **Agriculture** Cereals, sugar-cane and cotton are the only crops of any importance. Cattle rearing is becoming more widespread.
210	French and Kirundi (both off.); Swahili	Cath. 65%; Animist; Protestant	**Economy** Principally agrarian. **Agriculture** The main source of employment. The most important subsistence crops are sweet potatoes and cassava; coffee, tea and cotton are exported.
940	French and English (both off.); Fulani; Sao; Bamileke	Animist 40%; Mus. 22%; Cath. 21%	**Agriculture** A major sector of the domestic economy. Crops include cereals, cocoa, coffee, sugar-cane, palm-oil, cotton and bananas. Forests provide timber and caoutchouc. **Industry** The oil industry is of growing importance.
750	Portuguese (off.); Crioulu	Catholic	**Agriculture** Yields a variety of products, but in quantities insufficient to sustain the local population. **Economy** Export trade is boosted by the production of sea salt and fishing (tuna, lobster).
390	French (off.); Sangho (nat.), Sudanese dialects	Animist 57%; Prot. 15%; Mus. 8%	**Agriculture** Cereals, cassava and bananas are cultivated for domestic consumption; cotton, groundnuts, palm-oil and coffee are sold internationally. **Principal resources** Diamonds and gold are sold internationally. **Industry** Largely food processing.
220	French and Arabic (off.); other local languages	Muslim 50%; Animist 44%	**Agriculture** Cotton plantations are a highly profitable part of the economy. Cereal crops are also significant, as is fishing (on Chad's internal rivers and lakes). Animal farming is quite advanced. **Industry** Very limited.
500	French and Arabic (both off.); other local languages	Muslim	**Agriculture** The main economic activity, producing vanilla, cloves, ylang-ylang, copra, coffee, cocoa and bananas for export. Some fishing. **Industry** Generally quite undeveloped although the islands are beginning to attract tourists.
1120	French (off.); local languages	Animist 47%; Catholic 38%	**Economy** Oil is a major source of foreign revenue, thanks to reserves of petroleum and natural gas. **Agriculture** Well organized (mainly sugar-cane, coffee, cocoa, palm-oil and cassava); the forests provide timber for export.
600	Arabic and French (both off.); other local languages	Muslim	**Economy** Impoverished, largely as the land is so arid and infertile. Relies mainly on service industries, particularly the capital's port and airport. **Agriculture** Low rainfall restricts agriculture to nomadic animal grazing (sheep, goats, camels).
620	Arabic (off.); French and English used commercially	Muslim 90%; Christian 7%	**Agriculture** Concentrated along the banks of the Nile. Main crops: cereals, cotton and sugar-cane. **Mineral resources** Petrol, natural gas, iron, phosphates. **Economy** Tourism and tolls on the Suez Canal bring in foreign currency.

STATE (official name/ English translation)	CAPITAL ① inhabitants	AREA (sq km)	POPULATION	DENSITY (inhab/sq km)	LIFE EXPECT-ANCY (in years) M	F
EQUATORIAL GUINEA (República de Guinea Ecuatorial/Republic of Equatorial Guinea)	Malabo 30 700	28 051	356 000	13	44.4	47.6
ERITREA (Eritrea)	Asmara (Āsmera) 331 000	121 143	3 325 000	27	–	–
ETHIOPIA (Ityopya)	Addis Ababa 1 673 000	1 130 139	50 058 000	44	42.4	45.6
GABON (République Gabonaise/ Gabonese Republic)	Libreville 352 000	267 667	1 350 000	5	49.9	53.2
GAMBIA (Republic of the Gambia)	Banjul 44 500	11 295	884 000	78	41.4	44.6
GHANA (Republic of Ghana)	Accra 949 000	238 538	15 509 000	65	52.2	55.8
GUINEA (République de Guinée/ Republic of Guinea)	Conakry 705 000	245 857	7 052 000	28	42.0	43.0
GUINEA-BISSAU (República da Guiné-Bissau/ Republic of Guinea-Bissau)	Bissau 125 000	36 125	984 000	27	41.9	45.1
IVORY COAST (République de la Côte d'Ivoire/ Republic of the Ivory Coast)	Yamoussoukro 120 000	322 463	10 820 000	33	52.8	56.2
KENYA (Jamhuri ya Kenya/ Republic of Kenya)	Nairobi 1 429 000	582 646	23 183 000	40	56.5	60.5
LESOTHO (Muso oa Lesotho/ Kingdom of Lesotho)	Maseru 109 400	30 355	1 806 000	59	51.5	60.5
LIBERIA (Republic of Liberia)	Monrovia 465 000	111 369	2 520 000	23	53.9	56.3
LIBYA (Al Jamāhīrīya al 'Arabīya al-Lībīya ash Sha'bīya al-Ishtirākīya)	Tripoli (Tarābulus) 591 000	1 775 500	4 325 000	2	59.1	62.5
MADAGASCAR (Repoblika demokratika n'i Madagaskar/République démocratique de Madagascar)	Antananarivo (Tananarive) 1 050 000	587 041	11 493 000	19	54.0	57.0

GROSS NATIONAL PRODUCT ②	LANGUAGES	RELIGIONS	ECONOMY
330	Spanish (off.); Bubi; Fang; Pidgin English	Catholic 80%	**Agriculture** Cocoa and coffee are the most common plantation crops, followed by sugar-cane, bananas, palm-oil and coconuts. The country's main resource is its valuable timber (rosewood, ebony). **Industry** Almost none.
–	Tigrinya and Arabic (both off.); Italian	Coptic; Muslim	**Economy** Based on agriculture (cereals, citrus fruits, oilseed, cotton, tobacco, coffee), animal farming (sheep and goats), fishing and extracting sea salt. **Industry** Undergoing reconstruction.
120	Amharic (off.); Arabic; Oromo; other local languages	Coptic 55%; Muslim 35%	**Agriculture** The most profitable sector of the economy (coffee, tobacco, cotton, bananas and sugar-cane). Animals are reared extensively for their skins and leather. **Industry** Food processing and textile manufacture predominate.
3780	French (off.); Bantu (Fang)	Christian	**Economy** Depends on the forests, which provide valuable timber. **Agriculture** Practiced only at subsistence level. **Principal resources** Petroleum, natural gas, uranium, manganese and gold are lucratively mined and exported. ·
360	English (off.); Wolof; Mandinka; Fula	Muslim 95%; Christ. 4%	**Economy** Depends on the cultivation of groundnuts. Other crops include cotton, cereals and palm nuts. **Industry** Manufacturing centres on processing groundnuts. Tourism is a rapidly growing industry.
400	English (off.); Asante; Ewe; Ga	Christ. 52%; Animist 35%; Mus. 13%	**Economy** Ghana is the third leading producer of cocoa, which it exports worldwide. Fishing, forestry and mining (diamonds, gold, bauxite, petroleum and manganese) are also important.
450	French (off.); Sudanese languages	Muslim 85%; Animist 5%	**Economy** Most of the workforce is employed in agriculture. Groundnuts, citrus fruits, bananas, pineapple, coffee and palm-oil are exported. **Mineral resources** Guinea has large reserves of bauxite, which is exported in considerable bulk.
190	Portuguese (off.); Creole; Sudanese languages	Animist 65%; Muslim 30%	**Economy** Agricultural: the main products are groundnuts, palm-nuts, cashew nuts and cotton, which are processed locally and then exported. Cereals are widely cultivated. Many inhabitants engage in fishing and lumbering.
690	French (off.); local languages	Animist 37%; Mus. 34%; Cath. 22%	**Economy** Most revenue comes from agriculture (especially from coffee and cocoa, followed by oil and palm-nuts), lumbering (valuable wood and caoutchouc) and mining (petroleum, diamonds). **Industry** Expanding.
340	Swahili (off.); Kikuyu; Kamba; English	Animist; Cath. 21%; Prot. 15%	**Agriculture** Flourishing: the broad range of crops include cereals, coffee, tea, sugar-cane, pyrethrum, cotton and sisal. Animal farming is widespread. **Industry** Productive, especially food processing. Tourism brings in substantial revenue.
580	English; Sesotho	Christian 90%; Animist 6%	**Economy** Very impoverished. **Agriculture** Barely above subsistence level (cereals, legumes, fruit). Animal farming is widespread, wool and mohair are exported. **Industry** Some mining (precious stones). Tourism is profitable.
400	English (off.); Sudanese languages	Christian; Animist 20%; Mus. 15%	**Agriculture** Coffee, cocoa, rice, citrus fruits and cassava; plantation crops such as palm-oil and caoutchouc are significant. **Mineral resources** Iron ore, diamonds and gold are mined. **Industry** Manufacturing industries are developing.
5310	Arabic; other local languages	Muslim	**Economy** Depends on reserves of petroleum and natural gas. **Agriculture** Cereals, olives, grapes, citrus fruits and dates are among the main crops; animal farming is also practiced. **Industry** Centres on oil production.
210	Malagasy; French	Anim. 50%; Cath. 25%; Prot. 20%; Muslim 5%	**Economy** The island depends largely on agriculture; coffee, vanilla, cloves and pepper are the principal exports. Rice and cassava are cultivated for domestic consumption. **Industry** Mainly food processing.

STATE (official name/ English translation)	CAPITAL ① inhabitants	AREA (sq km) POPULATION		DENSITY (inhab/sq km)	LIFE EXPECT- ANCY (in years) M F	
MALAWI (Mfuko la Malaŵi/ Republic of Malawi)	**Lilongwe** 220 000	118 484	8 556 000	72	48.4	49.7
MALI (République du Mali/ Republic of Mali)	**Bamako** 646 200	1 240 142	8 299 000	6	45.0	47.0
MAURITANIA (Jumhūrīyat Mūrītānīya al-Islāmīya/Islamic Republic of Mauritania)	**Nouakchott** 393 000	1 030 700	2 036 000	2	45.0	48.0
MAURITIUS (Republic of Mauritius)	**Port Louis** 143 000	2 045	1 069 000	523	65.0	72.9
MOROCCO (Al Mamlakah al Maghribīya/ Kingdom of Morocco)	**Rabat** 556 000	458 730	25 698 000	56	61.6	65.0
MOZAMBIQUE (República de Moçambique/ Republic of Mozambique)	**Maputo** 1 070 000	799 380	16 084 000	20	46.9	50.2
NAMIBIA (Republic of Namibia/ Republiek van Namibie)	**Windhoek** 115 000	824 292	1 400 000	2	55.0	57.5
NIGER (République du Niger/ Republic of Niger)	**Niamey** 399 000	1 186 408	7 984 000	6	42.9	46.1
NIGERIA (Federal Republic of Nigeria)	**Abuja** 379 000	923 768	88 500 000	96	50.8	54.3
RWANDA (Republika y'u Rwanda/ République Rwandaise)	**Kigali** 234 000	26 338	7 150 000	271	48.8	52.2
SAO TOME E PRINCIPE (República Democrática de São Tomé e Príncipe)	**São Tomé** 35 000	964	123 000	127	64.0	67.0
SENEGAL (République du Sénégal/ Republic of Senegal)	**Dakar** 1 490 000	196 722	7 433 000	38	54.0	56.0
SEYCHELLES (Republic of Seychelles)	**Victoria** 24 300	453	68 000	150	65.3	74.0
SIERRA LEONE (Republic of Sierra Leone)	**Freetown** 470 000	71 740	4 260 000	59	41.4	44.6

GROSS NATIONAL PRODUCT ②	LANGUAGES	RELIGIONS	ECONOMY
230	English (off.); Chichewa (nat.); other local dialects	Animist; Catholic 19%	**Economy** Relatively poor. Tobacco, cotton, sugar-cane and tea are cultivated for export; maize is the principal subsistence crop. **Industry** Growing modestly, particularly the food processing, cement manufacture and tobacco sectors.
280	French (off.); Bambara; local languages	Muslim 90%; Animist 9%	**Economy** Extremely poor, and based almost entirely on agriculture. Cotton, rice, cassava and groundnuts are the main crops. Fishing is important, and sheep, goat and cattle farming is well developed (droughts notwithstanding).
510	Arabic (off.); French; Poular; Wolof; Soninke	Muslim	**Agriculture** Severe droughts have hampered arable farming: cereals and dates are almost the only crops. Deep-sea fishing and nomadic animal farming (cattle, sheep) are widespread. **Principal resources** Rich reserves of iron ore.
2420	English (off.); French; Creole; Hindi	Christ. 30%; Hindu 52%; Mus. 13%	**Economy** Depends on the production and export of sugar-cane, although there are also large plantations of tea, coffee and coco-palm. Fishing is profitable. **Industry** Mainly manufacturing; tourism is a significant source of revenue.
1030	Arabic (off.); Berber; French	Muslim	**Agriculture** Cereals, grapes, vegetables and fruit are cultivated. Animal farming is widespread (sheep, goats, cattle). **Principal resources** Phosphates. **Industry** Food manufacturing, textile and tanning industries. Tourism is important.
70	Portuguese (off.); other local languages	Animist 48%; Cath. 14%; Mus. 16%	**Agriculture** The main crops are cotton and sugar-cane; also tea, sisal, cassava, cashew nuts, cereals, bananas. **Mineral resources** Rich but under-exploited deposits of coal, diamonds and bauxite. **Industry** Largely food manufacturing.
1120	Afrikaans (off.); English; other local languages	Christian	**Economy** Depends on rich deposits of diamonds and uranium (plus copper, lead, zinc, silver and tin) which are exported internationally. **Agriculture** Animal farming and fishing are practiced widely. **Industry** Mainly food processing.
300	French (off.); Hausa; Tamashek; Poular; Djerma; Kanuri	Muslim; Animist 15%	**Economy** Uranium, the main mineral resource, is mined in substantial quantities, but agriculture employs the bulk of the population. Millet, sorghum, rice and cassava are the chief crops. Animals are farmed for their skins and leather.
290	English (off.); Sudanese languages (Hausa, Ibo, Yoruba)	Muslim 45%; Christian 38%	**Economy** In the past, agriculture predominated (cocoa, palm-oil, coconuts, groundnuts, caoutchouc and bananas), but oil is now the main source of revenue. **Industry** Mining (tin as well as oil) and food processing.
260	French; Kinyarwanda	Catholic 56%; Anim. 17%; Prot. 13%	**Agriculture** Coffee, tobacco, tea, pyrethrum and groundnuts are grown for cash; maize, rice, sorghum, sweet potatoes, cassava and bananas for subsistence. Some animal herding. **Principal resources** Tin, gold and tungsten.
350	Portuguese (off.); Creole	Catholic	**Agriculture** The mainstay of the economy. Cocoa, coffee, walnuts, palm-oil, coconuts, copra and bananas are the most important crops. Fishing is another source of revenue. **Industry** Scarcely developed.
720	French (off.); Sudanese languages (Wolof, nat.)	Muslim 85%	**Economy** Largely agrarian (groundnuts, cotton, cereals). Senegal is a leading producer of groundnuts. Fishing is important. **Principal resources** Phosphates. **Industry** Mainly groundnuts processing, oil production and tourism.
5110	Creole (off.); English; French	Catholic	**Agriculture** Coconut palms, cinnamon and vanilla are the principal crops. Fishing is also an important aspect of the economy. **Industry** About a third of the labour force is employed in the highly successful tourist industry.
210	English (off.); Krio; Sudanese languages	Animist 51%; Muslim 39%	**Mineral resources** The chief exports, particularly diamonds, rutile and bauxite. **Agriculture** Mainly at a subsistence level, the principal crops being cocoa, coffee and palm kernels. **Industry** Processing industries.

STATE (official name/ English translation)	CAPITAL ① inhabitants	AREA (sq km)	POPULATION	DENSITY (inhab/sq km)	LIFE EXPECT-ANCY (in years) M	F
SOMALIA (Jamhuuriyadda Diimoqraadiga Soomaaliya/ Somali Democratic Republic)	Mogadishu (Muqdisho) 500 000	637 657	6 760 000	11	43.4	46.6
SOUTH AFRICA (Republic of South Africa/ Republiek van Suid-Afrika)	Pretoria/Cape Town (Kaapstad)* 443 000/777 000	1 224 641	38 191 000	31	57.5	63.5
SUDAN (Jamhūrÿat es Sūdān/ Republic of Sudan)	Khartoum (Al Khar ṭūm) 557 000	2 505 813	25 941 000	10	52.0	54.0
SWAZILAND (Umbuso we Swatini/ Kingdom of Swaziland)	Mbabane 38 000	17 364	798 000	46	56.2	59.8
TANZANIA (Jamhuri ya Muungano wa Tanzania/United Republic of Tanzania)	Dodoma 204 000	939 470	26 353 000	28	51.3	54.7
TOGO (République Togolaise/ Togolese Republic)	Lomé 400 000	56 785	3 643 000	64	51.3	54.8
TUNISIA (Al Jumhūrīyah at Tūnisīyah/ Republic of Tunisia)	Tunis 626 000	163 610	8 293 000	51	64.9	66.4
UGANDA (Republic of Uganda)	Kampala 651 000	241 038	16 830 000	70	51.4	54.7
ZAIRE (République du Zaïre/ Republic of Zaïre)	Kinshasa 3 741 000	2 344 885	36 672 000	15	50.3	53.7
ZAMBIA (Republic of Zambia)	Lusaka 982 000	752 614	8 023 000	10	54.4	56.5
ZIMBABWE (Republic of Zimbabwe)	Harare 863 000	390 759	10 130 000	26	57.9	61.4

AFRICA		29 981 681	630 136 000	21
AFRICA Total ⓐ		30 249 096	632 915 000	21

GROSS NATIONAL PRODUCT ②	LANGUAGES	RELIGIONS	ECONOMY
150	Somali (off.); Arabic; Italian; English (adm.)	Muslim (Sunni)	**Economy** Depends on animal farming (cattle, sheep, goats, camels) and agriculture (cereals, cotton, sugar-cane, bananas). Both are major sources of employment. Fishing is on the increase.
2530	Afrikaans and English (both off.); other local languages	Protestant; Animist; Cath. 8%	**Economy** The most prosperous in Africa. The mining sector (gold, diamonds, uranium, platinum, coal, iron), industry (mechanical, chemical and textile) and agriculture (cereals, vegetables, fruit) are all flourishing.
400	Arabic (off.); other local dialects	Mus. 73%; Animist 17%; Cath. 6%	**Agriculture** Cotton is the most important crop; cereals, dates, sugar-cane and oilseed are also cutivated. Nomadic herding is widespread. Sudan is one of the world's largest producers of gum arabic. **Industry** Relatively undeveloped.
1060	English and siSwati	Christian 47%; Animist 40%	**Economy** Arable and animal farming, timber felling and mining are the main activities. **Agriculture** Sugar-cane and citrus fruits are cultivated widely. **Mineral resources** The country is quite rich in asbestos, carbon, diamonds and iron.
100	Swahili; English	Muslim; Christ. 30%; Hindu; Animist	**Agriculture** Coffee, tea, cotton, tobacco, sugar, sisal and cloves are grown for export. Animal farming and fishing are common. **Mineral resources** Diamonds and gold. **Industry** Food processing and textile production.
410	French (off.); Ewe; Poular; Hausa; Gour; Assirelii	Animist; Muslim 17%; Cath. 26%	**Agriculture** The population largely comprises subsistence farmers; coffee, cocoa, cotton, groundnuts and palm-oil are grown for export. **Mineral resources** Phosphates are the main export; iron ore is also mined. **Industry** Modest.
1510	Arabic (off.); French; Berber	Muslim	**Economy** Based on agriculture (cereals, olives, grapes, citrus fruits, dates) and mining; phosphates and petrol account for over a third of exports. Fishing is profitable. **Industry** Mainly food processing and metallurgy. Tourism is increasing.
160	English and Swahili (both off.); Luganda	Cath. 40%; Prot. 20%; Muslim 6%	**Agriculture** Coffee, tea, cotton, tobacco, cocoa and sugar-cane are cultivated for export, while maize, millet, sorghum and cassava are the main subsistence crops. **Industry** Well developed in the food and metallurgical fields.
220	French (off.); other local dialects	Cath. 40%; Prot. 29%; Animist	**Agriculture** Cassava, rice, maize and bananas are the chief subsistence crops; coffee, cotton, cocoa, tea, caoutchouc and palm-oil are exported. **Mineral resources** Tin, copper, diamonds, petroleum and zinc are mined for export.
420	English (off.); local languages include Lozi, Nyanja, Tonga	Prot. 34%; Cath. 26%; Animist 27%	**Economy** Depends on mining (copper, cobalt, manganese, lead, zinc, tin) and the related industries of metal and chemical processing. **Agriculture** Limited; maize, cassava, groundnuts and tobacco are the most common crops.
620	English (off.); local languages include Chishona and Sindebele	Animist; Prot. 17%; Cath. 12%	**Agriculture** Wheat, maize, cotton, sugar, coffee, soya and tobacco are the principal crops. **Mineral resources** Gold, asbestos, coal, iron, silver, tin, nickel, copper and cobalt are exported. **Industry** Manufacturing is developing slowly.

Ⓐ Includes Saint Helena, Comoros Is, Réunion I., Madeira, Canary Is, Ceuta, Melilla, Socotra, Western Sahara.

* Pretoria (administrative); Cape Town (legislative)

① The local form is given in brackets only when it differs from the English form

② Per inhabitant, in US$

STATE (official name/ English translation)	CAPITAL inhabitants	AREA (sq km)	POPULATION	DENSITY (inhab/sq km)	LIFE EXPECT-ANCY (in years) M	F
AUSTRALIA (Commonwealth of Australia)	Canberra 302 500	7 682 300	17 086 000	2	73.3	79.6
FIJI (Matanitu Ko Viti/ Republic of Fiji)	Suva 70 000	18 272	736 000	40	68.3	72.8
KIRIBATI (Republic of Kiribati)	Bairiki 2 100	849	72 000	85	50.6	55.6
MARSHALL ISLANDS (Republic of the Marshall Islands)	Dalap-Uliga-Darrit 17 600	181	44 000	243	61.0	64.0
MICRONESIA (Federated States of Micronesia)	Palikir —	707	111 000	157	64.0	68.1
NAURU (Republic of Nauru)	Yaren —	21	9 000	428	64.0	69.0
NEW ZEALAND (New Zealand)	Wellington 147 800	270 534	3 390 000	12	72.0	78.0
PALAU	Koror 10 500	487	15 000	31	—	—
PAPUA NEW GUINEA (Papua New Guinea)	Port Moresby 152 100	462 840	3 600 000	8	54.0	56.0
SOLOMON ISLANDS (Solomon Islands)	Honiara 35 300	28 369	319 000	11	59.9	61.4
TONGA (Pule'anga Tonga/ Kingdom of Tonga)	Nuku'alofa 28 900	748	96 000	128	61.0	64.8
TUVALU (The Tuvalu Islands)	Fongafale —	24	9 000	375	60.0	63.0
VANUATU (Ripablik Blong Vanuatu/ Republic of Vanuatu)	Port-Vila 19 300	12 189	147 000	12	61.1	59.3
WESTERN SAMOA (Malo Tuto'atasi/ Independent State of Western Samoa)	Apia 33 200	2 831	164 000	58	64.0	69.0

AUSTRALIA AND OCEANIA — 8 480 352 — 25 798 000 — 3

AUSTRALIA AND OCEANIA   Total Ⓐ — 8 942 252 — 29 128 000 — 3

© ISTITUTO GEOGRAFICO DE AGOSTINI S.p.A. - NOVARA

GROSS NATIONAL PRODUCT ①	LANGUAGES	RELIGIONS	ECONOMY
14 440	English	Protestant; Catholic 26%	**Economy** Based on agriculture (cereals, fruit, sugar-cane, cotton) and animal farming (sheep, cattle). **Mineral resources** Vast reserves of coal, natural gas, oil, nickel, gold, iron ore and bauxite. **Industry** All sectors expanding.
1 640	English, Fijian; Hindi	Methodist; Hindu 38%; Muslim	**Economy** Sustained by agriculture (sugar-cane, bananas, coconuts and potatoes) and fishing. Tourism also generates considerable revenue. **Mineral resources** Subsoil is rich in gold and silver. The island is heavily forested.
700	English (off.); I-Kiribati	Protestant; Catholic	**Agriculture** Most of the population is involved in agriculture and fishing. The principal crop is the coconut palm. **Industry** The tourist industry is expanding.
1 500	English (off.); Marshallese	Protestant; Catholic 8.5%	**Economy** Based on subsistence agriculture and fishing. Main crops are coconuts, copra, cassava and fruit. **Industry** Tourism is well developed.
1 500	English	Protestant; Catholic	**Economy** Most islanders are involved in fishing and cultivation (coconuts, copra, sweet potatoes, cassava, bananas). **Industry** The tourist industry is growing fast.
10 000	Nauruan (off.); English	Protestant; Catholic 24%	**Economy** Nauru is the wealthiest country in Oceania thanks to its rich phosphate deposits (which cover nearly 75% of the island). Phosphate mining accounts for three-quarters of the country's GDP.
11 800	English	Protestant; Catholic 15%	**Economy** Dominated by livestock farming, particularly sheep (for wool and meat) and cattle (dairy products and beef). **Agriculture** Well established. **Industry** Expanding, due in part to inexpensive hydroelectricity.
—	English; Palauan	Christian	**Economy** At subsistence level. The archipelago relies mainly on agriculture (potatoes, coconuts, cassava and bananas) and fishing. **Industry** Tourism is beginning to develop.
900	English (off.); Pidgin-English; Motu; other local dialects	Animist; Catholic 27%	**Economy** Essentially agricultural; sweet potatoes, cocoa, coffee and coconuts are the main crops. **Principal resources** Mining (especially gold, silver, copper) generates considerable revenue. The island is richly forested.
570	English (off.); Pidgin-English; Melanesian and Polynesian languages	Protestant; Catholic 18%	**Economy** The population is largely employed in cultivating coconut palms and sweet potatoes. Timber, fish and copra are the main exports. **Industry** Fishing is a major concern; a modest food processing industry has been established.
910	English; Tongan	Protestant; Catholic 13%	**Economy** Some 58% of the population is involved in agriculture (coconuts, potatoes, cassava and groundnuts). The chief exports are copra and coconuts. Fishing is also profitable. **Industry** Tourism is well established.
530	Tuvaluan; English	Protestant	**Economy** The two main sources of income are coconuts and fishing. The country relies on revenue from emigrants and foreign aid.
860	Bislama; English (off.); French (off.); other local dialects	Animist; Catholic 14%	**Economy** Based on subsistence agriculture and fishing. Main crops are coconut palm, cocoa, groundnuts and maize. The islands are densely forested. **Mineral resources** Primarily manganese.
720	Samoan (off.); English	Protestant; Catholic 22%	**Economy** Agriculture is the country's main resource, the principal crops being bananas, coconuts and cocoa. Fishing and pig farming are also well developed. **Industry** Confined to the manufacture of agricultural products.

Ⓐ Includes Norfolk I., Macquarie I., Cook Is, Niue I., Tokelau I., Pitcairn Is, New Caledonia, Wallis and Futuna, Polynesia, Clipperton, Guam, Hawaii, Midway Is, American Samoa, Wake Is, Mariana Is, Irian Jaya, Chilean Is.

① Per inhabitant, in US$1million

ANTARCTICA has an area of 14 107 637 sq km, including the islands and ice-shelf (13 176 727 sq km without the ice-shelf).

© ISTITUTO GEOGRAFICO DE AGOSTINI S.p.A. - NOVARA

NORTH AND CENTRAL AMERICA

STATE (official name/ English translation)	CAPITAL ① inhabitants	AREA (sq km)	POPULATION	DENSITY (inhab/sq km)	LIFE EXPECT- ANCY (in years) M	F
ANTIGUA AND BARBUDA (Antigua and Barbuda)	Saint John's 36 000	442	64 000	145	70.0	74.0
BAHAMAS (The Commonwealth of the Bahamas)	Nassau 172 000	13 939	259 000	18	69.0	76.0
BARBADOS (Barbados)	Bridgetown 7 600	431	258 000	598	72.9	77.9
BELIZE (Belize)	Belmopan 3 700	22 965	189 000	8	67.0	72.0
CANADA (Canada)	Ottawa 300 800	9 970 610	27 300 000	3	73.3	80.0
COSTA RICA (República de Costa Rica/ Republic of Costa Rica)	San José 297 000	51 100	3 064 000	60	72.4	77.0
CUBA (República de Cuba/ Republic of Cuba)	Havana (La Habana) 2 119 000	110 922	10 736 000	97	73.0	78.0
DOMINICA (Commonwealth of Dominica)	Roseau 15 900	751	71 000	94	73.0	79.0
DOMINICAN REPUBLIC (República Dominicana)	Santo Domingo 1 600 000	48 442	7 313 000	151	63.9	68.1
EL SALVADOR (República de El Salvador/ Republic of El Salvador)	San Salvador 481 000	21 041	5 392 000	256	63.0	68.0
GRENADA (State of Grenada)	Saint George's 7 500	344	101 000	293	69.0	74.0
GUATEMALA (República de Guatemala/ Republic of Guatemala)	Guatemala City 1 114 000	108 889	9 197 000	84	59.7	64.4
HAITI (République d'Haïti/ Republic of Haiti)	Port-au-Prince 514 000	27 400	6 625 000	242	53.1	56.4
HONDURAS (República de Honduras/ Republic of Honduras)	Tegucigalpa 608 000	112 088	4 708 000	42	61.9	66.1

NORTH AND CENTRAL AMERICA

GROSS NATIONAL PRODUCT ②	LANGUAGES	RELIGIONS	ECONOMY
4770	English (off.); Creole	Protestant	**Economy** Domestic economy relies primarily on tourism and secondarily on agriculture (cotton, sugar-cane, coconuts, vegetables and fruit). Fishing is well developed. **Industry** Limited to the manufacture of agricultural products and rum.
11 720	English (off.); Creole	Protestant; Catholic 22%	**Economy** The tourist industry is the main source of revenue. Agriculture (sugar-cane, tomatoes, pineapple), fishing (shellfish and turtles) and the production of sea-salt are also important.
6630	English	Protestant; Catholic 5%	**Economy** The island's economy is based entirely on sugar-cane. Maize, potatoes and cassava are produced for domestic consumption. Fishing is profitable. **Industry** Expanding. The tourist industry is highly developed.
2050	English (off.); Spanish; Creole	Catholic 58%; Protestant 28%	**Economy** Agriculture-based; citrus fruits, cereals (rice and maize), coconuts, bananas and sugar-cane are the main cash crops. Other activities include fishing, animal farming and lumbering (cedar, mahogany, pine and rosewood).
21 260	English; French	Catholic 46%; Protestant 41%	**Economy** Cereal crops dominate (wheat, oats, rye, barley, maize). Cattle and animal-fur farming are also widely practiced. **Principal resources** The vast forests are a rich asset. **Industry** All sectors are well established.
1930	Spanish	Catholic	**Economy** Primarily plantation agriculture (coffee, bananas, cocoa, sugar-cane, cotton and tobacco). Tuna-fishing and animal farming also generate considerable revenue. **Industry** Food processing is a principal industry.
2000	Spanish	Catholic	**Economy** The national wealth depends on sugar-cane (the main export), tobacco, coffee and fruit. Also, animal farming and fishing. **Industry** Nickel-mining, food processing, and the textile and tobacco industries are the chief industries.
2440	English (off.); French patois	Catholic	**Economy** Based on agriculture (bananas, citrus fruits, coconuts) and fishing. **Industry** The processing of agricultural products is developing rapidly. Tourism is also growing.
950	Spanish	Catholic	**Agriculture** Based on plantation crops (cocoa, sugar-cane, coffee, tobacco, coconuts). Also animal farming and fishing. **Mineral resources** Gold, silver and nickel are major exports. **Industry** Tourism brings in foreign revenue.
1070	Spanish; Nahua; Maya	Catholic	**Economy** The main resource of this agricultural country is maize, followed by rice, beans, coffee, sugar-cane, cotton and sesame. Forests yield cedar, mahogany and rosewood. **Industry** Modestly developed.
2180	English (off.); Creole; French patois	Catholic; Protestant 34%	**Economy** Agriculturally based. Citrus fruits, bananas, cocoa, coconuts, cotton, sugar-cane and nutmeg are cultivated. Fishing is an important pursuit. **Industry** Tourism is developing.
930	Spanish (off.); Mayan languages	Catholic; Protestant 25%	**Economy** Depends on plantation agriculture (bananas, coffee, sugar-cane, cotton, tobacco, and cocoa). Forests provide valuable wood, in particular mahogany and cedar. Sheep and cattle farming are profitable.
370	French; Creole	Catholic	**Economy** Essentially agricultural. The main crops are coffee, bananas and sisal, followed by cotton, sugar-cane, cocoa, citrus fruits and tobacco. **Principal resources** Bauxite is the sole mining resource of any significance.
570	Spanish (off.); other local languages	Catholic	**Agriculture** Bananas, coconuts, coffee and tobacco. **Principal resources** Timber (mahogany, cedar and pine). Gold, silver, lead, zinc and antimony are mined on a large scale. **Industry** Processing yields a high income.

STATE (official name/ English translation)	CAPITAL ① inhabitants	AREA (sq km) POPULATION		DENSITY (inhab/sq km)	LIFE EXPECT-ANCY (in years) M	F
JAMAICA (Jamaica)	Kingston 104 100	10 991	2 375 000	216	70.4	74.8
MEXICO (Estados Unidos Mexicanos/United Mexican States)	Mexico City (Ciudad de México) 8 237 000	1 972 547	82 151 000	41	66.5	73.1
NICARAGUA (República de Nicaragua/ Republic of Nicaragua)	Managua 682 000	130 682	3 999 000	31	64.8	67.7
PANAMA (República de Panamá/ Republic of Panama)	Panama City 411 000	77 082	2 466 000	32	70.1	74.1
SAINT CHRISTOPHER (KITTS) AND NEVIS (Federation of Saint Christopher and Nevis)	Basseterre 18 500	269	44 000	163	65.9	71.0
SAINT LUCIA (Saint Lucia)	Castries 51 200	616	153 000	248	68.0	74.8
SAINT VINCENT AND THE GRENADINES (Saint Vincent and the Grenadines)	Kingstown 26 500	389	108 000	277	68.0	72.0
UNITED STATES OF AMERICA (United States of America)	Washington 607 000	9 355 855	250 928 000	27	72.0	78.8

NORTH & CENTRAL AMERICA ⓐ   22 037 795   417 501 000   19
NORTH & CENTRAL AMERICA   Total ⓐ 24 227 189   422 159 000   17

GROSS NATIONAL PRODUCT ②	LANGUAGES	RELIGIONS	ECONOMY
1380	English	Protestant	**Economy** A leading producer of bauxite. **Agriculture** Plantation agriculture (tobacco, coffee, cocoa, bananas, sugar-cane, spices) is well developed. **Industry** Expanding. Tourism generates substantial foreign currency.
2870	Spanish (off.); Nahua; Maya	Catholic 90%	**Economy** Oil, silver, lead, gold and sulphur are the mainstays of the domestic economy. **Agriculture** A third of the population is in agriculture and animal farming. **Industry** Rapidly expanding. Tourism is well developed.
340	Spanish (off.); other local languages	Catholic	**Economy** Principally plantation agriculture (coffee, cotton, cocoa, sugar-cane, and bananas). The forests are rich in valuable wood (mahogany, cedar, rosewood). **Industry** Relatively undeveloped.
2180	Spanish (off.)	Catholic	**Economy** Sustained mainly by revenue raised by granting access to the Panama Canal. **Agriculture** Subsistence agriculture is practiced; large plantations growing bananas, coffee and cocoa also exist.
3960	English (off.); Creole	Protestant	**Agriculture** The economy's main source of revenue, with cotton and sugar-cane the chief crops. **Industry** Agricultural processing is developing modestly while the tourist industry is undergoing rapid expansion.
2500	English (off.); French patois	Catholic	**Agriculture** Domestic economy dominated by agriculture (potatoes, bananas, cocoa, coconuts and copra). Animal farming and fishing are developed. **Industry** Principally food processing and the production of fertilizers.
1730	English (off.); Creole	Protestant; Catholic 19%	**Agriculture** Plantation agriculture yields potatoes, bananas, coconuts, cotton and exotic fruit, largely for the overseas market. **Industry** Industry in general is developing; tourism is well established.
22 560	English	Protestant 53%; Catholic 26%	**Economy** The economy of the United States is the most developed in the world. It is founded on highly specialized agriculture, substantial mineral reserves and power resources, and impressive industrial organization.

Ⓐ Includes the Virgin Is, Puerto Rico, Anguilla, Cayman Is, Turks and Caicos, Bermuda, Montserrat, Guadeloupe, Martinique, St Pierre and Miquelon, North American Antilles, Greenland. Excludes the 16 759 sq km and 1 135 000 inhabitants of Hawaii, which is included in Oceania.

① The local form is given in brackets only when it differs from the English form

② Per inhabitant, in US$

SOUTH AMERICA

STATE (official name/ English translation)	CAPITAL inhabitants	AREA (sq km)	POPULATION	DENSITY (inhab/sq km)	LIFE EXPECT-ANCY (in years) M	F
ARGENTINA (República Argentina/ Argentine Republic)	**Buenos Aires** 2 961 000	2 780 092	32 713 000	12	68.0	74.0
BOLIVIA (República de Bolivia/ Republic of Bolivia)	**Sucre (legal); La Paz (admin.)** 101 000/126 000	1 098 581	7 612 000	7	50.9	55.4
BRAZIL (República Federativa do Brasil/Federative Republic of Brazil)	**Brasília** 1 596 000	8 511 996	146 000 000	17	63.5	69.1
CHILE (República de Chile/Republic of Chile)	**Santiago** 5 134 000	756 626	13 386 000	18	68.1	75.1
COLOMBIA (República de Colombia/ Republic of Colombia)	**Santa Fe de Bogotá** 4 922 000	1 141 748	33 613 000	29	66.4	72.3
ECUADOR (República del Ecuador/ Republic of Ecuador)	**Quito** 1 094 000	283 561	9 819 000	34	63.4	67.6
GUYANA (Cooperative Republic of Guyana)	**Georgetown** 200 000	214 970	760 000	3	61.0	68.0
PARAGUAY (República del Paraguay/ Republic of Paraguay)	**Asunción** 608 000	406 752	4 004 000	10	64.4	68.5
PERU (República del Perú/ Republic of Peru)	**Lima** 6 115 000	1 285 216	21 998 000	17	62.9	66.6
SURINAME (Republiek van Suriname/ Republic of Suriname)	**Paramaribo** 67 900	163 820	417 000	2	66.4	71.3
TRINIDAD AND TOBAGO (Republic of Trinidad and Tobago)	**Port of Spain** 50 900	5 123	1 253 000	244	69.7	74.7
URUGUAY (República Oriental del Uruguay/Eastern Republic of Uruguay)	**Montevideo** 1 248 000	176 215	3 112 000	17	68.9	75.3
VENEZUELA (República de Venezuela/ Republic of Venezuela)	**Caracas** 1 290 000	912 050	19 733 000	21	67.0	73.3
SOUTH AMERICA		17 736 750	294 420 000	16		
SOUTH AMERICA Total Ⓐ		17 833 382	294 762 000	16		

GROSS NATIONAL PRODUCT ①	LANGUAGES	RELIGIONS	ECONOMY
2780	Spanish (off.); Guarani; Quechua	Catholic 91%	**Economy** Traditionally farming (crops and animals) and the manufacture of pastoral and agricultural goods. **Industry** Petroleum output is rising; iron and steel, mechanical goods, textiles and food also of importance.
650	Spanish; Quechua; Aymará	Catholic 94%	**Principal resources** Minerals, including tin, gold, silver, bismuth, lead, zinc, tungsten, antimony and oil. **Agriculture** Currently at subsistence level, but animal husbandry (cattle, sheep) is developing rapidly.
2920	Portuguese (off.); Carib; Tupí	Catholic 88%	**Economy** Based on plantation crops (coffee, cocoa, sugar-cane, tobacco, cotton). **Industry** Food processing (by large, specialized companies) is the main activity. Industry is prosperous. The country is densely forested.
2160	Spanish (off.); Araucanian	Catholic 89%	**Economy** The most profitable sector is mining, particularly of copper, nitrates, oil, gold, silver, iron ore and coal. **Agriculture** Agronomy, animal farming and fishing are booming. **Industry** In a good position to grow.
1280	Spanish (off.); other local languages	Catholic 94%	**Economy** Principal export is coffee; other profitable cash crops include tobacco, cotton and sugar-cane. **Mineral resources** Gold, silver, platinum, emeralds and oil. **Industry** Relatively undeveloped.
1020	Spanish (off.); Quechua	Catholic 90%	**Economy** Relies on plantation crops: cocoa, coffee, sugar-cane, bananas, tobacco, cotton. **Mineral resources** Of considerable importance, principally oil, gold, silver and iron. **Industry** Developing modestly.
290	English (off.); Creole; Hindu; Urdu	Hindu 37%; Prot. 31%; Cath. 11%; Mus. 9%	**Agriculture** Mainly cane, rice, coffee, cassava and citrus fruits. **Mineral resources** Large quantities of bauxite (Guyana's main export), as well as gold and diamonds. **Industry** Limited to the production of agricultural goods.
1210	Spanish (off.); Guaraní	Catholic	**Economy** Essentially agricultural. Cotton, tobacco and fruit are the main exports, and timber. Cattle ranching also a major concern. **Industry** Growing as a result of inexpensive hydroelectric power.
1020	Spanish, Quechua, Aymará (all off.)	Catholic 92%	**Economy** Agriculture-based. Principal crops are cotton, sugar-cane, coffee and fruit. Animal farming is an important economic activity, and fishing even more so. **Mineral resources** Oil, copper and silver. **Industry** Prosperous.
3610	Dutch (off.); Carib; Creole	Hindu 26%; Cath. 22%; Mus. 19%; Prot. 18%	**Economy** Depends on agricultural products (especially rice, sugar-cane, coffee, citrus fruits, bananas and coconuts) and mining (bauxite, gold). **Industry** Limited to the production of agricultural goods.
3620	Englich (off.); Spanish; Hindu; Creole	Cath. 32%; Prot. 28%; Hindu 24%	**Economy** Industry has superseded agriculture as the main source of revenue due to rich deposits of oil, natural gas and asphalt. Other major industrial activities include refining and the production of petrochemicals and fertilizers.
2860	Spanish	Catholic	**Economy** Rearing livestock (sheep and cattle) and food processing are the chief economic activities in Uruguay, with wool, meat and hides the principal exports. **Agriculture** Also developing.
2610	Spanish (off.); Carib	Catholic 92%	**Economy** Previously relied on plantation crops, but petroleum production and the petrochemical industry now account for most export earnings. Fishing is also profitable. The country has considerable forest resources.

Ⓐ   Includes the Falkland Is, South American Antilles, Aruba and French Guiana

①   Per inhabitant, in US$

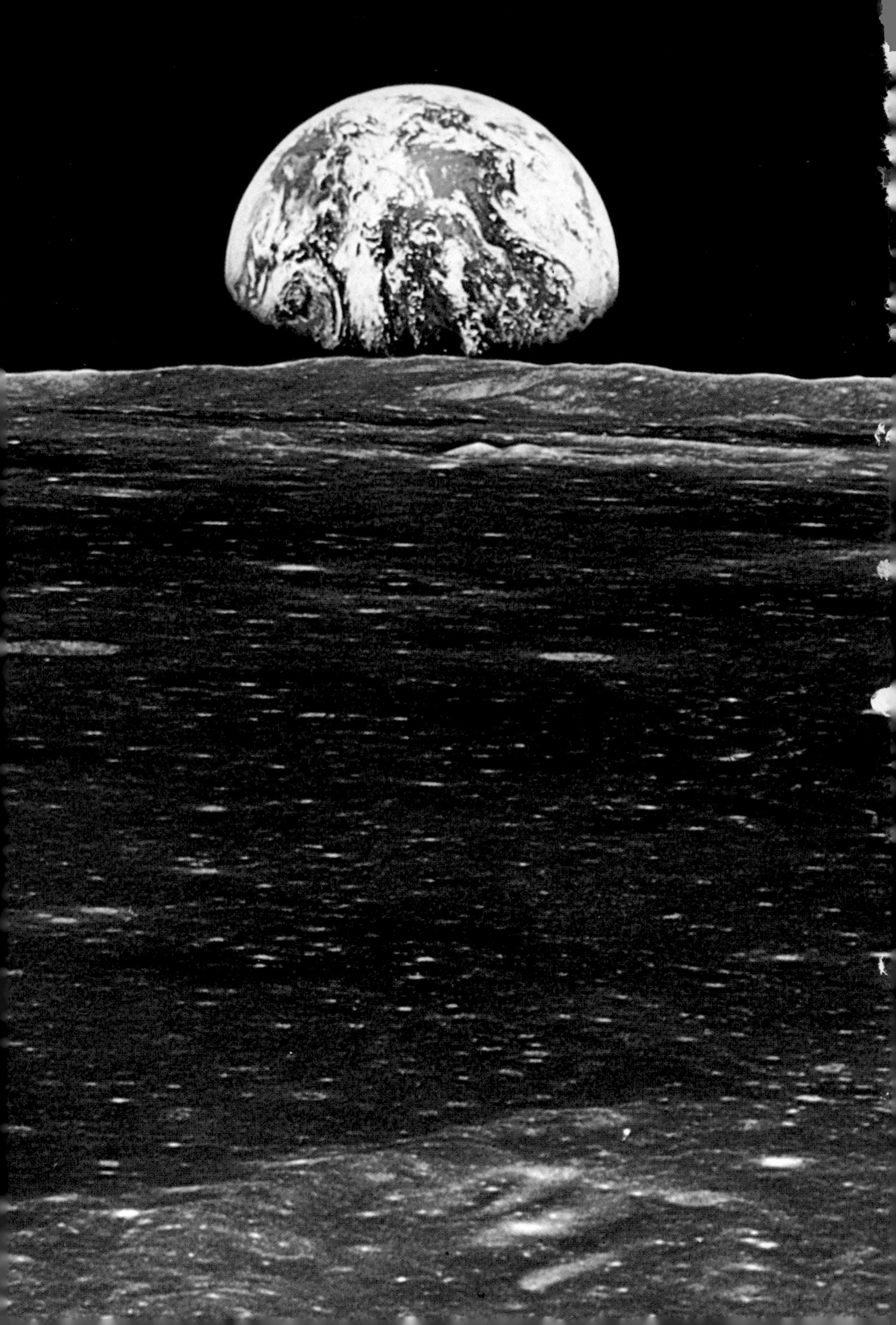

WORLD MAPS

Earth seen from the Moon
(image taken by astronauts aboard "Apollo 10" in May 1969)

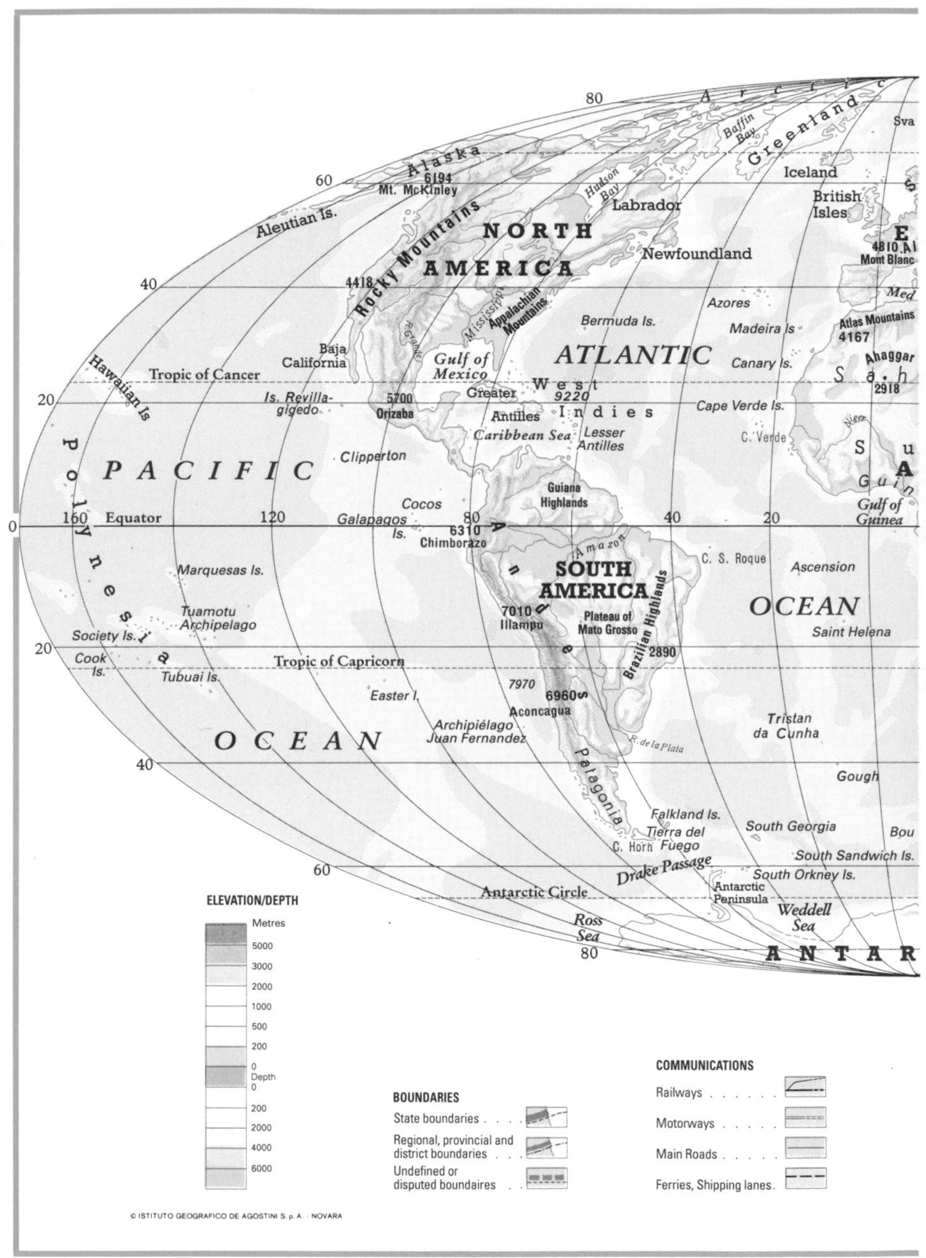

80

Arctic

Baffin
Bay

Greenland

Sva

Iceland

British
Isles

E

Alaska

60

6194
Mt. McKinley

Hudson
Bay

Labrador

4810
Mont Blanc

Aleutian Is.

NORTH

Newfoundland

Med

40

4418

AMERICA

Rocky Mountains

Appalachian Mountains

Azores

Atlas Mountains
4167

Bermuda Is.

Madeira Is.

Mississippi

ATLANTIC

Canary Is.

Ahaggar

Baja
California

Gulf of
Mexico

West

Sahara

2918

Tropic of Cancer

20

Is. Revilla-
gigedo

5700
Orizaba

9220

Indies

Greater
Antilles

Cape Verde Is.

S

u

Clipperton

Caribbean Sea

Lesser
Antilles

C. Verde

A

PACIFIC

Polynesia

Guiana
Highlands

Guinea

Gulf of
Guinea

0

160

Equator

120

Galapagos
Is.

80

6310
Chimborazo

Andes

40

20

Marquesas Is.

Amazon

SOUTH

C. S. Roque

Ascension

Tuamotu
Archipelago

7010
Illampu

AMERICA

Plateau of
Mato Grosso

OCEAN

Society Is.

Brazilian Highlands

Saint Helena

20

Cook
Is.

Tropic of Capricorn

2890

Tubuai Is.

7970

Easter I.

6960
Aconcagua

Tristan
da Cunha

OCEAN

Archipiélago
Juan Fernandez

R. de la Plata

40

Gough

Patagonia

Falkland Is.

Tierra del
C. Horn Fuego

South Georgia

Bou

60

Drake Passage

South Sandwich Is.

Antarctic Circle

South Orkney Is.

Antarctic
Peninsula

ELEVATION/DEPTH

Ross
Sea

80

Weddell
Sea

Metres

ANTAR

5000

3000

2000

1000

500

200

0
Depth
0

200

2000

4000

6000

BOUNDARIES

State boundaries . . . .

Regional, provincial and
district boundaries . . .

Undefined or
disputed boundaires . . .

COMMUNICATIONS

Railways . . . . .

Motorways . . . . .

Main Roads . . . . .

Ferries, Shipping lanes .

© ISTITUTO GEOGRAFICO DE AGOSTINI S.p.A. - NOVARA

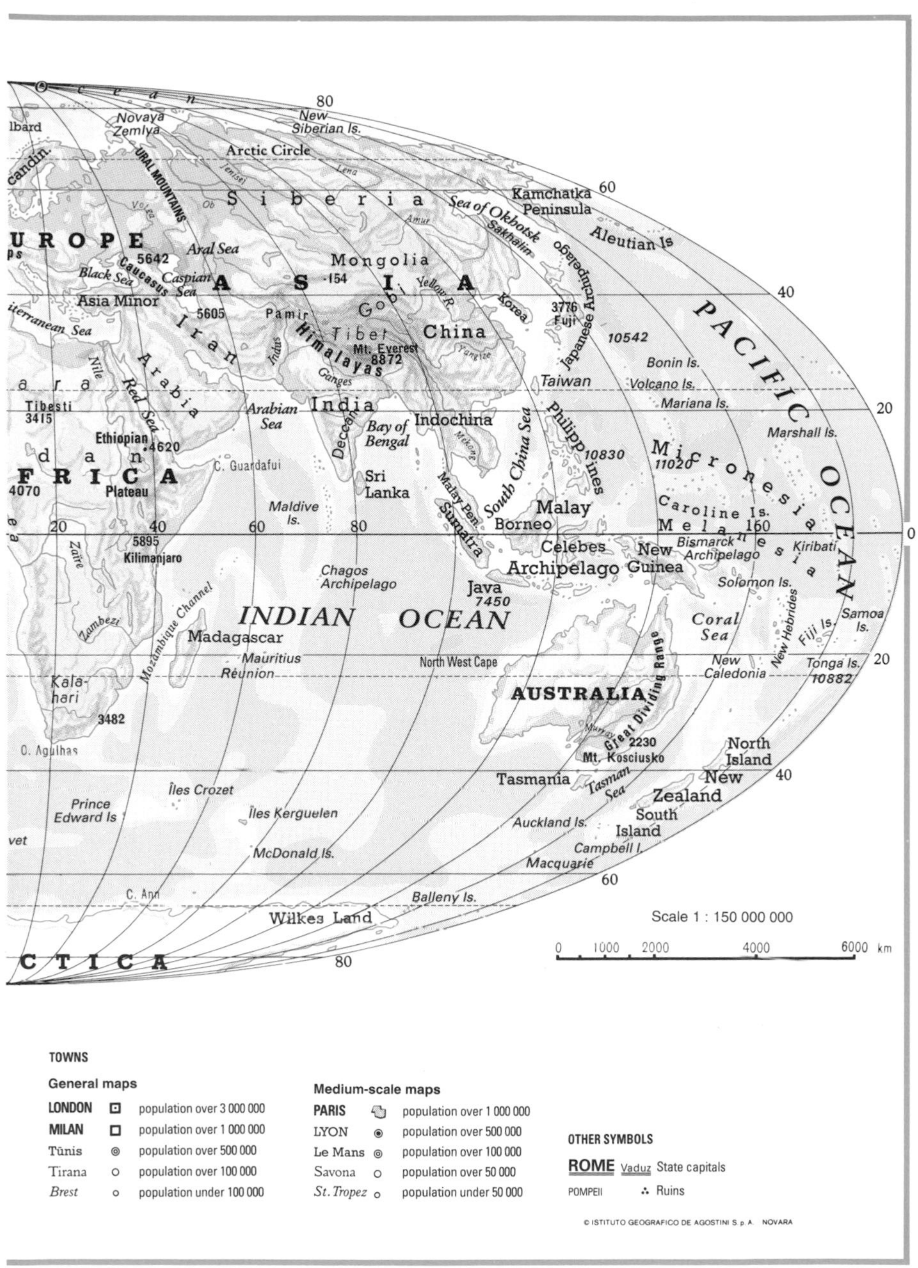

Scale 1 : 150 000 000

0   1000   2000   4000   6000 km

TOWNS

General maps

LONDON	▣	population over 3 000 000
MILAN	☐	population over 1 000 000
Tùnis	◉	population over 500 000
Tirana	○	population over 100 000
Brest	○	population under 100 000

Medium-scale maps

PARIS	▱	population over 1 000 000
LYON	◉	population over 500 000
Le Mans	◎	population over 100 000
Savona	○	population over 50 000
St. Tropez	○	population under 50 000

OTHER SYMBOLS

ROME <u>Vaduz</u> State capitals

POMPEII ∴ Ruins

© ISTITUTO GEOGRAFICO DE AGOSTINI S.p.A. NOVARA

43

1 GUYANA
2 SURINAME
3 French Guiana
4 UNITED KINGDOM
5 IRELAND
6 NETHERLANDS
7 BELGIUM
8 FRANCE
9 LUXEMBOURG
10 GERMANY
11 POLAND
12 ESTONIA
13 LATVIA
14 LITHUANIA
15 BELARUS
16 CZECH REPUBLIC
17 SLOVAKIA
18 AUSTRIA
19 HUNGARY
20 MOLDOVA
21 ROMANIA
22 SWITZERLAND
23 ITALY
24 SLOVENIA
25 CROATIA
26 BOSNIA-HERZEGOVINA
27 YUGOSLAVIA
28 MACEDONIA
29 ALBANIA
30 BULGARIA
31 GREECE
32 PORTUGAL
33 SPAIN
34 BURKINA
35 BENIN
36 CENTRAL AFRICAN REPUBLIC
37 CAMEROON
38 EQUATORIAL GUINEA
39 UGANDA
40 RWANDA
41 BURUNDI
42 MALAWI
43 ZIMBABWE
44 DJIBOUTI
45 ERITREA
46 OMAN
47 UNITED ARAB EMIRATES
48 QATAR
49 BAHRAIN
50 ARMENIA
51 GEORGIA
52 AZERBAIJAN
53 TURKMENISTAN
54 UZBEKISTAN
55 TAJIKISTAN
56 KYRGYZSTAN
57 BANGLADESH
58 CAMBODIA
59 British Indian Ocean Territory

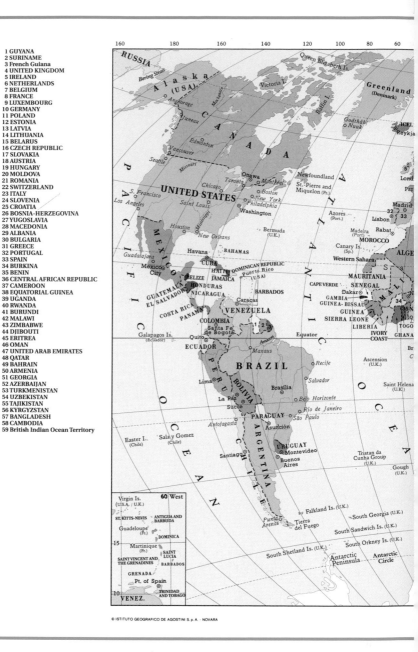

© ISTITUTO GEOGRAFICO DE AGOSTINI S. p. A. · NOVARA

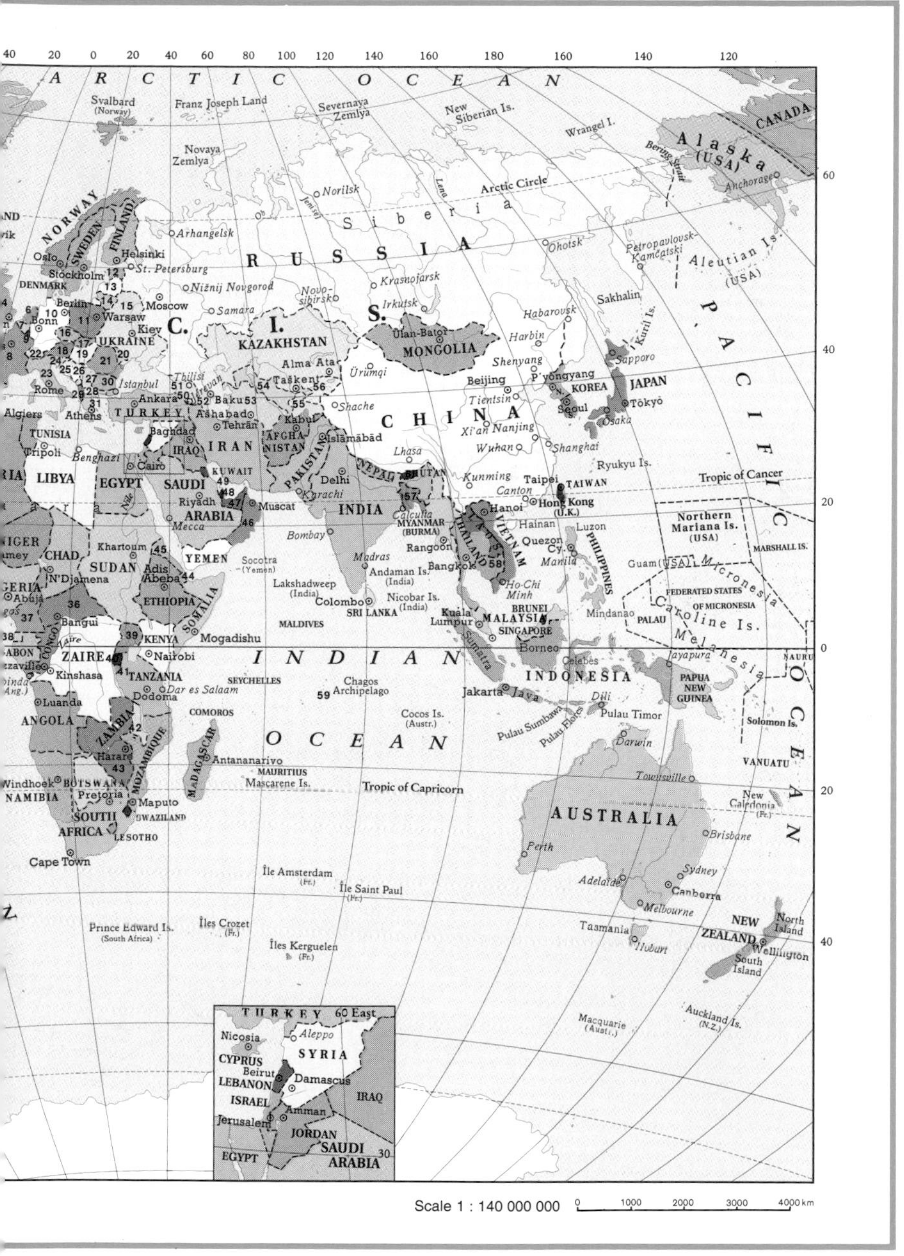

40 20 0 20 40 60 80 100 120 140 160 180 160 140 120

A R C T I C   O C E A N

Svalbard (Norway)   Franz Joseph Land   Severnaya Zemlya   New Siberian Is.   Wrangel I.   CANADA

Novaya Zemlya   Arctic Circle   Bering Str.   Alaska (USA)

ND   Arhangelsk   Norilsk   Ohotsk   Petropavlovsk Kamčatski   Anchorage   60

rik   NORWAY   S i b e r i a   Aleutian Is. (USA)

Oslo   Helsinki   R U S S I A   PACIFIC

Stockholm   St. Petersburg   Niznij Novgorod   Novo-sibirsk   Krasnojarsk   Habarovsk   Sakhalin

DENMARK   13   Moscow   Irkutsk   Kuril Is.

Berlin   15   Samara   Harbin   Sapporo   40

Bonn   11   Warsaw   Kiev   C. I. S.   Ulan-Bator   Shenyang   P'yongyang   JAPAN

UKRAINE   KAZAKHSTAN   MONGOLIA   Beijing   KOREA   Tokyo

Alma Ata   Urümqi   Tientsin   Seoul   Osaka

Istanbul   Tbilisi   Taskent   54   56   Shache   Xi'an Nanjing   Shanghai

Rome   Ankara   Baku   55   CHINA   Wuhan

TURKEY   Ashabad   Kabul   Lhasa   Ryukyu Is.

Algiers   Athens   Baghdad   Tehrān   AFGHA-NISTAN   Islamabad   Kunming   Taipei   Tropic of Cancer

TUNISIA   IRAQ   IRAN   PAKIS-   Delhi   NEPAL   BHUTAN   Canton   TAIWAN

Tripoli   Benghazi   Cairo   KUWAIT   Karachi   Hanoi   Hong Kong (U.K.)   Northern Mariana Is. (USA)

IA   LIBYA   EGYPT   SAUDI   Riyadh   Muscat   INDIA   MYANMAR (BURMA)   Hainan   Guam (USA)   MARSHALL IS.

Mecca   ARABIA   Bombay   Rangoon   Madras   Bangkok   Quezon   PHILIPPINES   Micronesia

IGER   CHAD   Khartoum   YEMEN   Socotra (Yemen)   Lakshadweep (India)   THAILAND   VIETNAM   Manila   FEDERATED STATES OF MICRONESIA

SUDAN   Adis Abeba   Colombo   Nicobar Is. (India)   Ho-Chi Minh   Mindanao   PALAU   Caroline Is.

ERIA   ETHIOPIA   SRI LANKA   MALAYSIA   BRUNEI   Melanesia

Bangui   KENYA   SOMALIA   MALDIVES   Kuala Lumpur   SINGAPORE   Borneo   Jayapura   NAURU

ABON   ZAIRE   Nairobi   I N D I A N   Sumatra   Celebes   INDONESIA   PAPUA NEW GUINEA   Solomon Is.

Kinshasa   TANZANIA   SEYCHELLES   Chagos Archipelago   Jakarta   Java   Dili   Pulau Timor   Darwin

Luanda   Dar es Salaam   Dodoma   COMOROS   59   Cocos Is. (Austr.)   Pulau Sumbawa   Pulau Flores   VANUATU

ANGOLA   ZAMBIA   Harare   MADAGASCAR   O C E A N   Antananarivo   Townsville   New Caledonia (Fr.)   20

Windhoek   BOTSWANA   Pretoria   MOZAMBIQUE   MAURITIUS   Mascarene Is.   Tropic of Capricorn   AUSTRALIA   Brisbane

NAMIBIA   SOUTH AFRICA   SWAZILAND   LESOTHO   Perth   Sydney

Cape Town   Île Amsterdam (Fr.)   Île Saint Paul (Fr.)   Adelaide   Canberra   NEW ZEALAND   North Island

Prince Edward Is. (South Africa)   Îles Crozet (Fr.)   Îles Kerguelen b (Fr.)   Tasmania   Melbourne   Hobart   South Island   Wellington   40

Macquarie (Aust.)   Auckland Is. (N.Z.)

T U R K E Y   60 East

Nicosia   Aleppo

CYPRUS   SYRIA

Beirut   Damascus

LEBANON

ISRAEL   IRAQ

Jerusalem   Amman

EGYPT   JORDAN   SAUDI   30   ARABIA

Scale 1 : 140 000 000   0   1000   2000   3000   4000 km

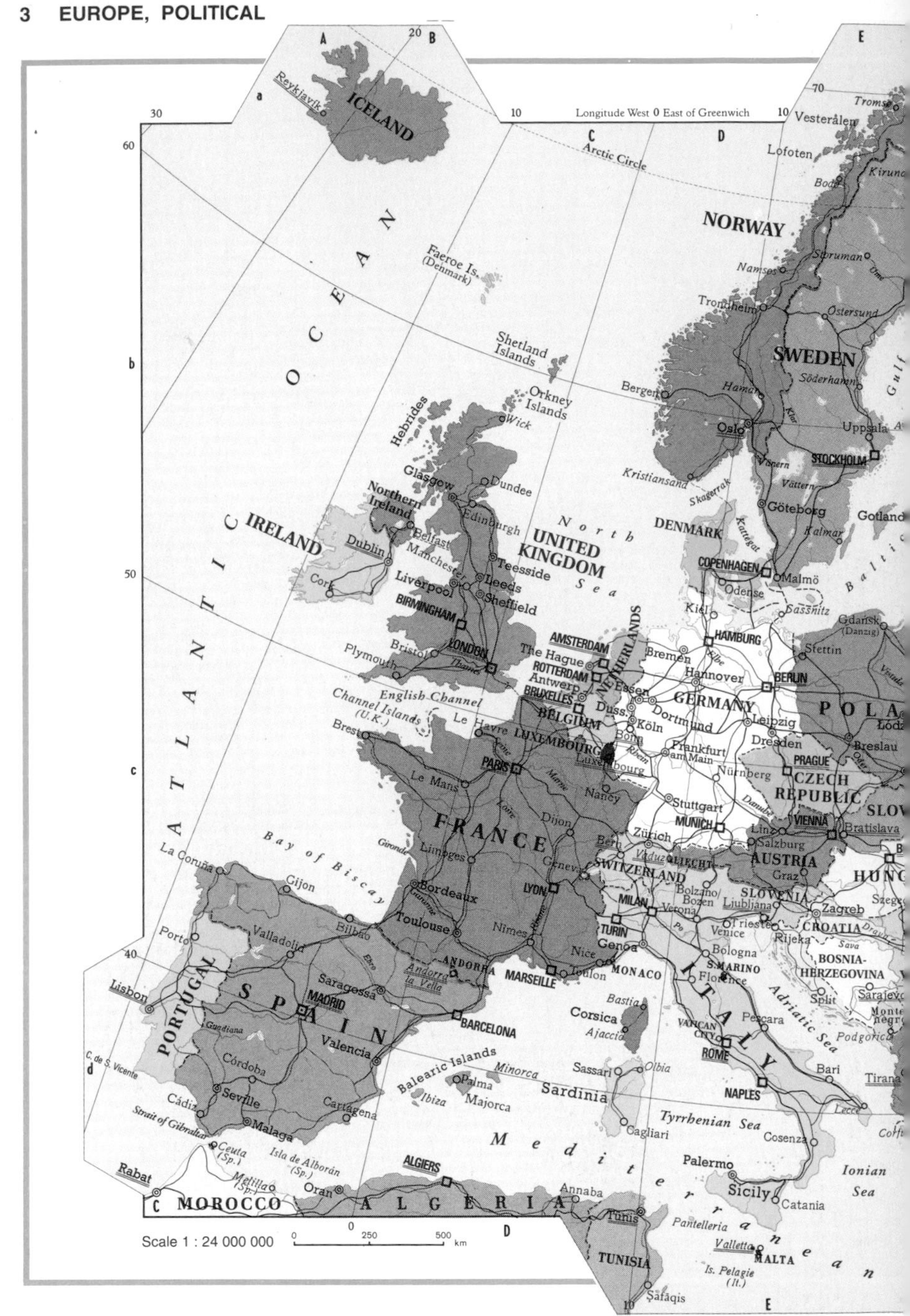
Longitude West 0 East of Greenwich
Arctic Circle
ICELAND
Reykjavík
ATLANTIC OCEAN
Faeroe Is.
(Denmark)
Shetland Islands
Orkney Islands
Hebrides
Wick
NORWAY
Vesterålen
Tromsø
Lofoten
Bodø
Kiruna
Storuman
Namsos
Trondheim
Östersund
SWEDEN
Söderhamn
Bergen
Hamar
Oslo
Uppsala
STOCKHOLM
Vänern
Vättern
Kristiansand
Skagerrak
Göteborg
Kattegat
Kalmar
Gotland
DENMARK
COPENHAGEN
Malmö
Odense
Kiel
Sassnitz
Baltic
Gdańsk
(Danzig)
Glasgow
Dundee
Edinburgh
Northern Ireland
Belfast
IRELAND
Dublin
Cork
UNITED KINGDOM
North Sea
Manchester
Teesside
Liverpool
Leeds
Sheffield
BIRMINGHAM
Bristol
LONDON
Thames
Plymouth
English Channel
Channel Islands
(U.K.)
Brest
Le Havre
AMSTERDAM
The Hague
ROTTERDAM
Antwerp
BRUXELLES
BELGIUM
NETHERLANDS
LUXEMBOURG
Luxembourg
Bremen
HAMBURG
Elbe
Hannover
BERLIN
Stettin
Essen
Düss.
Dortmund
Köln
Bonn
GERMANY
Leipzig
Dresden
Frankfurt am Main
Rhein
Nürnberg
Stuttgart
MUNICH
Danube
PRAGUE
CZECH REPUBLIC
POLAND
Łódź
Breslau
PARIS
Seine
Le Mans
Marne
Nancy
Loire
FRANCE
Dijon
Bay of Biscay
Gironde
Limoges
Bordeaux
Garonne
Toulouse
LYON
Geneva
Bern
Zürich
Vaduz
LIECHT.
SWITZERLAND
Linz
Salzburg
VIENNA
Bratislava
AUSTRIA
Graz
HUNGARY
Bolzano/Bozen
SLOVENIA
Ljubljana
Zagreb
CROATIA
Sava
Rijeka
Trieste
Venice
MILAN
Verona
TURIN
Po
Genoa
Nice
Bologna
S.MARINO
Florence
BOSNIA-HERZEGOVINA
Sarajevo
Split
Montenegro
Podgorica
Adriatic Sea
Nîmes
Rhône
MARSEILLE
Toulon
MONACO
ANDORRA
Andorra la Vella
La Coruña
Gijon
Porto
Valladolid
Bilbao
Ebro
Saragossa
PORTUGAL
Lisbon
SPAIN
MADRID
Guadiana
BARCELONA
Valencia
C. de S. Vicente
Córdoba
Seville
Cádiz
Malaga
Cartagena
Strait of Gibraltar
Ceuta
(Sp.)
Isla de Alborán
(Sp.)
Melilla
(Sp.)
Rabat
MOROCCO
Oran
ALGIERS
ALGERIA
Annaba
Balearic Islands
Minorca
Palma
Ibiza
Majorca
Corsica
Bastia
Ajaccio
Sassari
Olbia
Sardinia
Cagliari
ITALY
Pescara
VATICAN CITY
ROME
NAPLES
Bari
Tirana
Lecce
Tyrrhenian Sea
Cosenza
Palermo
Sicily
Catania
Ionian Sea
Mediterranean
Tunis
TUNISIA
Pantelleria
Valletta
MALTA
Is. Pelagie
(It.)
Şafāqis
Scale 1 : 24 000 000
0 250 500 km

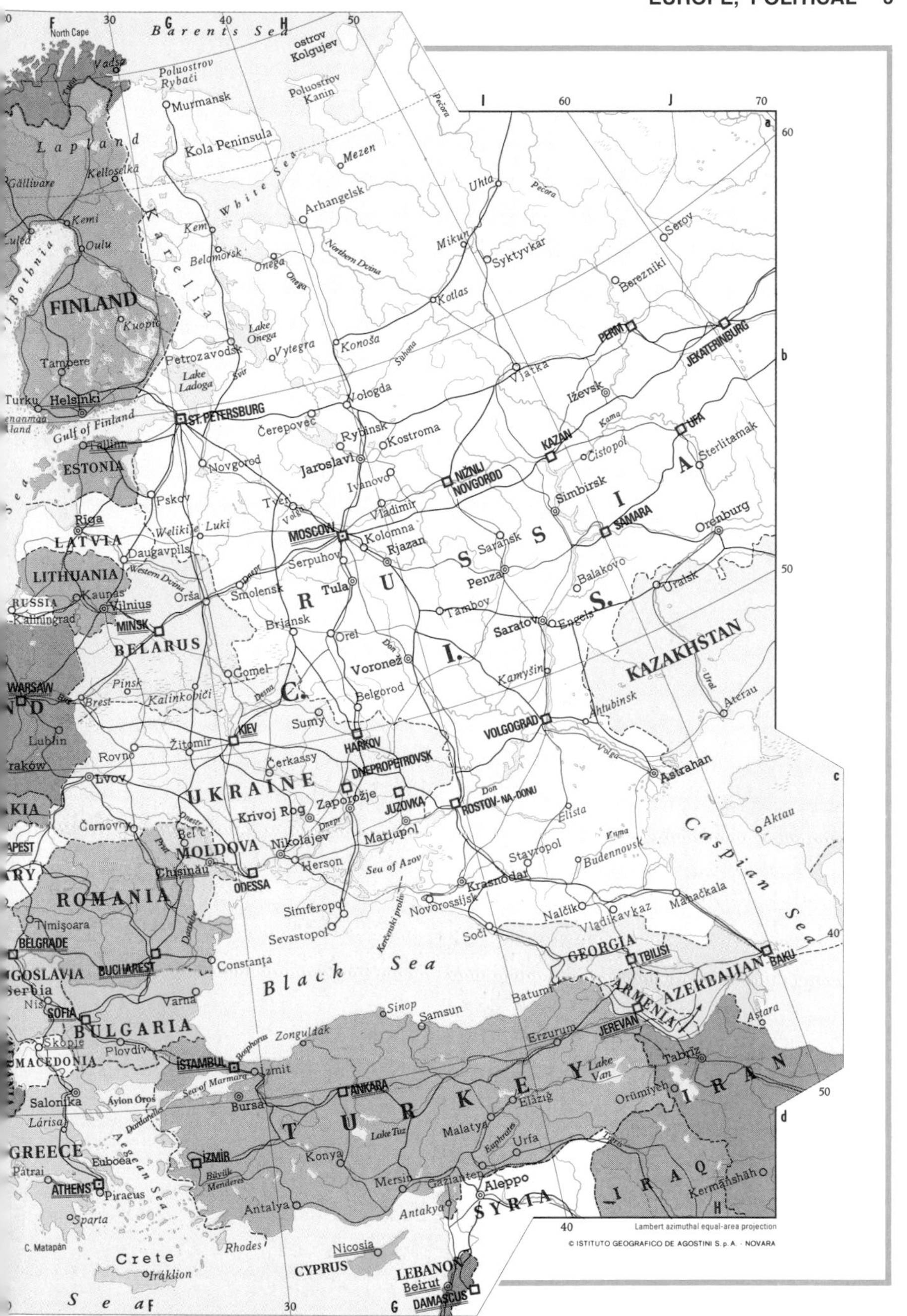
Barents Sea
North Cape
ostrov Kolgujev
Poluostrov Rybači
Poluostrov Kanin
Murmansk
Kola Peninsula
Lapland
White Sea
Mezen
Arhangelsk
Kemi
Oulu
Gulf of Bothnia
FINLAND
Kuopio
Tampere
Turku
Helsinki
Gulf of Finland
Tallinn
ESTONIA
Karelia
Kem
Belomorsk
Onega
Lake Onega
Petrozavodsk
Lake Ladoga
Vytegra
ST. PETERSBURG
Novgorod
Pskov
Riga
LATVIA
Daugavpils
LITHUANIA
Kaunas
Vilnius
Kaliningrad
RUSSIA
MINSK
BELARUS
Pinsk
Brest
WARSAW
Lublin
Kraków
Lvov
Rovno
Žitomir
KIEV
Kalinkoviči
Gomel
Orša
Smolensk
Brjansk
Orel
Tula
Kursk
Voronež
Belgorod
Sumy
HARKOV
Čerkassy
DNEPROPETROVSK
UKRAINE
Zaporožje
Krivoj Rog
JUZOVKA
Mariupol
Nikolajev
Herson
ODESSA
MOLDOVA
Chişinău
Černovcy
ROMANIA
Timişoara
BELGRADE
BUCHAREST
Constanța
YUGOSLAVIA
Serbia
Niš
SOFIA
BULGARIA
Varna
Plovdiv
Skopje
MACEDONIA
Salonika
Áyion Óros
Lárisa
GREECE
Euboea
Pátrai
ATHENS
Piraeus
Sparta
C. Matapán
Crete
Iráklion
Rhodes
Aegean Sea
Sea of Marmara
ISTAMBUL
Bosphorus
Izmit
Bursa
İZMİR
Dardanelles
Antalya
Konya
Mersin
Gaziantep
Antakya
Aleppo
SYRIA
Nicosia
CYPRUS
LEBANON
Beirut
DAMASCUS
ANKARA
TURKEY
Lake Tuz
Malatya
Elâzığ
Urfa
Euphrates
Erzurum
Lake Van
Samsun
Sinop
Zonguldak
Black Sea
Sevastopol
Simferopol
Kerčenskij proliv
Sea of Azov
Novorossijsk
Krasnodar
Soči
Batumi
GEORGIA
TBILISI
ARMENIA
JEREVAN
AZERBAIJAN
BAKU
Astara
Tabrīz
Orūmīyeh
IRAN
IRAQ
Kermānshāh
Nal'čik
Vladikavkaz
Mahačkala
Caspian Sea
Aktau
Stavropol
Budennovsk
Elista
ROSTOV-NA-DONU
Don
VOLGOGRAD
Kamyšin
Astrahan
Volga
Aktubinsk
Atarau
KAZAKHSTAN
Ural
Uralsk
Saratov
Engels
Balakovo
Penza
Tambov
Saransk
Rjazan
RUSSIA
Serpuhov
Kolomna
MOSCOW
Tver'
Vladimir
Ivanovo
Jaroslavl
Kostroma
Rybinsk
Čerepovec
Vologda
Konoša
Suhona
Kotlas
Northern Dvina
Mikun
Syktyvkar
Uhta
Pečora
NIŽNIJ NOVGOROD
Simbirsk
SAMARA
KAZAN
Čistopol
Kama
Iževsk
Vjatka
PERM
Berezniki
Serov
JEKATERINBURG
UFA
Sterlitamak
Orenburg
Lambert azimuthal equal-area projection
© ISTITUTO GEOGRAFICO DE AGOSTINI S.p.A. - NOVARA

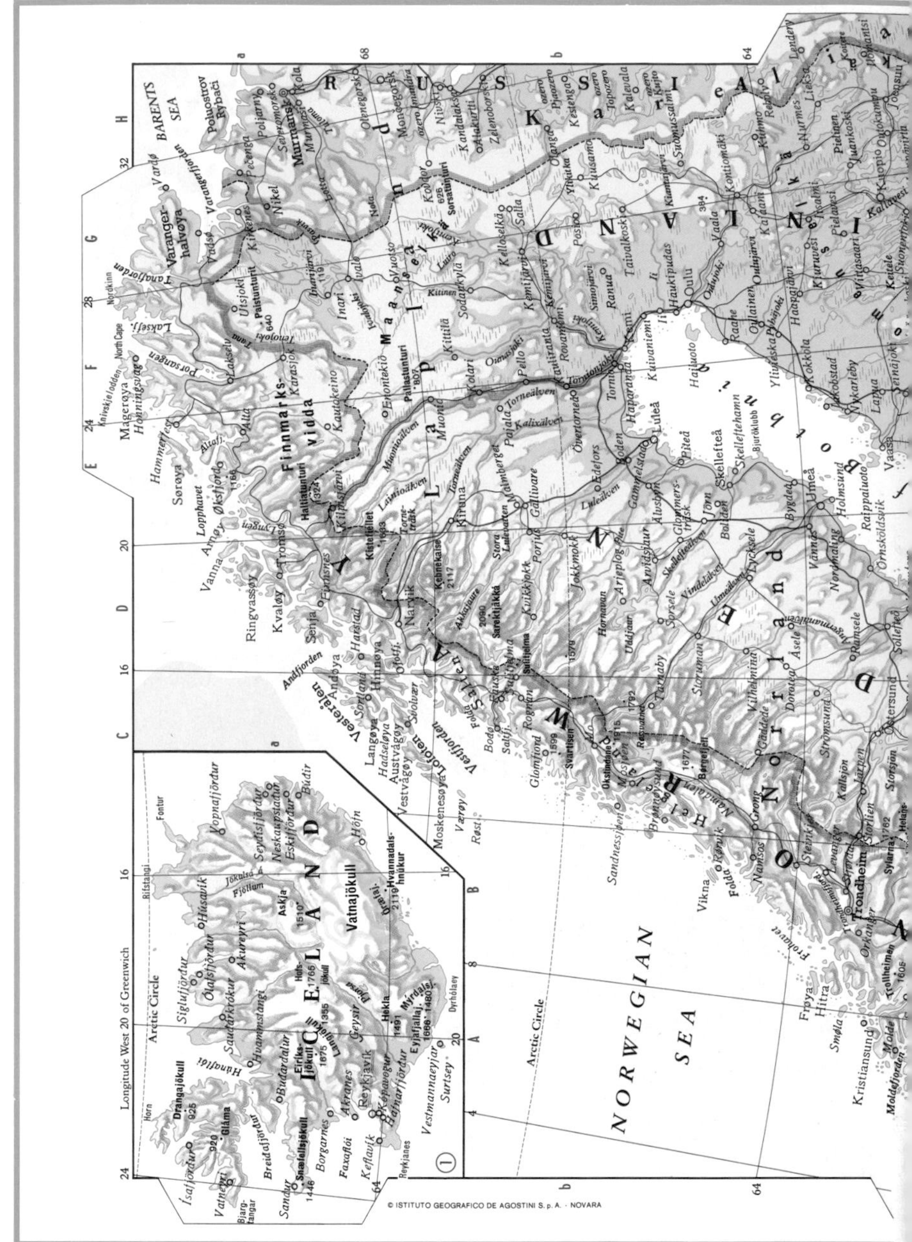

© ISTITUTO GEOGRAFICO DE AGOSTINI S. p. A. - NOVARA

BARENTS SEA
NORWEGIAN SEA
ICELAND
Vatnajökull
Hvannadalshnúkur
Reykjavík
Akureyri
Húsavík
Arctic Circle
Longitude West 20 of Greenwich
Finnmarksvidda
Varangerhalvøya
Murmansk
Vardø
Vadsø
Kirkenes
Nikel
Hammerfest
Tromsø
Narvik
Kiruna
Gällivare
Luleå
Oulu
Umeå
Trondheim
Kristiansund
Molde
Östersund
Vesterålen
Lofoten
Senja
Kebnekaise
North Cape
Magerøya
Karasjok
Kautokeino
Inari
Rovaniemi
Kemi
Tornio
Haparanda
Skellefteå
Vaasa
Kokkola
Kajaani
Kuopio
Namsos
Bodø
Mo
Harstad
Alta
Lakselv
Sodankylä
Kittilä
Kemijärvi
Ranua
Arvidsjaur
Jokkmokk
Storuman
Vilhelmina
Sorsele
Lycksele
Örnsköldsvik
Sollefteå
Surtsey
Vestmannaeyjar
Hekla
Keflavík
Grong
Frøya
Hitra
Smøla

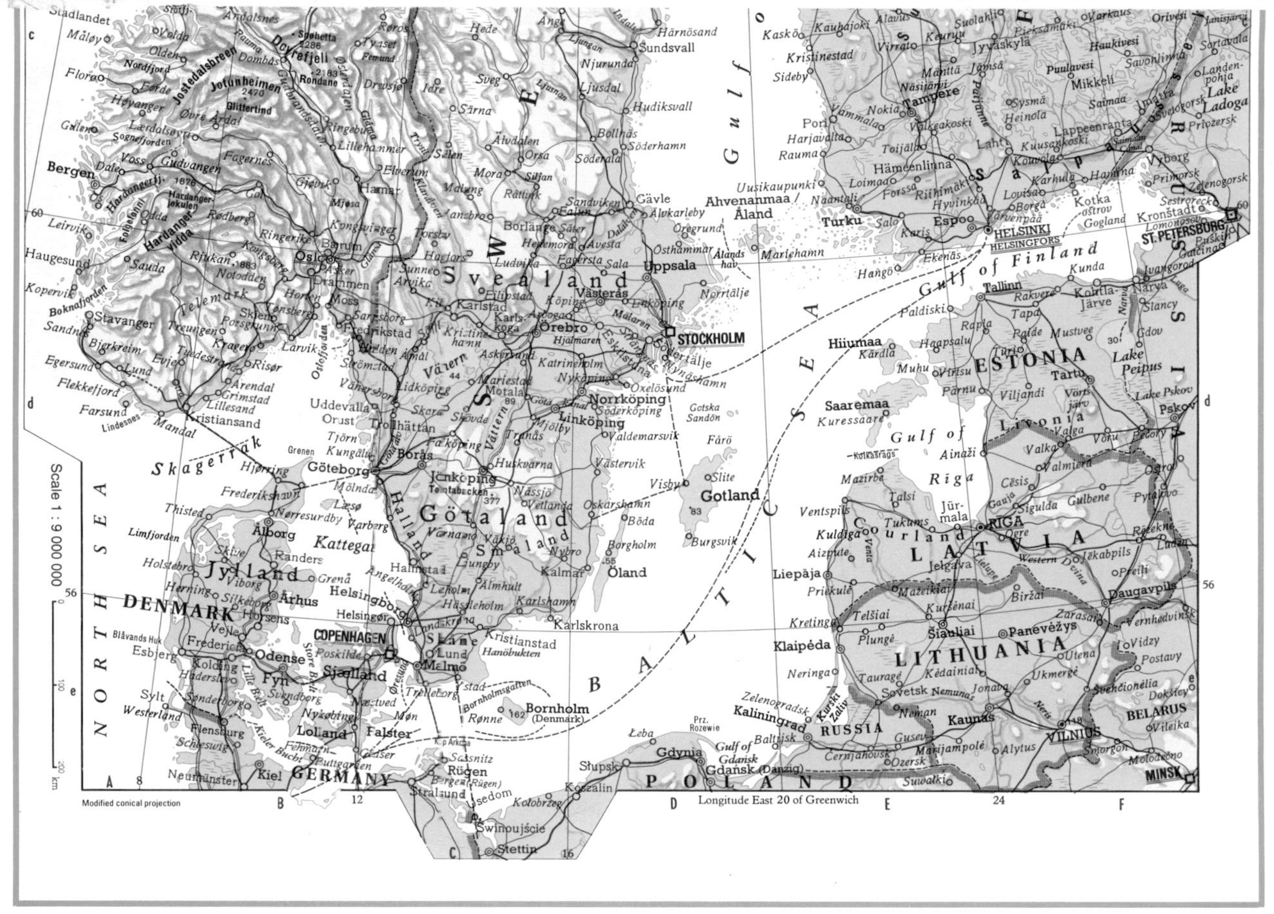
Scale 1 : 9 000 000
0 100 200 km
Modified conical projection
Longitude East 20 of Greenwich
NORTH SEA
Skagerrak
Kattegat
Gulf of Bothnia
Gulf of Finland
Gulf of Riga
BALTIC SEA
DENMARK
ESTONIA
LATVIA
LITHUANIA
BELARUS
RUSSIA
POLAND
GERMANY
Svealand
Götaland
Småland
Halland
Jylland
Courland
Livonia
Oslo
STOCKHOLM
HELSINKI
HELSINGFORS
ST. PETERSBURG
Tallinn
RIGA
VILNIUS
MINSK
COPENHAGEN
Göteborg
Bergen
Stavanger
Kristiansand
Uppsala
Västerås
Örebro
Norrköping
Linköping
Jönköping
Borås
Turku
Tampere
Espoo
Gotland
Öland
Saaremaa
Hiiumaa
Bornholm
(Denmark)
Ahvenanmaa / Åland
Lake Ladoga
Lake Peipus
Kaliningrad
Klaipėda
Kaunas
Šiauliai
Panevėžys
Liepāja
Daugavpils
Gdańsk (Danzig)
Gdynia
Malmö
Helsingborg
Århus
Ålborg
Odense
Fyn
Sjælland
Lolland
Falster
Rügen
Kiel
Stettin

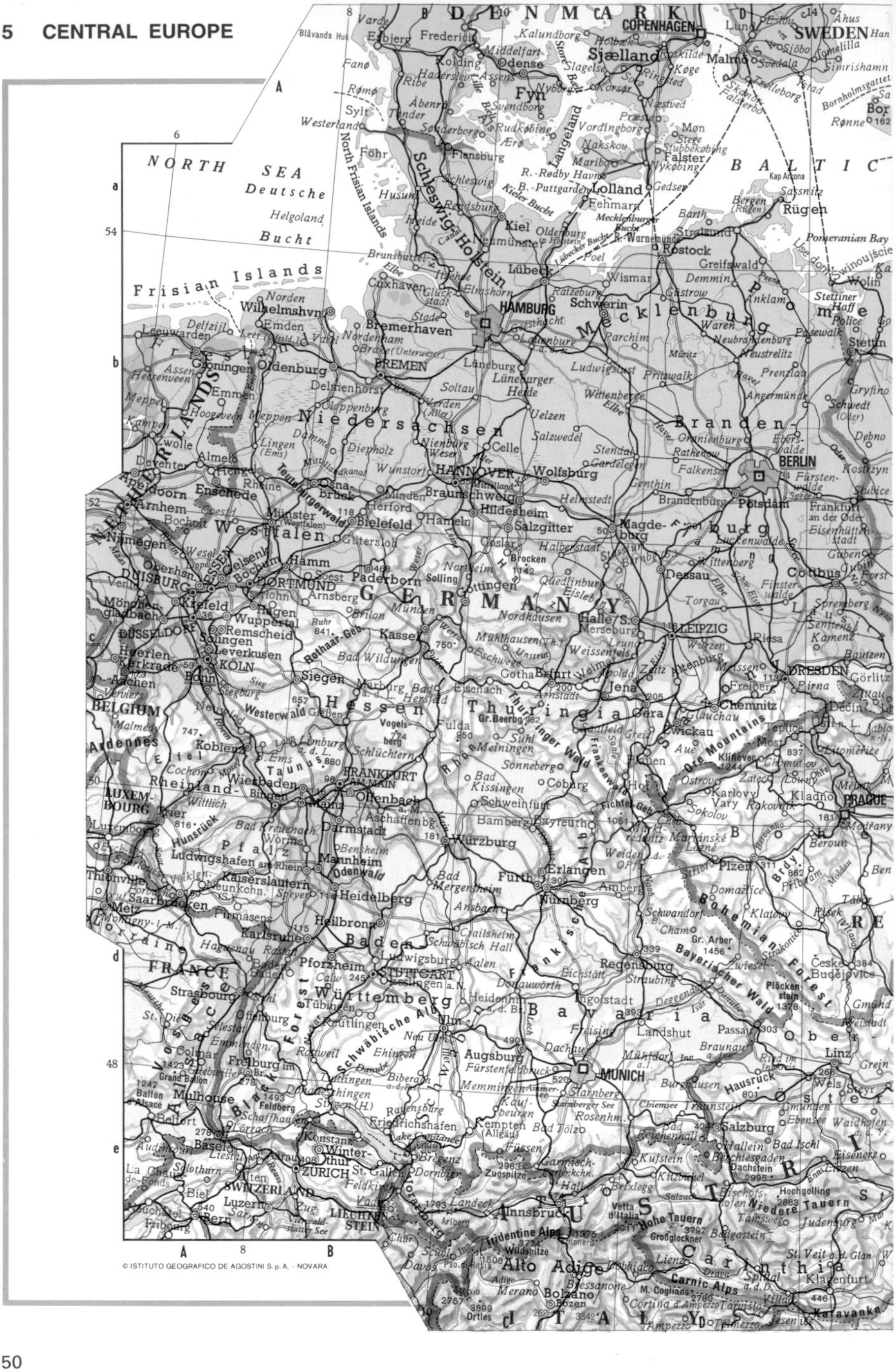

NORTH SEA
Deutsche
Helgoland
Bucht

Frisian Islands

DENMARK
COPENHAGEN
SWEDEN

BALTIC

Schleswig-Holstein

HAMBURG
BREMEN
BREMERHAVEN
Wilhelmshvn
Emden
Oldenburg
Groningen

NIEDERSACHSEN

HANNOVER
Wolfsburg
Hildesheim
Salzgitter
Braunschweig
Bielefeld
Osnabrück

Westfalen
DORTMUND
DUISBURG
DÜSSELDORF
KÖLN
Bonn
Aachen

BELGIUM
Ardenne

LUXEMBOURG

FRANCE

Koblenz
Wiesbaden
FRANKFURT
Offenbach
Darmstadt
Mannheim
Ludwigshafen
Heidelberg
Kaiserslautern
Saarbrücken
Karlsruhe
Pforzheim
STUTTGART
Württemberg
Baden
Freiburg
Mulhouse

Basel
ZURICH
SWITZERLAND
LIECHTENSTEIN
Bern

GERMANY

Kassel
Göttingen
Hessen
Würzburg
Nürnberg
Erlangen
Fürth
Augsburg
MUNICH
Bavaria
Regensburg
Ingolstadt
Landshut
Passau
Salzburg
Innsbruck

Thuringia
LEIPZIG
Halle
Dessau
Magdeburg
DRESDEN
Chemnitz
Gera
Jena
Erfurt

Brandenburg
BERLIN
Potsdam
Frankfurt an der Oder
Cottbus

Rostock
Mecklenburg
Schwerin
Wismar
Lübeck
Stralsund
Greifswald
Rügen

BOHEMIA
PRAGUE
Plzeň
Bohemian Forest
Karlovy Vary
České Budějovice

AUSTRIA
Linz

ITALY
Bolzano
Carnic Alps
Klagenfurt

© ISTITUTO GEOGRAFICO DE AGOSTINI S.p.A. · NOVARA

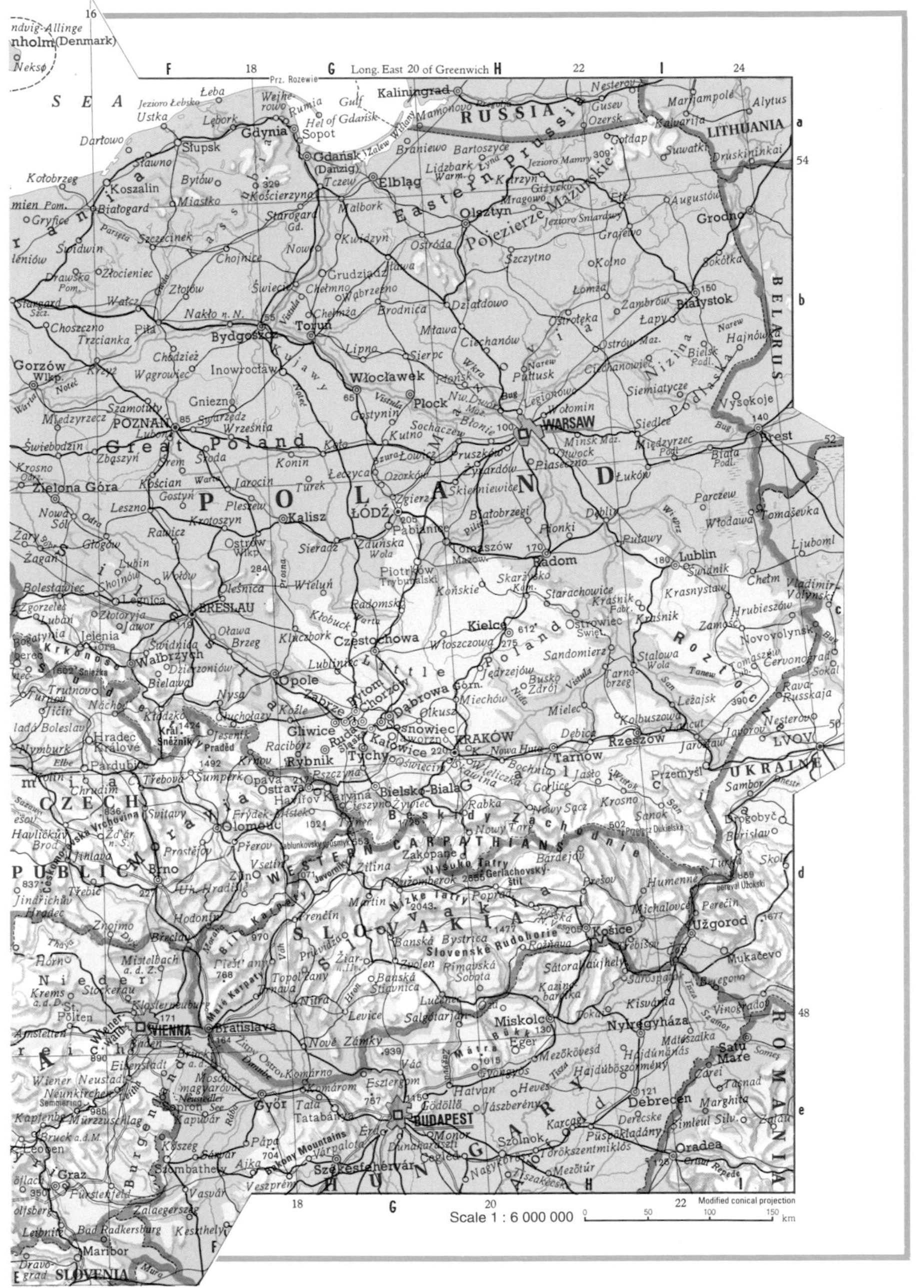
Long. East 20 of Greenwich
POLAND
RUSSIA
LITHUANIA
BELARUS
UKRAINE
ROMANIA
SLOVAKIA
CZECH REPUBLIC
HUNGARY
WARSAW
BUDAPEST
VIENNA
BRESLAU
KRAKÓW
Scale 1 : 6 000 000
Modified conical projection

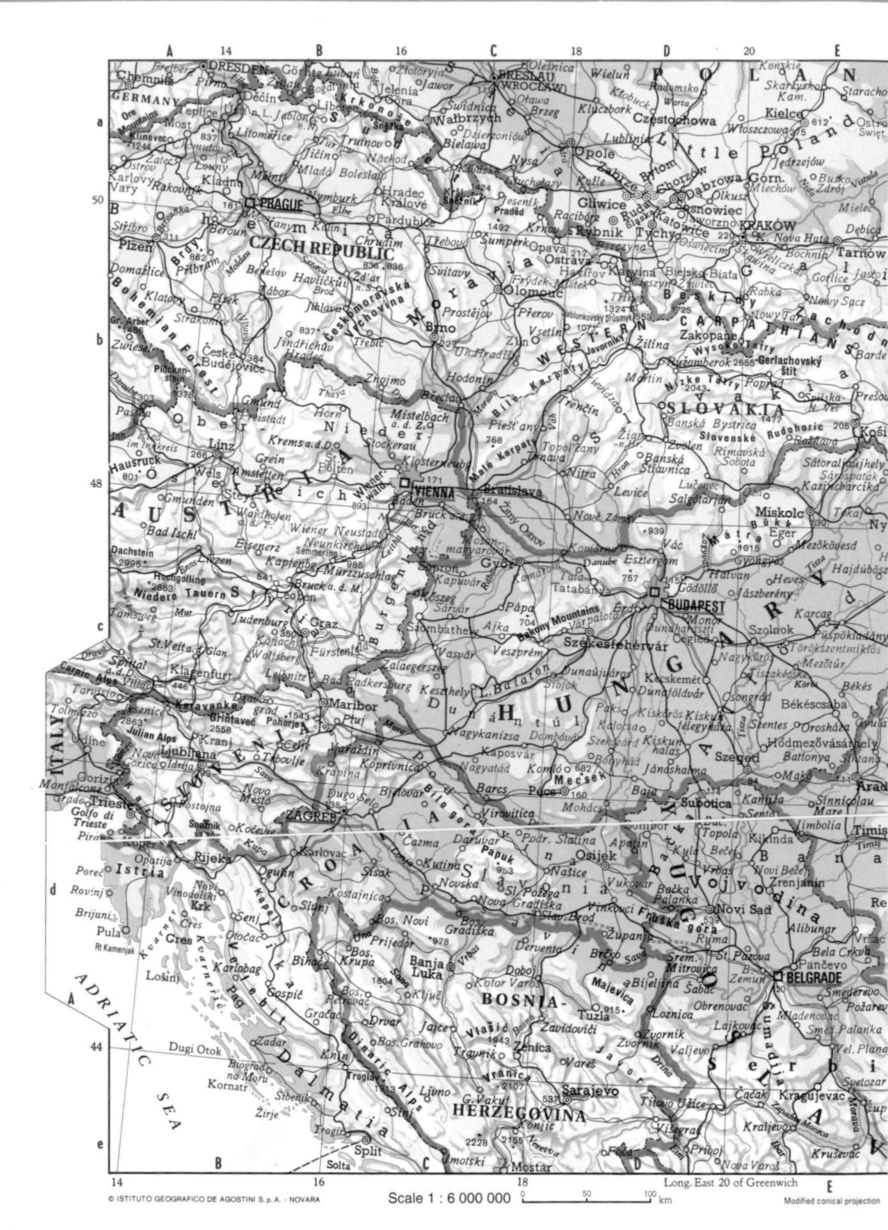

Scale 1 : 6 000 000

Long. East 20 of Greenwich

© ISTITUTO GEOGRAFICO DE AGOSTINI S.p.A. - NOVARA

Modified conical projection

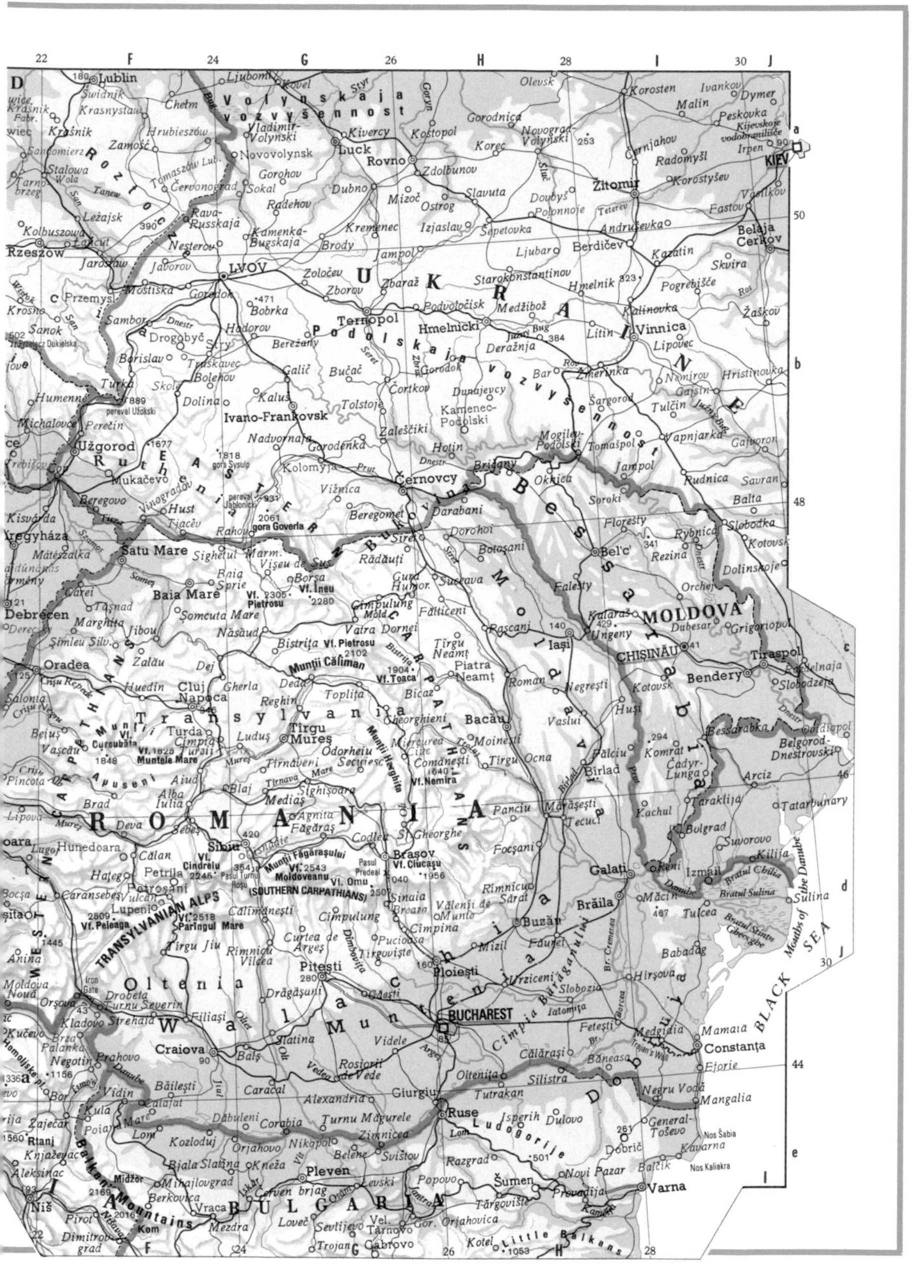

Lublin
Chełm
Volynskaja vozvyšennost
Kovel
Luck
Rovno
Kivercy
Kostopol
Gorodnica
Novograd-Volynskij
Korosten
Malin
Ivankov
Dymer
Kijevskoje vodochranilišče
KIEV
Irpen
Radomyšl
Korostyšev
Žitomir
Vladimir-Volynskij
Novovolynsk
Zamość
Hrubieszów
Krasnystaw
Kraśnik
Stalowa Wola
Tarnobrzeg
Leżajsk
Kolbuszowa
Łańcut
Rzeszów
Jarosław
Przemyśl
Krosno
Sanok
Roztocze
Sokal
Červonograd
Gorohov
Radehov
Rava-Russkaja
Kamenka-Bugskaja
Nesterov
Javorov
LVOV
Mostiska
Gorodok
Sambor
Drogobyč
Stryj
Borislav
Truskavec
Bolehov
Dolina
Kaluš
Turka
Skole
Bobrka
Brody
Dubno
Mizoč
Ostrog
Slavuta
Zdolbunov
Kremenec
Izjaslav
Šepetovka
Polonnoje
Berdičev
Andruševka
Fastov
Belaja Cerkov
Kazatin
Skvira
Ljubar
Starokonstantinov
Hmelnik
Pogrebišče
Zoločev
Zborov
Zbaraž
UKRAINE
Ternopol
Podvoločisk
Medžibož
Hmelnicki
Deražnja
Litin
Vinnica
Lipovec
Podolskaja vozvyšennost
Berežany
Galič
Bučač
Gorodok
Čortkov
Dunajevcy
Kamenec-Podolski
Bar
Žmerinka
Šargorod
Tulčin
Nemirov
Gajsin
Hristinovka
Ivano-Frankovsk
Tolstoje
Zaleščiki
Nadvornaja
Gorodenka
Kolomyja
Hotin
Mogilev-Podolski
Tomašpol
Jampol
Vapnjarka
Gajvoron
Černovcy
Vižnica
Oknica
Soroki
Rudnica
Savran
Balta
Humenné
Michalovce
Perečin
Užgorod
Mukačevo
Ruthenia
Vinogradov
Hust
Beregovo
Tjačev
Rahov
gora Goverla
EASTERN CARPATHIANS
Tisza
Kisvárda
Nyíregyháza
Mátészalka
Satu Mare
Sighetul Marm.
Vişeu de Sus
Baia Sprie
Borşa
Baia Mare
Vf. Pietrosu
Vf. Ineu
Carei
Tăşnad
Şomcuta Mare
Năsăud
Debrecen
Marghita
Jibou
Şimleu Silv.
Zalău
Dej
Oradea
Huedin
Cluj Napoca
Gherla
Bistriţa
Vf. Pietrosu
Munţii Călimani
Vf. Toaca
Bukovina
Siret
Rădăuţi
Suceava
Gura Humor.
Câmpulung Mold.
Vatra Dornei
Fălticeni
Dorohoi
Botoşani
Darabani
Bessarabia
Moldavia
Bel'c'
Floreşty
Faleşty
Rybnica
Kotovsk
Dolinskoje
Rezina
Orchej
MOLDOVA
Dubesar
Grigoriopol
Kalaraš
Ungeny
Iaşi
CHIŞINĂU
Tiraspol
Bendery
Kotovsk
Slobodzeja
Dnestr
Belgorod-Dnestrovski
Bessarabka
Ovidiopol
Hînceşti
Huşi
Komrat
Čadyr-Lunga
Arciz
Taraklija
Tatarbunary
Kachul
Bolgrad
Suvorovo
Izmail
Kilija
Reni
Danube
Bratul Chilia
Bratul Sulina
Sulina
Bratul Sfintu Gheorghe
Mouths of the Danube
BLACK SEA
Tîrgu Neamţ
Piatra Neamţ
Roman
Paşcani
Negreşti
Vaslui
Bacău
Moineşti
Bicaz
Toplița
Gheorghieni
Miercurea Ciuc
Comăneşti
Tîrgu Ocna
Odorheiu Secuiesc
Vf. Nemira
Munţii Harghita
CARPATHIANS
Bîrlad
Bîrlad
Panciu
Mărăşeşti
Tecuci
Focşani
Galaţi
Brăila
Măcin
Tulcea
Babadag
Rimnicu Sărat
Buzău
Făurei
Mizil
Ploieşti
Urziceni
Slobozia
Hîrşova
Cîmpia Bărăganului
Fetești
Medgidia
Constanţa
Mamaia
Eforie
Mangalia
Negru Vodă
Trajan's Wall
Transylvania
Reghin
Tîrgu Mureş
Luduş
Turda
Cîmpia Turzii
Vf. Curcubăta
Vf. Muntele Mare
Apuseni
Aiud
Blaj
Tîrnăveni
Mediaş
Sighişoara
Alba Iulia
Brad
Deva
Hunedoara
Călan
Sibiu
Vf. Cindrelu
Vf. Moldoveanu
Munţii Făgăraşului
Făgăraş
Agnita
Codlea
Braşov
Sf. Gheorghe
Vf. Ciucaşu
Pasul Predeal
Vf. Omu
SOUTHERN CARPATHIANS
Sinaia
Breaza
Vălenii de Munte
Cîmpina
Hațeg
Petrila
Petroşani
Lupeni
Vf. Peleaga
Vf. Paringul Mare
TRANSYLVANIAN ALPS
Caransebeş
Lugoj
Tîrgu Jiu
Rîmnicu Vîlcea
Cîmpulung
Curtea de Argeş
Pitești
Tîrgovişte
Găeşti
Drăgăşani
ROMANIA
Oltenia
Walachia
Muntenia
BUCHAREST
Iatomiţa
Orşova
Drobeta Turnu Severin
Strehaia
Filiaşi
Craiova
Balş
Slatina
Videle
Roşiorii de Vede
Alexandria
Giurgiu
Olteniţa
Călăraşi
Silistra
Tutrakan
Dobrogea
Turnu Măgurele
Zimnicea
Corabia
Dăbuleni
Caracal
Băileşti
Calafat
Vidin
Kula
Lom
Kozloduj
Orjahovo
Nikopol
Belene
Svištov
Ruse
Isperih
Dulovo
Razgrad
Ludogorije
General-Toševo
Dobrič
Kavarna
Balčik
Nos Šabla
Nos Kaliakra
Novi Pazar
Varna
Provadija
Šumen
Popovo
Tărgovište
Kamčija
Pleven
Levski
Červen brjag
Bjala Slatina
Knezha
Mihajlovgrad
Berkovica
Vraca
Mezdra
Loveč
Sevlijevo
Vel. Tărnovo
Gor. Orjahovica
Gabrovo
Trojan
Kotel
Little Balkans
BULGARIA
Balkan Mountains
Midžor
Kom
Niš
Pirot
Dimitrovgrad
Aleksinac
Knjaževac
Zaječar
Rtanj
Negotin
Prahovo
Bor
Kučevo
Moldova Nouă
Anina
Reşiţa
Iron Gate
Kladovo

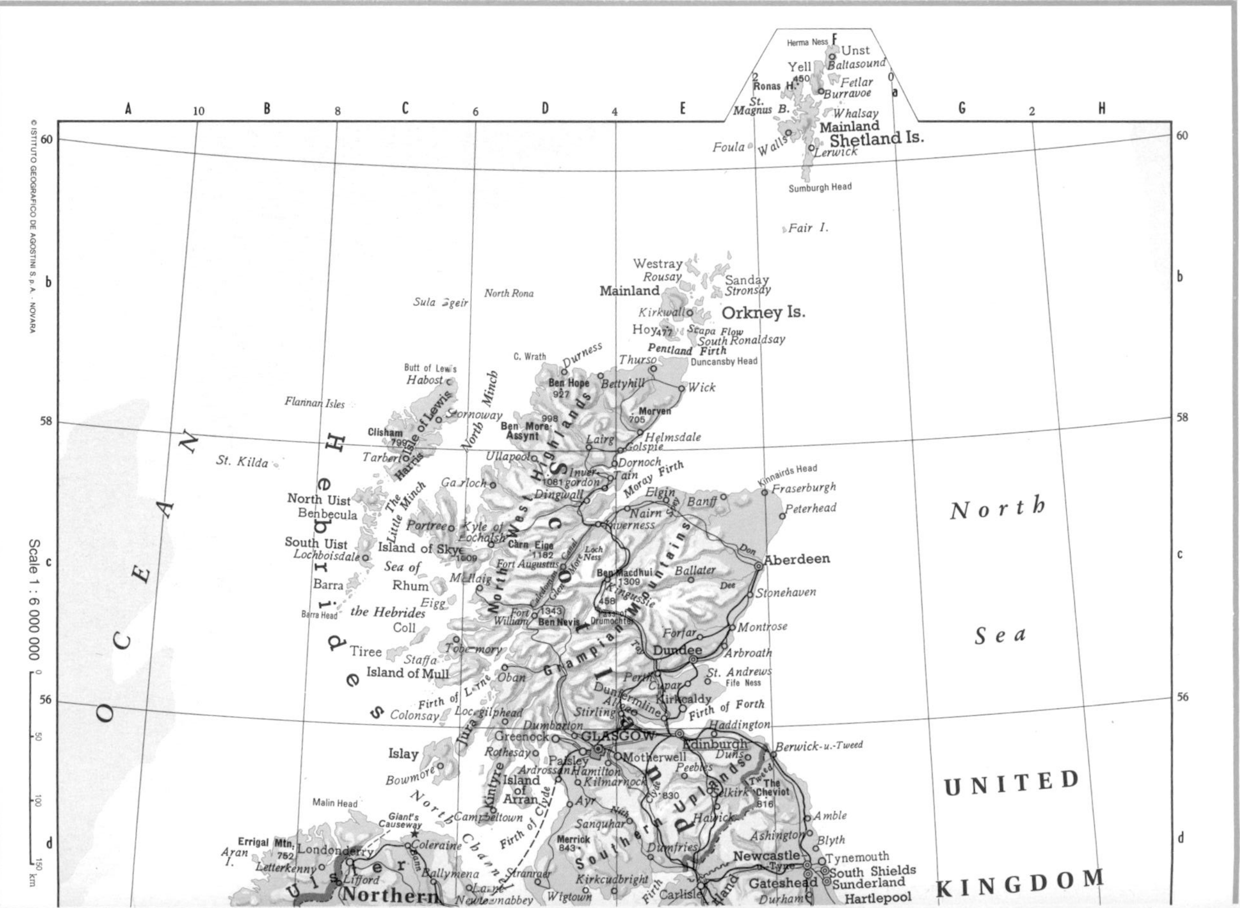
North Sea
UNITED KINGDOM
Shetland Is.
Mainland
Herma Ness
Unst
Baltasound
Yell
Ronas H.
Fetlar
Burravoe
St. Magnus B.
Whalsay
Walls
Lerwick
Foula
Sumburgh Head
Fair I.
Orkney Is.
Westray
Rousay
Sanday
Stronsay
Mainland
Kirkwall
Hoy
Scapa Flow
South Ronaldsay
Pentland Firth
Duncansby Head
Thurso
Wick
Durness
C. Wrath
North Rona
Sula Sgeir
Butt of Lewis
Habost
Stornoway
North Minch
Isle of Lewis
Harris
Clisham
Tarbert
Flannan Isles
St. Kilda
The Little Minch
North Uist
Benbecula
South Uist
Lochboisdale
Barra
Barra Head
Hebrides
Sea of the Hebrides
Island of Skye
Portree
Kyle of Lochalsh
Rhum
Eigg
Coll
Tiree
Staffa
Island of Mull
Tobermory
Oban
Firth of Lorne
Colonsay
Jura
Lochgilphead
Islay
Bowmore
Kintyre
Campbeltown
Island of Arran
Firth of Clyde
North Channel
Scotland
North West Highlands
Grampian Mountains
Southern Uplands
Ben Hope
Bettyhill
Morven
Helmsdale
Ben More Assynt
Lairg
Golspie
Dornoch
Ullapool
Gairloch
Invergordon
Tain
Moray Firth
Dingwall
Carn Eige
Fort Augustus
Caledonian Canal
Glen More
Loch Ness
Mallaig
Fort William
Ben Nevis
Pass of Drumochter
Ben Macdhui
Kingussie
Inverness
Nairn
Elgin
Banff
Kinnairds Head
Fraserburgh
Peterhead
Don
Aberdeen
Ballater
Dee
Stonehaven
Montrose
Forfar
Dundee
Arbroath
Perth
Cupar
St. Andrews
Fife Ness
Kirkcaldy
Dunfermline
Alloa
Stirling
Firth of Forth
Haddington
Dumbarton
Greenock
GLASGOW
Edinburgh
Berwick-u.-Tweed
Rothesay
Paisley
Motherwell
Duns
Peebles
Tweed
The Cheviot
Ardrossan
Hamilton
Kilmarnock
Selkirk
Ayr
Hawick
Sanquhar
Nith
Amble
Ashington
Blyth
Merrick
Dumfries
Newcastle
Tyne
Tynemouth
South Shields
Sunderland
Gateshead
Durham
Hartlepool
Kirkcudbright
Carlisle
Wigtown
Stranraer
Malin Head
Giant's Causeway
Coleraine
Errigal Mtn.
Aran I.
Londonderry
Letterkenny
Lifford
Ulster
Northern
Ballymena
Larne
Newtownabbey
OCEAN
© ISTITUTO GEOGRAFICO DE AGOSTINI S. p. A. - NOVARA
Scale 1 : 6 000 000
0 50 100 150 km

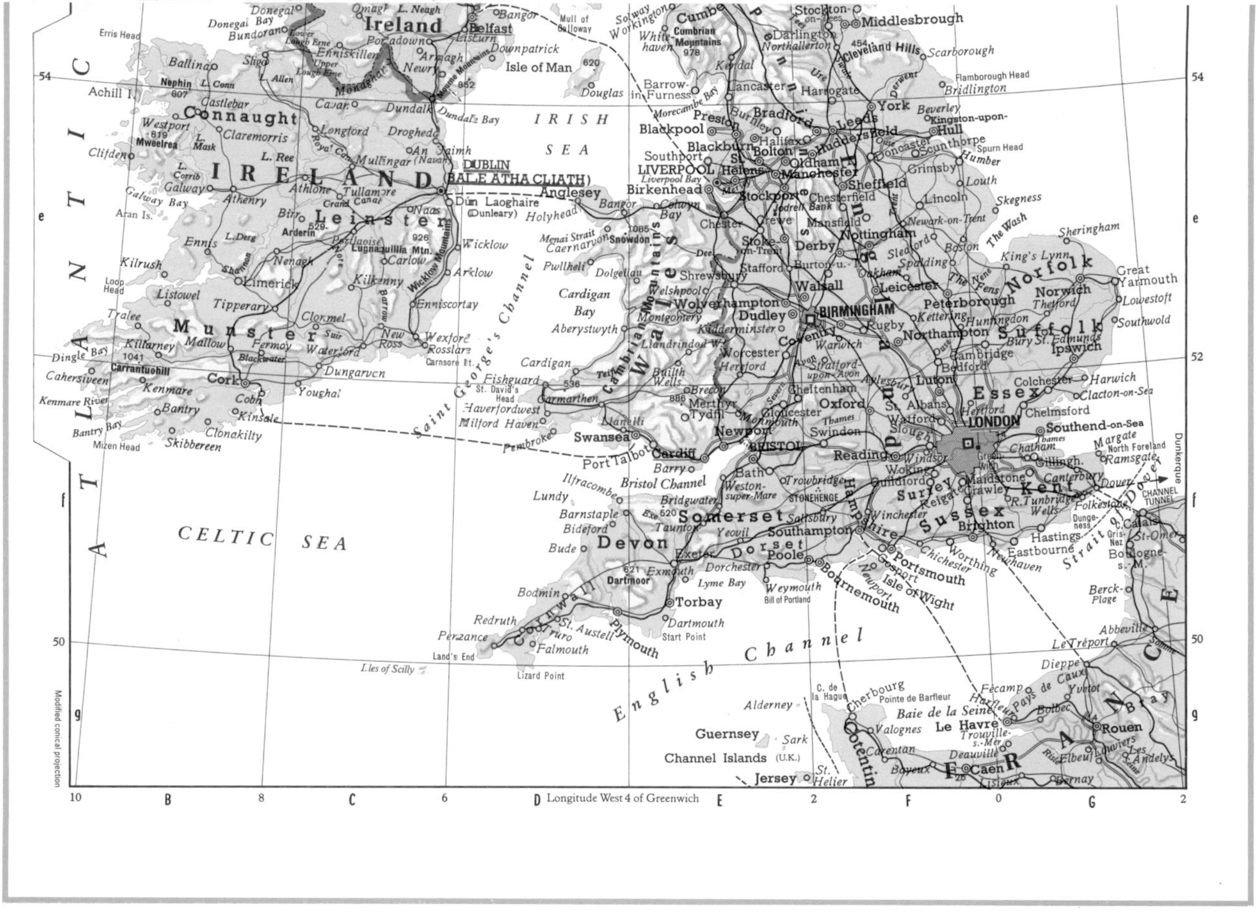
ATLANTIC
IRELAND
Ireland
Connaught
Leinster
Munster
DUBLIN
BAILE ATHA CLIATH
Belfast
Cork
Limerick
Galway
Waterford
Wexford
Isle of Man
Anglesey
IRISH SEA
CELTIC SEA
Saint George's Channel
Bristol Channel
English Channel
Strait of Dover
Wales
England
LIVERPOOL
Manchester
Leeds
Sheffield
BIRMINGHAM
LONDON
BRISTOL
Cardiff
Swansea
Plymouth
Southampton
Portsmouth
Bournemouth
Isle of Wight
Middlesbrough
York
Hull
Nottingham
Leicester
Norwich
Ipswich
Southend-on-Sea
Brighton
Norfolk
Suffolk
Essex
Kent
Sussex
Surrey
Hampshire
Dorset
Somerset
Devon
Cornwall
Guernsey
Jersey
Channel Islands (U.K.)
FRANCE
Le Havre
Rouen
Caen
Cotentin
Dunkerque
CHANNEL TUNNEL
Modified conical projection
Longitude West 4 of Greenwich

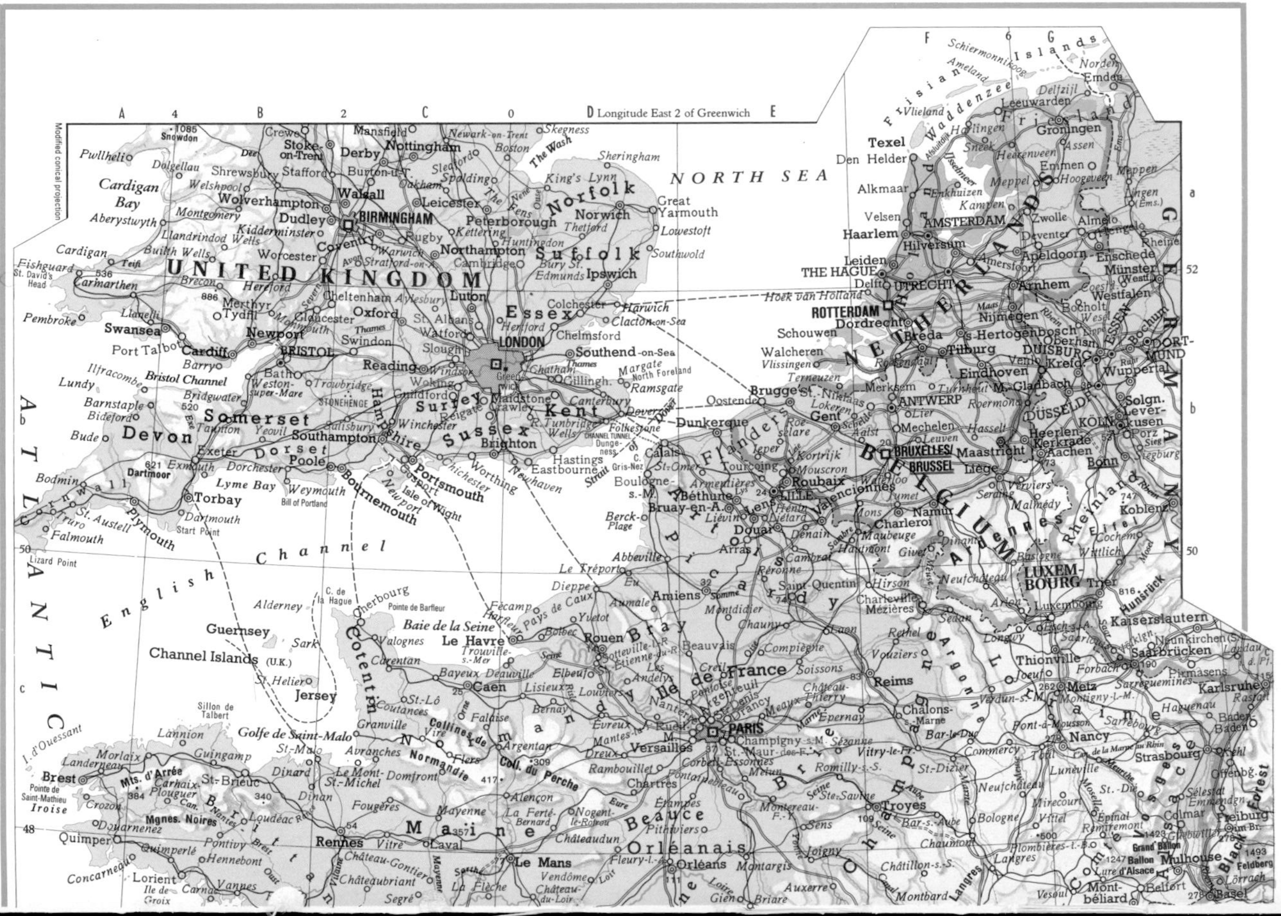
Longitude East 2 of Greenwich
NORTH SEA
ATLANTIC
English Channel
UNITED KINGDOM
NETHERLANDS
BELGIUM
GERMANY
LUXEMBOURG
Île de France
Normandie
Bretagne
Picardy
Champagne
Lorraine
Orléanais
Maine
Beauce
Cotentin
Black Forest
LONDON
PARIS
BRUXELLES/BRUSSEL
AMSTERDAM
THE HAGUE
ROTTERDAM
BIRMINGHAM
BRISTOL
Channel Islands (U.K.)
Guernsey
Jersey
Isle of Wight
Bristol Channel
Cardigan Bay
Lyme Bay
Baie de la Seine
Golfe de Saint-Malo
Strait of Dover
Modified conical projection

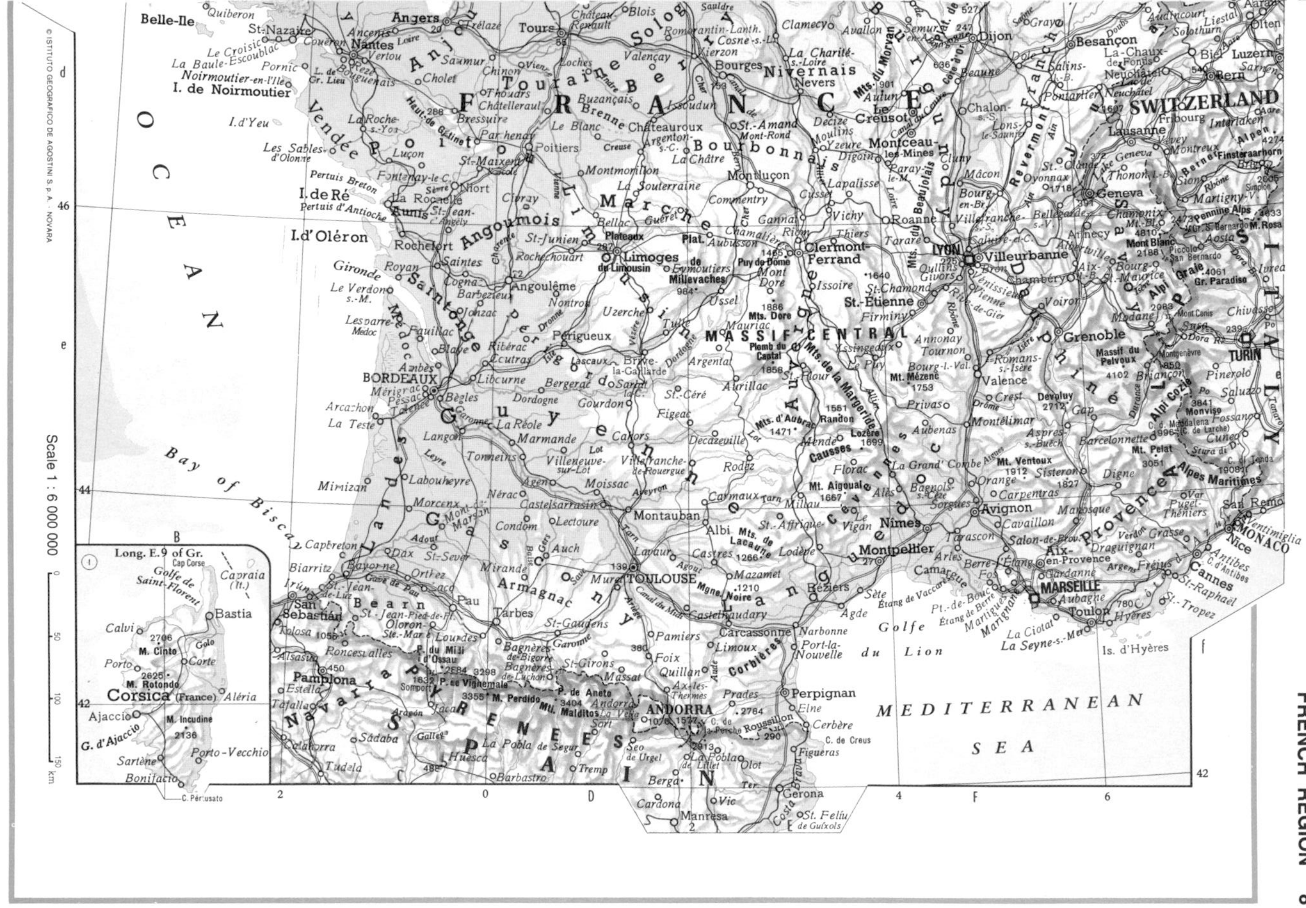

Scale 1 : 6 000 000

0   50   100   150 km

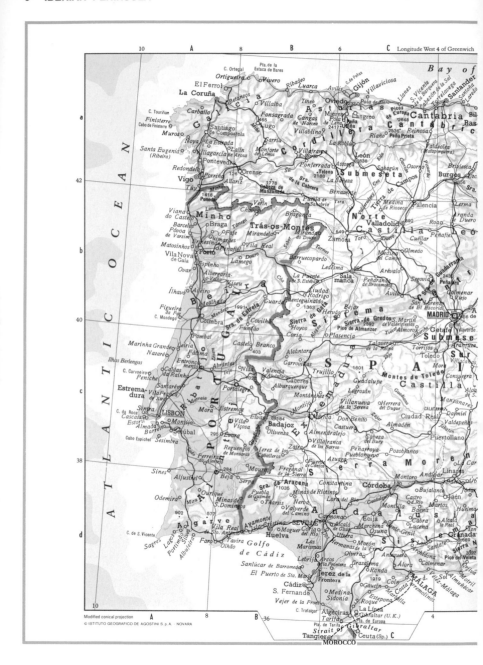

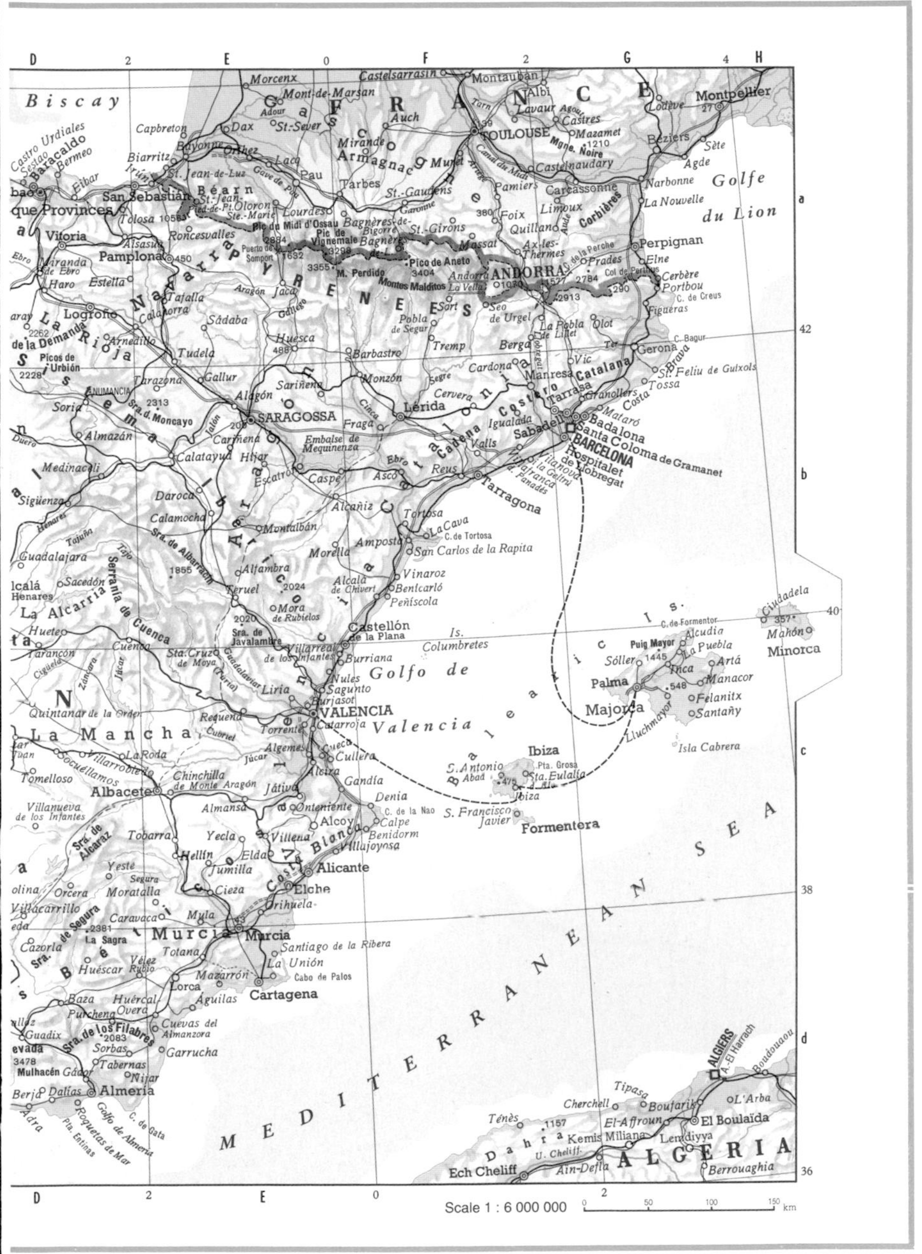
Biscay
FRANCE
Golfe du Lion
Montpellier
Toulouse
Castelsarrasin
Montauban
Mont-de-Marsan
Albi
Castres
Mazamet
Auch
Dax
Bayonne
Biarritz
Pau
Tarbes
Lourdes
Carcassonne
Narbonne
Béziers
Sète
Agde
La Nouvelle
Perpignan
Elne
Cerbère
Portbou
C. de Creus
Figueras
Gerona
Olot
Vic
Manresa
Berga
Tremp
Lérida
Tarrasa
Sabadell
Granollers
Mataró
Badalona
Santa Coloma de Gramanet
BARCELONA
Hospitalet de Llobregat
Tarragona
Reus
Valls
Costa Brava
St. Feliu de Guíxols
Tossa
ANDORRA
PYRENEES
Pic de Aneto
3404
M. Perdido
3355
Montes Malditos
Seo de Urgel
Huesca
Barbastro
Monzón
Fraga
Caspe
Alcañiz
Tortosa
Amposta
San Carlos de la Rapita
C. de Tortosa
Vinaroz
Benicarló
Peñíscola
Castellón de la Plana
Villarreal de los Infantes
Burriana
Nules
Sagunto
Burjasot
VALENCIA
Catarroja
Torrente
Golfo de Valencia
Is. Columbretes
Cullera
Alcira
Gandía
Játiva
Denia
C. de la Nao
Calpe
Benidorm
Villajoyosa
Alcoy
Onteniente
Villena
Elda
Alicante
Elche
Orihuela
Murcia
Cartagena
Cabo de Palos
La Unión
Mazarrón
Lorca
Águilas
Almería
Golfo de Almería
C. de Gata
Baleares Is.
Ibiza
Formentera
Majorca
Palma
Sóller
Inca
Alcudia
Puig Mayor
1445
Manacor
Felanitx
Santañy
Isla Cabrera
Minorca
Mahón
Ciudadela
MEDITERRANEAN SEA
ALGERIA
ALGIERS
El Boulaïda
Ech Cheliff
Tipasa
Cherchell
SARAGOSSA
Pamplona
Logroño
Vitoria
San Sebastián
Tolosa
Tudela
Soria
Teruel
Cuenca
Albacete
Calatayud
Daroca
Medinaceli
Sigüenza
Guadalajara
La Alcarria
La Mancha
Serranía de Cuenca
Almansa
Hellín
Jumilla
Yecla
Cieza
Tobarra
Sra. de Segura
Cazorla
La Sagra
Huéscar
Baza
Guadix
Sra. de los Filabres
Sorbas
Garrucha
Tabernas
Mulhacén
3478
Scale 1 : 6 000 000
0 50 100 150 km

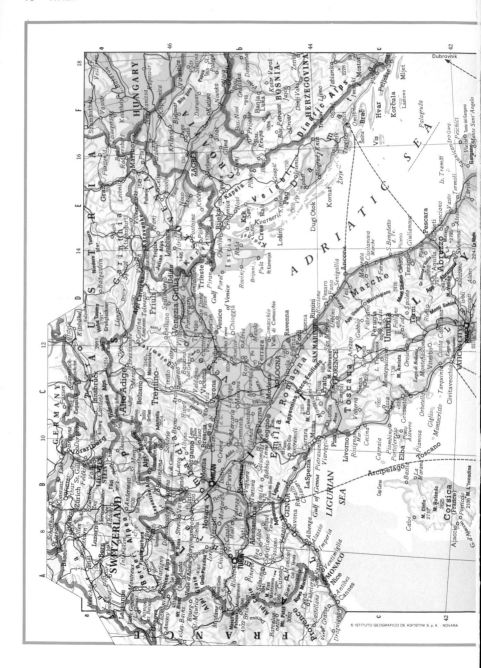

© ISTITUTO GEOGRAFICO DE AGOSTINI S.p.A. - NOVARA

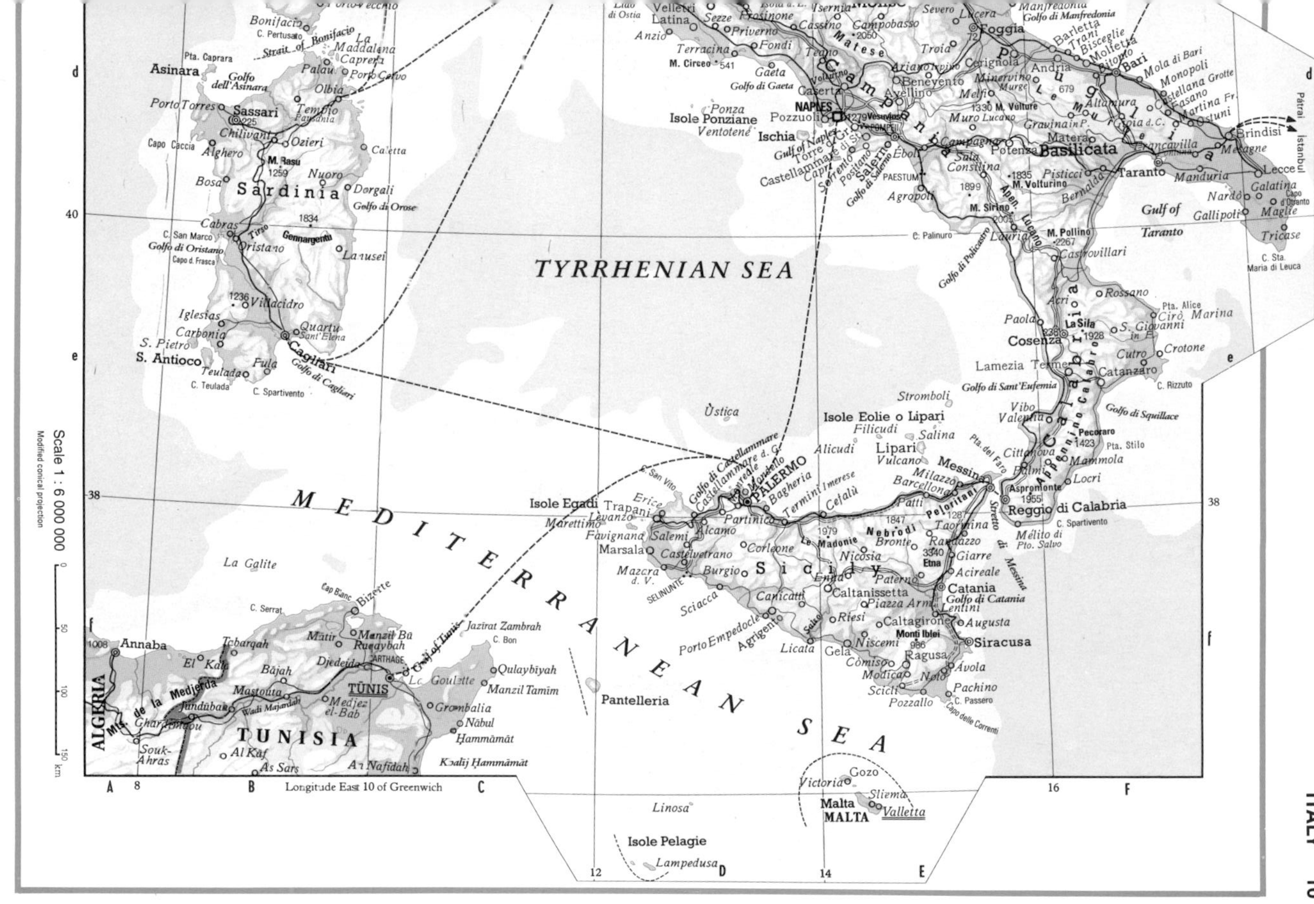
TYRRHENIAN SEA
MEDITERRANEAN SEA
Sardinia
Sicily
TUNISIA
ALGERIA
MALTA
NAPLES
PALERMO
Cagliari
Sassari
Messina
Catania
Siracusa
Reggio di Calabria
Bari
Brindisi
Taranto
Foggia
Tūnis
Annaba
Isole Eolie o Lipari
Isole Egadi
Isole Pelagie
Pantelleria
Longitude East 10 of Greenwich
Scale 1 : 6 000 000
Modified conical projection

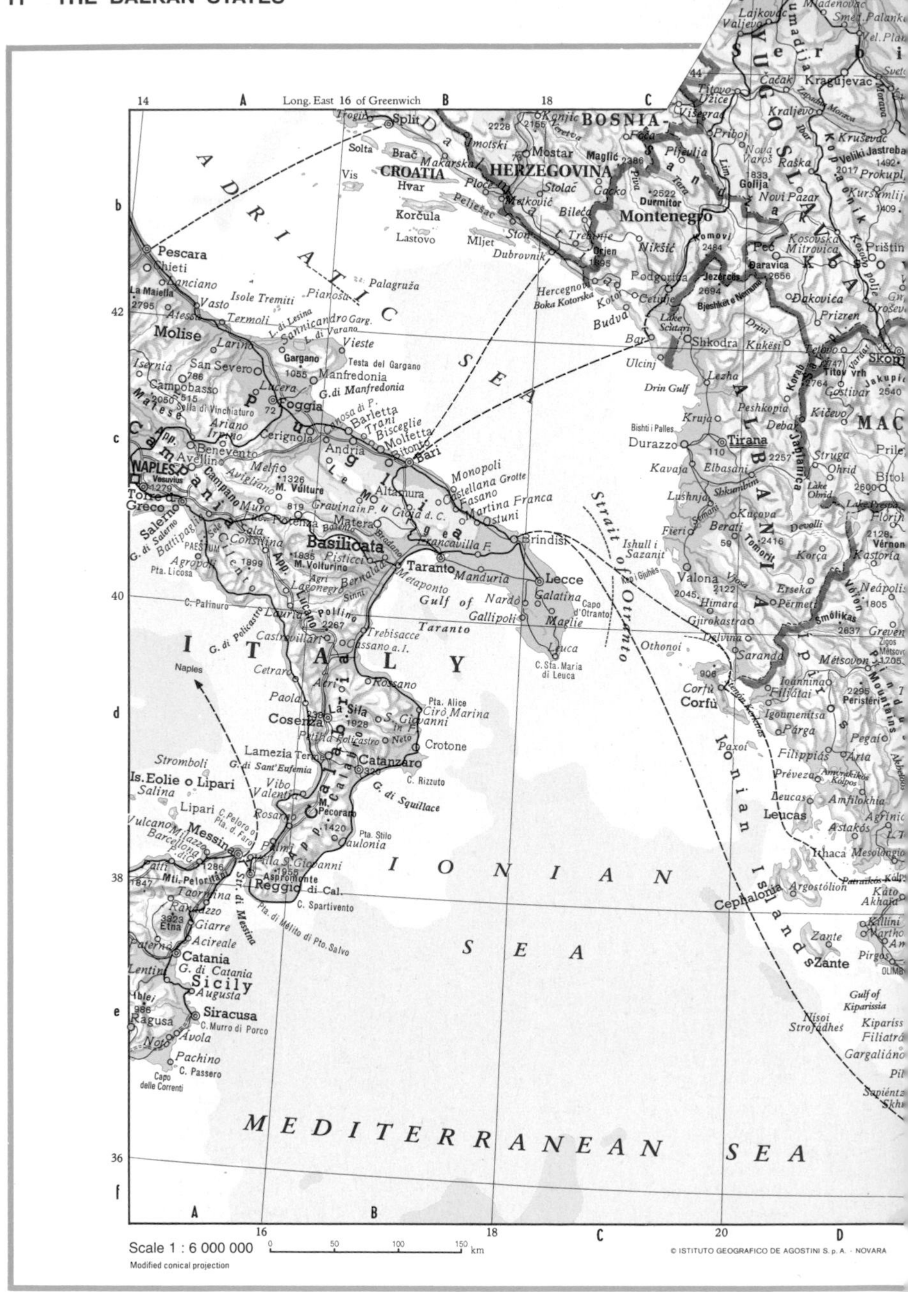

Scale 1 : 6 000 000

0 50 100 150 km

Modified conical projection

© ISTITUTO GEOGRAFICO DE AGOSTINI S.p.A. · NOVARA

ROMANIA

BUCHAREST

BULGARIA

SOFIA

BLACK
SEA

GREECE

TURKEY

ISTANBUL
(CONSTANTINOPLE)

SALONIKA

ATHENS

Sea of Marmara

Crete

Rhodes

Cythera

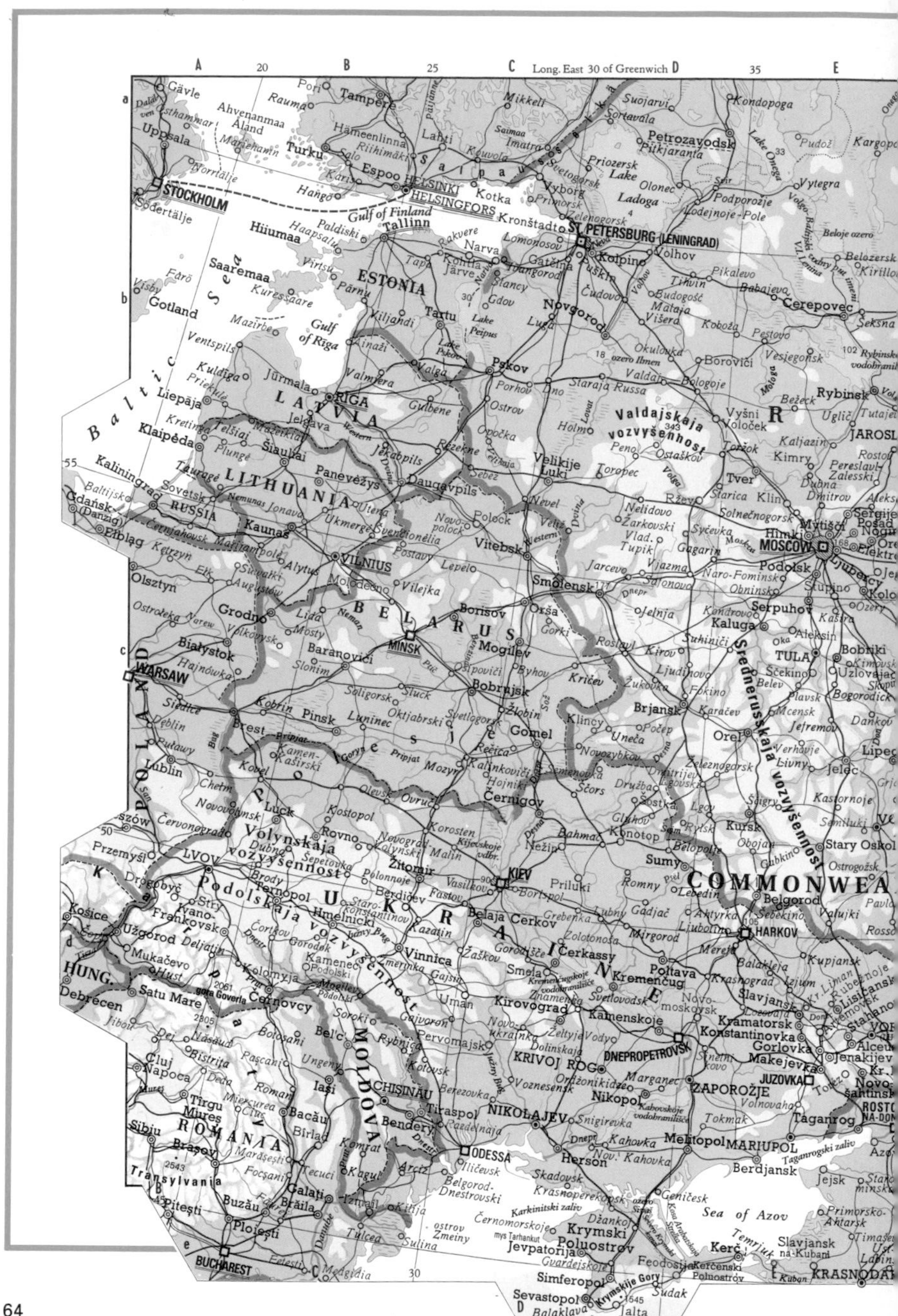
Long. East 30 of Greenwich
Baltic Sea
Gulf of Finland
Gulf of Riga
Sea of Azov
ESTONIA
LATVIA
LITHUANIA
RUSSIA
BELARUS
UKRAINE
MOLDOVA
ROMANIA
POLAND
HUNG.
COMMONWEA
STOCKHOLM
HELSINKI
HELSINGFORS
Tallinn
RIGA
VILNIUS
MINSK
WARSAW
KIEV
CHIŞINĂU
BUCHAREST
MOSCOW
ST PETERSBURG (LENINGRAD)
ODESSA
HARKOV
DNEPROPETROVSK
ZAPOROŽJE
KRIVOJ ROG
NIKOLAJEV
JUZOVKA
MARIUPOL
KRASNODAR
Gävle
Uppsala
Södertälje
Gotland
Saaremaa
Hiiumaa
Åland
Turku
Tampere
Lahti
Espoo
Kotka
Vyborg
Petrozavodsk
Lake Ladoga
Lake Onega
Lake Peipus
Narva
Tartu
Pärnu
Pskov
Novgorod
Ventspils
Liepāja
Klaipėda
Kaliningrad
Šiauliai
Panevėžys
Kaunas
Daugavpils
Grodno
Białystok
Brest
Pinsk
Gomel
Mogilev
Vitebsk
Smolensk
Tver
Kaluga
Tula
Brjansk
Kursk
Orel
Sumy
Poltava
Kremenčug
Kirovograd
Vinnica
Žitomir
Rovno
Luck
Lvov
Ternopol
Černovcy
Iaşi
Tiraspol
Bendery
Herson
Nikopol
Melitopol
Berdjansk
Taganrog
Kerč
Simferopol
Sevastopol
Jalta
Feodosija
Jevpatorija
Krymski Poluostrov
Galaţi
Brăila
Ploieşti
Braşov
Cluj Napoca
Satu Mare
Debrecen
Lublin
Valdajskaja vozvyšennost
Srednerusskaja vozvyšennost
Volynskaja vozvyšennost
Podolskaja vozvyšennost
Polesje
Carpathians
Transylvania
Kharkiv
Donetsk

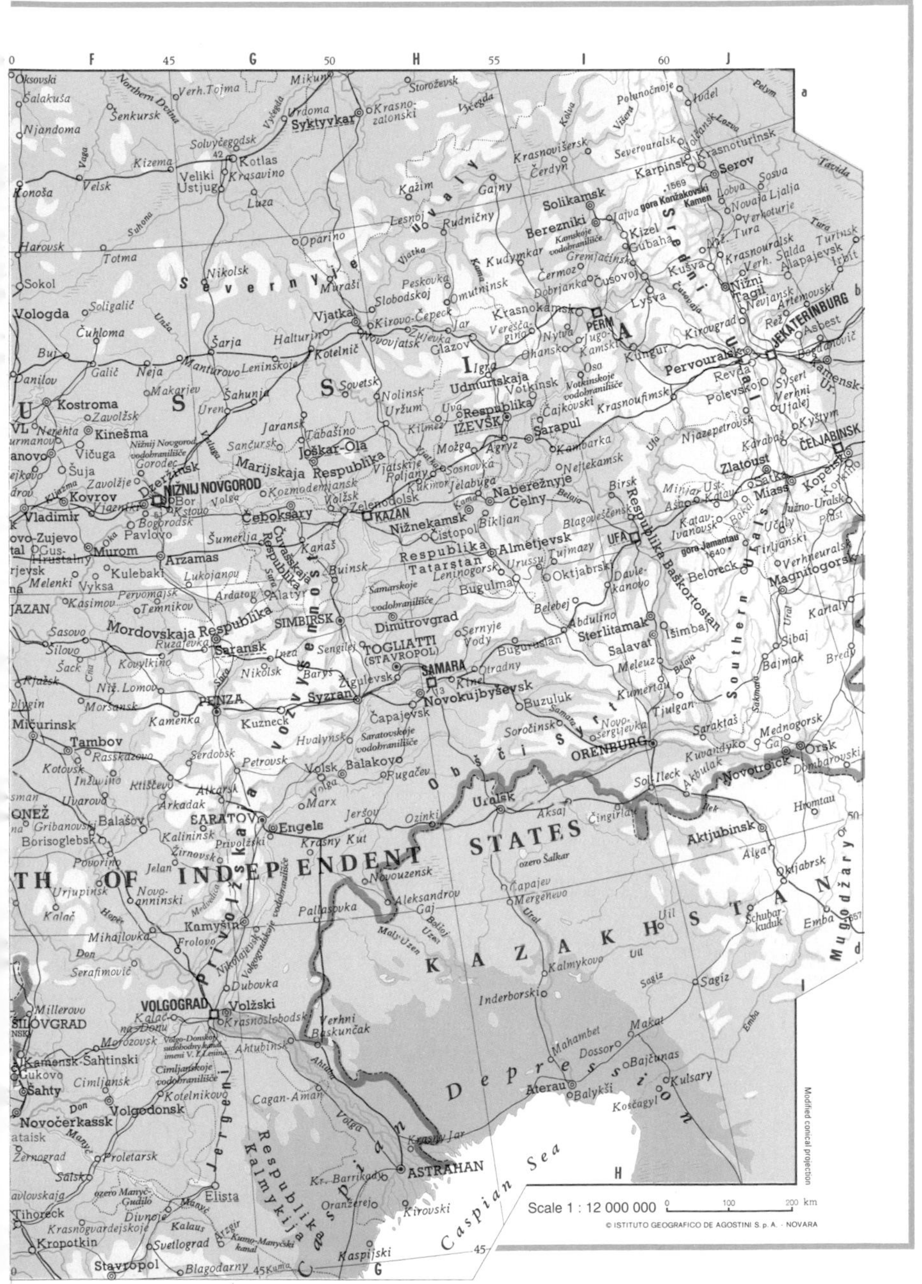

Scale 1 : 12 000 000

0   100   200 km

© ISTITUTO GEOGRAFICO DE AGOSTINI S.p.A. - NOVARA

Modified conical projection

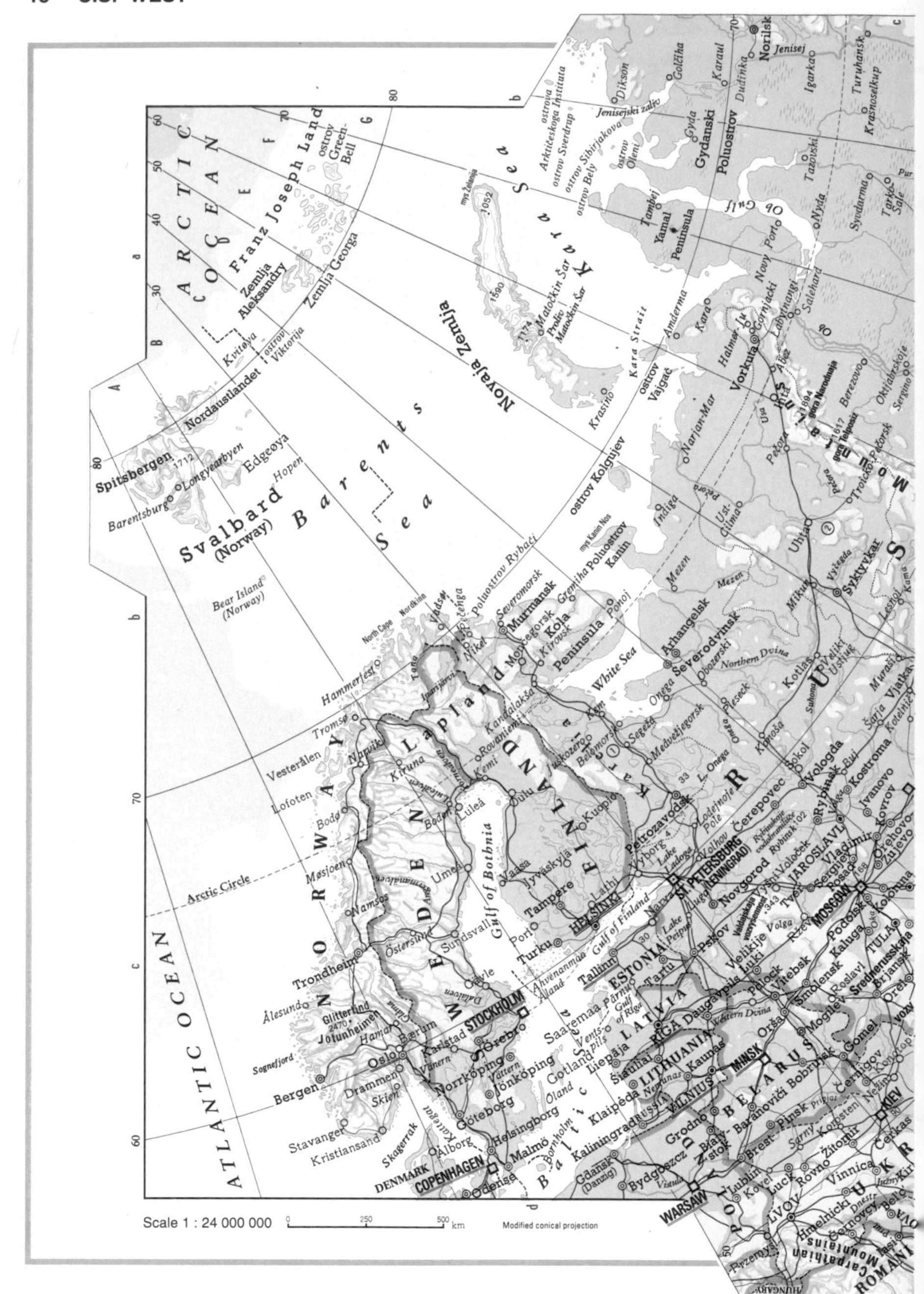

ARCTIC OCEAN

Franz Joseph Land

ostrova ostrova Arktičeskogo Instituta
ostrov Sibirjakova
ostrov Bely
ostrov Oleni

Bell
Green-
Bell

Zemlja
Aleksandry

Zemlja Georga

Kutelva
Knitelva
ostrov Viktorija

Kara
Sea

Tambej
Yamal
Peninsula

Dikson

Goltiha
Karaul

Jenisejskij zaliv

Sydarma

Novy Porto

Gydanski

Poluostrov

Jenisej
Igarka

Turuhansk
Krasnojarsk

Norilsk

Dudinka

Nordaustlandet

Spitsbergen

Barentsburgo

Longyearbyen

Svalbard
(Norway)

Edgeøya

Hopen

Novaja Zemlja

Barents
Sea

ostrov Kolgujev

mys Kanin Nos

Kanin
Peninsula

Kara Strait
ostrov
Vajgač

Krasino

Amderma
Kara

Usa
Pečora

Narjan-Mar

Indiga

Mezen

White Sea

Kola
Peninsula (Pana)

Bear Island
(Norway)

North Cape
Hammerfest
Tromsø

poluostrov Rybačij
Severomorsk
Murmansk
Kola

Monmanska

Kandalakša

Vorkuta

Ust-Usa

Uhta

Vyksa

Syktyvkar

Vesterålen
Lofoten
Bodø
Mosjøen

Namsos
Trondheim
Ålesund
Jotunheim
Sognefjord
Bergen

Arctic Circle

NORWAY

SWEDEN
LAPLAND

Kiruna

Luleå
Umeå
Östersund

Karlstad
STOCKHOLM
Norrköping
Jönköping
Göteborg

Oslo
Drammen
Skien
Stavanger
Kristiansand
Skagerrak

Hammerfest

FINLAND
KARELIA

Rovaniemi
Kemi
Oulu

Tampere
Turku
HELSINKI
Gulf of Finland

Gulf of Bothnia

Vaasa

Pori

Lake
Ladoga

Onega

Onega

Northern Dvina

Arhangelsk
Severodvinsk

Kotlas

Vel'sk

Vologda

Čerepovec

ST PETERSBURG
LENINGRAD
Novgorod

YAROSLAVL'
Rybinsk
Tver'
Ivanovo

MOSCOW

Velikie Luki

TULA

Kaluga

RUSSIA

ATLANTIC OCEAN

Halden
ESTONIA
Tallinn
Tartu

Saaremaa
LATVIA
RIGA

Western Dvina

Pskov

Vitebsk

Smolensk

Mogilev

Orel

LITHUANIA
Kaunas
Klaipeda
VILNIUS

Liepaja

Baltic Sea

Kaliningrad

Gdańsk
(Danzig)

Grodno
Brest

MINSK
BELARUS
Bobrujsk
Gomel'

KIEV

UKRAINE

DENMARK
COPENHAGEN
Odense
Ålborg
Malmö
Helsingborg

Bornholm

WARSAW
POLAND

L'VOV

Carpathian
Mountains

ROMANIA

HUNGARY

Scale 1 : 24 000 000   Modified conical projection

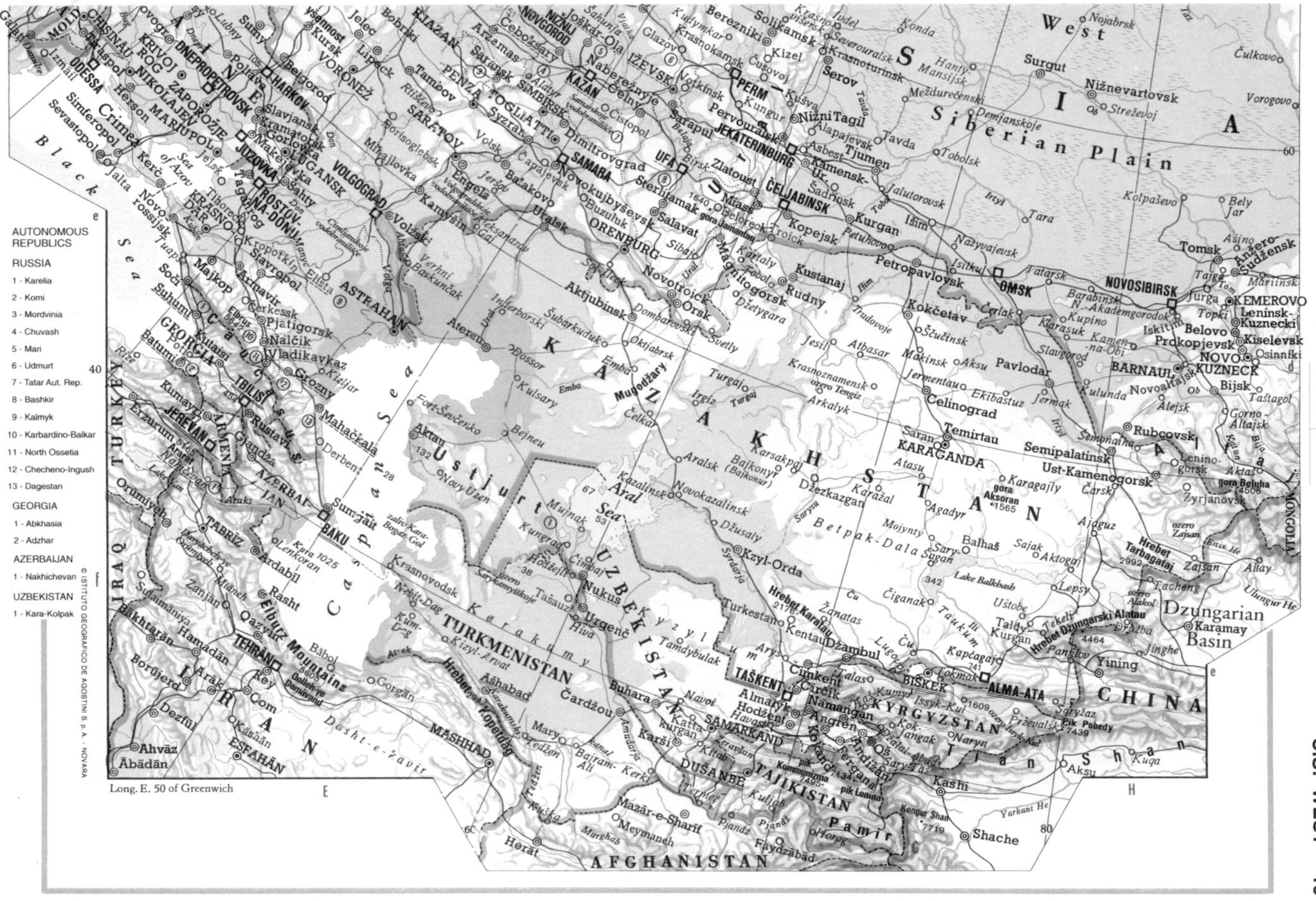

AUTONOMOUS
REPUBLICS

RUSSIA
1 - Karelia
2 - Komi
3 - Mordvinia
4 - Chuvash
5 - Mari
6 - Udmurt
7 - Tatar Aut. Rep.
8 - Bashkir
9 - Kalmyk
10 - Karbardino-Balkar
11 - North Ossetia
12 - Chechenia-Ingush
13 - Dagestan

GEORGIA
1 - Abhasia
2 - Adzhar

AZERBAIJAN
1 - Nakhichevan

UZBEKISTAN
1 - Kara-Kolpak

Long. E. 50 of Greenwich

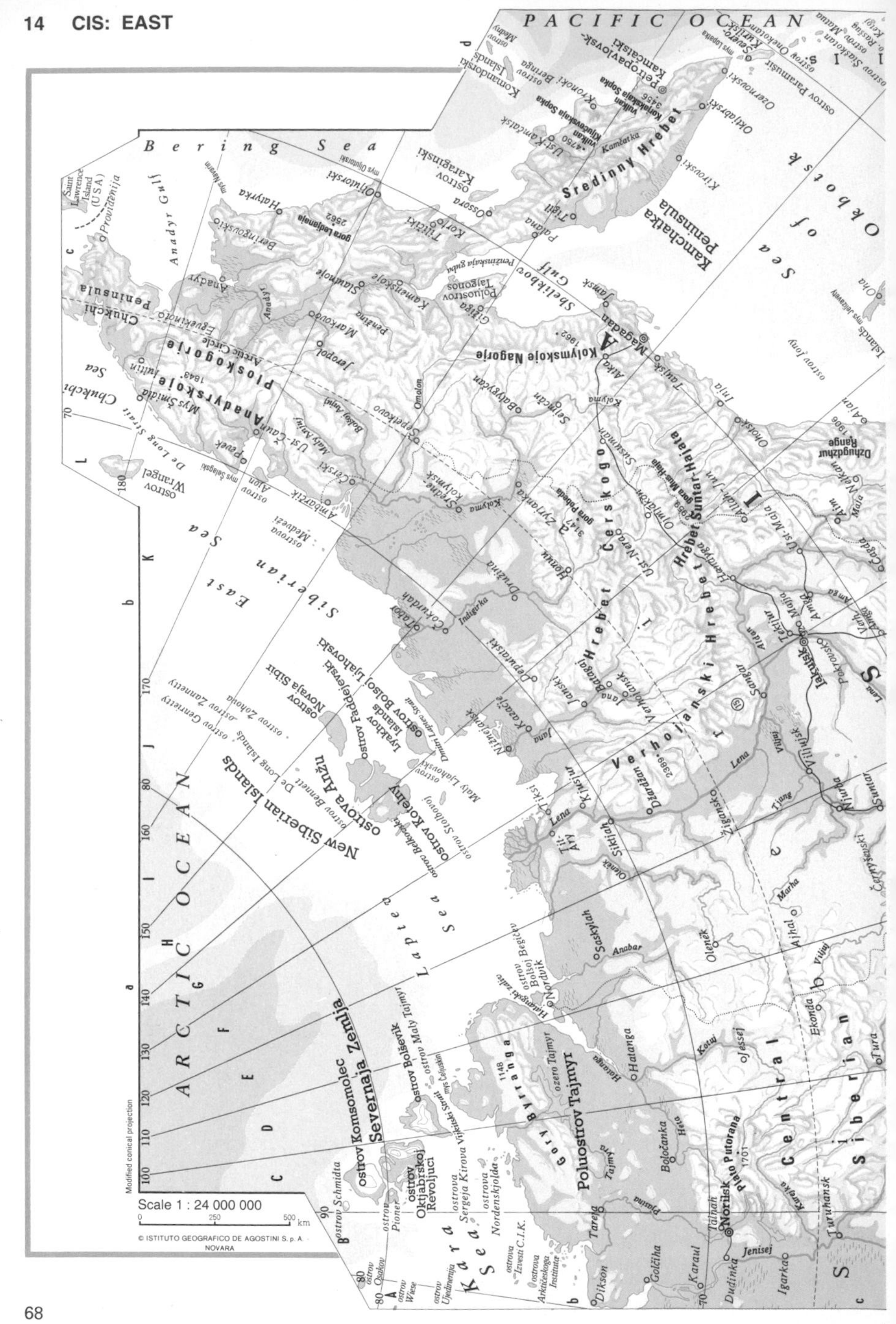

PACIFIC OCEAN

Bering Sea

Arctic Circle

Chukchi Sea

ARCTIC OCEAN

East Siberian Sea

New Siberian Islands

Laptev Sea

Kara Sea

Sredinny Hrebet

Kamchatka Peninsula

Sea of Okhotsk

Kolymskoje Nagorje

Hrebet Cerskogo

Verhojanski Hrebet

Hrebet Suntar-Hajata

Central Siberian Plateau

Ploskogorje

Anadyrskoje

Chukchi peninsula

Komsomolec Severnaja Zemlja

Poluostrov Tajmyr

Modified conical projection

Scale 1 : 24 000 000

0   250   500 km

© ISTITUTO GEOGRAFICO DE AGOSTINI S.p.A. -
NOVARA

68

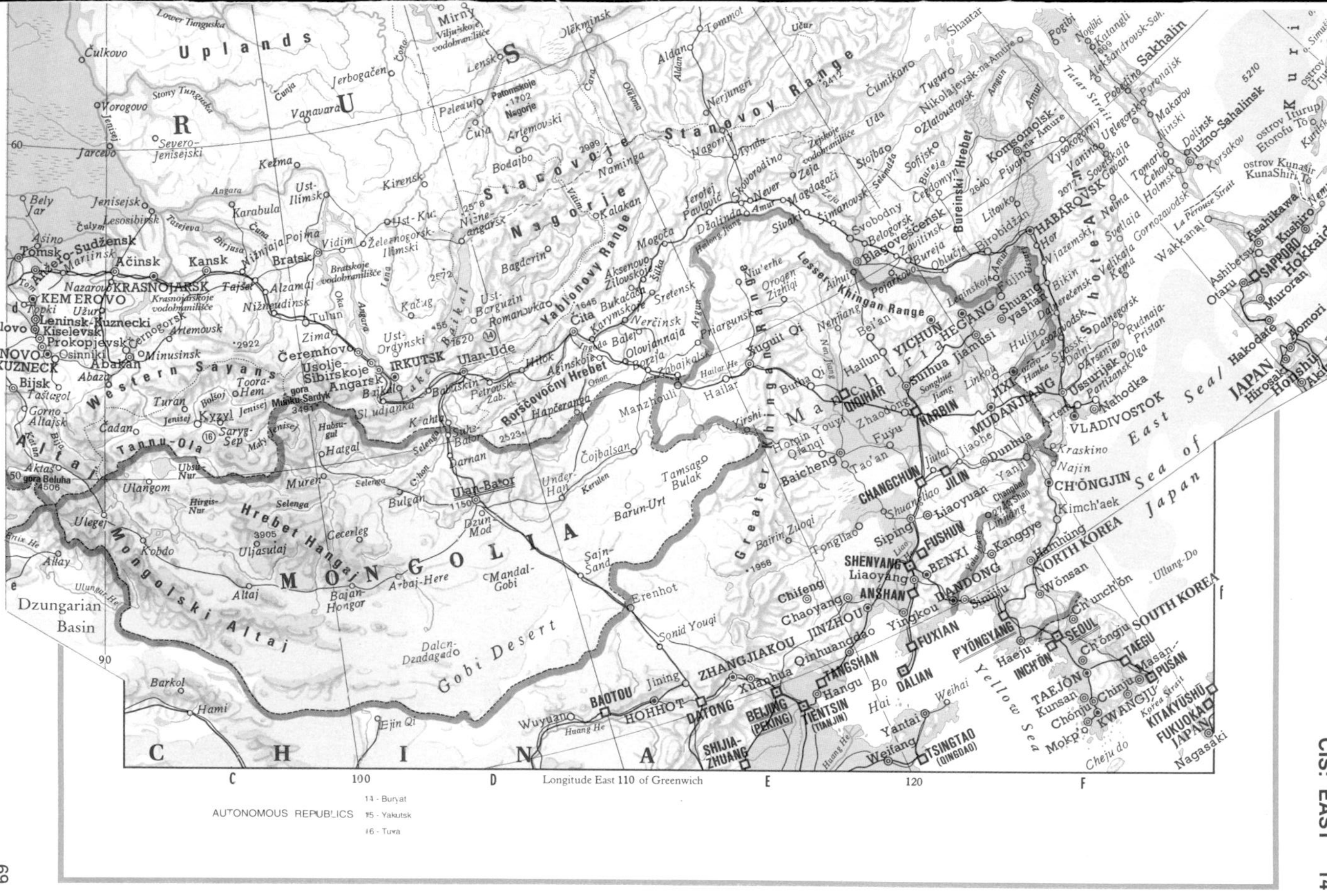

Longitude East 110 of Greenwich

AUTONOMOUS REPUBLICS
14 - Buriat
15 - Yakutia
16 - Tuva

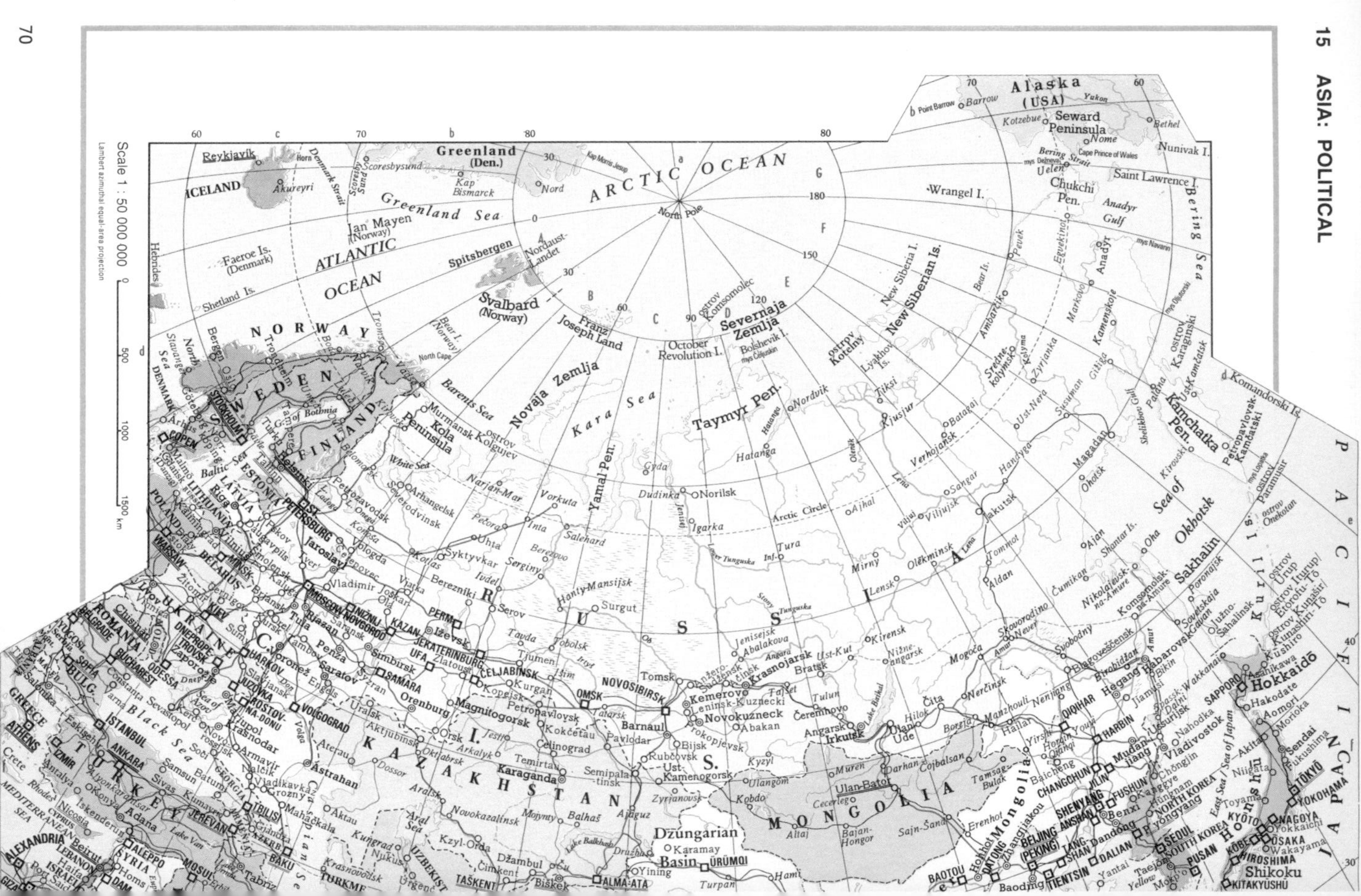

P A C I F I C

Kurils Is.

Bering Sea

Alaska (USA)

Seward Peninsula

Chukchi Pen.

ARCTIC OCEAN

North pole

Wrangel I.

New Siberian Is.

New Siberia I.

Severnaja Zemlja

Taymyr Pen.

Kara Sea

Novaja Zemlja

Yamal Pen.

Franz Joseph Land

Barents Sea

Svalbard (Norway)

Spitsbergen

Greenland (Den.)

Greenland Sea

ATLANTIC OCEAN

Jan Mayen (Norway)

ICELAND

Reykjavik

Denmark Strait

Faeroe Is. (Denmark)

Shetland Is.

Hebrides

North Sea

NORWAY

SWEDEN

FINLAND

DENMARK

Stockholm

ESTONIA

LATVIA

LITHUANIA

POLAND

Warsaw

Baltic Sea

PETERSBURG

MOSCOW

U. S. S. R.

KAZAKHSTAN

UZBEKISTAN

TASHKENT

Caspian Sea

Black Sea

ROMANIA

Bucharest

BULG.

GREECE

ATHENS

ISTANBUL

TURKEY

MEDITERRANEAN SEA

Crete

MONGOLIA

Ulan-Bator

Dzungarian Basin

URUMQI

Sea of Japan

Sakhalin

HOKKAIDO

Sapporo

HONSHU

TOKYO

Sea of Okhotsk

Kamchatka Pen.

Bering Sea

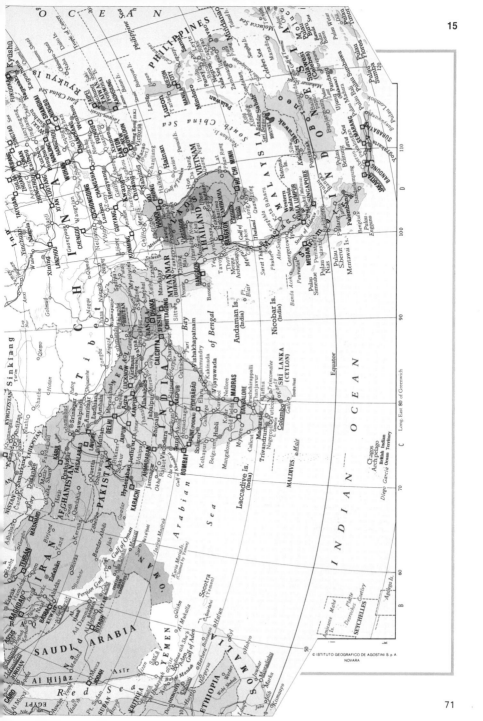

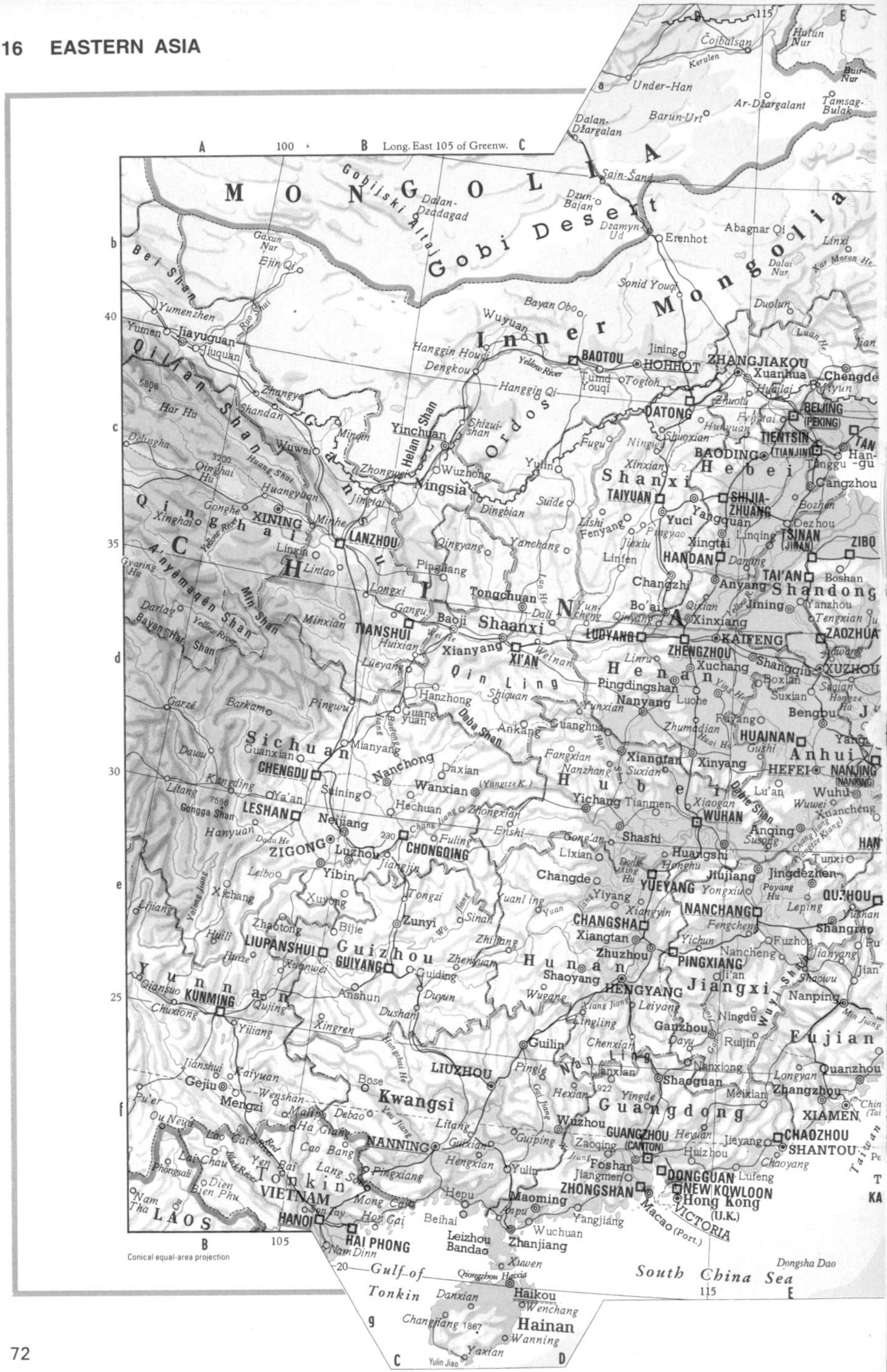

Long. East 105 of Greenw.

M O N G O L I A

Gobijskij Altaj

Gobi Desert

I n n e r   M o n g o l i a

Dalan-Dzadagad

Sain-Sand

Dzun-Bajan

Dzamyn-Ud

Erenhot

Abagnar Qi

Linxi

Dalai Nur

Duolun

Sonid Youqi

Bayan Obo

Wuyuan

BAOTOU   HOHHOT

ZHANGJIAKOU

Xuanhua   Chengde

Jining

Umd Togtoh

DATONG

Yumen   Jiayuguan   Yumenzhen

Qilian Shan

Gaxun Nur

Ejin Qi

Bei Shan

Hanggin Houqi

Dengkou

Hanggin Qi

Shizui-shan

Yinchuan   Helan Shan

O r d o s

Fugu

Ningvu

Shuozhou

BEIJING (PEKING)

TIENTSIN (TIANJIN)   TAN-gu

Han-gu

Cangzhou

Bozhou

Zhangye   shandan   Minqin   Wuwei

Huang Shui

Qinghai Hu

Gonghe   Minhe   XINING

LANZHOU   Linxia   Lintao

Lintao   C H   Lintao

Anyemaqen Shan

Gyaring Hu   Min Shan

Wuzhong   Ningxia

Zhongning   Jingtai   Yulin   Suide

Dingbian

Pingliang   Qingyang   Yanchang

Yanan

Xinxian

BAODING

S h a n x i   H e b e i

TAIYUAN   Yuci   Yangquan

Lishi   Fenyang   Zhangguan   Linqing

SHIJIA-ZHUANG

Jiexiu   Fuyang

Linfen   Xingtai   HANDAN   Daming

Changzhi   Anyang

SINAN   ZIBO

Boshan

TAI'AN   S h a n d o n g

Jining   Yanzhou

Bo'ai   Qixian

LUOYANG   ZHENGZHOU   Xinxiang   KAIFENG   ZAOZHUANG   XUZHOU

Tongchuan

Longxi   Tianshui

Gangu   Baoji

Minxian   Huixian   Dali

Lüeyang   Hanzhong   Xianyang   XI'AN

Qin Ling   Shiquan   Ankang

Nanzhang   Xiangfan

Linru   H e n a n

Pingdingshan   Nanyang   Luohe

Zhumadian

Boxian

Suxian   Bengbu

HUAINAN   Gushi

A n h u i

HEFEI   NANJING (NANKING)

Daba Shan   Yunyang

Daxian   (Yangtze K.)   Fangxian

Xiangtan   Xinyang   Lu'an

Wuwei   Wuhu   Xuancheng

S i c h u a n

Guanxian   Mianyang

CHENGDU   Nanchong

Suining

Neijiang   Hechuan

Wanxian   Zhongxian   Yichang   Tianmen   Xiaogan   Shan

Fuling   Enshi   WUHAN

H u b e i

Shashi   Anqing   HAN

ZIGONG   Luzhou   CHONGQING

Yibin   Xuyong   Tongzi   Yuanling   Changde   Huangshi   Jiujiang   Jingdezhen   QUZHOU

Leibo   Bijie   Zunyi   Sinan   Zhijiang   Lixian   Gong'an   Yongxiu   Leping   Shangrao

Xichang   Zhaotong   Yiyang   Xiangyin   Fengcheng   Fuzhou   Tianyang

Yanhe   NANCHANG

G u i z h o u   CHANGSHA   Yichun   Jiangshan

LIUPANSHUI   GUIYANG   Zhenyuan   Xiangtan   Zhuzhou   PINGXIANG   Nanping   F u j i a n

Guiding   Duyun   H u n a n   J i a n g x i

Anshun   Shaoyang   HENGYANG   Ganzhou   Quanzhou

KUNMING   Xingren   Dushan   Wugang   Leiyang   Ningdu   Ruijin   Longyan   Zhangzhou

Y u n n a n   Chuxiong   Yiliang   Zuling   Chenxian   Nanxiong   Meixian   Shaoguan

Guilin   Pingle   XIAMEN

LIUZHOU   Nan Ling   G u a n g d o n g   CHAOZHOU   SHANTOU

Jianshui   Kaiyuan   Wenshan   Malipo   Debao   Litang   Hexian   Yingde   Chaoyang   Taixan

Gejiu   Mengzi   Bose   Guiping   Wuzhou   GUANGZHOU (CANTON)   Heyuan   Jieyang

Ha Giang   Cao Bang   NANNING   Hengxian   Yulin   Zaoqing   FOSHAN   Huizhou   Lufeng

Pingxiang   Hepu   Maoming   ZHONGSHAN   DONGGUAN   NEW KOWLOON   Hong Kong (U.K.)

T o n k i n   Mong Cai   Yangjiang   Macao (Port.)   VICTORIA

VIETNAM   HANOI   Beihai   Wuchuan   Zhanjiang

L A O S   HAI PHONG   Leizhou Bandao

Gulf of Tonkin   Xuwen   South China Sea

Danxian   Haikou   Wenchang   Dongsha Dao

Changjiang   Hainan   Wanning

Yulin Jiao   Taixan

Conical equal-area projection

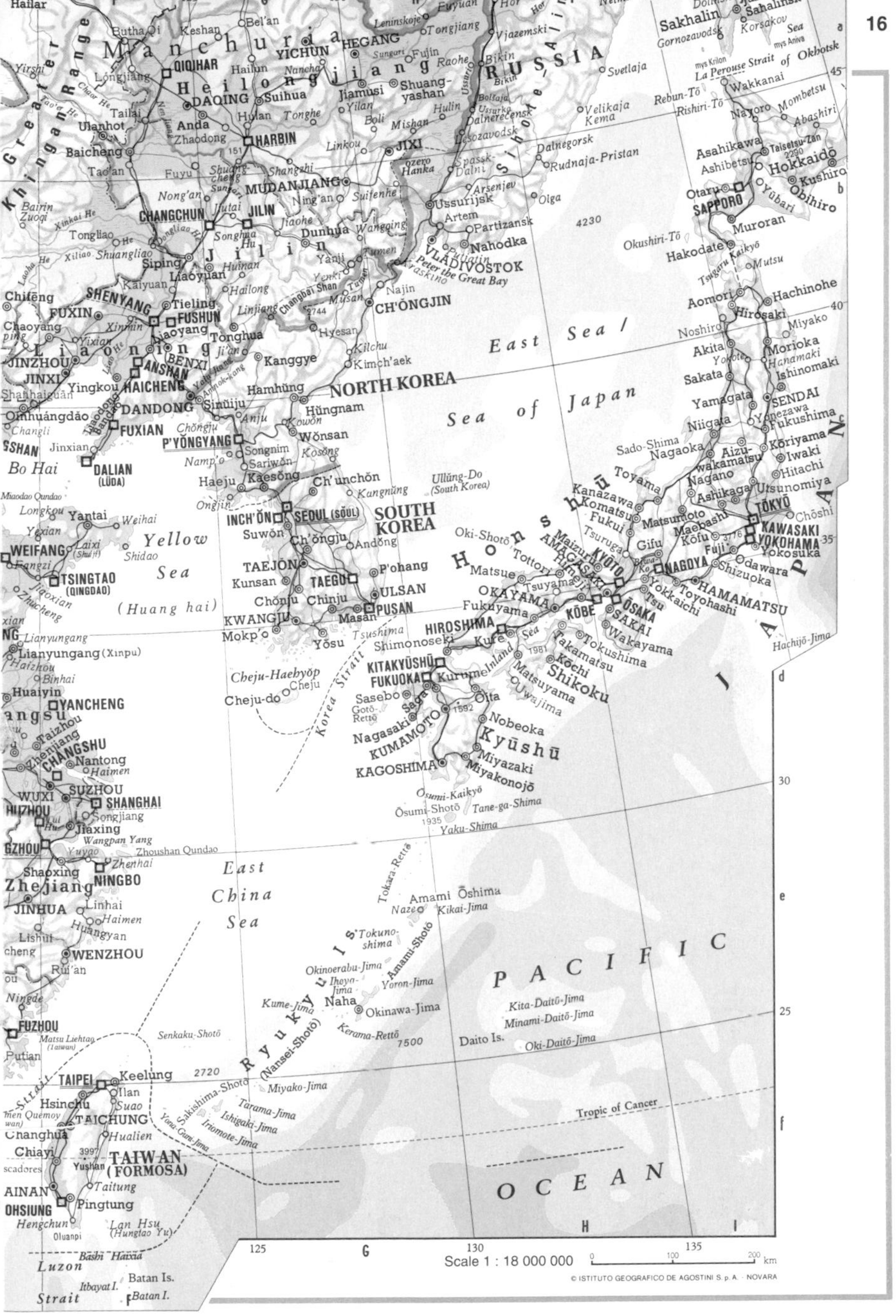

Hailar
Manchuria
Great Khingan Range
QIQIHAR
DAQING
Heilongjiang
YICHUN
HEGANG
Jiamusi
Shuangyashan
HARBIN
JIXI
MUDANJIANG
CHANGCHUN
JILIN
Jilin
Siping
SHENYANG
FUSHUN
FUXIN
Liaoning
JINZHOU
ANSHAN
HAICHENG
DANDONG
FUXIAN
DALIAN
(LÜDA)
Bo Hai
RUSSIA
Sikhote-Alin
Ussurijsk
Nahodka
VLADIVOSTOK
Peter the Great Bay
CH'ŎNGJIN
NORTH KOREA
Hamhŭng
Hŭngnam
Wŏnsan
P'YŎNGYANG
Kaesŏng
SEOUL (SŎUL)
INCH'ŎN
SOUTH KOREA
TAEJŎN
TAEGU
P'ohang
ULSAN
PUSAN
KWANGJU
Mokp'o
Yŏsu
Cheju-do
Korea Strait
Tsushima
Yellow Sea
(Huang hai)
Yantai
WEIFANG
TSINGTAO
(QINGDAO)
Lianyungang (Xinpu)
YANCHENG
CHANGSHU
SUZHOU
SHANGHAI
WUXI
NINGBO
Zhejiang
WENZHOU
FUZHOU
East China Sea
TAIPEI
Keelung
TAICHUNG
TAIWAN
(FORMOSA)
Pingtung
Luzon Strait
Batan Is.
East Sea /
Sea of Japan
Ullŭng-Do
(South Korea)
Sakhalin
Južno-Sahalinsk
Sea of Okhotsk
La Perouse Strait
Wakkanai
Hokkaidō
Asahikawa
SAPPORO
Otaru
Kushiro
Obihiro
Muroran
Hakodate
Tsugaru Kaikyō
Aomori
Hirosaki
Hachinohe
Akita
Morioka
SENDAI
Niigata
Sado-Shima
Fukushima
Kōriyama
Toyama
Kanazawa
Honshū
Nagano
Utsunomiya
TŌKYŌ
KAWASAKI
YOKOHAMA
Yokosuka
Fuji
Shizuoka
HAMAMATSU
NAGOYA
Gifu
KYŌTO
ŌSAKA
KŌBE
SAKAI
Wakayama
OKAYAMA
HIROSHIMA
Matsue
Shimonoseki
KITAKYŪSHŪ
FUKUOKA
Kurume
Shikoku
Tokushima
Takamatsu
Kōchi
Matsuyama
Kyūshū
Nagasaki
KUMAMOTO
Ōita
Nobeoka
Miyazaki
Miyakonojō
KAGOSHIMA
Ōsumi-Kaikyō
Tane-ga-Shima
Yaku-Shima
JAPAN
Hachijō-Jima
Amami Ōshima
Ryukyu Is (Nansei-Shotō)
Okinawa-Jima
Naha
Daito Is.
Tropic of Cancer
PACIFIC OCEAN
Scale 1 : 18 000 000
0 100 200 km
© ISTITUTO GEOGRAFICO DE AGOSTINI S.p.A. - NOVARA

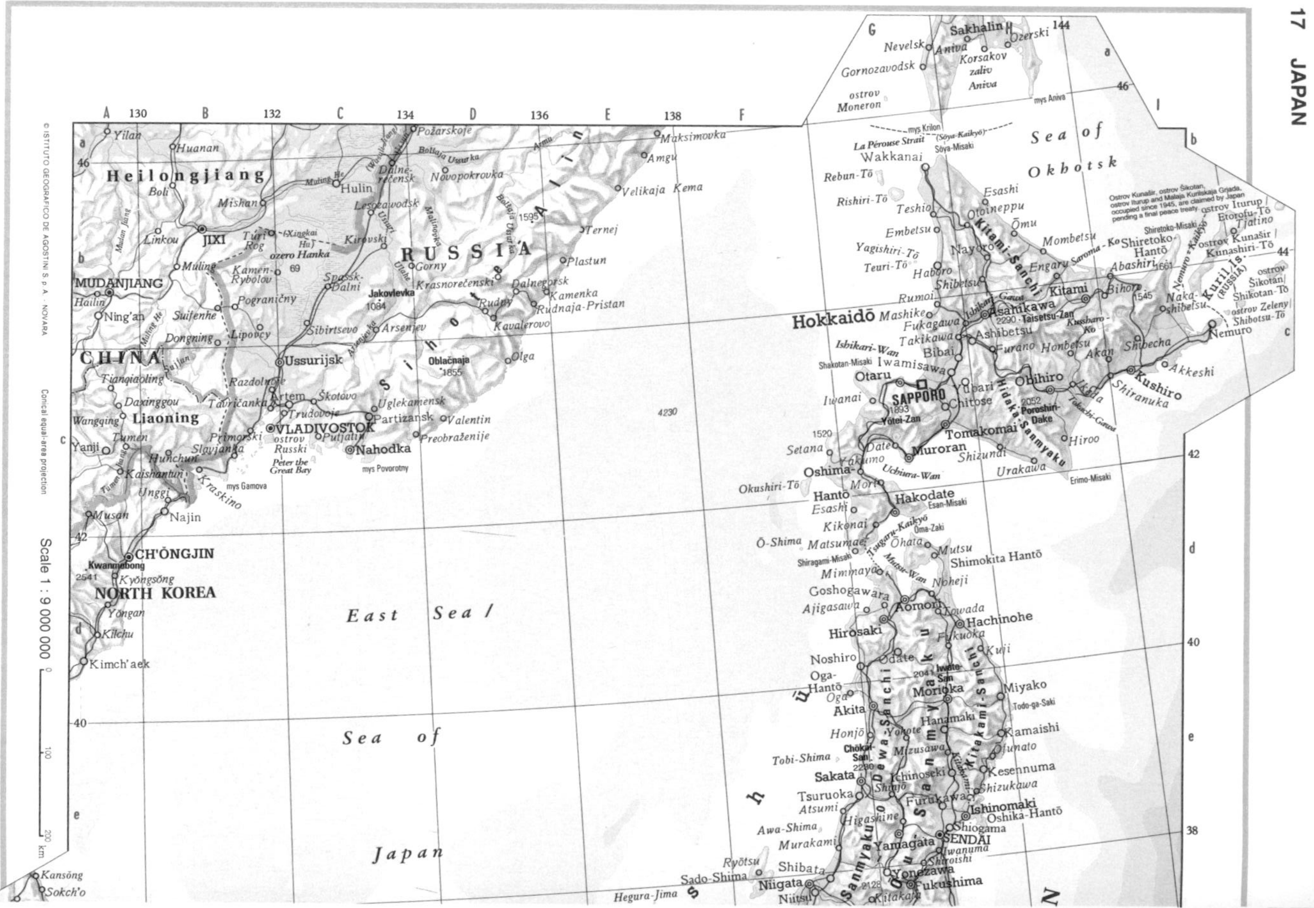
Sea of Okhotsk
East Sea / Sea of Japan
RUSSIA
Sihote-Alin
CHINA
NORTH KOREA
Heilongjiang
Liaoning
Hokkaidō
SAPPORO
Otaru
Asahikawa
Kitami
Obihiro
Kushiro
Nemuro
Muroran
Tomakomai
Hakodate
Aomori
Hachinohe
Hirosaki
Morioka
Akita
Sakata
Yamagata
SENDAI
Fukushima
Niigata
Sado-Shima
VLADIVOSTOK
Ussurijsk
Nahodka
CH'ŎNGJIN
JIXI
MUDANJIANG
Sakhalin
La Pérouse Strait
Wakkanai
Kuril Is. (RUSSIA)
Ostrov Kunašir, ostrov Šikotan, ostrov Iturup and Malaja Kurilskaja Grjada, occupied since 1945, are claimed by Japan pending a final peace treaty
© ISTITUTO GEOGRAFICO DE AGOSTINI S.p.A. - NOVARA
Conical equal-area projection
Scale 1 : 9 000 000
0 100 200 km

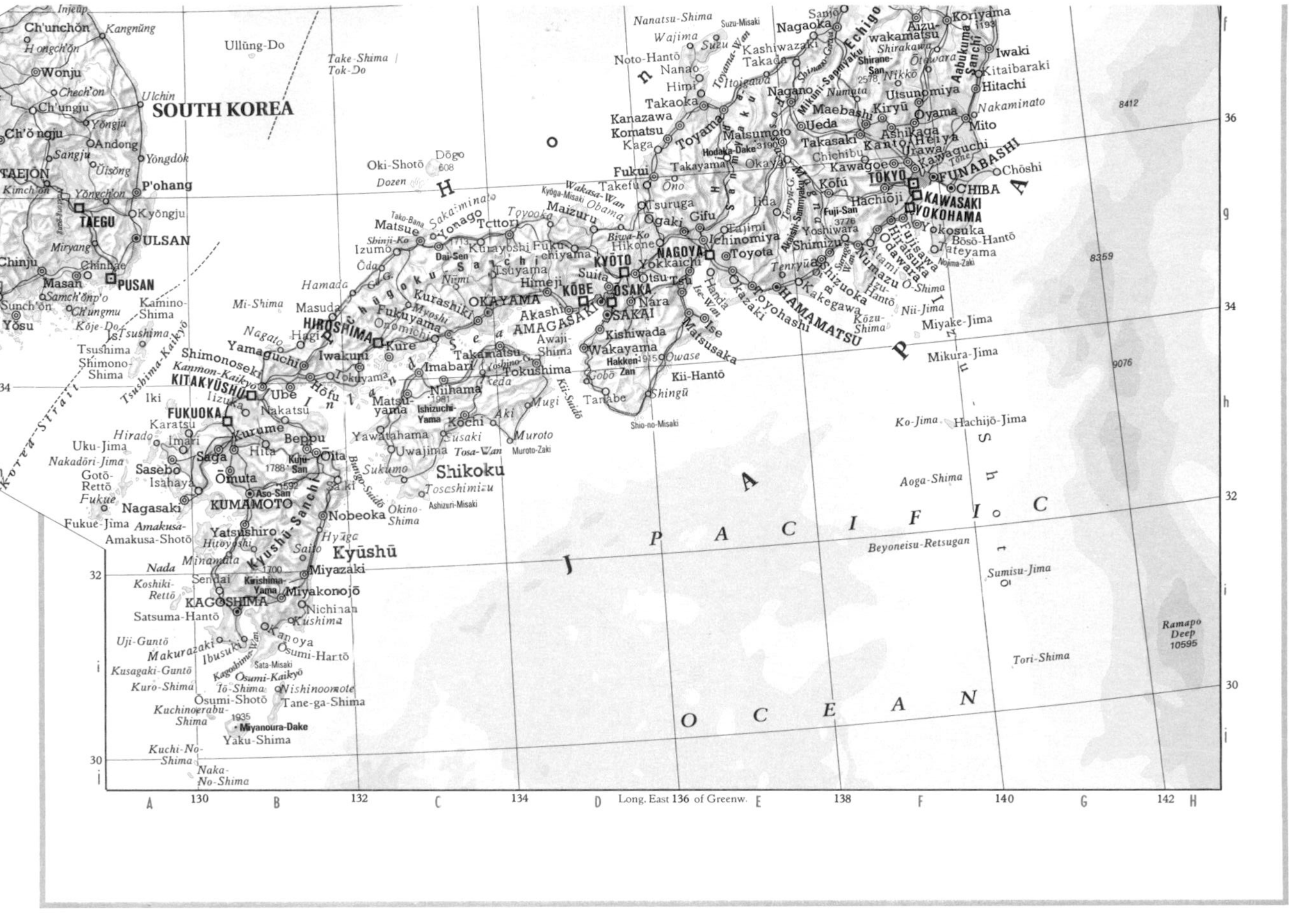
SOUTH KOREA
Ch'unchŏn
Wonju
Ch'ŏngju
TAEJŎN
TAEGU
ULSAN
PUSAN
P'ohang
Masan
Chinju
Yŏsu
Ullŭng-Do
Take-Shima / Tok-Do
Oki-Shotō
Tsushima
Tsushima-Kaikyō
Korea Strait
Iki
Kyūshū
Shikoku
KITAKYŪSHŪ
FUKUOKA
Shimonoseki
Kammon-Kaikyō
Nagasaki
Sasebo
Saga
Kurume
Ōmuta
KUMAMOTO
Aso-San
Yatsushiro
KAGOSHIMA
Miyazaki
Miyakonojō
Nobeoka
Ōita
Beppu
Kyūshū-Sanchi
Satsuma-Hantō
Ōsumi-Hantō
Ōsumi-Shotō
Tane-ga-Shima
Yaku-Shima
Miyanoura-Dake 1935
HIROSHIMA
Kure
Iwakuni
Yamaguchi
Ube
Hōfu
Matsue
Izumo
Yonago
Tottori
Dai-Sen
Matsuyama
Imabari
Niihama
Ishizuchi-Yama 1981
Kōchi
Takamatsu
Tokushima
Uwajima
Muroto-Zaki
Ashizuri-Misaki
Bungo-Suidō
Kii-Suidō
OKAYAMA
Kurashiki
Fukuyama
Himeji
Akashi
KŌBE
AMAGASAKI
ŌSAKA
SAKAI
KYŌTO
Nara
Wakayama
Kishiwada
Biwa-Ko
Maizuru
Tsuruga
Ōgaki
Gifu
NAGOYA
Yokkaichi
Toyota
Okazaki
Toyohashi
HAMAMATSU
Shizuoka
Ise
Matsusaka
Kii-Hantō
Shio-no-Misaki
Ise-Wan
Kanazawa
Komatsu
Fukui
Takaoka
Toyama
Noto-Hantō
Nagano
Matsumoto
Hodaka-Dake 3190
Takayama
Kōfu
Fuji-San 3776
Numazu
Izu-Hantō
Maebashi
Takasaki
Utsunomiya
Nikkō
Nagaoka
Aizu-wakamatsu
Kōriyama
Iwaki
Hitachi
Mito
TŌKYŌ
KAWASAKI
YOKOHAMA
Yokosuka
CHIBA
FUNABASHI
Chōshi
Bōsō-Hantō
Hachiōji
Ō-Shima
Nii-Jima
Kōzu-Shima
Miyake-Jima
Mikura-Jima
Hachijō-Jima
Ko-Jima
Aoga-Shima
Beyoneisu-Retsugan
Sumisu-Jima
Tori-Shima
Ramapo Deep 10595
PACIFIC OCEAN
Long. East 136 of Greenw.

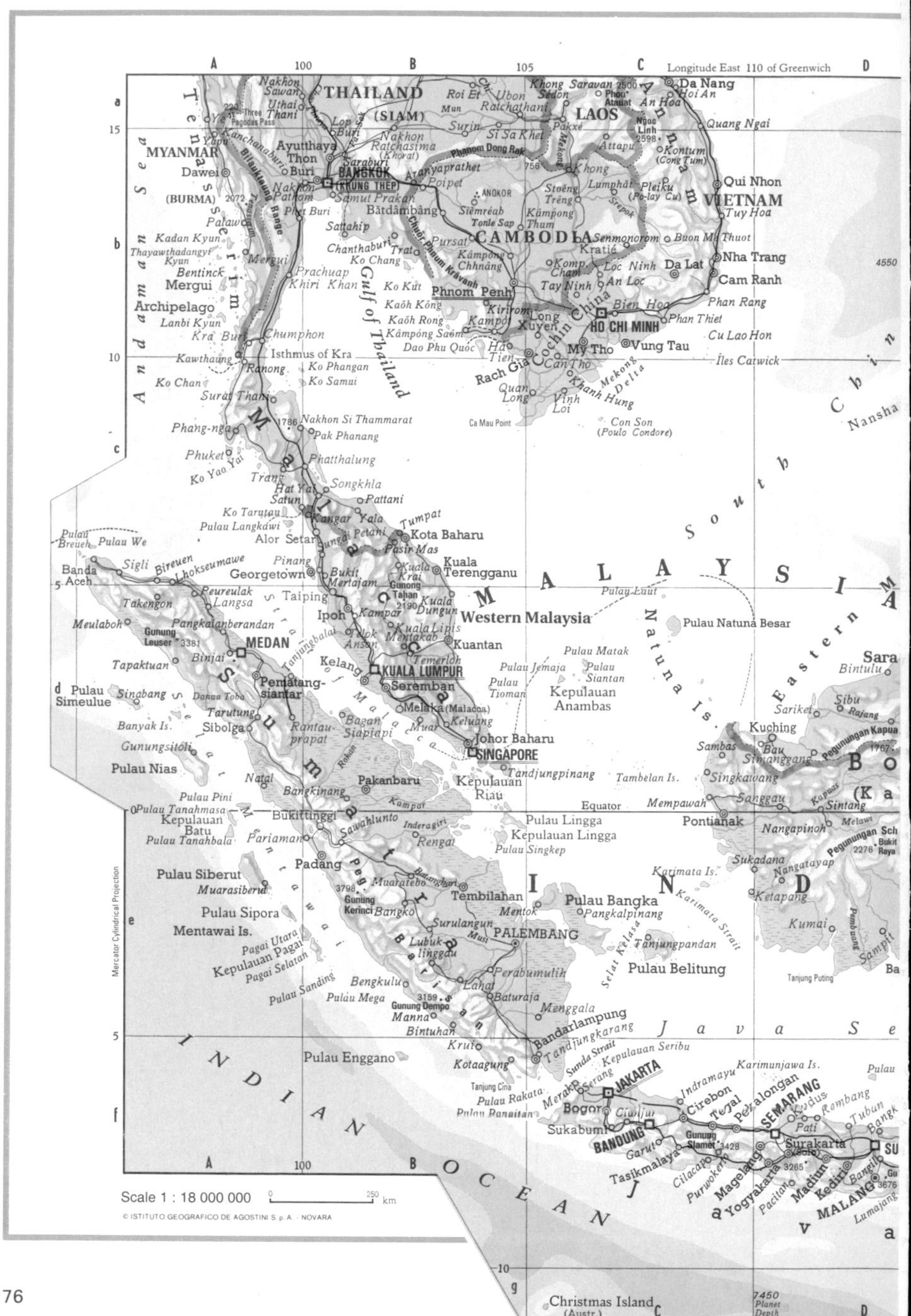
Longitude East 110 of Greenwich
THAILAND
(SIAM)
LAOS
CAMBODIA
VIETNAM
MYANMAR
(BURMA)
BANGKOK
(KRUNG THEP)
Phnom Penh
HO CHI MINH
Da Nang
Qui Nhon
Nha Trang
Cam Ranh
Da Lat
Vung Tau
Gulf of Thailand
Andaman Sea
Mergui Archipelago
Isthmus of Kra
Georgetown
Kota Baharu
Kuala Terengganu
Kuantan
KUALA LUMPUR
Seremban
Melaka (Malacca)
Johor Baharu
SINGAPORE
Western Malaysia
MALAYSIA
South China Sea
Natuna Is.
Pulau Natuna Besar
Kepulauan Anambas
Kuching
Pontianak
MEDAN
Pematang-siantar
Pakanbaru
Padang
PALEMBANG
Pulau Bangka
Pulau Belitung
Bengkulu
Bandarlampung
JAKARTA
Bogor
BANDUNG
SEMARANG
Surakarta
Yogyakarta
MALANG
Java Sea
Pulau Nias
Pulau Siberut
Pulau Sipora
Mentawai Is.
Pulau Enggano
INDIAN OCEAN
Christmas Island
(Austr.)
Equator
Mercator Cylindrical Projection
Scale 1 : 18 000 000
© ISTITUTO GEOGRAFICO DE AGOSTINI S.p.A. - NOVARA

120 Calayan
Dalupiri Babuyan Is.
Babuyan Channel Camiguin
Bangui Escarpada Point
Laoag Aparri
Vigan Tuguegarao
S. Fernando
Bangued Bontoc
Lingayen Gulf Mount Pulog 2930
Bolinao Baguio Ilagan
S. Carlos Bayombong
Tarlac San Jose Dagupan
S. Fernando Cabanatuan
Scarborough Reef
Olongapo Polillo Is.
QUEZON CITY
MANILA Sta Cruz Lamon Bay
Manila Bay Cavite S. Pablo Daet
Tagaytay City Lucena Naga Catanduanes
Batangas Boac Marin- Virac
Calapan duque Legazpi
Mindoro Mount Sibuyan Burias Bulan Sorsogon
Halcon S. Tablas Masbate Loaog
Busuanga Mindoro Strait Mashate Sea Calbayog
Calamian Group Kalibo Masbate Samar
Culion Panay Roxas Catbalogan
Linapacan S. Jose de Iloilo Tacloban
Taytay Buenavista Cadiz Leyte
Cuyo Is. Bacolod S. Carlos Baybay
Dumaran Guimaras Toledo Cebu
Palawan 1693 Negros Bohol Dinagat 10830
Puerto Princesa Dumaguete Tagbilaran Siargao
Cagayan Is. Bayawan Siquijor Gingoog Surigao 10 400
Mount Mantalingajan Dipolog Cagayan Tandag
2054 5575 de Oro Butuan
Balabac Ozamis Malaybalay
Bugsuk Pagadian Iligan
Balabac Strait San Miguel Is. Cotabato Mount Mindanao
Balambangan Pulau Cagayan Moro Gulf Apo DAVAO
Kudat Banggi Sulu Zamboanga 2954 Digos
Kota Pulau Basilan City Datu Piang Mati
Kinabalu Jambongan Pangutaran Group Basilan (Dulawan) General
Gunong Kinabalu Jolo Santos Malita
Sabah 4101 Sandakan Jolo Group 6220 Davao Gulf
Beaufort Samales Tinaca Point
Melalap Tapul Group Group Sarangani Is.
Bandar Lahad
Seri Begawan Sipitang Datu Pulau Miangas
Luton Weston Tawitawi Pulau-Pulau Nanusa
Miri BRUNEI Sibutu Is. Group Sulu Archipelago Kepulauan Talaud
wak Gunong Murud 2423 Tawau Kepulauan Kawio
Penambo Range Celebes 1860 Pulau Kaburuang
Tarakan Sea Pulau Sangihe 3800
Kapit Tanjungselor Pulau Makalehi Pulau
Hulu 2988 Pulau Maratua Pulau Siau Morotai
Tanjungredeb Pulau Tahulandang Selat Morotai
Sangkulirang Tolitoli Paleleh Manado Galela
ONE Dongeala Minahassa Tondano Gunong Klabat 4970 Ternate Halmahera
Purukcahu Bukit Malino Gorontalo 2027 1639 Kau
Muaratewe Tomini Bohontehu Soasiu Weda Pulau Gebe Pulau
Samarinda Teluk Tomini Molukka 4180 Makian Waigeo
Balikpapan Kepulauan Togian Pulau Kayoa Sea Sorong
I N D O N E S I A
Tanjung Palu Poh Pulau Batudaka Luwuk Pulau Peleng Kepulauan Pulau Bacan Sula Pulau Batanta Dampier Strait
Tahan Gunong Waikana Poso Banggai Pulau Kasiruta Labuha Salawati Klamono
Balabalangan Kepulauan Obi Pulau Kofiau Pulau Misool
Kotabaru Sulawesi Banggai Pulau Taliabu Misool
Pulau Laut (Celebes) Mamuju Wotu Malili Sanana Ceram Sea
Pulau Sebuku Majene Palopo Gunong Saroako Danau Sanana Namlea Piru 3010 Bula
Kepulauan Laut Kecil Mekongka Towuti 5800 Pulau Mangole Boano Ceram
2700 Kendari Pulau Manui Geser
Parepare Singkang Kolaka Pulau Amahai
Watampone Wowoni Pulau Kelang Ambon
UJUNG PANDANG 2871 (Bone) Raha Buru Pulau Bandanaira
(MAKASAR) Bantaeng Pulau Buton Ambelau Bandanaira Kepulauan Banda
Bawean Selat Selajar Kabaena Banggawangi Banda Kepulauan
Pulau Madura Benteng Baubau Kepulauan Sea Kepulauan Manuk Tayanda
Pamekasan Kepulauan Selajar Pulau Binongko Tukangbesi Lucipara Penju Pulau
Sepanjang Kangean Serua
SURABAYA Pulau Tanahjampea Pulau Nila
Probolinggo Pulau Kangean Kepulauan Kangean Kepulauan Barat Daya Pulau Teun
Bali Sea Pulau Kalao Pulau Damar Pulau Babar
Banyuwangi Singaraja Pulau Moyo 3142 Pulau Kalaotoa Larantuka Kepulauan Romang Wetar
Bondowoso Denpasar Sangeang Pulau Adonara Pulau Lomblen Pulau Wetar Pulau Moa
Bali 3726 Gunong Rinjani Raba Komodo 6960 Pulau Flores Alor Pulau Ataoro Leti Is.
Pulau Lombok Pulau Bali Ruteng Ende Maumere Pantar Dili 2960
Pulau Sumbawa Sumbawa Pulau Sumba Sumba Strait Savu Okusi
Waikabubak Waingapu Sea Kupang Pulau Timor
Mataram 1225 Pulau Sumba Pulau Sawu T i m o r
Pulau Lombok Pulau Raijua Pulau Roti S e a

115 E 120 F 125 G 130

77

© ISTITUTO GEOGRAFICO DE AGOSTINI S.p.A. - NOVARA

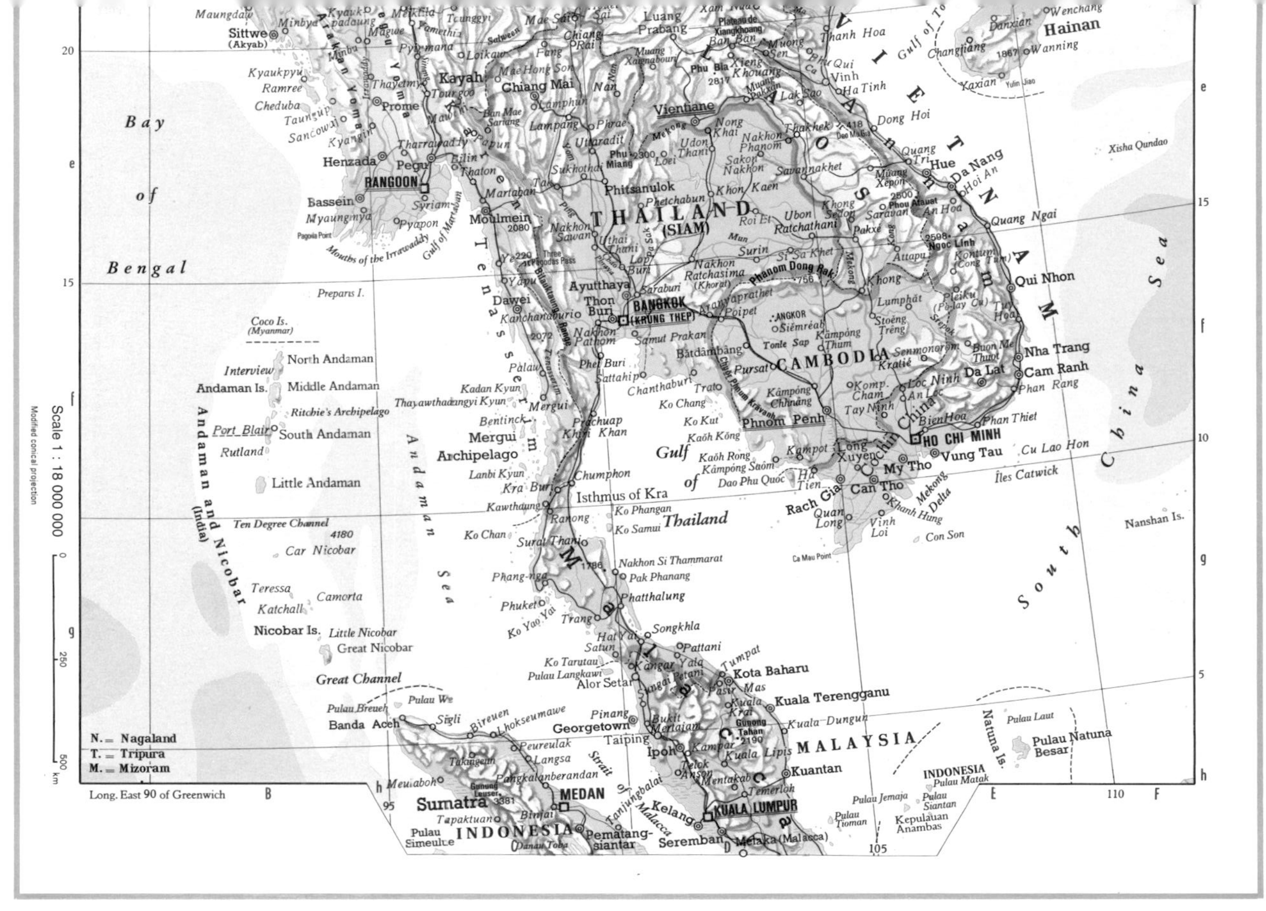

Scale 1 : 18 000 000

0   250   500 km

Modified conical projection

Long. East 90 of Greenwich

N. = Nagaland
T. = Tripura
M. = Mizoram

Andaman and Nicobar
(India)

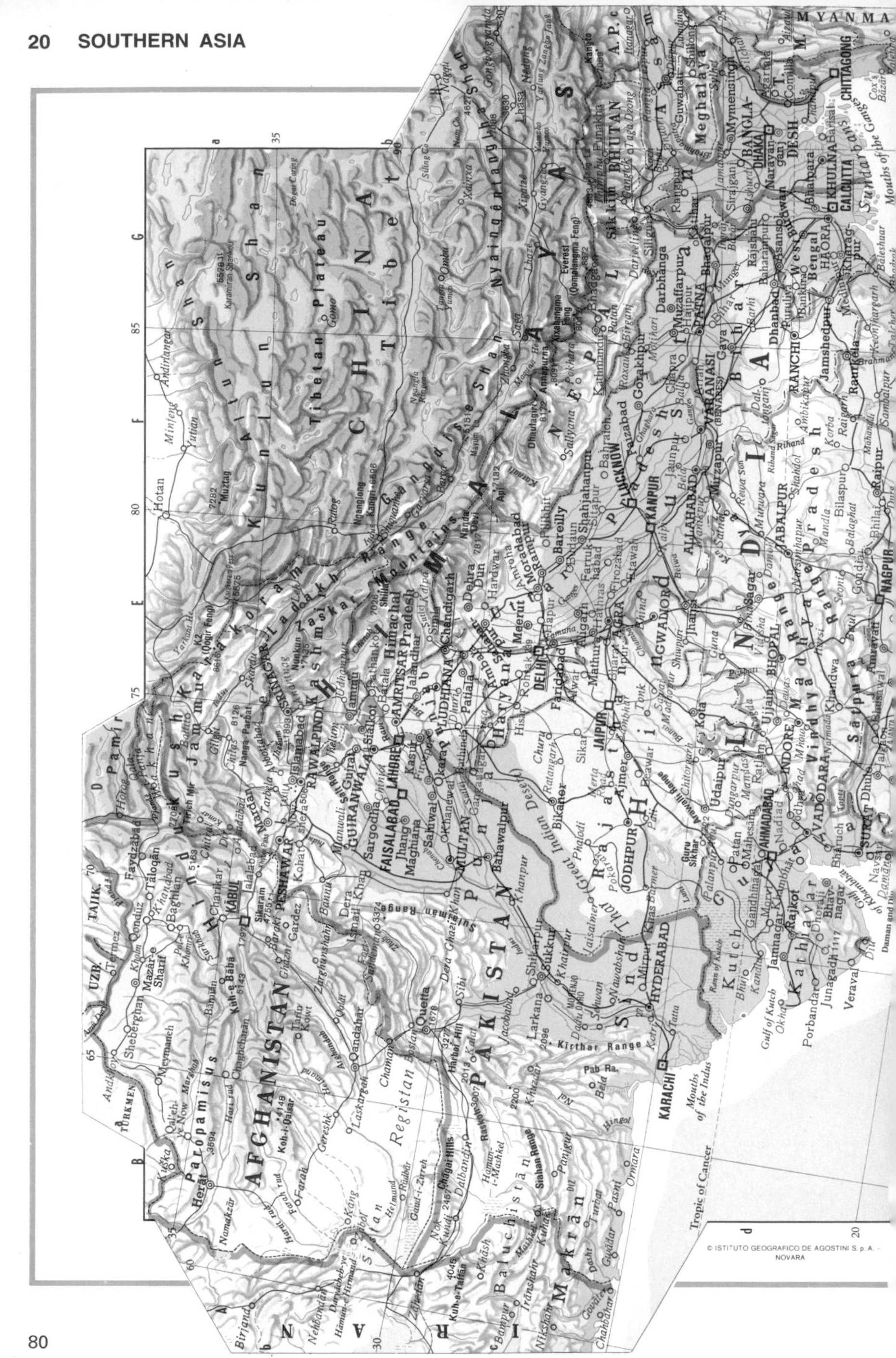
AFGHANISTAN
PAKISTAN
INDIA
CHINA
NEPAL
BHUTAN
BANGLADESH
MYANMA
IRAN
TURKMEN.
UZB.
TAJIK.
Tibetan Plateau
Kunlun Shan
Karakoram Range
Hindu Kush
Himalaya
Paropamisus
Thar (Great Indian) Desert
Tropic of Cancer
Mouths of the Indus
Mouths of the Ganges
Gulf of Kutch
Rann of Kutch
Kirthar Range
Sulaiman Range
Aravalli Range
Vindhya Range
Satpura Range
KABUL
PESHAWAR
RAWALPINDI
Islamabad
LAHORE
FAISALABAD
MULTAN
HYDERABAD
KARACHI
Quetta
Herat
Qandahar
DELHI
AGRA
JAIPUR
JODHPUR
AHMADABAD
VADODARA
SURAT
INDORE
BHOPAL
KANPUR
LUCKNOW
ALLAHABAD
VARANASI
PATNA
CALCUTTA
HAORA
KHULNA
DHAKA
CHITTAGONG
NAGPUR
JABALPUR
RANCHI
Kathmandu
Everest
Lhasa
Hotan
K2
Tropic of Cancer

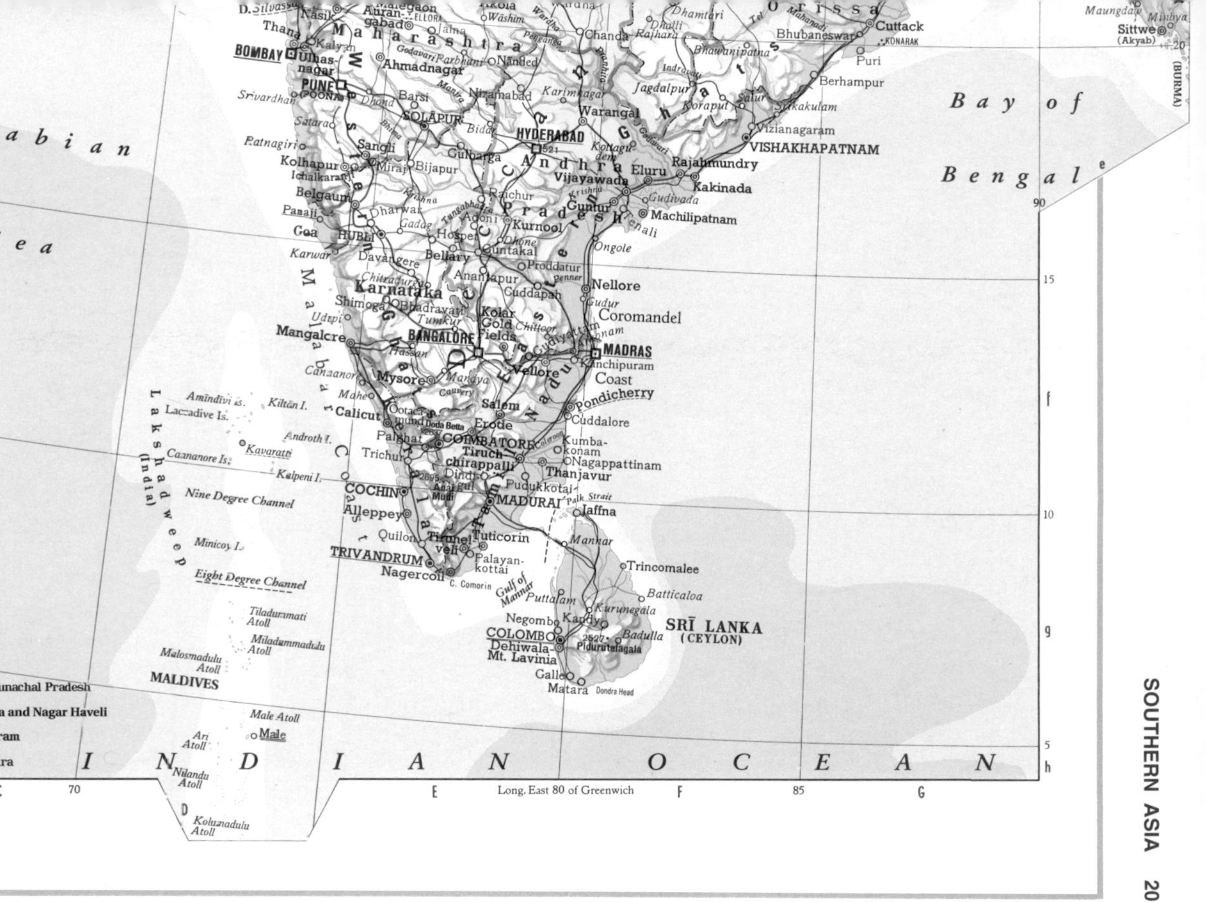

(BURMA)

Maungdaw Minbya
Sittwe
(Akyab)

Bay of Bengal

O R I S S A

Cuttack
Bhubaneswar
Puri
Berhampur

VISHAKHAPATNAM

Rajahmundry
Kakinada
Machilipatnam

Eluru
Vijayawada
Coromandel
Coast

HYDERABAD

Nellore
MADRAS
Kanchipuram
Pondicherry
Cuddalore
Nagapattinam
Thanjavur
Jaffna

SRĪ LANKA
(CEYLON)

Trincomalee
Batticaloa

BANGALORE
MYSORE
Salem
Erode
Tiruchirappalli
MADURAI
Tuticorin

Negombo
COLOMBO
Dehiwala-
Mt. Lavinia
Galle
Matara

COCHIN
Alleppey
TRIVANDRUM
Nagercoil
C. Comorin

Mangalore

Calicut

M a l a b a r   C o a s t

BOMBAY
PUNE
Goa

A r a b i a n

S e a

Aminduvi Is.
Laccadive Is.
Androth I.
Kavaratti
Kalpeni I.
Minicoy I.

Tiladummati Atoll
Mihammadu Atoll

Malosmadulu Atoll
Arī Atoll
Nilandu Atoll
Kolumadulu Atoll

Male Atoll
Malé

MALDIVES

L a k s h a d w e e p
(India)

I N D I A N   O C E A N

Long. East 80 of Greenwich

A. P. = Arunachal Pradesh
D. = Dādra and Nagar Havell
M. = Mizoram
T. = Tripura

Scale 1 : 18 000 000
Modified conical projection

0   250   500 km

81

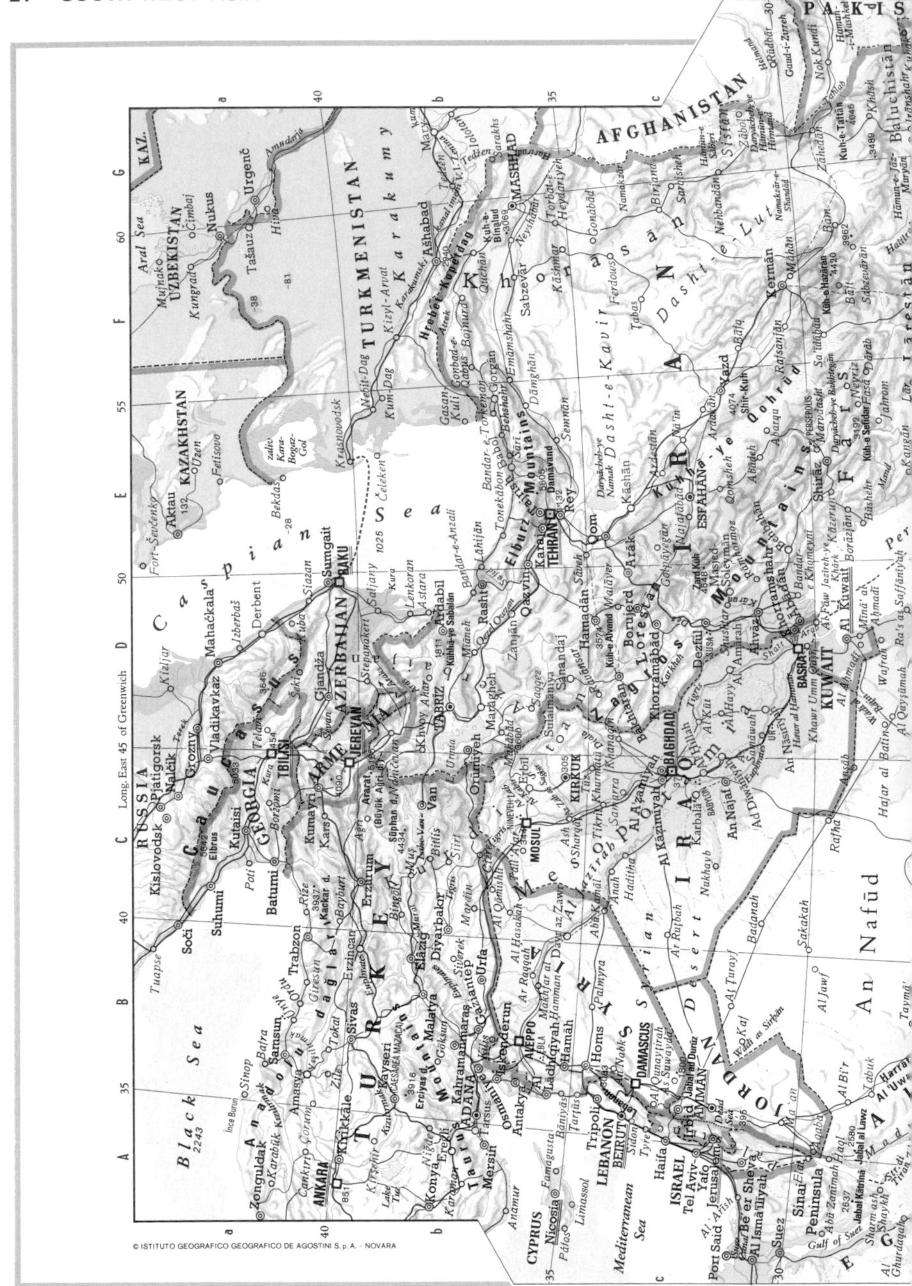

© ISTITUTO GEOGRAFICO GEOGRAFICO DE AGOSTINI S.p.A. - NOVARA

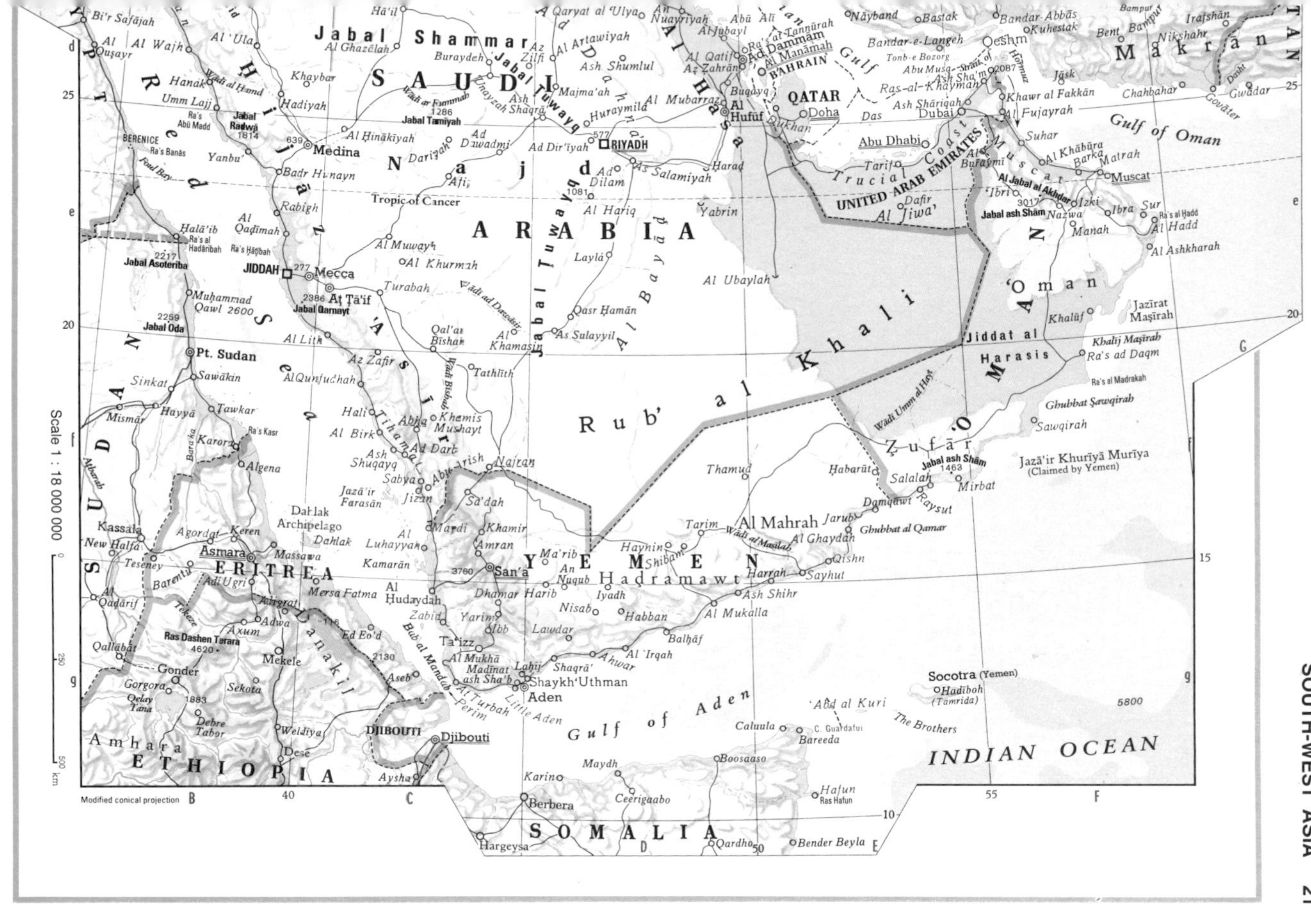

SAUDI ARABIA
UNITED ARAB EMIRATES
QATAR
BAHRAIN
OMAN
YEMEN
ERITREA
DJIBOUTI
ETHIOPIA
SOMALIA
SUDAN
INDIAN OCEAN
Gulf of Oman
Gulf of Aden
Red Sea
Rub' al Khali
Al Hijaz
Najd
Jabal Shammar
Ad Dahna
Jabal Tuwayq
Tihamat 'Asir
Hadramawt
Al Mahrah
Zufar
Jiddat al Harasis
Trucial Coast
Muscat
Makran
Danakil
Amhara
RIYADH
Mecca
Medina
JIDDAH
At Ta'if
Doha
Abu Dhabi
Dubai
Aden
San'a
Djibouti
Asmara
Pt. Sudan
Berbera
Hargeysa
Socotra (Yemen)
Jaza'ir Khuriya Muriya (Claimed by Yemen)
Tropic of Cancer
Scale 1 : 18 000 000
0
250
500 km
Modified conical projection

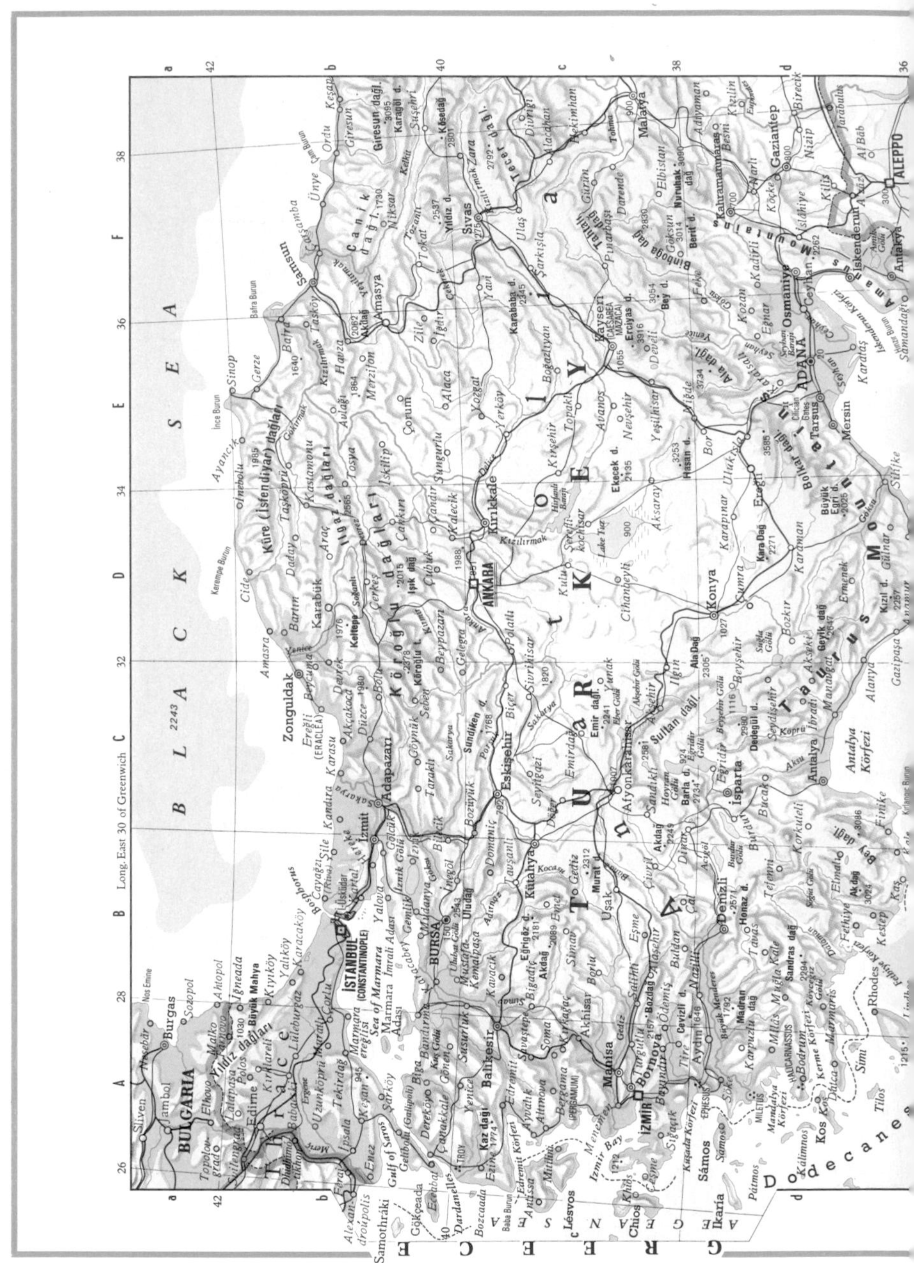
B L A C K S E A
T U R K E Y
ANKARA
İSTANBUL (CONSTANTINOPLE)
İZMİR
BURSA
ADANA
ALEPPO
BULGARIA
Sea of Marmara
Long. East 30 of Greenwich

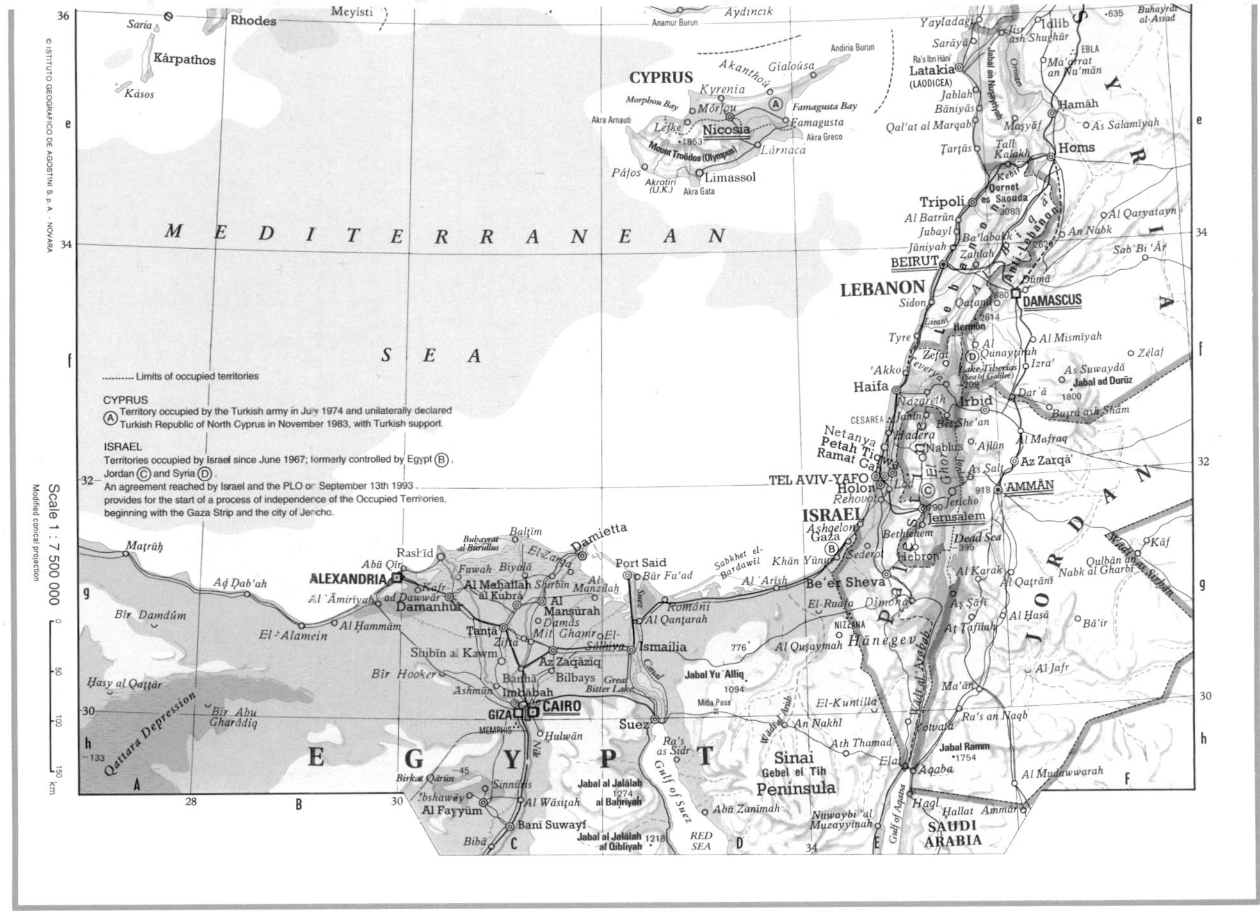

Scale 1 : 7 500 000

0   50   100   150 km

Modified conical projection

CYPRUS
- - - - - - - Limits of occupied territories

Ⓐ Territory occupied by the Turkish army in June 1974 and unilaterally declared
Ⓑ Turkish Republic of North Cyprus in November 1983, with Turkish support.

ISRAEL
Territories occupied by Israel since June 1967; formerly controlled by Egypt Ⓑ.
Jordan Ⓒ and Syria Ⓓ
Ⓔ An agreement reached by the PLO or September 13th 1993
provides for the start of a process of independence of the Occupied Territories,
beginning with the Gaza Strip and the city of Jericho.

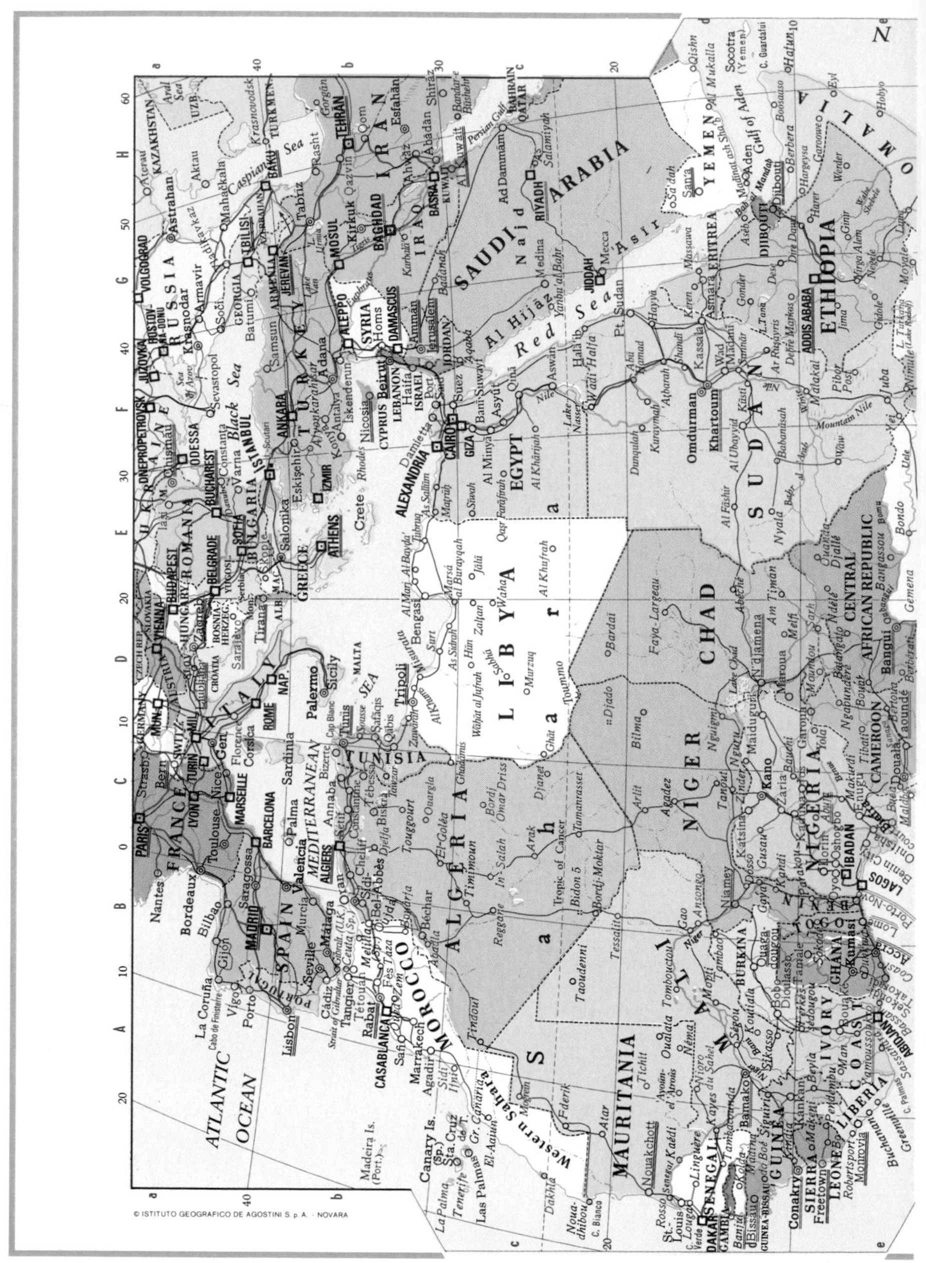
ATLANTIC OCEAN
MEDITERRANEAN SEA
Black Sea
Caspian Sea
Red Sea
Gulf of Aden
Persian Gulf
FRANCE
SPAIN
PORTUGAL
ITALY
GREECE
TURKEY
SYRIA
IRAQ
IRAN
SAUDI ARABIA
YEMEN
EGYPT
LIBYA
TUNISIA
ALGERIA
MOROCCO
Western Sahara
MAURITANIA
MALI
NIGER
CHAD
SUDAN
ETHIOPIA
ERITREA
DJIBOUTI
SOMALIA
NIGERIA
CAMEROON
CENTRAL AFRICAN REPUBLIC
SENEGAL
GUINEA
SIERRA LEONE
LIBERIA
IVORY COAST
GHANA
BURKINA
Tropic of Cancer
Sahara
© ISTITUTO GEOGRAFICO DE AGOSTINI S. p. A. - NOVARA

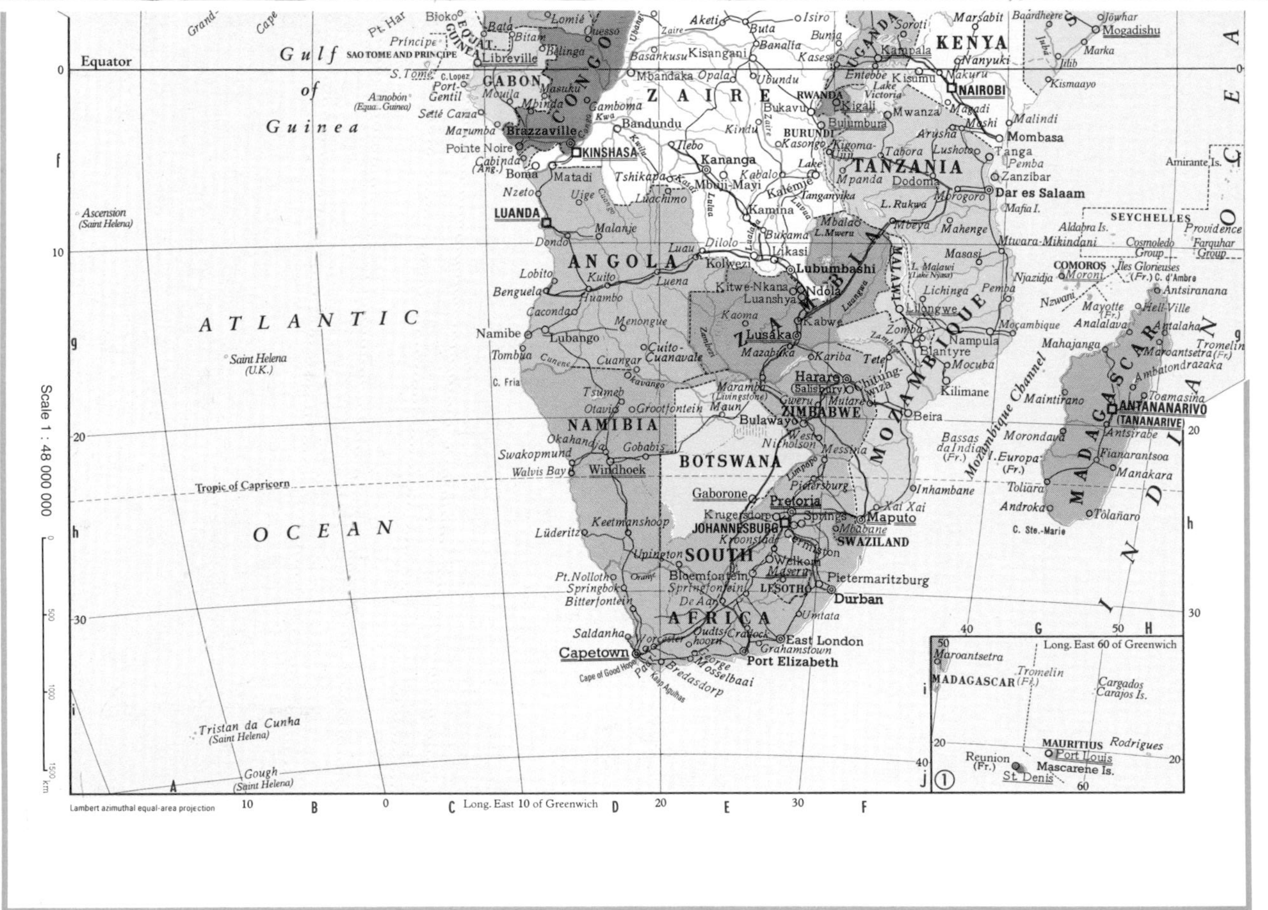

Gulf of Guinea
ATLANTIC
OCEAN
INDIAN
Equator
Tropic of Capricorn
SAO TOME AND PRINCIPE
EQUAT. GUINEA
Bioko
GABON
Libreville
CONGO
Brazzaville
KINSHASA
ZAIRE
Cabinda (Ang.)
LUANDA
ANGOLA
NAMIBIA
Windhoek
Walvis Bay
BOTSWANA
Gaborone
SOUTH AFRICA
Pretoria
JOHANNESBURG
LESOTHO
Maseru
SWAZILAND
Mbabane
Maputo
Durban
East London
Port Elizabeth
Capetown
Cape of Good Hope
UGANDA
Kampala
KENYA
NAIROBI
Mombasa
Mogadishu
RWANDA
Kigali
BURUNDI
Bujumbura
TANZANIA
Dar es Salaam
Zanzibar
Dodoma
ZAMBIA
Lusaka
Lubumbashi
MALAWI
Lilongwe
Blantyre
ZIMBABWE
Harare (Salisbury)
Bulawayo
MOZAMBIQUE
Beira
Mozambique Channel
MADAGASCAR
ANTANANARIVO (TANANARIVE)
COMOROS
Moroni
SEYCHELLES
MAURITIUS
Port Louis
Reunion (Fr.)
St. Denis
Mascarene Is.
Saint Helena (U.K.)
Ascension (Saint Helena)
Tristan da Cunha (Saint Helena)
Gough (Saint Helena)
Long. East 10 of Greenwich
Long. East 60 of Greenwich
Lambert azimuthal equal-area projection
Scale 1 : 48 000 000
0 500 1000 1500 km

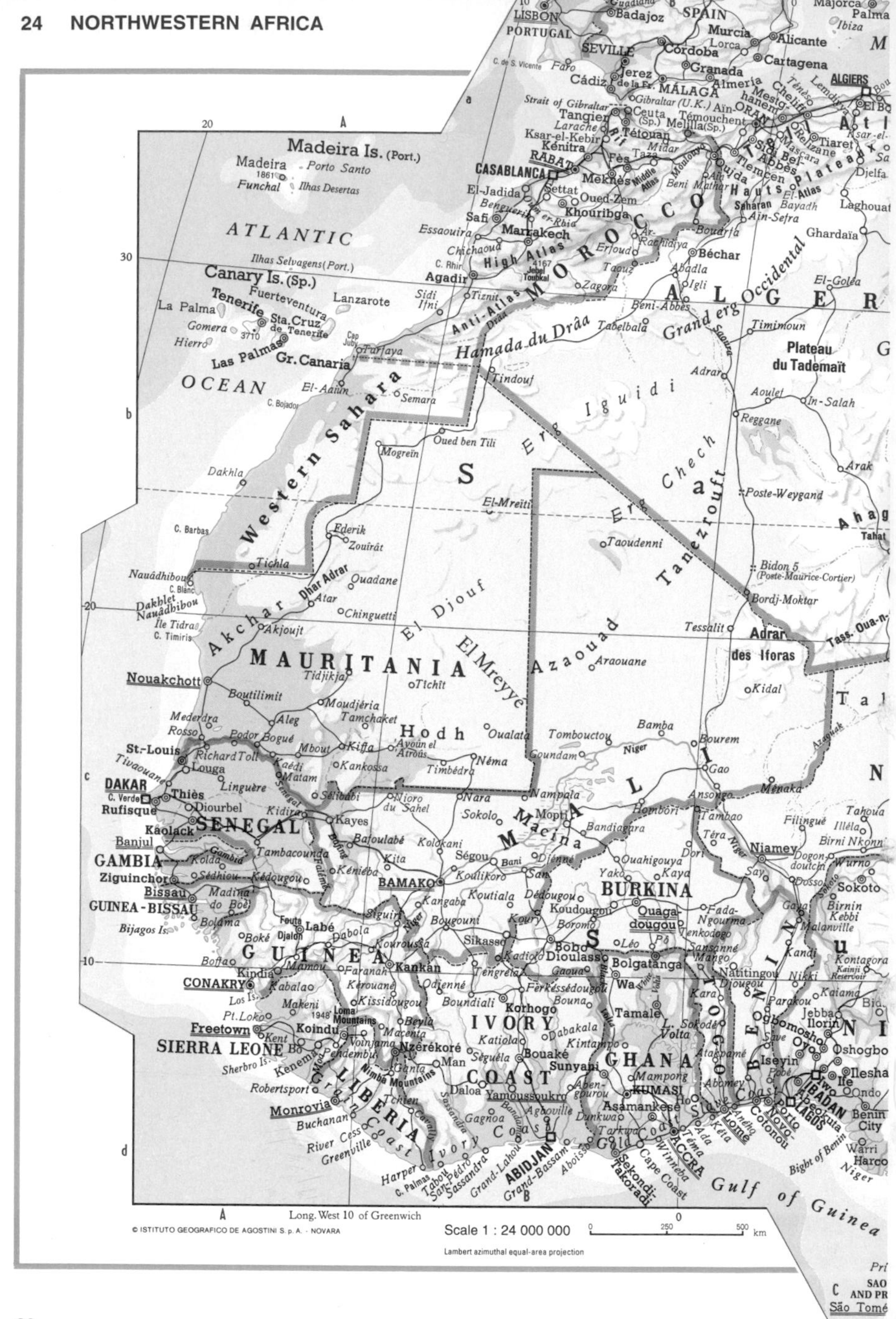

Scale 1 : 24 000 000
Lambert azimuthal equal-area projection

© ISTITUTO GEOGRAFICO DE AGOSTINI S.p.A. - NOVARA

Long. West 10 of Greenwich

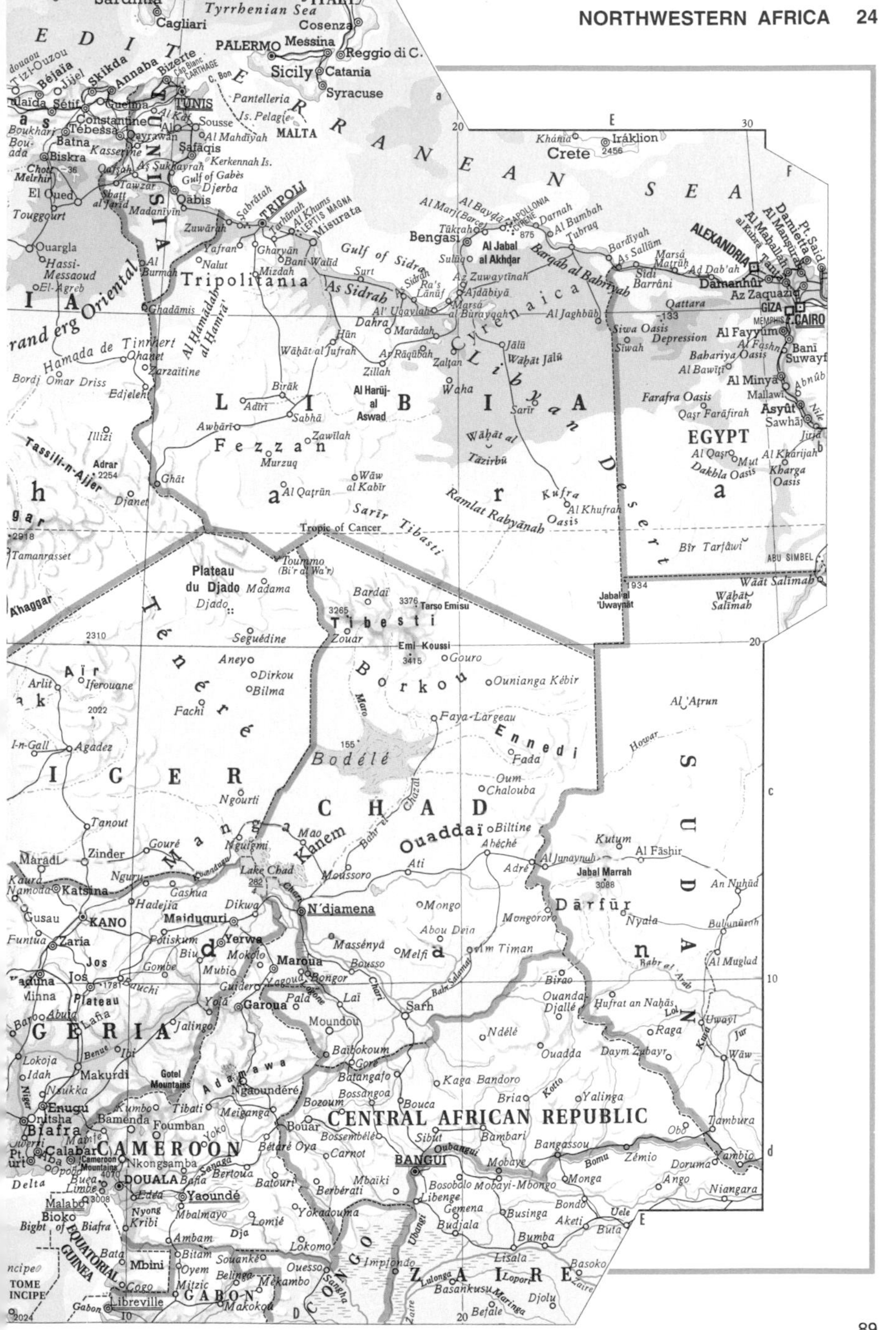
Sardinia
Cagliari
Tyrrhenian Sea
ITALY
Cosenza
PALERMO
Messina
Reggio di C.
Sicily
Catania
Syracuse
Pantelleria
Is. Pelagie
MALTA
Béjaïa
Jijel
Skikda
Annaba
Bizerte
TUNIS
Sétif
Constantine
Guelma
Tébessa
Sousse
Al Mahdīyah
Batna
Biskra
Kasserine
Şafāqis
Kerkennah Is.
Gulf of Gabès
Djerba
Chott Melrhir
El Oued
Touggourt
Qābis
Madanīyīn
Zuwārah
Şabrātah
TRIPOLI
Tarhūnah
Al Khums
LEPTIS MAGNA
Misurata
Ouargla
Hassi-Messaoud
El-Agreb
Grand erg Oriental
Ghadāmis
Yafran
Gharyān
Nalut
Banī Walīd
Mizdah
Tripolitania
Al Hamādah al Hamrā'
Hamada de Tinrhert
Ohanet
Zarzaïtine
Bordj Omar Driss
Edjeleh
Gulf of Sidra
Surt
As Sidrah
Ra's Lānūf
Bengasi
Tūkrah
Al Marj (Barce)
Al Bayḑā
APOLLONIA
CYRENE
Darnah
Al Bumbah
Tubruq
Al Jabal al Akhḑar
Sulūq
Az Zuwaytīnah
Ajdābiyā
Al 'Uqaylah
Marsá al Burayqah
Dahra
Marādah
Cyrenaica
Al Jaghbūb
Hūn
Wāḩāt al Jufrah
Ar Rāqūbah
Zillah
Zaltan
Jālū
Wāḩāt Jālū
Libyan Desert
Birāk
Adīrī
Sabhā
Al Harūj-al Aswad
LIBYA
Awbārī
Fezzan
Zawīlah
Murzuq
Waha
Sarīr
Wāḩāt al Tāzirbū
Illizi
Tassili-n-Ajjer
Adrar 2254
Ghāt
Djanet
Wāw al Kabīr
Al Qaţrūn
Sahara
Ramlat Rabyānah
Kufra Oasis
Al Khufrah
Sarīr Tibasti
Tropic of Cancer
Tamanrasset
Ahaggar
Crete
Khaniá
Iráklion
2456
MEDITERRANEAN SEA
ALEXANDRIA
Damietta
Pt. Said
Al Manşūrah
Al Maḩallah al Kubrá
Ţanţā
Bardīyah
As Sallūm
Marsá Maţrūh
Ad Dab'ah
Sīdi Barrâni
Damanhûr
Az Zaqaziq
Qattara Depression
-133
GIZA
MEMPHIS
CAIRO
Siwa Oasis
Sīwah
Al Fayyūm
Al Fashn
Banī Suwayf
Bahariya Oasis
Al Bawīţī
Al Minyā
Abnûb
Mallawī
Farafra Oasis
Qaşr Farāfirah
Asyûţ
Sawhāj
Nile
Jirjā
EGYPT
Al Qaşr
Mut
Dakhla Oasis
Al Khārijah
Kharga Oasis
Bīr Tarfāwī
ABU SIMBEL
Wāat Salīmah
Wāḩāt Salīmah
1934
Jabal al 'Uwaynāt
Plateau du Djado
Djado
Madama
Toummo (Bi'r al Wa'r)
Bardaï
3376 Tarso Emisu
3265
Tibesti
Zouar
Seguédine
2310
Emi Koussi 3415
Gouro
Aneyo
Dirkou
Bilma
Ténéré
Aïr
Arlit
Iferouane
2022
Fachi
Borkou
Ounianga Kébir
Al 'Aţrun
Faya-Largeau
Ennedi
Fada
Bodélé
155
Agadez
In-Gall
NIGER
Ngourti
Oum Chalouba
SUDAN
CHAD
Tanout
Manga
Mao
Kanem
Bahr el Ghazal
Ouaddaï
Biltine
Abéché
Zinder
Gouré
Nguigmi
Maradi
Lake Chad
282
Moussoro
Ati
Adré
Al Junaynah
Kutum
Al Fāshir
Jabal Marrah 3088
Dārfūr
An Nuhūd
Katsina
Nguru
Gashua
Hadejia
KANO
Dikwa
Maiduguri
Yerwa
N'djamena
Mongo
Mongororo
Nyala
Gusau
Zaria
Funtua
Potiskum
Massénya
Abou Deia
Am Timan
Melfi
Kaduna
Jos
Plateau
1781
Bauchi
Gombe
Biu
Mokolo
Mubi
Maroua
Bousso
Bongor
Bahr al Arab
Al Muglad
Minna
Guider
Yagoua
Logone
Pala
Laï
Chari
Bahr Salamat
Birao
Ouanda Djallé
Ḩufrat an Naḩās
Raga
Baro
Abuja
Lafia
NIGERIA
Jalingo
Yola
Garoua
Moundou
Sarh
Ndélé
Lokoja
Idah
Benue
Ibi
Makurdi
Gotel Mountains
Adamawa
Baïbokoum
Gore
Ouadda
Daym Zubayr
Wāw
Nsukka
Enugu
Onitsha
Biafra
Calabar
Niger
Batangafo
Ngaoundéré
Kaga Bandoro
Bossangoa
Bouca
Bria
Yalinga
Kumbo
Tibati
Meiganga
Bamenda
Foumban
Bozoum
Bouar
CENTRAL AFRICAN REPUBLIC
Tambura
Yambio
CAMEROON
Nkongsamba
Cameroon Mountains 4070
Bétaré Oya
Bossembélé
Sibut
Bambari
Bangassou
Carnot
Oubangui
BANGUI
Mobaye
Bomu
Zémio
Doruma
DOUALA
Bafia
Bertoua
Batouri
Mbaïki
Berbérati
Bosobolo
Mobayi-Mbongo
Monga
Ango
Niangara
Buea
Limbe
Edéa
Yaoundé
Malabo
3008
Bioko
Bight of Biafra
Nyong
Kribi
Mbalmayo
Lomié
Yokadouma
Libenge
Gemena
Businga
Bondo
Aketi
Uele
Buta
EQUATORIAL GUINEA
Ambam
Dja
Bata
Mbini
Bitam
Oyem
Souanké
Lokomo
Budjala
Bumba
Ouesso
Impfondo
Lisala
Basoko
Zaire
Mitzic
Belinga
Mékambo
Sangha
CONGO
ZAIRE
Lopori
Lulonga
Basankusu
Maringa
Djolu
Befale
TOME
PRINCIPE
2024
GABON
Libreville
Gabon
Cogo
Makokou
Delta

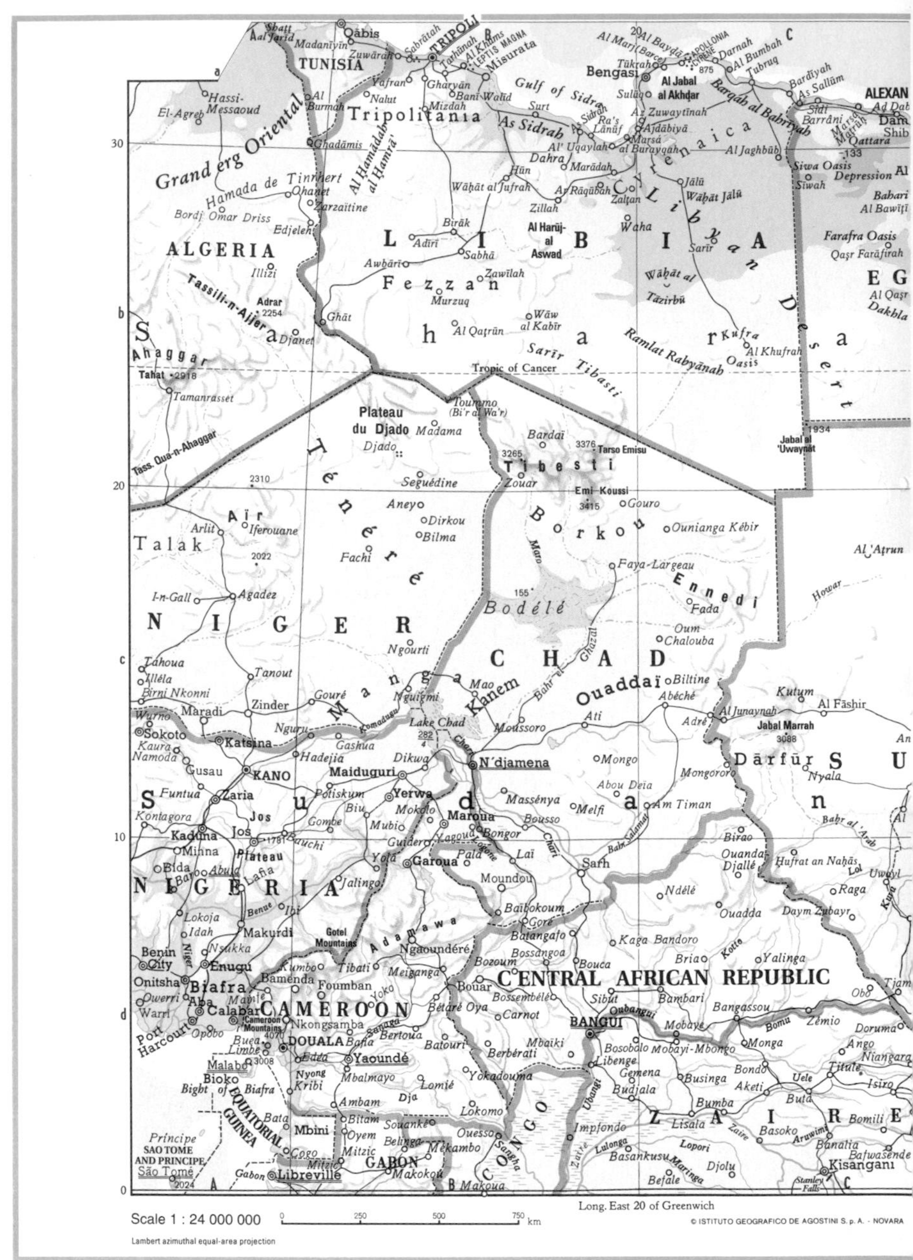

Scale 1 : 24 000 000

0   250   500   750 km

Lambert azimuthal equal-area projection

Long. East 20 of Greenwich

© ISTITUTO GEOGRAFICO DE AGOSTINI S. p. A. - NOVARA

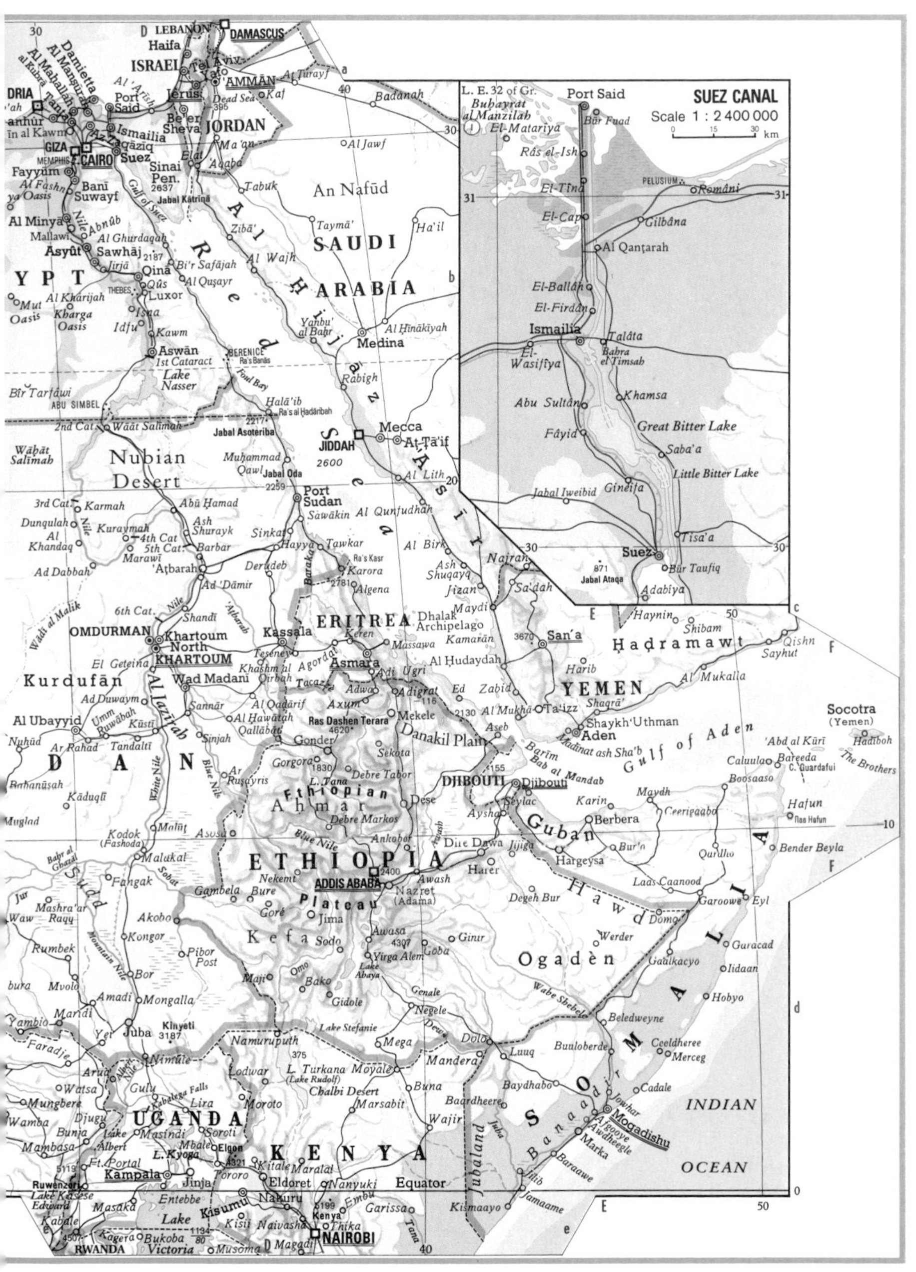

SUEZ CANAL
Scale 1 : 2 400 000
L. E. 32 of Gr.
Port Said
Bûr Fuad
El-Matarîya
Râs el-Ish
PELUSIUM
Români
El-Tîna
El-Cap
Gilbâna
Al Qanţarah
El-Ballâh
El-Firdân
Ismailia
Talâta
El-Wasifîya
Bahra el Timsah
Abu Sultân
Khamsa
Fâyid
Great Bitter Lake
Saba'a
Little Bitter Lake
Jabal Iweibid
Gineifa
Tîsa'a
Suez
Bûr Taufiq
Jabal Ataqa
Adabiya
LEBANON
DAMASCUS
Haifa
ISRAEL
Tel Aviv-Yafo
'AMMĀN
Jerusalem
Dead Sea
JORDAN
Beer Sheva
Elat
'Aqaba
Damietta
Al Manşūrah
Al Maḩallah al Kubrá
Ţanţā
Port Said
Ismailia
Az Zaqāziq
GIZA
CAIRO
Suez
MEMPHIS
Fayyūm
Sinai Pen.
Banī Suwayf
Jabal Kātrīnā
Al Minyā
Mallawī
Asyût
Sawhāj
Jirjā
Qinā
Qûs
Luxor
THEBES
Al Khārijah
Kharga Oasis
Isnā
Idfu
Kawm
Aswān
1st Cataract
Lake Nasser
BERENICE
Bīr Tarfāwi
ABU SIMBEL
2nd Cat.
Wādī Ḩalfā
Nubian Desert
3rd Cat.
Karmah
Dunqulah
Kuraymah
4th Cat.
5th Cat.
Marawī
Barbar
'Aţbarah
Abū Ḩamad
Ad Dabbah
Ad Dāmir
6th Cat.
Shandī
OMDURMAN
Khartoum
North
KHARTOUM
El Geteina
Kurdufān
Wad Madanī
Ad Duwaym
Al Ubayyid
Sannār
Kūstī
Al Jazīrah
Sinjah
Kāduqlī
Kodok
(Fashoda)
Malakal
Fangak
Akobo
Kongor
Rumbek
Pibor Post
Bor
Amadi
Mongalla
Maridi
Yei
Juba
Kinyeti
3187
Nimule
Arua
Gulu
Lira
Moroto
UGANDA
Soroti
Elgon
Masindi
L. Kyoga
Kampala
Jinja
Entebbe
Masaka
Kabale
Mbarara
Ruwenzori
RWANDA
Lake Victoria
Bukoba
Musoma
KENYA
Kitale
Eldoret
Nakuru
Kisumu
Kisii
Naivasha
Nairobi
NAIROBI
Thika
Nanyuki
Equator
Garissa
Kismaayo
Marsabit
Wajir
L. Turkana
(Lake Rudolf)
Chalbi Desert
Lodwar
Moyale
Mandera
Buna
Namuruputh
SAUDI ARABIA
An Nafūd
Al Jawf
Tabūk
Taymā'
Ḩā'il
Al Wajh
Yanbu' al Baḩr
Medina
Al Ḩijāz
Rābigh
Mecca
JIDDAH
Aţ Ţā'if
Al Lith
Al Qunfudhah
'Asīr
Najrān
Jīzān
Red Sea
Port Sudan
Sawākin
Tawkar
Karora
ERITREA
Asmara
Keren
Massawa
Dhalak Archipelago
Kassala
Al Qaḑārif
Gonder
Ras Dashen Terara
4620
L. Tana
Debre Tabor
Mekele
Danakil Plain
Dese
Ethiopian Plateau
ETHIOPIA
ADDIS ABABA
Awash
Nazret (Adama)
Harer
Dire Dawa
Jijiga
Gambela
Jima
Kefa
Sodo
Awasa
Ogadèn
Gode
Negele
Mega
Dolo
Luuq
DJIBOUTI
Djibouti
Seylac
Berbera
Hargeysa
Guban
Hawd
YEMEN
San'a
Ṣa'dah
Al Ḩudaydah
Ta'izz
Aden
Al Mukalla
Ḩadramawt
Gulf of Aden
Bab al Mandab
Socotra
(Yemen)
The Brothers
Boosaaso
Bender Beyla
Garoowe
Eyl
Gaalkacyo
Hobyo
Beledweyne
SOMALIA
Mogadishu
Marka
Baraawe
Jamaame
Baydhabo
Jubaland
INDIAN OCEAN

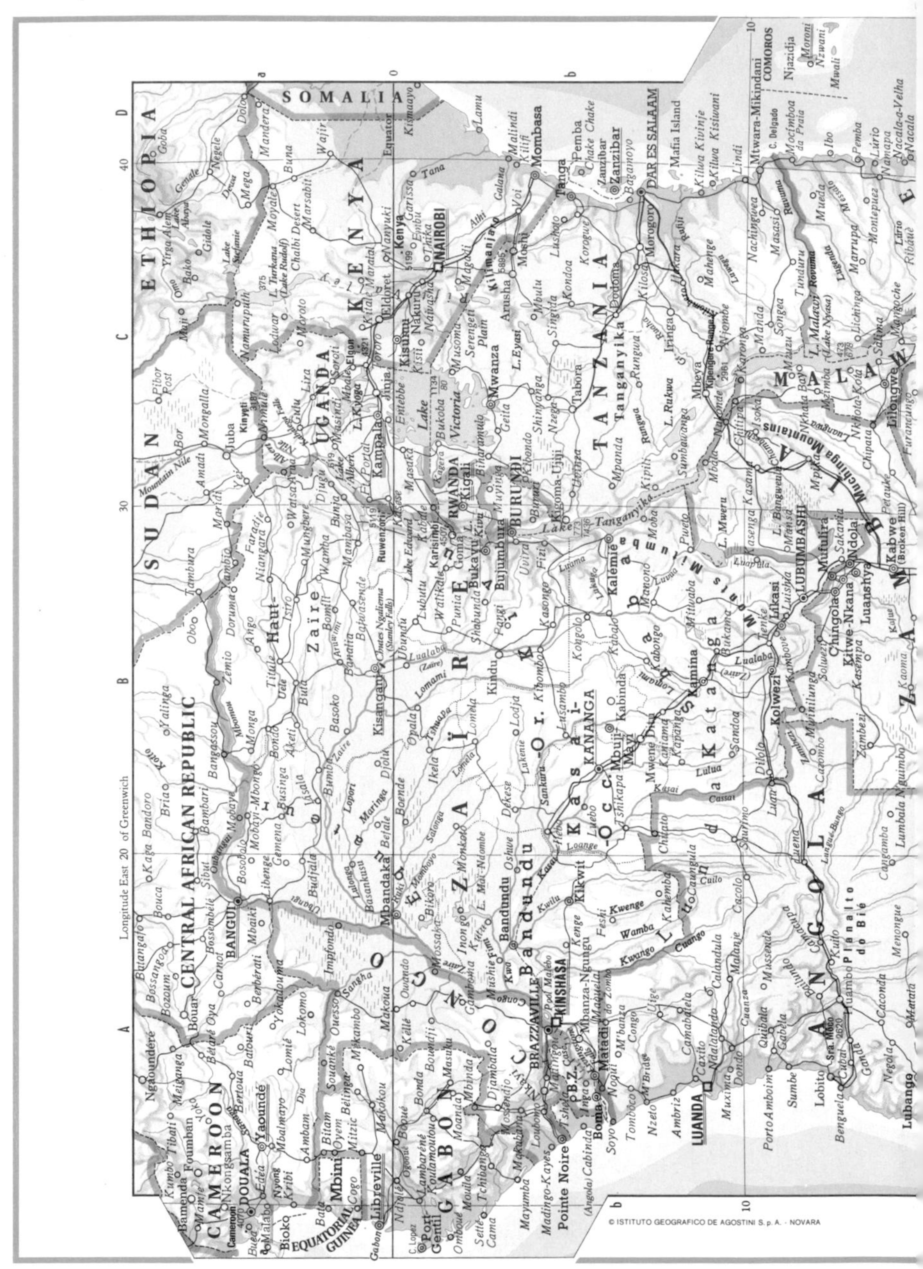
ETHIOPIA
SOMALIA
KENYA
SUDAN
UGANDA
CENTRAL AFRICAN REPUBLIC
CAMEROON
EQUATORIAL GUINEA
GABON
CONGO
ZAÏRE
RWANDA
BURUNDI
TANZANIA
ZAMBIA
MALAWI
ANGOLA
COMOROS
NAIROBI
KAMPALA
BANGUI
Yaoundé
Libreville
BRAZZAVILLE
KINSHASA
LUANDA
DAR ES SALAAM
Lake Victoria
Lake Tanganyika
L. Malawi (Lake Nyasa)
Kilimanjaro 5895
Mombasa
Zanzibar
Kisangani
Lubumbashi
Kananga
Mbuji-Mayi
Bujumbura
Kigali
Pointe Noire
Matadi
Lobito
Benguela
Huambo
Longitude East 20 of Greenwich
Equator
© ISTITUTO GEOGRAFICO DE AGOSTINI S. p. A. - NOVARA

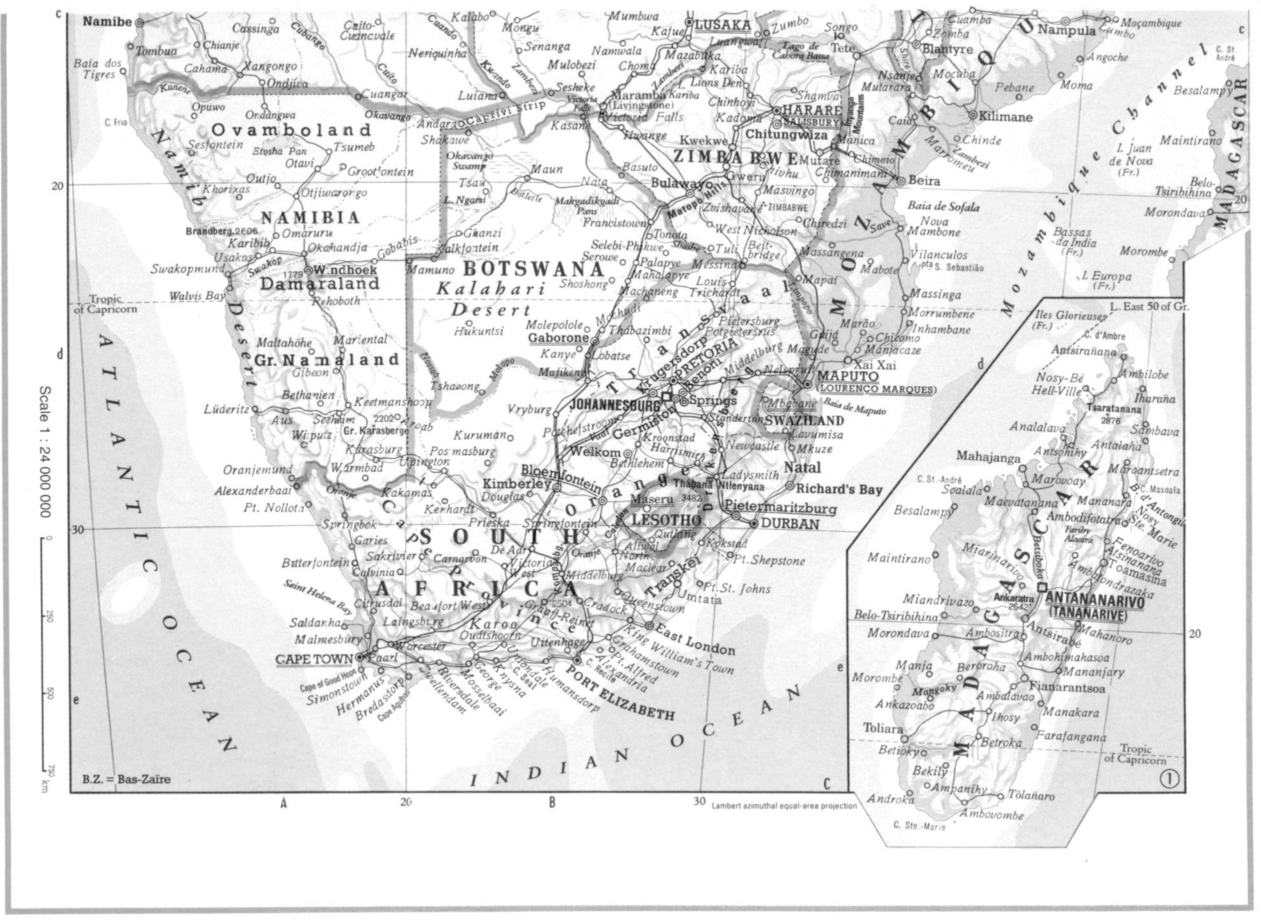
ATLANTIC OCEAN
INDIAN OCEAN
Mozambique Channel
NAMIBIA
BOTSWANA
ZIMBABWE
MOZAMBIQUE
SOUTH AFRICA
LESOTHO
SWAZILAND
MADAGASCAR
Ovamboland
Damaraland
Gr. Namaland
Namib Desert
Kalahari Desert
Transvaal
Natal
Transkei
Cape Province
LUSAKA
HARARE (SALISBURY)
MAPUTO (LOURENÇO MARQUES)
PRETORIA
JOHANNESBURG
Gaborone
Maseru
Windhoek
CAPE TOWN
PORT ELIZABETH
East London
DURBAN
Pietermaritzburg
Bloemfontein
Kimberley
Bulawayo
Beira
Blantyre
Nampula
Kilimane
ANTANANARIVO (TANANARIVE)
Tropic of Capricorn
L. East 50 of Gr.
Lambert azimuthal equal-area projection
B.Z. = Bas-Zaïre
Scale 1 : 24 000 000
0 250 500 750 km

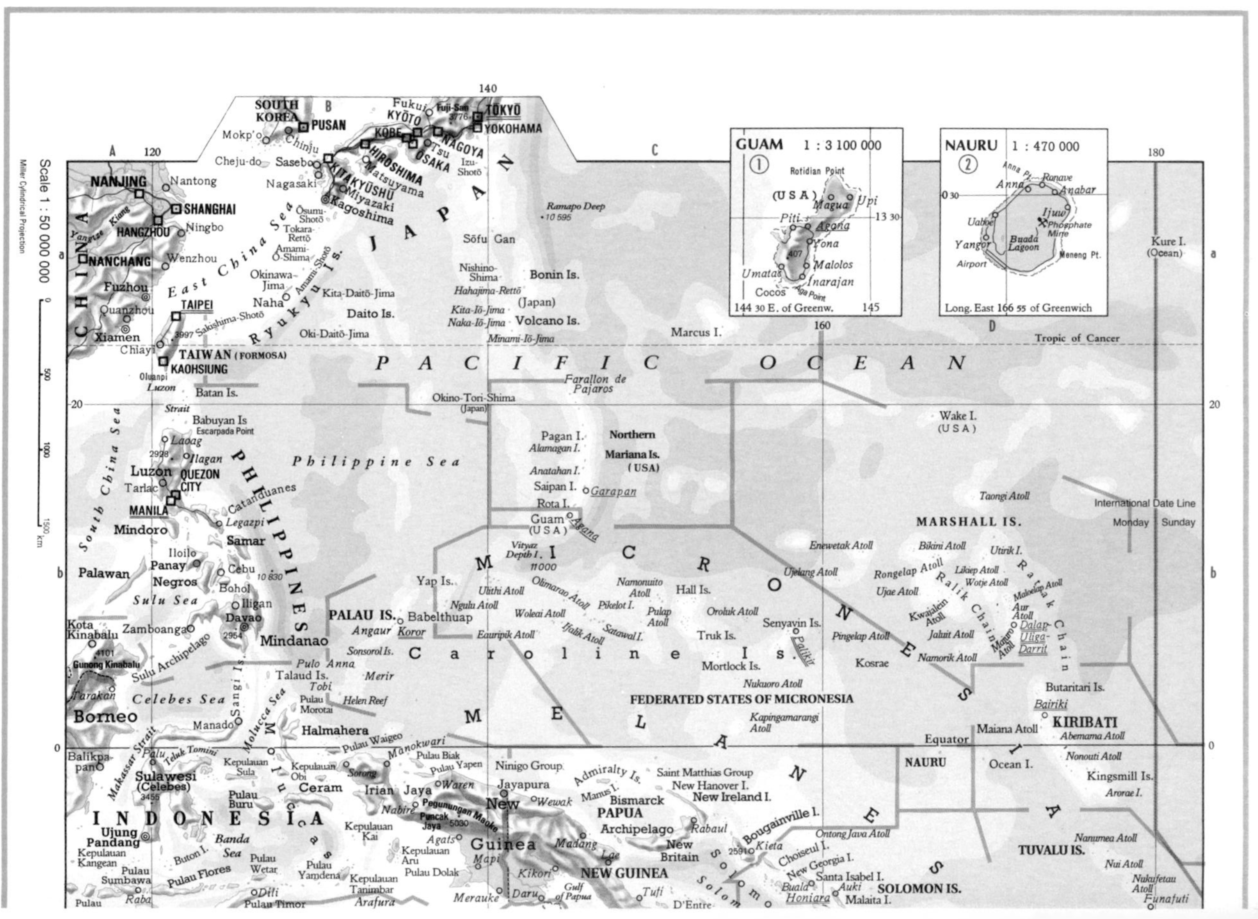

NAURU 1 : 470 000
②
Aiwa Pt.   Anabar
Anna   Ijuw
             Anibare
Uaboe   Meneng Pt.
Baudi
Lagoon   Yaren
        Airport
Long. East 166 55 of Greenwich

GUAM 1 : 3 100 000
①
Ritidian Point
(U S A) Yigo   Upi   13 30
         Agana   Anigua
Piti Agana Inarajan
Umatac Cocos I.   Abo Point
144 30 E. of Greenw. 145

NORTHERN
Mariana Is.
(USA)

FEDERATED STATES OF MICRONESIA

Scale 1 : 50 000 000   0   500   1000   1500 km

Miller Cylindrical Projection

PACIFIC OCEAN

MARSHALL IS.

KIRIBATI

TUVALU IS.

NAURU

SOLOMON IS.

Tropic of Cancer

Equator

International Date Line

C H I N A
NANJING
SHANGHAI
HANGZHOU
NANCHANG
Nantong
Ningbo
Wenzhou
Quanzhou
Xiamen
Fuzhou

JAPAN
TOKYO
YOKOHAMA
NAGOYA
OSAKA
KOBE
KYŌTO
HIROSHIMA
Nagasaki
Kagoshima
KYŪSHŪ

SOUTH KOREA
PUSAN

TAIWAN (FORMOSA)
TAIPEI
KAOHSIUNG

PHILIPPINES
MANILA
QUEZON CITY
Luzon
Mindoro
Palawan
Panay
Cebu
Negros
Samar
Bohol
Mindanao
Davao
Zamboanga

INDONESIA
Borneo
Sulawesi (Celebes)
Halmahera
Ujung Pandang

NEW GUINEA
PAPUA
New Britain
Bismarck Archipelago

South China Sea
Sulu Sea
Celebes Sea
Molucca Sea
Banda Sea
Philippine Sea
East China Sea

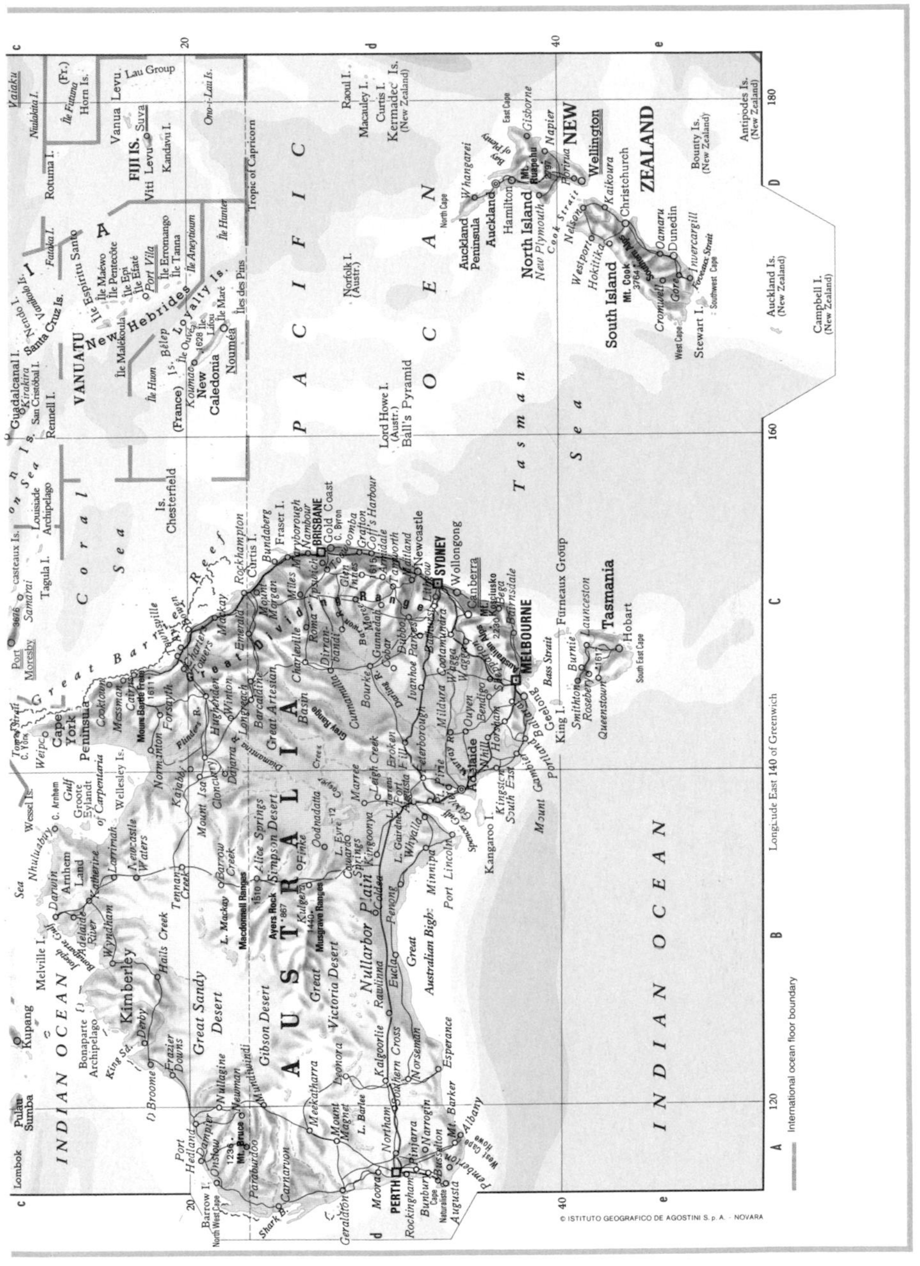

© ISTITUTO GEOGRAFICO DE AGOSTINI S. p. A. - NOVARA

International ocean floor boundary

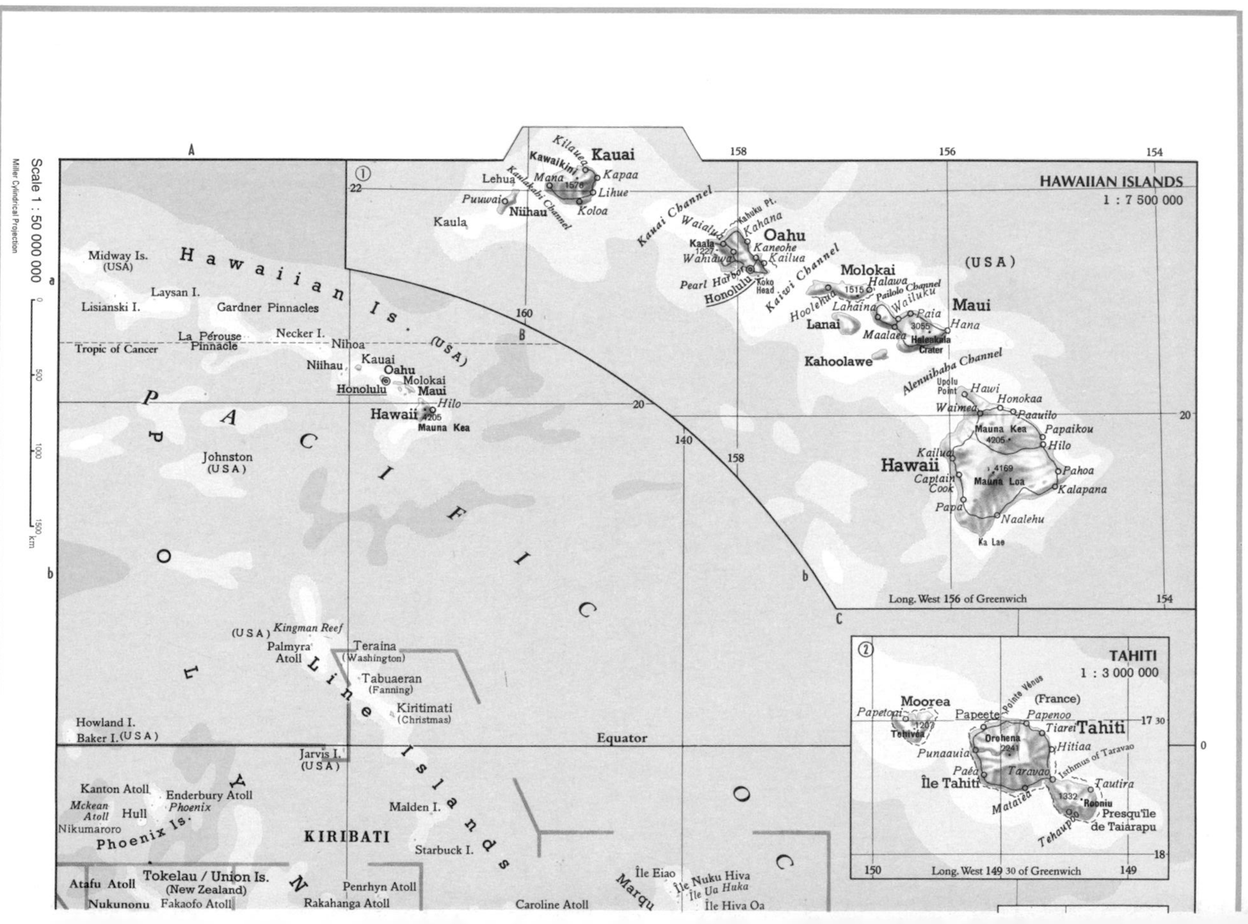

HAWAIIAN ISLANDS
1 : 7 500 000

(USA)

Kauai
Kilauea
Kawaihau
Kapaa
Lihue
Koloa
Lehua
Mana
Niihau
Puuwai
Kekaha
Kaula

Kaena Pt.
Waialua
Kahuku
Oahu
Mokuleia
Kaneohe
Waipahu
Wahiawa
Kailua
Honolulu
Pearl Harbor
Kapaa
Koko Head

Molokai
Kaunakakai
Hoolehua
Maunaloa
Kalaupapa
Halawa

Lanai
Lanai City

Kahoolawe

Maui
Wailuku
Kahului
Lahaina
Makawao
Hana
Wailua
Kipahulu
Haleakala Crater

Hawaii
Waimea
Honokaa
Papaikou
Hilo
Pahoa
Kalapana
Naalehu
Ka Lae
Waipio
Hilo
Mauna Kea
Mauna Loa
Kailua
Captain Cook
Papa

Molokai Channel
Kalohi Channel
Kaiwi Channel
Kailiki Channel
Auau Channel
Pailolo Channel
Kealaikahiki Channel
Alalakeiki Channel
Alenuihaha Channel

Long. West 156 of Greenwich

TAHITI
1 : 3 000 000
(France)

Moorea
Papetoai
Teavaro
Afareaitu

Île Tahiti
Papenoo
Orofara
Papeete
Faaa
Punaauia
Paea
Papara
Mataiea
Taravao
Tiarei
Hitiaa
Tautira
Tevaitoa
Teahupoo
Presqu'île de Taiarapu

Tahiti

Île Eiao
Nuku Hiva
Ua Huka
Ua Haka
Île Hiva Oa

Marquises

Caroline Atoll

Starbuck I.

Malden I.

KIRIBATI

Penrhyn Atoll

Rakahanga Atoll

Equator

Line Islands

Teraina
(Washington)
Tabuaeran
(Fanning)
Kiritimati
(Christmas)

Jarvis I.
(USA)

Kingman Reef
(USA)
Palmyra
Atoll

Hawaiian Is. (USA)
Nihoa
Necker I.
La Pérouse
Pinnacle
Gardner Pinnacles
Niihau
Kauai
Oahu
Honolulu
Molokai
Maui
Hawaii
Hilo
Mauna Kea
Laysan I.
Lisianski I.
Midway Is.
(USA)
Tropic of Cancer

Johnston
(USA)

Howland I.
Baker I. (USA)

Kanton Atoll
Mckean
Atoll
Nikumaroro
Enderbury Atoll
Phoenix
Hull
Nukumono
Fakaofo Atoll
Phoenix Is.
Tokelau / Union Is.
(New Zealand)
Atafu Atoll

P A C I F I C   O C E A N

P O L Y N E S I A

Scale 1 : 50 000 000

0   500   1000   1500 km

Miller Cylindrical Projection

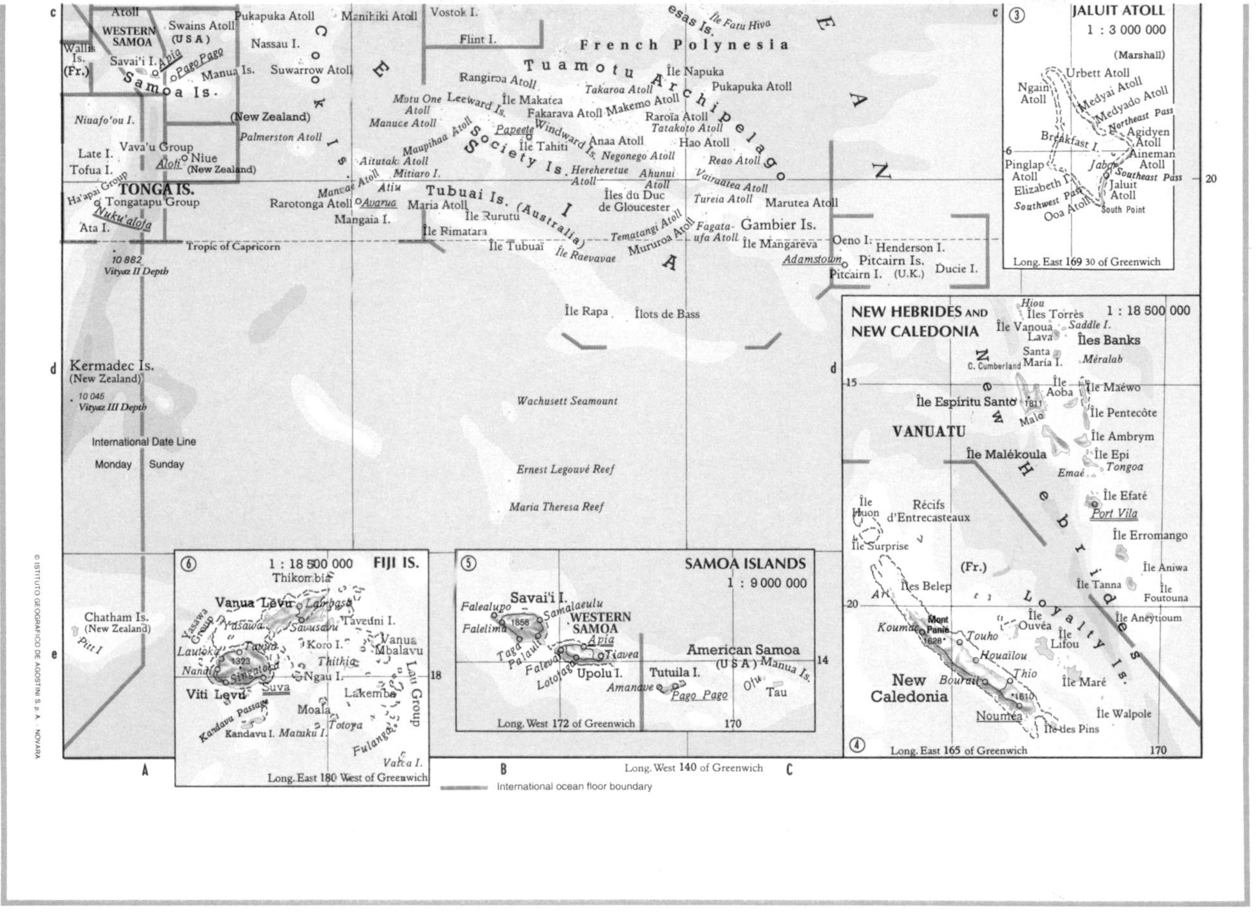

JALUIT ATOLL
1 : 3 000 000
(Marshall)

Urbert Atoll
Ngatik Atoll
Medyato Atoll
Northeast Pass
Apedyen Atoll
Ainemon Atoll
Brigiktaet I.
Jaboldik Atoll
Pinglap I.
Jabor I.
Jaluit Atoll
Elizabeth Atoll
Jaluit Atoll
Southwest pass
Ooa Atoll
South Point
Long. East 169 30 of Greenwich

FRENCH POLYNESIA

Tuamotu Archipelago
Society Is.
Tubuai Is. (Australia)

NEW HEBRIDES AND NEW CALEDONIA
1 : 18 500 000

Hiou
Iles Torrès
Saddle I.
Ile Vanua Lava
 Iles Banks
Santa Maria I.
Méralab
C. Cumberland Santo
Espiritu Santo
Ile Maewo
Aoba
Ile Pentecôte
Malo
Ile Ambrym
Mao
Emae
Tongoa
Ile Epi
Ile Malékoula
Ile Efaté
Port Vila
Ile Erromango
Ile Aniwa
Ile Tanna
Ile Futuna
Ile Anetyioum

H e b r i d e s

L o y a l t y   I s.
Ile Aneytioum
Ouvéa
Lifou
Ile Maré
Ile des Pins
Ile Walpole

Récifs
Iles Belep
Ile Huon d'Entrecasteaux
Ile Surprise
Koumac
Touho
Tiga
Houailou
Thio
New Caledonia
Mont Panié
Nouméa

VANUATU

NEW Caledonia

Long. East 165 of Greenwich

SAMOA ISLANDS
1 : 9 000 000

WESTERN SAMOA
Savai'i I.
Faleolupo
Fagamalo
Falealupo
Matautu
Faleolo
Apia
Upolu I.
Falealili
American Samoa
(U.S.A.)
Tutuila I.
Pago Pago
Amanave
Manu'a Is.
Ofu
Olosega
Tau
Long. West 170 of Greenwich

Iles Marquises
Ile Fatu Hiva

Ile Rapa
Ilots de Bass

Wachusett Seamount

Ernest Legouvé Reef

Maria Theresa Reef

FIJI IS.
1 : 18 500 000

Thikombia I.
Vanua Levu
Yasawa
Koro I.
Vanua I.
Lau Group
Tuvutha
Vanua Vatu
Koro Sea
Kandavu
Mataiku I.
Moala
Totoya
Lakemba
Matuku
Vatoa I.
Viti Levu
Suva
Nandi
Lautoka
Prasam
Kanara
Kandavu I.
Tropic of Capricorn
Long. East 180 West of Greenwich

International ocean floor boundary

International Date Line
Monday Sunday

Kermadec Is.
(New Zealand)
10 045
Vanua III Depth

Chatham Is.
(New Zealand)
Pitt I.

WESTERN SAMOA (USA)
Swains Atoll
Savai'i I.
Apia
Pago Pago
Manua Is.
Samoa Is.

Atoll
Wallis Is. (Fr.)
Vava'u Group
Niuafo'ou I.
Late I.
Tofua I.
Ha'apai Group
Tongatapu Group
Nuku'alofa
Ata I.
TONGA IS.
10 882
Vanua II Depth

Cook Is. (New Zealand)
Pukapuka Atoll
Nassau I.
Suwarrow Atoll
Palmerston Atoll
Niue (New Zealand)
Rarotonga Atoll
Mangaia I.
Manuae Atoll
Aitutaki Atoll
Atiu
Mauke
Mitiaro I.
Mangaia
Takutea

Flint I.
Manihiki Atoll
Vostok I.

Starbuck I.

Rangiroa Atoll
Makatea
Ile Napuka
Fakarava Atoll
Makemo Atoll
Anaa Atoll
Raroia Atoll
Takaroa Atoll
Takume Atoll
Pukapuka Atoll
Hao Atoll
Reao Atoll
Tatakoto Atoll
Motu One Atoll
Manuae Atoll
Bora Bora
Windward Is.
Leeward Is.
Papeete
Ile Tahiti
Tetiaroa I.
Turia Atoll
Vanavana Atoll
Herehéretue Atoll
Ahunui Atoll
Iles du Duc de Gloucester
Temataangi Atoll
Fagatau Atoll
Ile Mangaréva
Marutea Atoll
Maria Atoll
Ile Rurutu
Ile Tubuai
Ile Raivavae
Mururoa
u/a Atoll
Gambier Is.
Oeno I.
Henderson I.
Adamstown
Pitcairn Is.
Ducie I.
Pitcairn I. (U.K.)

Long. West 140 of Greenwich

Long. West 172 of Greenwich

© ISTITUTO GEOGRAFICO DE AGOSTINI S. p. A. · NOVARA

Arafura Se

Cobourg Peninsula
Dundas Str.
Melville I.
Milikapiti
Van Diemen Gulf
Goulburn Is.
Bathurst I.
Clarence Str.
Maningrida
Rum Jungle
Darwin
Batchelor
Arnhem Land
Adelaide River
Port Keats
Pine Creek
Daly R.
Katherine
Roper
Roper Valley
Matarinka
Larrimah
Birdum
Daly Waters
Newcastle Waters

INDIAN OCEAN

Cartier I.
Scott Reef
Browse I.
Admiralty Gulf
C. Londonderry
Kalumburu
Joseph Bonaparte Gulf
Wyndham
Kununurra
Victoria R.
Bonaparte Archipelago
Adele I.
Kuri Bay
Collier B.
Mt. Hann. 776
KIMBERLEY
Victoria Riv. Downs

C. Lévêque
Yampi Sd.
King Sd.
King Leopold Ranges
Mt. Ord 936
Kimberley Plateau 900
Ord River
Wave Hill

Lacepede Is.
Derby
Fitzroy Crossing
Halls Creek
Margaret River

Northern

Broome
Roebuck B.
Lagrange
Fitzroy R.
Tanami
Tennant Creek
Tanami Desert

Frazier Downs
Eighty Mile Beach
Gregory L.
The Granites
Lander R.
Barrow Creek

Port Hedland
Shay Gap
De Grey R.
Great Sandy Desert
Percival Lakes
L. Mackay
Yuendumu
Territor

Dampier Archipelago
Monte Bello Is.
Wickham
Roebourne
Marble Bar
L. Waukarly-carly
Macdonnell Ranges
Mt. Zeil
Alice Springs

Barrow I.
Dampier
Nullagine
L. Dora
L. Auld

Exmouth Gulf
North West Cape
Exmouth
Pannawonica
Fortescue R.
Wittenoom
Roy Hill
Haasts Bluff 1510
Mt. 1480

Learmouth
Onslow
Mt. Bruce 1236
Hamersley Range
Tom Price
Newman
L. Disappointment
L. Macdonald

Brockman 1235
Ashburton R.
Paraburdoo
Mundiwindi
L. Hopkins
L. Neale
L. Amadeus
Ehrundra
Henbury
Finke

Uaroo
Tropic of Capricorn
Western
Gibson Desert
Peterman Ranges
Ayers Rock 867
Mt. Woodroffe 1440
Kulgera

L. Mc Leod
Minilya
Mt. Augustus 1106
Carnegie
Warburton Mission
Musgrave Ranges
De Rose Hill
Abminga

Carnarvon
Gascoyne Junction
Gascoyne R.
Peak Hill
AUST
R

Geograp. Channel
Naturaliste Channel
Shark Bay
Wooramel R.
L. Gregory
L. Carnegie
L. Wells
Oodnada
Edwards

Dirk Hartog I.
Denham
Meekatharra
Wiluna
Australia
Great Victoria Desert
Serpentine Lakes

Cue
L. Yeo
Coober Pedy

Northampton
L. Austin
Mount Magnet
Sandstone
Agnew
Laverton
Rason L.
South A

Geraldton
Houtman Abrolhos
Mullewa
Morawa
Yalgoo
Leonora
L. Carey
L. Minigwal

Dongara
Three Springs
Payne's Find
L. Barlee
Menzies
L. Rebecca
Nullarbor Plain
Ooldea
Tarcoola
L. Everard

Watheroo
Moora
Lancelin
Dalwallinu
Kalannie
L. Moore
Kalgoorlie
Zanthus
Haig
Forrest
Yalata
Penong
Ceduna

Mukinbudin
Bullfinch
Coolgardie
Kambalda
Rawlinna
Cockleblddy
Eucla
Fowler's Bay
Nuyts Archipelago
Streaky Bay
Minn

Kalamunda
Northam
Merredin
Southern Cross
Widgiemooltha
L. Cowan
Balladonia
Great
Investigator Group
Elliston

PERTH
Beverley
Brookton
Kondinin
Norseman
L. Dundas
Cum

Rockingham
Mandurah
Narrogin
Newdegate
Australian Bight
Port Lin

Bunbury
Collie
Wagin
Katanning
Ravensthorpe
Esperance 585
C. Arid
C

Busselton
Cape Naturaliste
Blackwood R.
Bridgetown
Gnowangerup
Hopetoun
Archipelago of the Recherche

Augusta
C. Leeuwin
Pemberton
Stirling Range 1109
Mount Barker
Albany

Denmark
Pt. d'Entrecasteaux
West Cape Howe
King George Sound

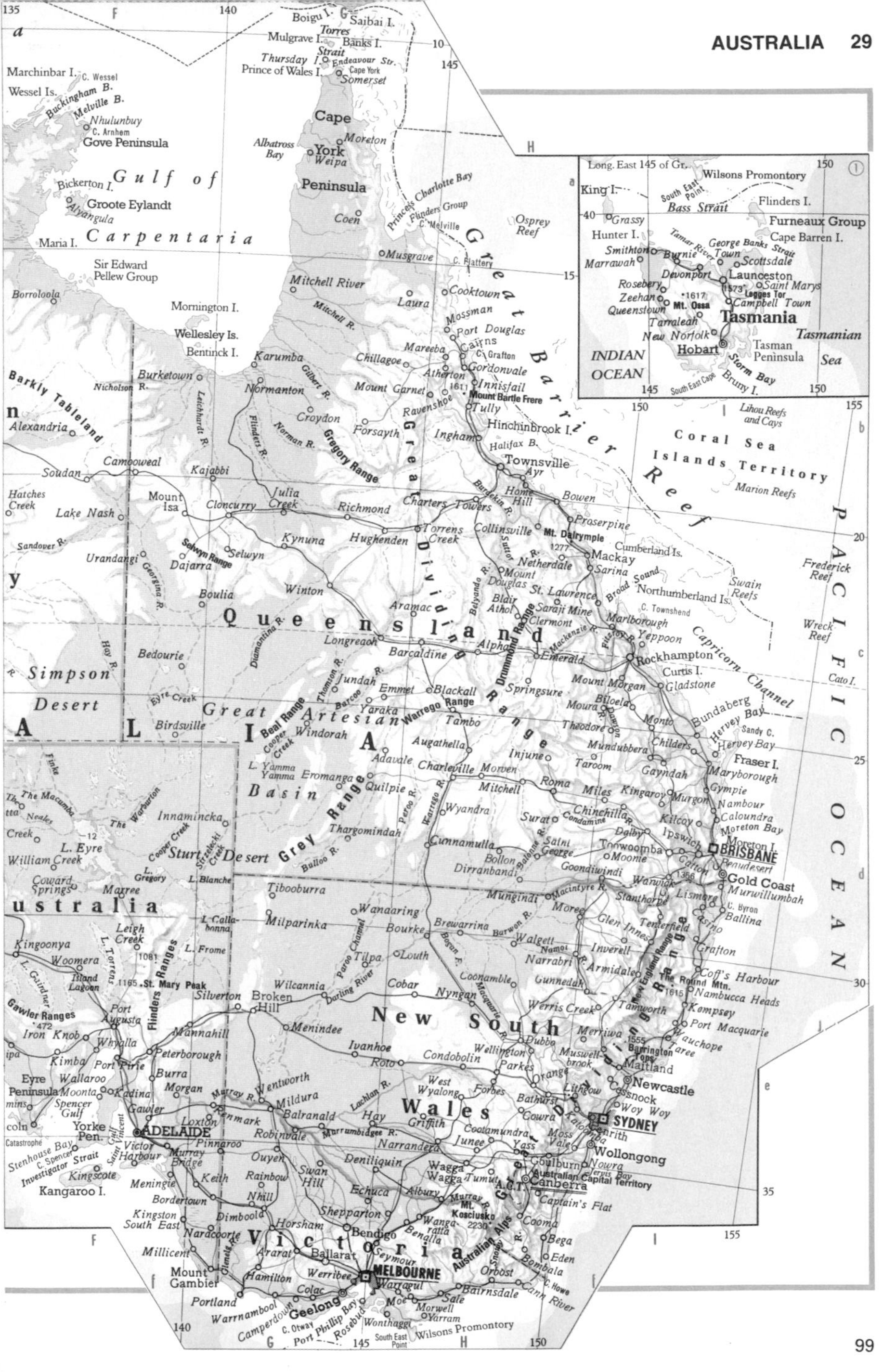

135   f   140
a
Boigu I.
Mulgrave I. Saibai I.
Torres   Banks I.   10
Thursday   Strait
Marchinbar I. C. Wessel   Prince of Wales I. Endeavour Str. 145
Wessel Is.   C. Arnhem   Cape York   Somerset
Buckingham   B.
Melville B.
Nhulunbuy   Cape   Moreton
C. Arnhem   York   Albatross
Gove Peninsula   Bay   Weipa
Bickerton I.   Gulf of   Peninsula
Groote Eylandt   Princess Charlotte Bay   Osprey
Angurugu   Coen   C. Melville   Reef
Maria I.   Carpentaria   Flinders Group
Sir Edward   Mitchell River   Cooktown
Borroloola   Pellew Group   Laura   Mossman
Mornington I.   Mitchell R.   Port Douglas
Wellesley Is.   Chillagoe   Mareeba   Cairns
Barkly Tableland   Bentinck I.   Karumba   Atherton   Gordonvale
Nicholson R.   Normanton   Mount Garnet   1611   Innisfail
n   Leichhardt R.   Croydon   Mount Bartle Frere   Tully
Alexandria   Forsayth   Ravenshoe   Hinchinbrook I.
Soudan   Camooweal   Norman R.   Ingham
Hatches   Kajabbi   Gregory Range   Halifax B.
Creek   Lake Nash   Cloncurry   Julia   Richmond   Charters Towers   Townsville
Sandover R.   Mount   Creek   Hughenden   Collinsville   Ayr
Urandangi   Isa   Kynuna   Torrens   Mt Dalrymple   Bowen
y   Dajarra   Selwyn   Creek   1277   Proserpine
Boulia   Winton   Netherdale   Mackay
Simpson   Aramac   Blair   St. Lawrence   Cumberland Is.
Bedourie   Longreach   Athol   Clermont   Sarina   Northumberland Is.
Desert   Barcaldine   Alpha   Emerald   Marlborough   C. Townshend
Birdsville   Jundah   Emmet   Blackall   Springsure   Yeppoon
A   L   Windorah   Yaraka   Tambo   Mount Morgan   Rockhampton
Simpson   Eyre Creek   Barcoo R.   Augathella   Injune   Moura   Gladstone
Desert   Bedourie   Beal Range   Theodore   Monto   Bundaberg
Sturt's Desert   Quilpie   Charleville   Morven   Taroom   Mundubbera   Childers
Innamincka   Eromanga   Mitchell   Roma   Miles   Kingaroy   Maryborough
ustralia   Thargomindah   Wyandra   Surat   Chinchilla   Murgon   Gympie
Tibooburra   Cunnamulla   Saint   Dalby   Nambour
Milparinka   Bollon   George   Toowoomba   Caloundra
Wanaaring   Dirranbandi   Goondiwindi   Ipswich   BRISBANE
Bourke   Brewarrina   Mungindi   Warwick   Gold Coast
Tilpa   Walgett   Moree   Stanthorpe   Murwillumbah
Louth   Narrabri   Inverell   Glen Innes   Tenterfield   C. Byron
Wilcannia   Cobar   Gunnedah   Armidale   Grafton   Ballina
Broken   Nyngan   Werris Creek   Tamworth   Coff's Harbour
Hill   Tamworth   Kempsey   Nambucca Heads
New   South   Wales   Port Macquarie
Condobolin   Wellington   Gloucester
Iron Knob   Ivanhoe   Parkes   Orange   Muswellbrook   Maitland
Whyalla   Roto   Forbes   Bathurst   Cessnock   Newcastle
Kimba   Burra   West   Cowra   Lithgow   Woy Woy
Port Pirie   Morgan   Wyalong   Young   SYDNEY
Wallaroo   Moonta   Hay   Griffith   Yass   Wollongong
Kadina   Murray R.   Wentworth   Narrandera   Canberra   A.C.T.
ADELAIDE   Mildura   Balranald   Junee   Australian Capital Territory
Victor   Loxton   Robinvale   Deniliquin   Wagga Wagga   Captain's Flat
Harbour   Renmark   Swan   Tumut
Pinnaroo   Ouyen   Hill   Echuca   Albury   Cooma
Meningie   Keith   Rainbow   Nhill   Shepparton   Benalla   Kosciusko 2230   Bega
Kangaroo I.   Bordertown   Horsham   Bendigo   Wangaratta   Eden
Kingston   Dimboola   Ararat   Ballarat   Seymour   Bairnsdale
South East   Victoria   MELBOURNE
Millicent   Hamilton   Werribee   Warragul
Mount   Colac   Geelong   Morwell   Sale
Gambier   Portland   Warrnambool   C. Otway   Port Phillip Bay   Wonthaggi   Wilsons Promontory
140   145   150

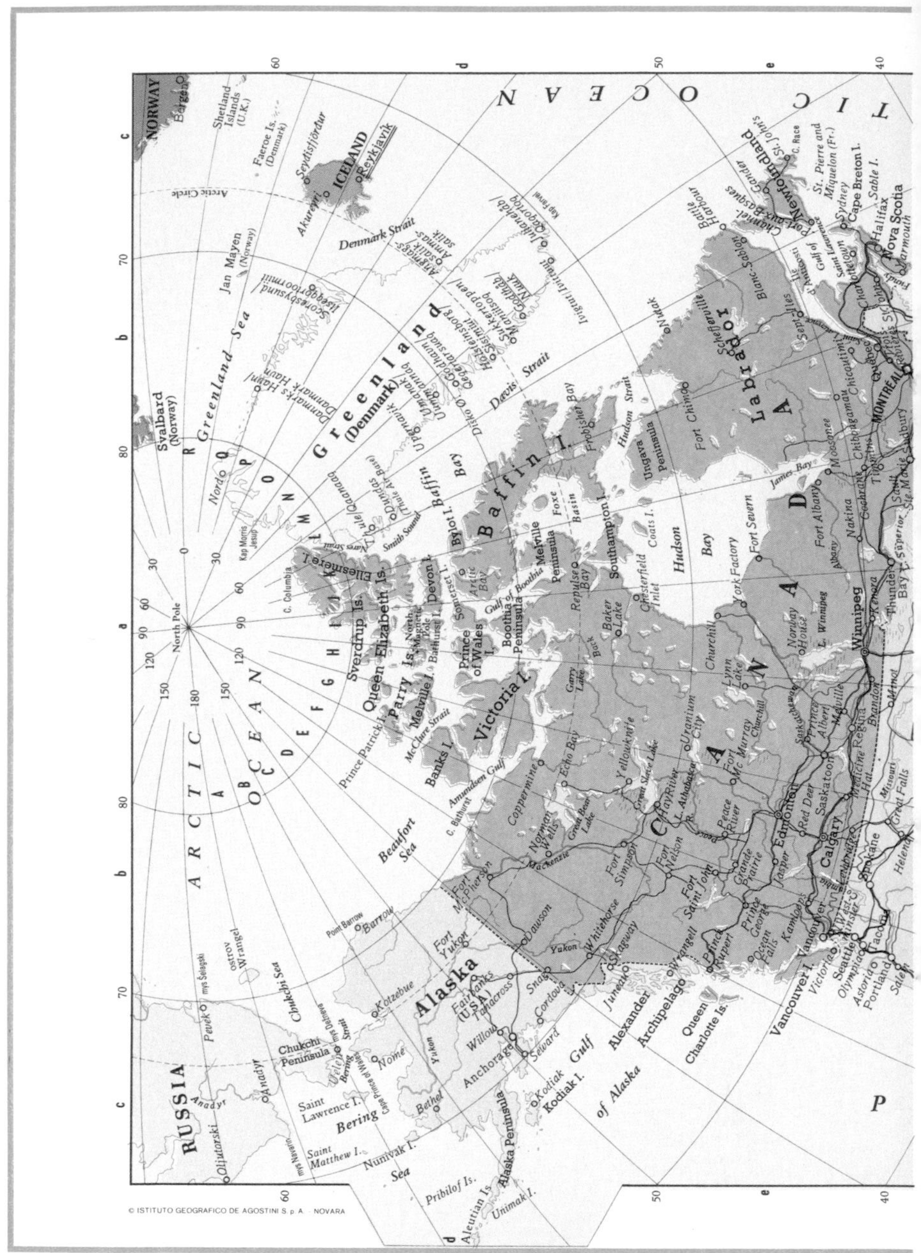
ARCTIC OCEAN
Greenland (Denmark)
ICELAND
Reykjavik
NORWAY
Svalbard (Norway)
Greenland Sea
Denmark Strait
Davis Strait
Baffin Bay
Baffin I.
Hudson Bay
Hudson Strait
Labrador
Newfoundland
Nova Scotia
CANADA
Victoria I.
Queen Elizabeth Is.
Ellesmere I.
Beaufort Sea
Alaska
Gulf of Alaska
Bering Sea
Chukchi Sea
RUSSIA
Winnipeg
Edmonton
Calgary
Vancouver
Seattle
MONTREAL
North Pole
Arctic Circle

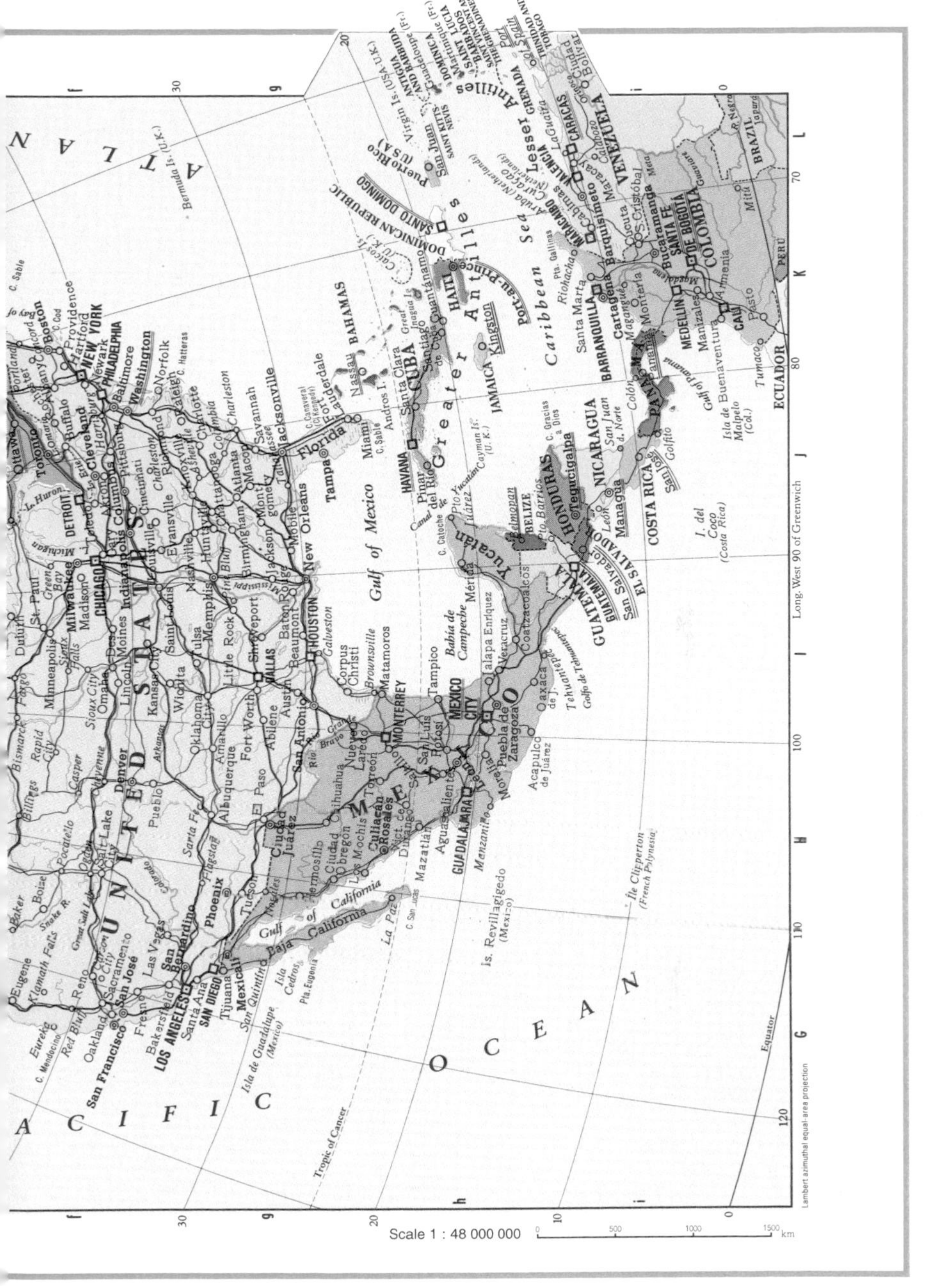
UNITED STATES
MEXICO
PACIFIC OCEAN
ATLANTIC
Gulf of Mexico
Caribbean Sea
Greater Antilles
Lesser Antilles
Gulf of California
CUBA
HAVANA
BAHAMAS
HAITI
DOMINICAN REPUBLIC
SANTO DOMINGO
JAMAICA
Kingston
Puerto Rico (U.S.A.)
San Juan
BELIZE
Belmopan
GUATEMALA
HONDURAS
Tegucigalpa
EL SALVADOR
San Salvador
NICARAGUA
Managua
COSTA RICA
San José
PANAMA
VENEZUELA
CARACAS
COLOMBIA
SANTA FE DE BOGOTA
ECUADOR
BRAZIL
PERU
NEW YORK
PHILADELPHIA
Washington
Boston
CHICAGO
DETROIT
HOUSTON
DALLAS
LOS ANGELES
SAN DIEGO
San Francisco
San José
Denver
Phoenix
Miami
New Orleans
Jacksonville
Tampa
MONTERREY
MEXICO CITY
GUADALAJARA
Bermuda Is. (U.K.)
Tropic of Cancer
Equator
Long. West 90 of Greenwich
Lambert azimuthal equal-area projection

Scale 1 : 48 000 000 0 500 1000 1500 km

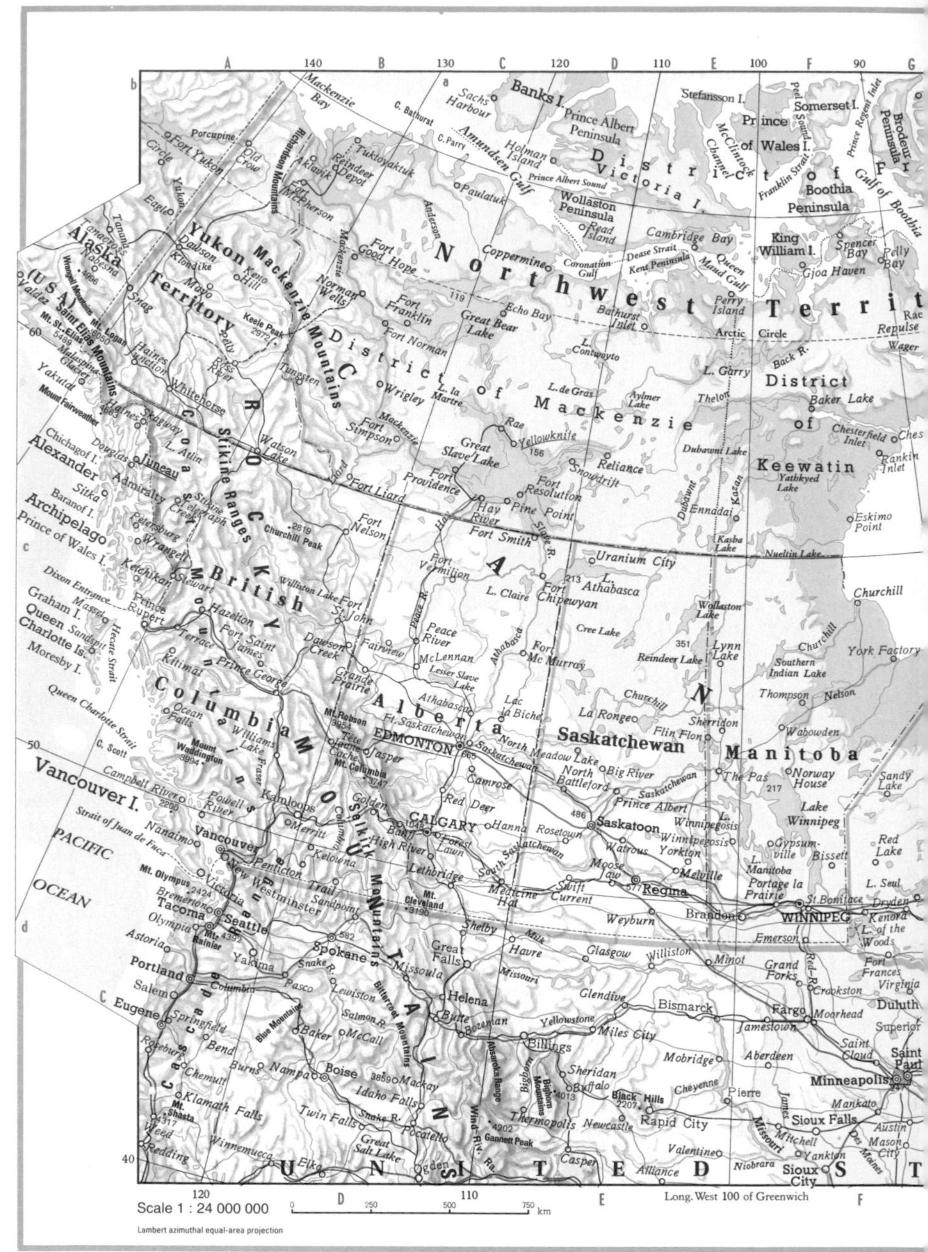

Scale 1 : 24 000 000

Lambert azimuthal equal-area projection

Long. West 100 of Greenwich

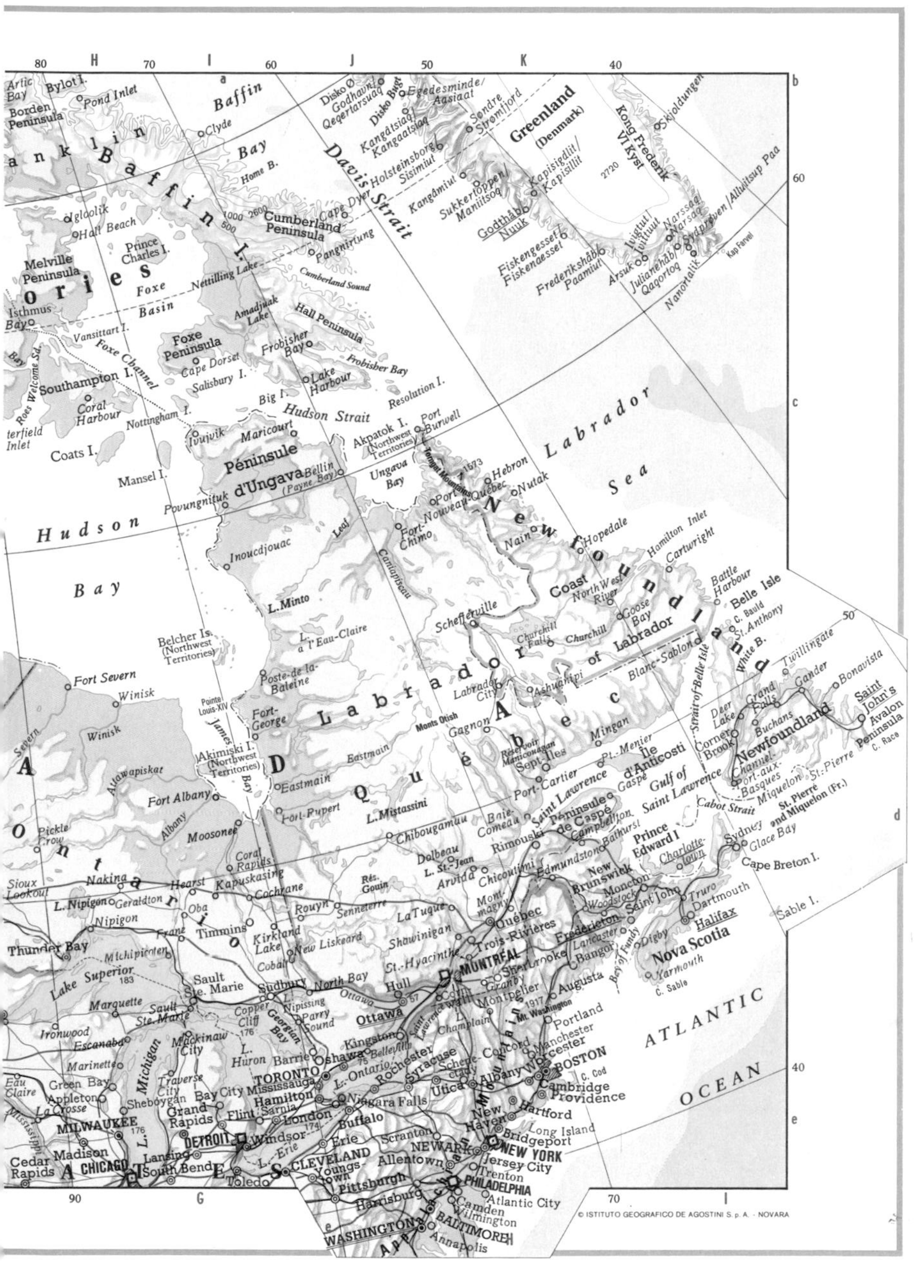
Baffin Bay
Davis Strait
Greenland (Denmark)
Cumberland Peninsula
Melville Peninsula
Foxe Basin
Foxe Peninsula
Southampton I.
Hall Peninsula
Hudson Strait
Labrador Sea
Péninsule d'Ungava
Ungava Bay
Hudson Bay
Newfoundland
Labrador
Québec
Ontario
Gulf of Saint Lawrence
Nova Scotia
New Brunswick
Prince Edward I.
Lake Superior
L. Michigan
L. Huron
L. Ontario
L. Erie
Toronto
Montréal
Québec
Ottawa
Boston
New York
Chicago
Detroit
Cleveland
Philadelphia
Washington
Atlantic Ocean
© ISTITUTO GEOGRAFICO DE AGOSTINI S. p. A. - NOVARA

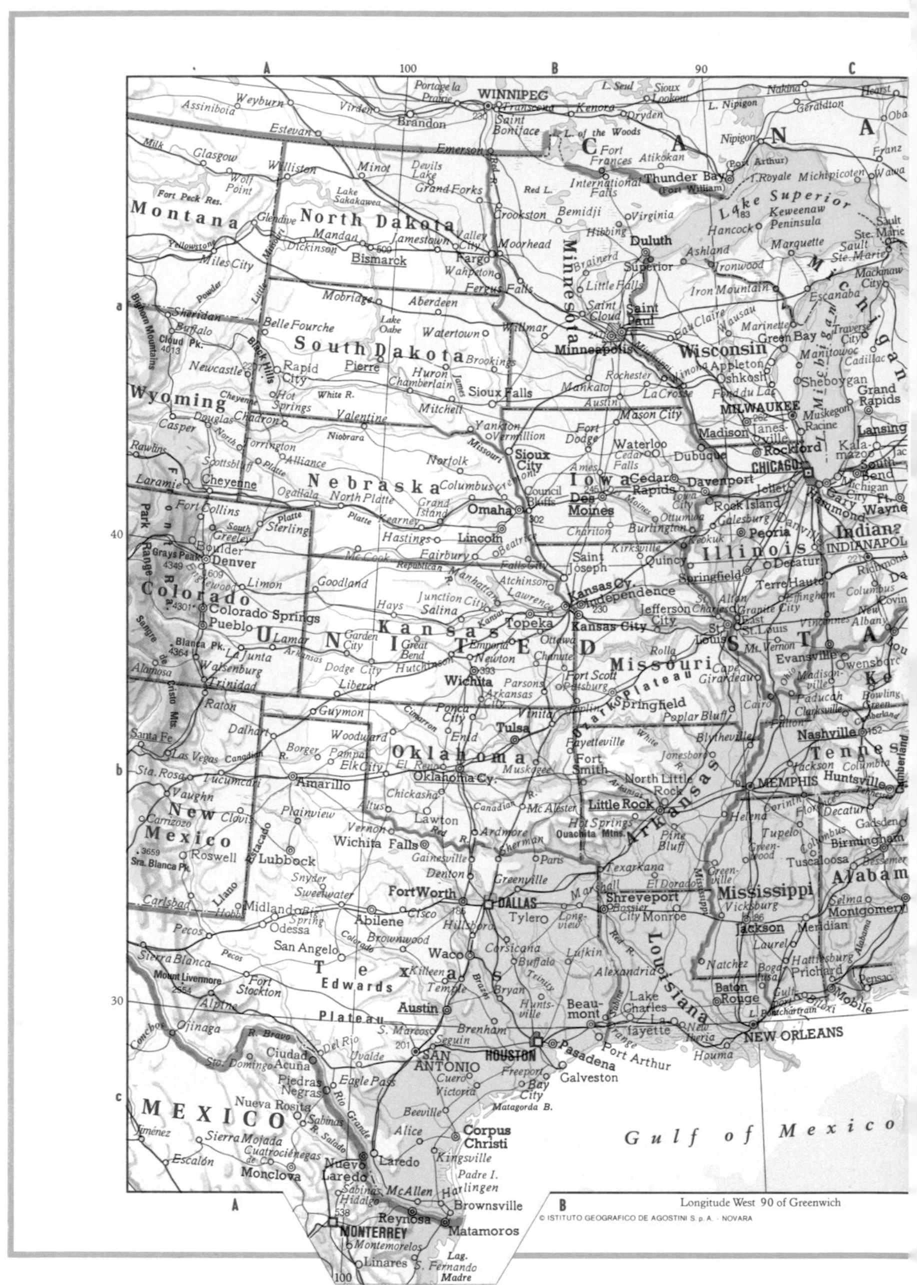
A
100
B
90
C
a
40
b
30
c
WINNIPEG
Brandon
Weyburn
Estevan
Emerson
Kenora
Dryden
Thunder Bay
(Fort William)
Lake Superior
Keweenaw Peninsula
Marquette
Duluth
Superior
Minot
Williston
Glasgow
Montana
North Dakota
Bismarck
Mandan
Dickinson
Jamestown
Fargo
Moorhead
Grand Forks
Minnesota
Saint Paul
Minneapolis
Saint Cloud
Brainerd
Rochester
Mankato
Wisconsin
Green Bay
Appleton
Oshkosh
Madison
MILWAUKEE
Racine
Rockford
CHICAGO
Michigan
Grand Rapids
Lansing
Sheboygan
Manitowoc
South Dakota
Pierre
Rapid City
Aberdeen
Watertown
Huron
Mitchell
Sioux Falls
Brookings
Wyoming
Casper
Cheyenne
Laramie
Sheridan
Buffalo
Newcastle
Nebraska
Lincoln
Omaha
North Platte
Grand Island
Kearney
Hastings
Columbus
Norfolk
Sioux City
Iowa
Des Moines
Cedar Rapids
Waterloo
Dubuque
Davenport
Mason City
Fort Dodge
Council Bluffs
Ottumwa
Burlington
Peoria
Illinois
Springfield
Quincy
Decatur
Indiana
INDIANAPOLIS
Terre Haute
Evansville
Colorado
Denver
Boulder
Fort Collins
Greeley
Sterling
Colorado Springs
Pueblo
Limon
Trinidad
Walsenburg
La Junta
Kansas
Topeka
Salina
Wichita
Hutchinson
Dodge City
Liberal
Goodland
Hays
Junction City
Manhattan
Emporia
Newton
Kansas City
Independence
Saint Joseph
Jefferson City
Missouri
Springfield
St. Louis
Rolla
Cape Girardeau
Poplar Bluff
UNITED STATES
Oklahoma
Oklahoma Cy.
Tulsa
Enid
Ponca City
Lawton
Chickasha
Muskogee
McAlester
Ardmore
Guymon
Woodward
Elk City
Arkansas
Little Rock
North Little Rock
Fort Smith
Fayetteville
Pine Bluff
Hot Springs
Jonesboro
Texarkana
El Dorado
MEMPHIS
Nashville
Tennessee
Jackson
Huntsville
Mississippi
Jackson
Vicksburg
Meridian
Tupelo
Hattiesburg
Alabama
Birmingham
Tuscaloosa
Montgomery
Mobile
Louisiana
Shreveport
Monroe
Alexandria
Baton Rouge
Lafayette
Lake Charles
NEW ORLEANS
Houma
New Mexico
Santa Fe
Las Vegas
Tucumcari
Clovis
Roswell
Carlsbad
Amarillo
Lubbock
Plainview
Wichita Falls
Abilene
Midland
Odessa
San Angelo
Fort Worth
DALLAS
Denton
Tyler
Waco
Texas
Austin
SAN ANTONIO
HOUSTON
Pasadena
Galveston
Beaumont
Port Arthur
Corpus Christi
Laredo
Brownsville
Victoria
Edwards Plateau
MEXICO
Nuevo Laredo
MONTERREY
Monclova
Matamoros
Reynosa
Gulf of Mexico
Longitude West 90 of Greenwich
© ISTITUTO GEOGRAFICO DE AGOSTINI S. p. A. - NOVARA

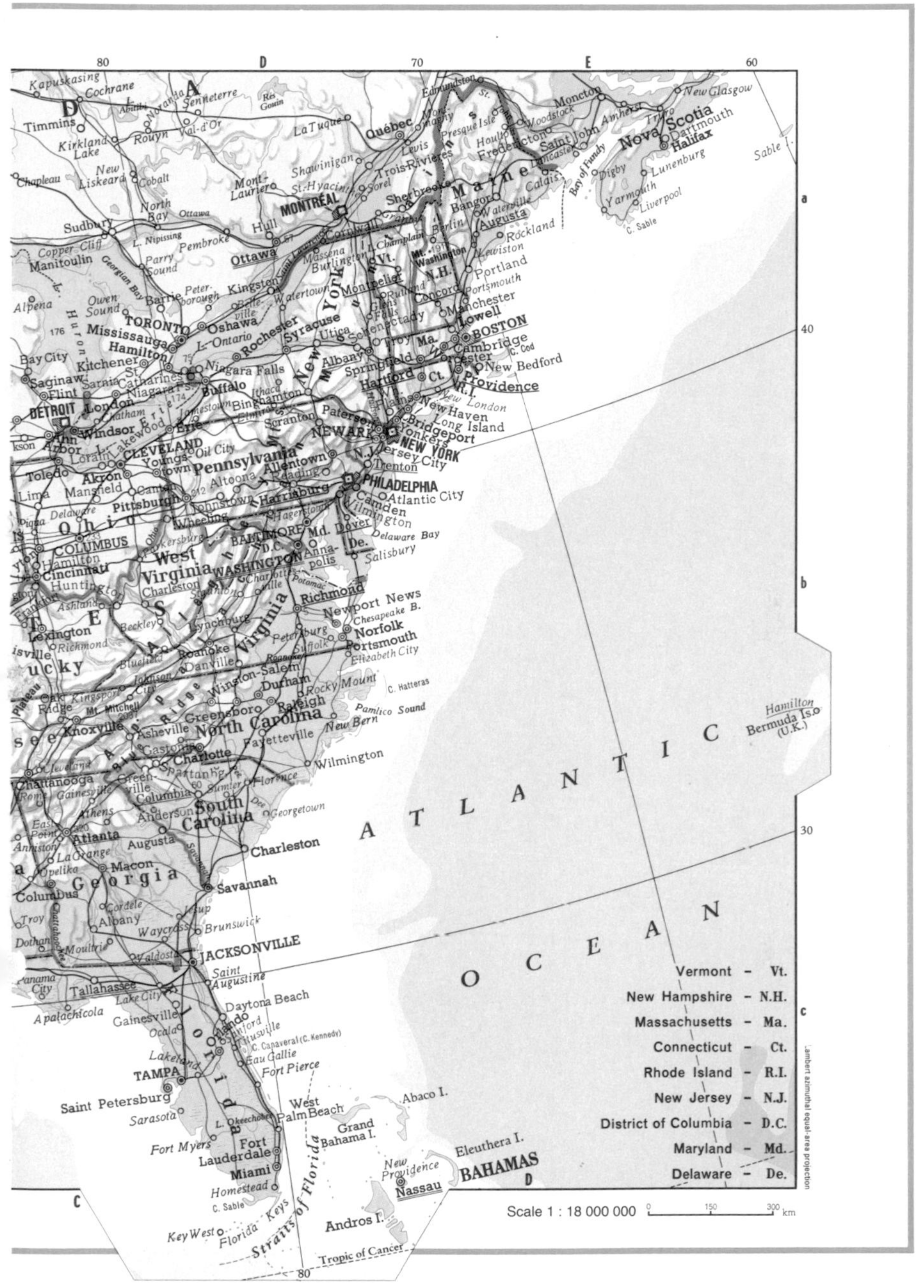

Vermont – Vt.
New Hampshire – N.H.
Massachusetts – Ma.
Connecticut – Ct.
Rhode Island – R.I.
New Jersey – N.J.
District of Columbia – D.C.
Maryland – Md.
Delaware – De.

Scale 1 : 18 000 000

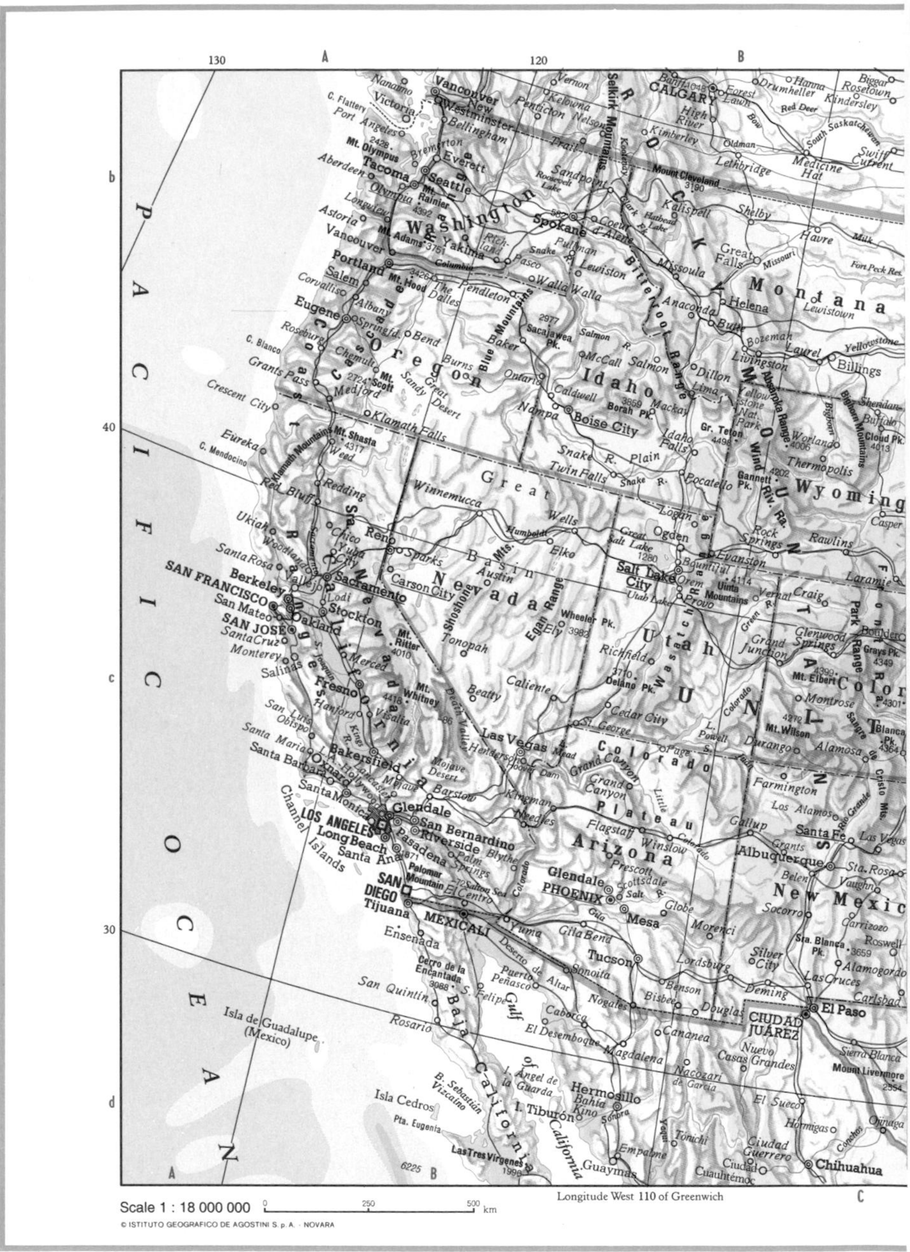

Scale 1 : 18 000 000

© ISTITUTO GEOGRAFICO DE AGOSTINI S.p.A. - NOVARA

Longitude West 110 of Greenwich

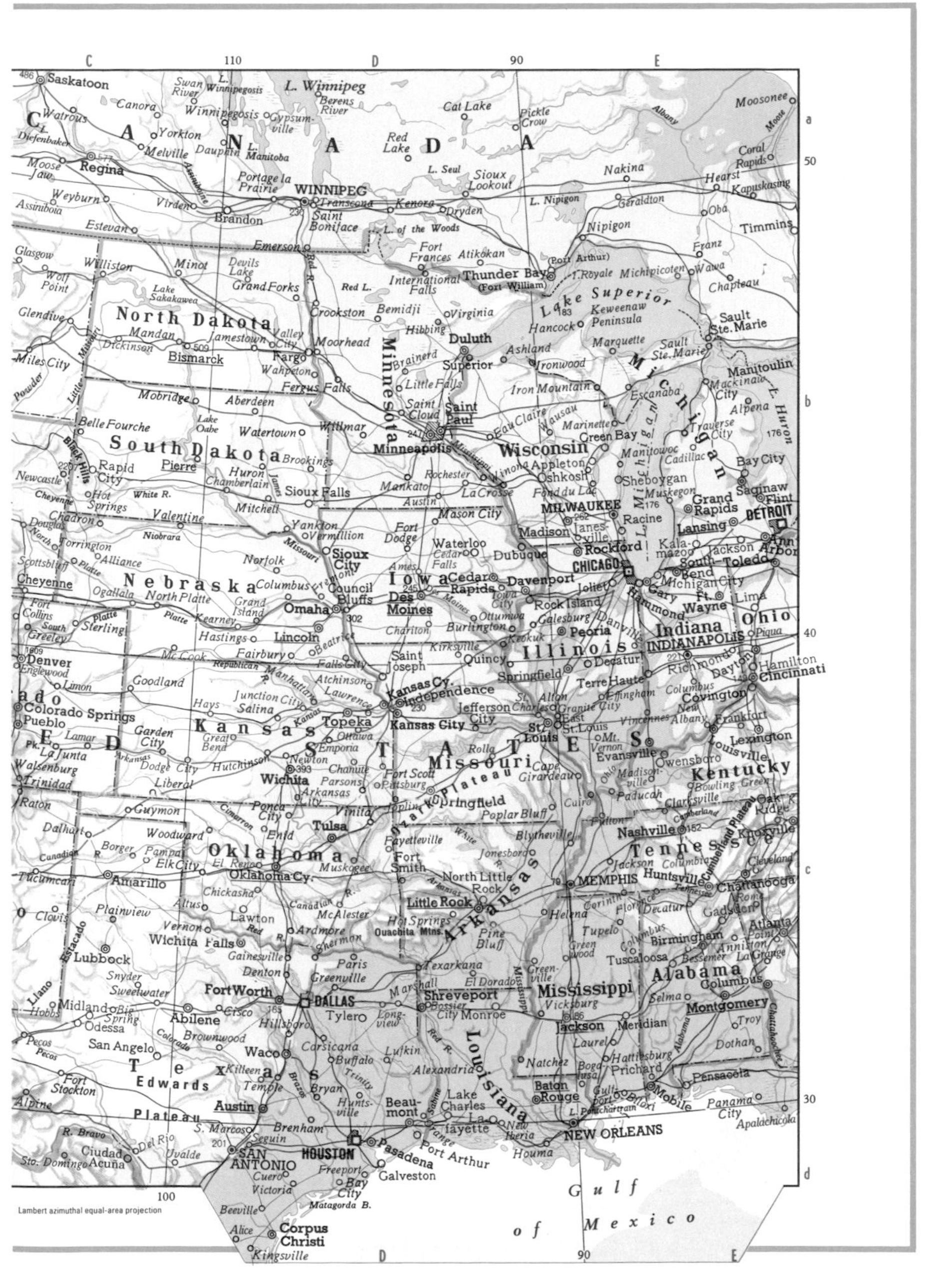
CANADA
UNITED STATES
North Dakota
South Dakota
Nebraska
Kansas
Oklahoma
Texas
Minnesota
Iowa
Missouri
Arkansas
Louisiana
Wisconsin
Illinois
Michigan
Indiana
Ohio
Kentucky
Tennessee
Mississippi
Alabama
Lake Superior
L. Winnipeg
L. Huron
Gulf of Mexico
Ozark Plateau
Edwards Plateau
Cumberland Plateau
WINNIPEG
Regina
Saskatoon
Minneapolis
Saint Paul
Duluth
Thunder Bay
MILWAUKEE
CHICAGO
DETROIT
Des Moines
Omaha
Lincoln
Kansas City
St. Louis
INDIANAPOLIS
Cincinnati
Toledo
Wichita
Tulsa
Oklahoma Cy.
Amarillo
Lubbock
Fort Worth
DALLAS
Austin
SAN ANTONIO
HOUSTON
Corpus Christi
Shreveport
Little Rock
MEMPHIS
Nashville
Jackson
Baton Rouge
NEW ORLEANS
Montgomery
Birmingham
Atlanta
Chattanooga
Knoxville
Louisville
Lexington
Frankfort
Springfield
Peoria
Topeka
Bismarck
Pierre
Cheyenne
Denver
Colorado Springs
Pueblo
Lambert azimuthal equal-area projection

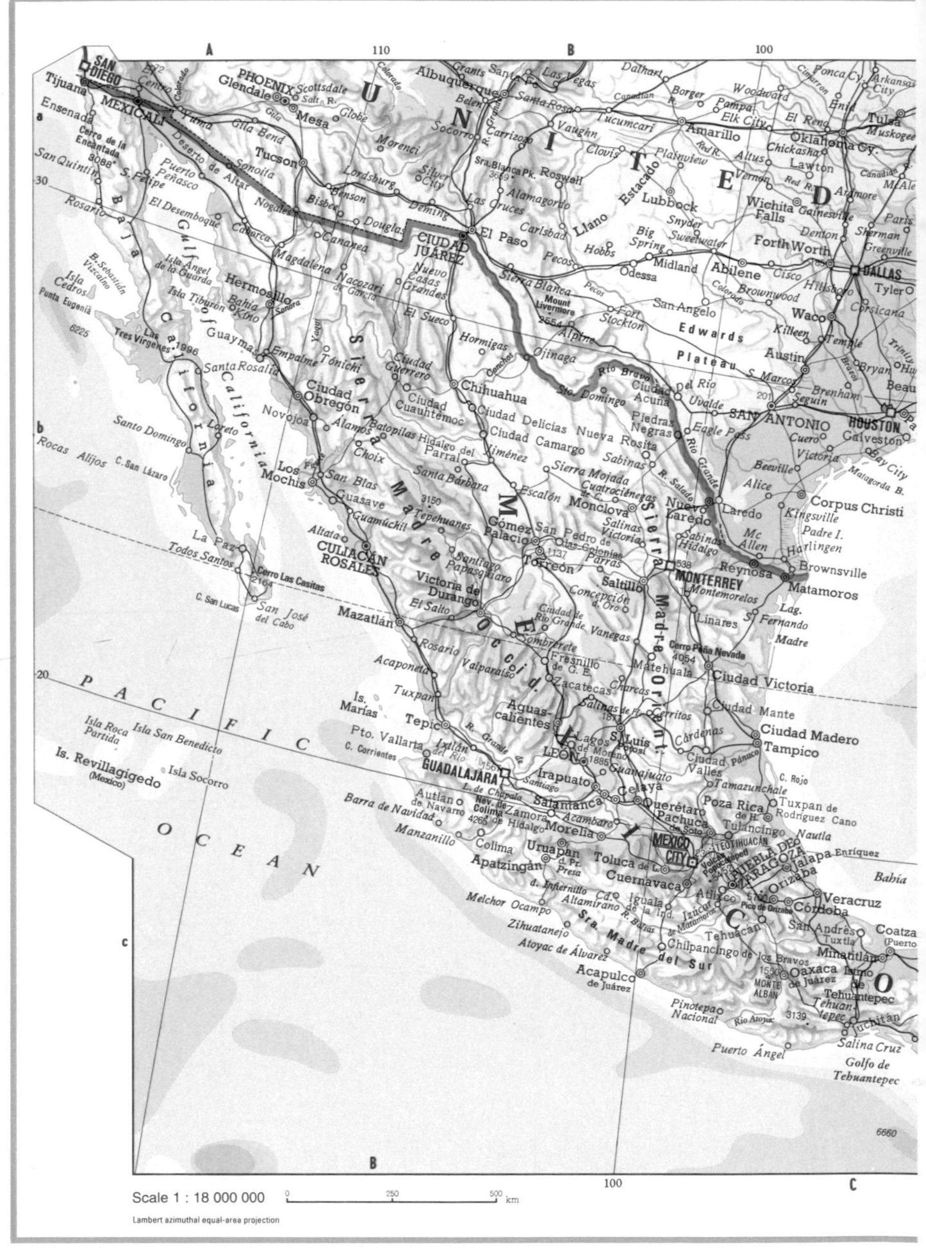

Scale 1 : 18 000 000

0   750   500 km

Lambert azimuthal equal-area projection

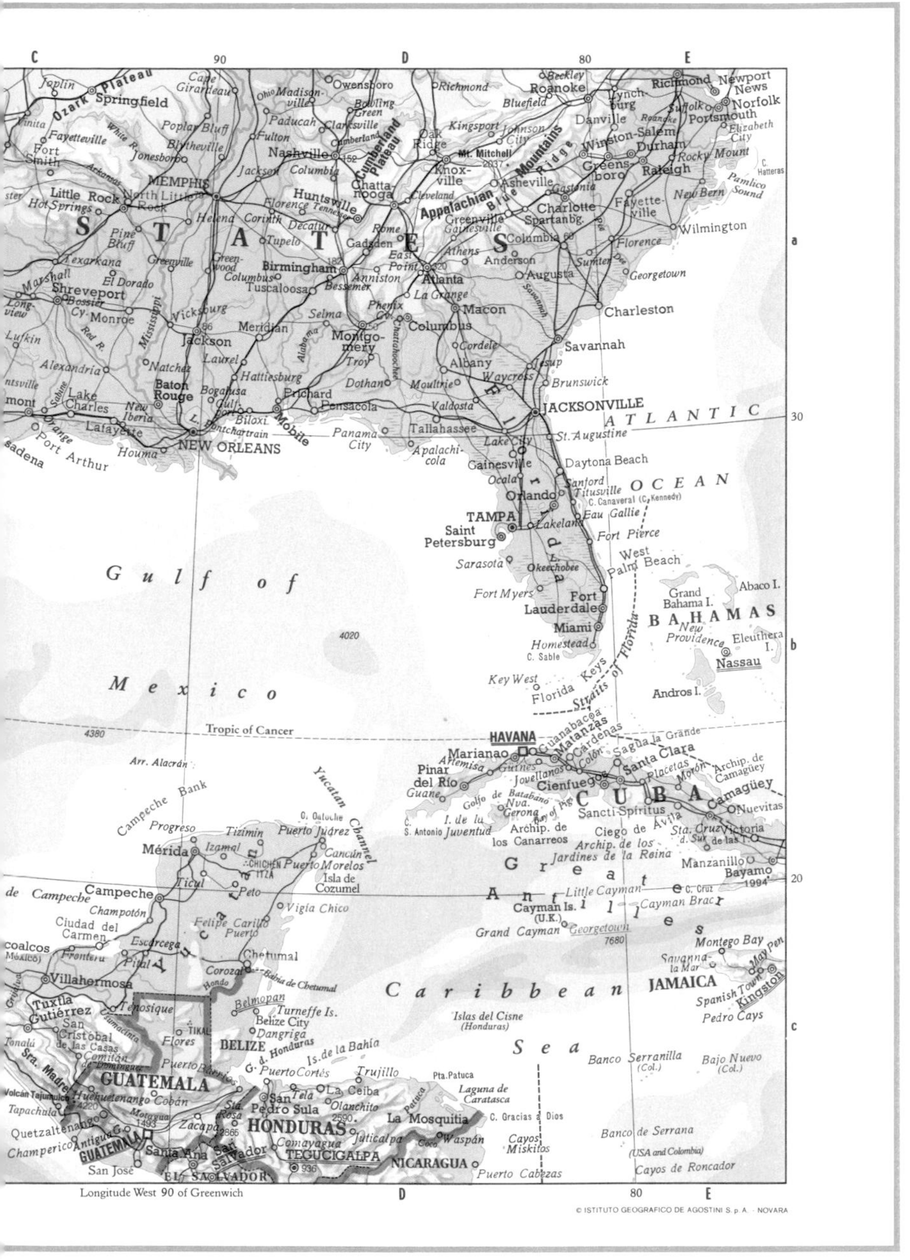

C 90 D 80 E

Joplin Plateau Cape Girardeau Owensboro Richmond Beckley Roanoke Richmond Newport News
Springfield Ohio Madisonville Bowling Green Bluefield Lynchburg Suffolk Norfolk
Ozark Plateau Poplar Bluff Paducah Clarksville Kingsport Johnson Danville Roanoke Portsmouth Elizabeth City
Anita Fayetteville Fort Smith Jonesboro Blytheville Fulton Nashville Oak Ridge Mt. Mitchell 2037 Winston-Salem Durham Rocky Mount
Little Rock North Little Rock MEMPHIS Jackson Columbia Chattanooga Knoxville Asheville Greensboro Raleigh Hatteras
Hot Springs Helena Corinth Decatur Cleveland Appalachian Charlotte Fayetteville New Bern Pamlico Sound
Pine Bluff Tupelo Rome Gadsden Athens Gainesville Columbia Spartanburg Wilmington
S T A T E S Birmingham Anniston East Point Atlanta Anderson Sumter Georgetown
Texarkana Greenville Greenwood Columbus Tuscaloosa Bessemer La Grange Augusta
El Dorado Shreveport Bossier Monroe Meridian Selma Phenix Columbus Macon Charleston
Longview Cy Vicksburg Jackson Montgomery Troy Columbus Cordele Savannah
Lufkin Alexandria Natchez Laurel Hattiesburg Dothan Albany Waycross Jesup Brunswick
ntsville Lake Charles New Iberia Baton Rouge Bogalusa Prichard Pensacola Moultrie Valdosta Lake City
mont Port Arthur Houma Biloxi Mobile Panama City Tallahassee Apalachicola JACKSONVILLE
sadena Lafayette NEW ORLEANS Lake Pontchartrain St. Augustine ATLANTIC 30
Gainesville
Ocala Daytona Beach OCEAN
Sanford
Orlando C. Canaveral (C. Kennedy)
TAMPA Titusville
Saint Petersburg Lakeland Eau Gallie
G u l f o f Sarasota Okeechobee Fort Pierce
Fort Myers West Palm Beach
Fort Lauderdale Grand Bahama I. Abaco I.
4020 Miami B A H A M A S
Homestead New Providence Eleuthera I.
M e x i c o C. Sable Key West Nassau
Florida Keys Andros I.
4380 Tropic of Cancer Straits of Florida
Arr. Alacrán HAVANA Matanzas Sagua la Grande Archip.
Marianao Cárdenas de Camagüey
Pinar Artemisa Güines Santa Clara
del Río Jovellanos Placetas Morón Camagüey
Yucatán Channel Guane Golfo de Batabanó Cienfuegos C U B A Nuevitas
Campeche Bank G. Ostoche Gerona I. de la Sancti Spíritus Sta. Cruz
Progreso Tizimín Puerto Juárez S. Antonio Juventud Archip. de Clego de Ávila del Sur de la Victoria
Mérida Izamal los Canarreos Archip. de los Manzanillo
CHICHEN ITZA Cancún Jardines de la Reina Bayamo
de Campeche Ticul Peto Isla de G r e a t 1994 20
Campeche Champotón Cozumel A n t i l l e s Little Cayman Sta. Cruz
Ciudad del Vigía Chico Cayman Is. Cayman Brac
Carmen Felipe Carillo (U.K.)
coalcos Frontera Puerto Grand Cayman Georgetown Montego Bay
México) Chetumal 7680 Savannala-Mar JAMAICA Spanish Town Kingston
Villahermosa Corozal Bahía de Chetumal C a r i b b e a n JAMAICA Pedro Cays
Tuxtla Belmopan Turneffe Is. Islas del Cisne
Gutiérrez Atenosique TIKAL Belize City (Honduras) S e a Banco Serranilla Bajo Nuevo
Cristóbal de las Casas Flores Dangriga (Col.) (Col.)
Comitán BELIZE G. de Honduras Banco de Serrana
Volcán Tajumulco Cobán Puerto Cortés Is. de la Bahía Pta. Patuca (USA and Colombia)
Quetzaltenango Zacapa Puerto Barrios San Pedro Sula La Ceiba Trujillo Laguna de Cayos de Roncador
GUATEMALA Antigua Santa Ana Olanchito Caratasca C. Gracias a Dios
Tapachula HONDURAS La Mosquitia Cayos
Champerico GUATEMALA EL SALVADOR Comayagua Juticalpa Waspán Miskitos
San José TEGUCIGALPA NICARAGUA
Puerto Cabezas

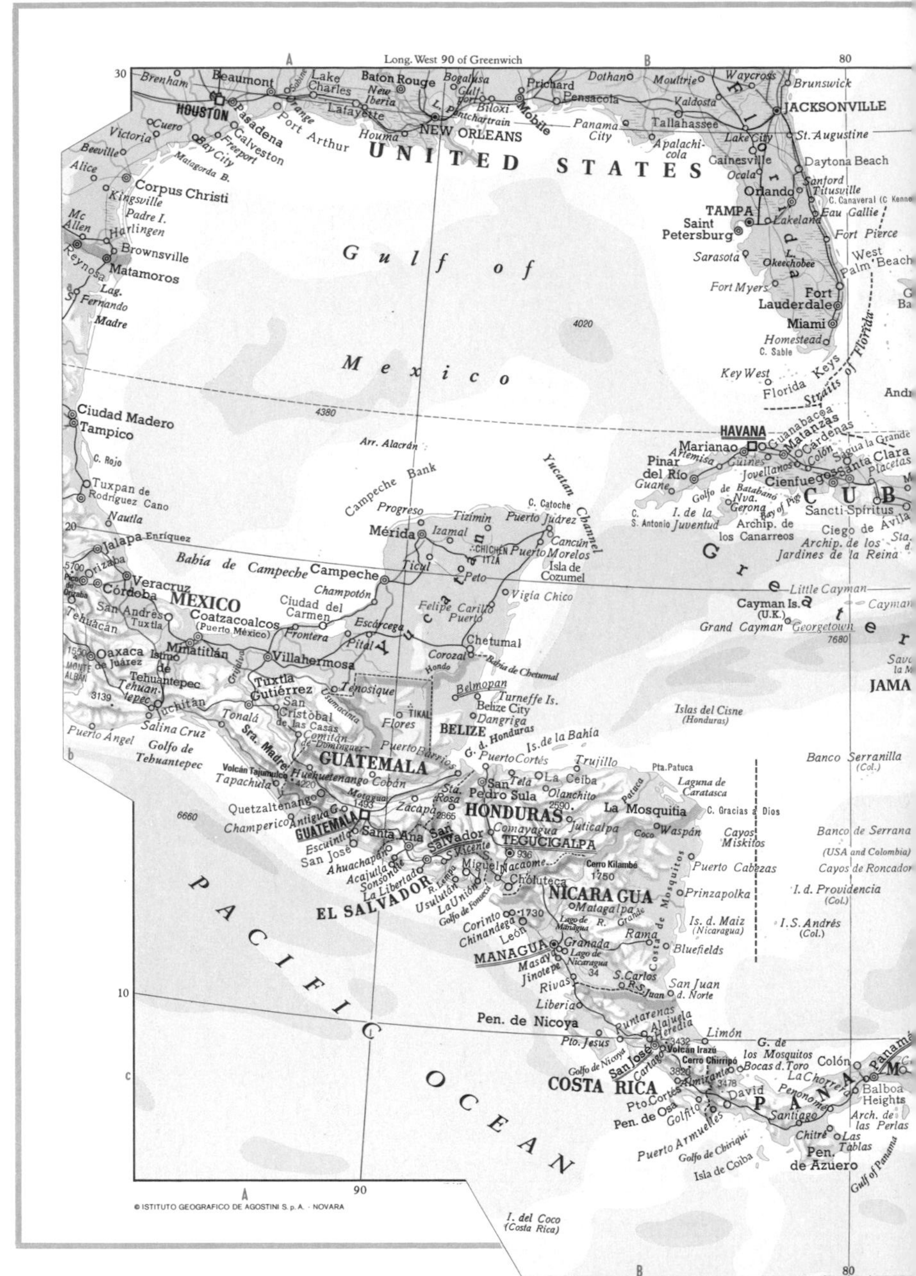

Long. West 90 of Greenwich
A
B
80
30
20
10
Brenham
Beaumont
Lake Charles
Baton Rouge
Bogalusa
Gulfport
Biloxi
Mobile
Prichard
Pensacola
Dothan
Moultrie
Waycross
Brunswick
HOUSTON
Pasadena
Galveston
Freeport
Bay City
Matagorda B.
Port Arthur
Lafayette
New Iberia
Houma
L. Pontchartrain
NEW ORLEANS
Panama City
Tallahassee
Apalachicola
Valdosta
JACKSONVILLE
St. Augustine
Victoria
Cuero
Beeville
Alice
UNITED STATES
Gainesville
Ocala
Daytona Beach
Sanford
Titusville
Orlando
C. Canaveral
Eau Gallie
Corpus Christi
Kingsville
Padre I.
Mc Allen
Harlingen
Brownsville
Reynosa
Matamoros
Lag.
S. Fernando
Madre
TAMPA
Saint Petersburg
Lakeland
Fort Pierce
Sarasota
L. Okeechobee
West Palm Beach
Fort Myers
Fort Lauderdale
Miami
Homestead
C. Sable
Florida
Gulf of Mexico
4020
Key West
Florida Keys
Straits of Florida
Ciudad Madero
Tampico
4380
HAVANA
Marianao
Guanabacoa
Matanzas
Cárdenas
Artemisa
Güines
Colón
Sagua la Grande
Santa Clara
Placetas
Pinar del Río
Jovellanos
Cienfuegos
Guane
Golfo de Batabanó
Nva. Gerona
Bay of Pigs
CUBA
C. Rojo
Arr. Alacrán
Campeche Bank
Yucatan Channel
Tuxpan de Rodríguez Cano
Nautla
Progreso
Tizimín
C. Catoche
Puerto Juárez
C. S. Antonio
I. de la Juventud
Archip. de los Canarreos
Sancti-Spíritus
Ciego de Avila
Archip. de los Jardines de la Reina
Mérida
Izamal
Chichén Itzá
Cancún
Puerto Morelos
Isla de Cozumel
Jalapa Enríquez
Bahía de Campeche
Campeche
Ticul
Peto
Yucatan
Orizaba
Pico de Orizaba
5700
Veracruz
Córdoba
MEXICO
Champotón
Ciudad del Carmen
Vigía Chico
Felipe Carillo Puerto
Little Cayman
Cayman Is. (U.K.)
Grand Cayman
Georgetown
7680
San Andrés Tuxtla
Tehuacán
Coatzacoalcos (Puerto México)
Frontera
Escárcega
Pital
Chetumal
Oaxaca de Juárez
Monte Albán
1550
Minatitlán
Istmo de Tehuantepec
Villahermosa
Corozal
Bahía de Chetumal
Hondo
Tuxtla Gutiérrez
Tehuantepec
3139
Juchitán
Tenosique
Usumacinta
Belmopan
Turneffe Is.
Belize City
Dangriga
Tonalá
San Cristóbal de las Casas
Tikal
Flores
BELIZE
Islas del Cisne (Honduras)
Salina Cruz
Puerto Ángel
Golfo de Tehuantepec
Comitán de Domínguez
Puerto Barrios
G. d. Honduras
Is. de la Bahía
Sra. Madre
GUATEMALA
Puerto Cortés
Trujillo
Pta. Patuca
Banco Serranilla (Col.)
Volcán Tajumulco
4220
Tapachula
Huehuetenango
Cobán
San Pedro Sula
Tela
La Ceiba
Olanchito
Laguna de Caratasca
Quetzaltenango
Motagua
1493
Sta. Rosa
2590
Patuca
6660
Zacapa
2865
HONDURAS
La Mosquitia
C. Gracias á Dios
Champerico
Antigua G.
GUATEMALA
Santa Ana
San Salvador
Comayagua
Juticalpa
Coco
Waspán
Cayos Miskitos
Banco de Serrana (USA and Colombia)
Escuintla
San José
TEGUCIGALPA
936
Ahuachapán
Acajutla
Sonsonate
La Libertad
S. Vicente
S. Miguel
Nacaome
Cerro Kilambé
1750
Puerto Cabezas
Cayos de Roncador
EL SALVADOR
Usulután
La Unión
Golfo de Fonseca
Choluteca
NICARAGUA
Matagalpa
Prinzapolka
I. d. Providencia (Col.)
PACIFIC OCEAN
Corinto
Chinandega
1730
León
Lago de Managua
R. Grande
Costa de Mosquitos
Is. d. Maíz (Nicaragua)
I. S. Andrés (Col.)
MANAGUA
Masaya
Jinotepe
Granada
Lago de Nicaragua
34
Rama
Bluefields
Rivas
S. Carlos
R. S. Juan
San Juan d. Norte
Liberia
Pen. de Nicoya
Puntarenas
Alajuela
Heredia
Limón
Pto. Jesus
Golfo de Nicoya
San José
Cartago
3432
Volcán Irazú
Cerro Chirripó
3820
3478
G. de los Mosquitos
Bocas d. Toro
Colón
Panamá
COSTA RICA
Pto. Cortés
Almirante
David
La Chorrera
Balboa Heights
Penonomé
PANAMA
Pen. de Osa
Golfito
Santiago
Arch. de las Perlas
Puerto Armuelles
Golfo de Chiriquí
Chitré
Las Tablas
Isla de Coiba
Pen. de Azuero
Gulf of Panama
90
I. del Coco (Costa Rica)
Savanna la Mar
JAMAICA
Greater
© ISTITUTO GEOGRAFICO DE AGOSTINI S. p. A. - NOVARA

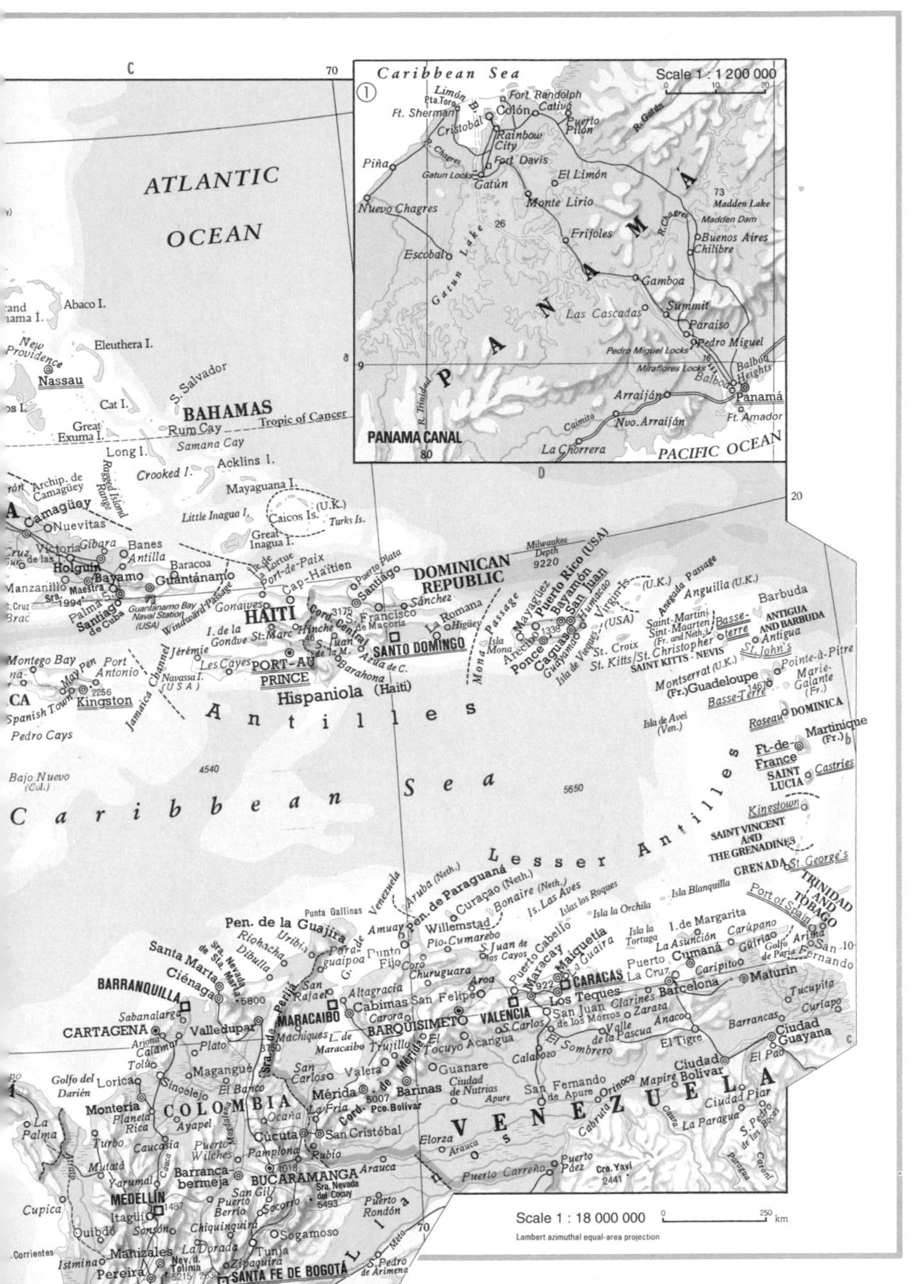

ATLANTIC
OCEAN

Inset: PANAMA CANAL

Caribbean Sea

Scale 1 : 1 200 000

Limón
Pta. Toro
Ft. Sherman
Fort Randolph
Colón
Catival
Cristóbal
Rainbow City
Puerto Pilón
R. Gatún
Piña
Chagres
Fort Davis
Gatún Locks
El Limón
Nuevo Chagres
Gatún
Monte Lirio
Madden Lake
Madden Dam
73
Buenos Aires
Chilibre
Escobal
Frijoles
Gamboa
Las Cascadas
Summit
Paraiso
Pedro Miguel Locks
Pedro Miguel
Miraflores Locks
Balboa Heights
Arraiján
Balboa
Panamá
Nvo. Arraiján
Ft. Amador
PANAMA CANAL
80
Coimta
La Chorrera
PACIFIC OCEAN

PANAMA

BAHAMAS

Abaco I.
New Providence
Eleuthera I.
Nassau
Cat I.
S. Salvador
Great Exuma I.
Rum Cay
Tropic of Cancer
Samana Cay
Long I.
Crooked I.
Acklins I.
Mayaguana I.
Little Inagua I.
Caicos Is. (U.K.)
Turks Is.
Great Inagua I.

Archip. de Camagüey
Camagüey
Nuevitas
Victoria de las
Gibara
Banes
Antilla
Holguín
Baracoa
Manzanillo
Bayamo
Guantánamo
Port-de-Paix
Puerto Plata
Santiago
DOMINICAN REPUBLIC
Milwaukee Depth 9220
Puerto Rico (USA)
Anguilla (U.K.)
Barbuda
Maestra
Palma
Cord.
Cap-Haïtien
San Francisco
Sánchez
Mayagüez
San Juan
(U.K.)
ANTIGUA
Santiago
Guantánamo Bay Naval Station (USA)
Gonaïves
HAITI
de Macorís
La Romana
Higüey
Ponce
Caguas
St. Croix
Saint-Martin (Fr. and Neth.)
Basse-Terre
ANTIGUA AND BARBUDA
Brac
I. de la Gonâve
St-Marc
San Juan de la M.
SANTO DOMINGO
Isla Mona
Mona Passage
Isla de Vieques (USA)
St. Kitts/St. Christopher
SAINT KITTS - NEVIS
St. John's
Montego Bay
Pen. Port Antonio
Jérémie
Navassa I. (USA)
Barahona
Guaira de C.
Guayama
St. Croix
Montserrat (U.K.)
Pointe-à-Pitre
Marie-Galante (Fr.)
CA
Spanish Town
Kingston
2256
Les Cayes
PORT-AU-PRINCE
Hispaniola (Haïti)
(Fr.)Guadeloupe
Basse-Terre
Pedro Cays
Jamaica
Isla de Avel (Ven.)
Roseau
DOMINICA

A n t i l l e s

Bajo Nuevo (Col.)
4540
C a r i b b e a n   S e a
5650
Ft-de-France
Martinique (Fr.)
SAINT LUCIA
Castries

L e s s e r   A n t i l l e s
Kingstown
SAINT VINCENT AND THE GRENADINES
GRENADA
St. George's
TRINIDAD AND TOBAGO
Port of Spain

Pen. de la Guajira
Punta Gallinas
Aruba (Neth.)
Pen. de Paraguaná
Curaçao (Neth.)
Bonaire (Neth.)
Is. Las Aves
Islas los Roques
Isla Blanquilla
Santa Marta
Riohacho
Urbia
Amuay
Willemstad
Plo. Cumarebo
S. Juan de los Cayos
Isla la Orchila
I. de Margarita
La Asunción
Carúpano
Güiria
Maturín
BARRANQUILLA
Ciénaga
Dibulla
Punta Fijo
Churuguara
Puerto Cabello
La Guaira
Maiquetía
Cumaná
Caripito
San Fernando
CARTAGENA
Sabanalarga
San Rafael
Altagracia
Maracay
CARACAS
Los Teques
La Cruz
Golfo de Paria
Tucupita
Curiapo
Valledupar
Cabimas
San Felipe
VALENCIA
San Juan de los Morros
Barcelona
Maturín
Machiques
L. de Maracaibo
BARQUISIMETO
San Carlos
Clarines
Barrancas
MARACAIBO
Trujillo
Zaraza
Anaco
Ciudad Guayana
Golfo del Darién
Loricao
Magangué
Plato
Tocuyo
Acarigua
Valle de la Pascua
El Tigre
Ciudad Bolívar
Monteria
El Banco
Valera
Ciudad de Nutrias
Calabozo
Sombrero
Ciudad Piar
Planeta Rica
Mérida
Barinas
San Fernando de Apure
Mapire
COLOMBIA
La Fría
Pco. Bolívar
Guanare
Elorza
VENEZUELA
MEDELLÍN
Cúcuta
San Cristóbal
Pamplona
Arauca
Cabruta
La Paragua
Barranca bermeja
Rubio
Puerto Carreño
Puerto Páez
Cro. Yaví 2441
BUCARAMANGA
Socorro
Tunja
SANTA FE DE BOGOTÁ

Scale 1 : 18 000 000   0   250 km

Lambert azimuthal equal-area projection

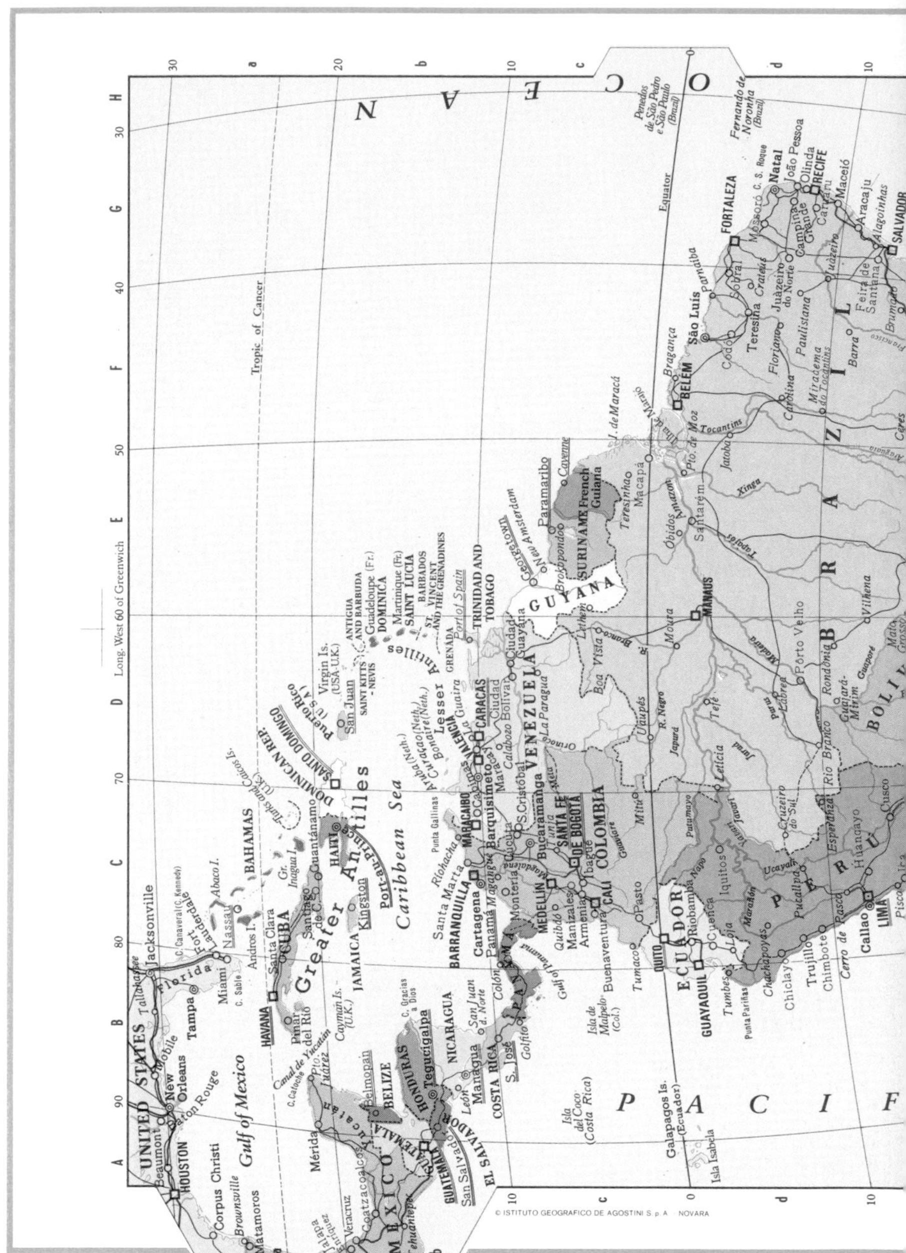
Long. West 60 of Greenwich
Tropic of Cancer
Equator
UNITED STATES
MEXICO
GUATEMALA
BELIZE
HONDURAS
EL SALVADOR
NICARAGUA
COSTA RICA
PANAMA
CUBA
BAHAMAS
JAMAICA
HAITI
DOMINICAN REP.
COLOMBIA
VENEZUELA
GUYANA
SURINAME
French Guiana
ECUADOR
PERU
BRAZIL
TRINIDAD AND TOBAGO
Gulf of Mexico
Caribbean Sea
Greater Antilles
Lesser Antilles
HOUSTON
New Orleans
Tampa
Miami
Jacksonville
HAVANA
Kingston
Port-au-Prince
SANTO DOMINGO
CARACAS
BOGOTA
QUITO
GUAYAQUIL
LIMA
MANAUS
BELÉM
São Luís
FORTALEZA
Natal
RECIFE
SALVADOR
Paramaribo
Cayenne
Georgetown
Galapagos Is. (Ecuador)
Isla del Coco (Costa Rica)
Fernando de Noronha (Brazil)
Penedos de São Pedro e São Paulo (Brazil)
© ISTITUTO GEOGRAFICO DE AGOSTINI S.p.A. NOVARA

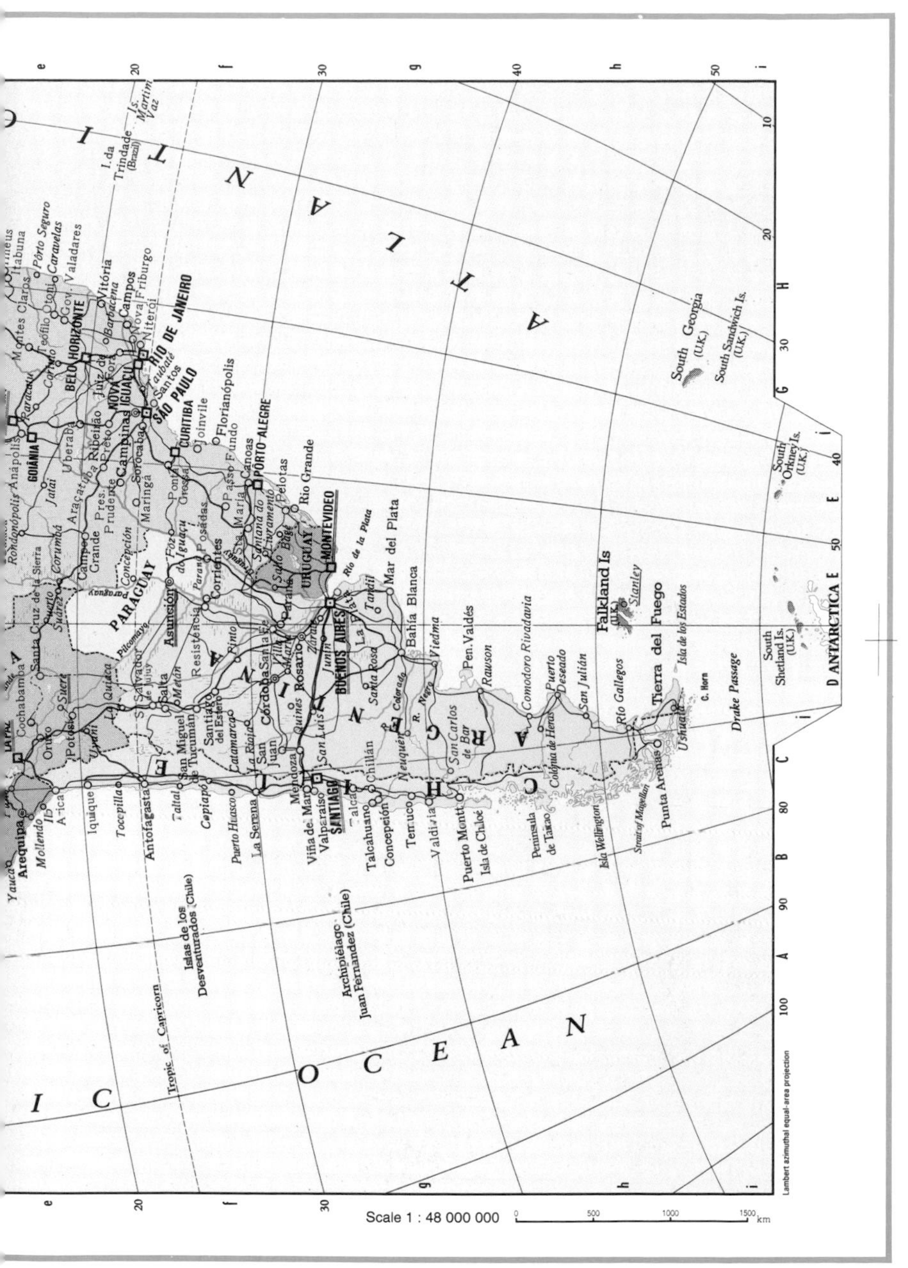
ATLANTIC
PACIFIC OCEAN
PARAGUAY
Asunción
URUGUAY
MONTEVIDEO
ARGENTINA
BUENOS AIRES
CHILE
SANTIAGO
RIO DE JANEIRO
SÃO PAULO
BELO HORIZONTE
CURITIBA
PÔRTO ALEGRE
GOIÂNIA
NOVA IGUAÇU
Arequipa
Cochabamba
Sucre
Potosí
Arica
Iquique
Tocopilla
Antofagasta
Taltal
Copiapó
La Serena
Viña del Mar
Valparaíso
Talca
Talcahuano
Concepción
Temuco
Valdivia
Puerto Montt
Isla de Chiloé
Salta
San Miguel de Tucumán
Santiago del Estero
Catamarca
La Rioja
San Juan
Mendoza
San Luis
Córdoba
Rosario
Santa Fe
Paraná
Corrientes
Resistencia
Posadas
Mar del Plata
Bahía Blanca
Viedma
Rawson
Comodoro Rivadavia
Puerto Deseado
San Julián
Río Gallegos
Punta Arenas
Ushuaia
Tierra del Fuego
Isla de los Estados
C. Horn
Drake Passage
Falkland Is
Stanley
South Georgia (U.K.)
South Sandwich Is. (U.K.)
South Orkney Is. (U.K.)
South Shetland Is. (U.K.)
ANTARCTICA
Islas de los Desventurados (Chile)
Archipiélago Juan Fernández (Chile)
I. da Trindade (Brazil)
Tropic of Capricorn
Río de la Plata
Scale 1 : 48 000 000
Lambert azimuthal equal-area projection

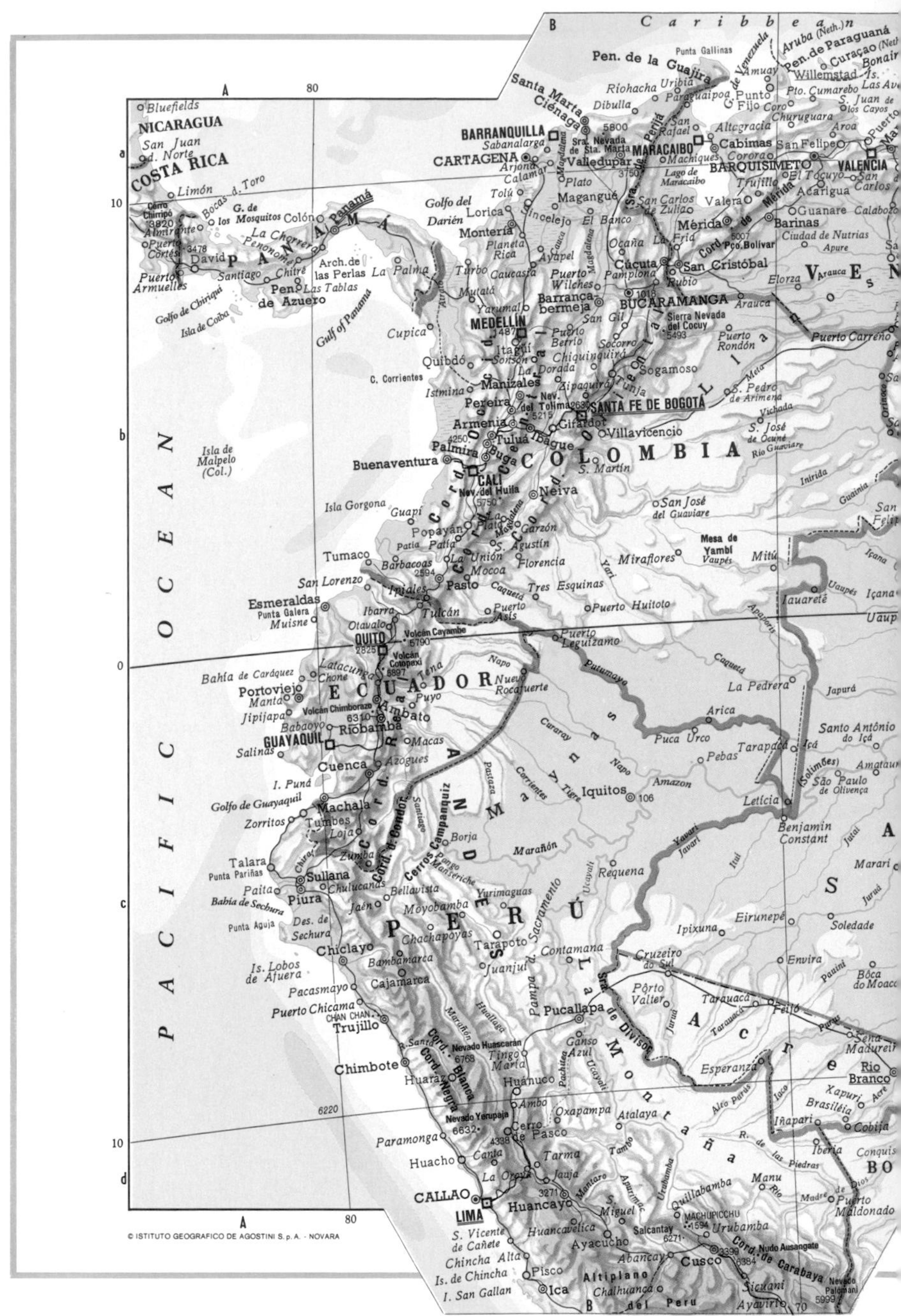

Caribbean
Pen. de la Guajira
Punta Gallinas
Aruba (Neth.)
Pen. de Paraguaná
Curaçao (Neth.)
Bonaire
Willemstad
Santa Marta
Ciénaga
Ríohacha
Uribia
Dibulla
Paraguaipoa
Punto Fijo
Coro
Pto. Cumarebo
Las Aves
S. Juan de los Cayos
Churuguara
Aroa
San Felipe
Puerto
VALENCIA
BARRANQUILLA
Sabanalarga
CARTAGENA
Arjona
Calamar
5800
Sra. Nevada de Sta. Marta
Valledupar
MARACAIBO
Machiques
Lago de Maracaibo
Cabimas
Corora
BARQUISIMETO
El Tocuyo
San Carlos
Altagracia
Trujillo
Acarigua
Guanare
Calabozo
Plato
Magangué
San Carlos de Zulia
Valera
Mérida
Barinas
Ciudad de Nutrias
Apure
Golfo del Darién
Tolú
Lorica
Sincelejo
El Banco
Montería
Planeta Rica
Ayapel
Ocaña
La Fría
Pco. Bolívar
5007
Cúcuta
San Cristóbal
Pamplona
Rubio
Elorza
Arauca
Turbo
Caucasia
Puerto Wilches
Mutatá
Barrancabermeja
BUCARAMANGA
Sierra Nevada del Cocuy
5493
Puerto Rondón
Puerto Carreño
Cupica
MEDELLÍN
Itagüí
Sonsón
Puerto Berrío
Socorro
Chiquinquirá
Quibdó
La Dorada
Sogamoso
C. Corrientes
Istmina
Manizales
Zipaquirá
Tunja
S. Pedro de Arimena
Pereira
Nev. del Tolima
5215
SANTA FE DE BOGOTÁ
Vichada
Armenia
Girardot
Villavicencio
S. José de Ocuné
Tuluá
Ibagué
Palmira
Buga
Buenaventura
COLOMBIA
S. Martín
CALI
Nev. del Huila
5750
Neiva
Isla Gorgona
Guapí
San José del Guaviare
Popayán
Garzón
Patía
S. Agustín
Mesa de Yambí
Tumaco
Barbacoas
La Unión
Florencia
Miraflores
Mitú
Vaupés
2594
Mocoa
Pasto
Tres Esquinas
San Lorenzo
Ipiales
Caquetá
Esmeraldas
Punta Galera
Muisne
Ibarra
Tulcán
Puerto Asís
Puerto Huitoto
Iauaretê
Otavalo
QUITO
Volcán Cayambe
5790
Puerto Leguízamo
Volcán Cotopaxi
5897
Latacunga
Bahía de Caráquez
Chone
ECUADOR
Nuevo Rocafuerte
Portoviejo
Manta
Puyo
Putumayo
La Pedrera
Japurá
Jipijapa
Volcán Chimborazo
6310
Ambato
Babahoyo
Riobamba
Arica
Santo Antônio do Içá
GUAYAQUIL
Macas
Salinas
Puca Urco
Tarapacá
Pebas
Cuenca
Azogues
Napo
São Paulo de Olivença
I. Puná
Amazon
Golfo de Guayaquil
Iquitos
106
Machala
Leticia
Zorritos
Tumbes
Loja
Benjamin Constant
Borja
Marañón
Talara
Punta Pariñas
Zumba
Sullana
Requena
Paita
Chulucanas
Piura
Bahía de Sechura
Bellavista
Yurimaguas
Jaén
Moyobamba
PERU
Eirunepé
Soledade
Punta Aguja
Des. de Sechura
Chachapoyas
Tarapoto
Ipixuna
Chiclayo
Contamana
Cruzeiro do Sul
Envira
Is. Lobos de Afuera
Bambamarca
Juanjuí
Cajamarca
Pacasmayo
Pôrto Valter
Tarauacá
Feijó
Puerto Chicama
CHAN CHAN
Trujillo
Pucallpa
Acre
Sena Madureira
Nevado Huascarán
6768
Ganso Azul
Tingo María
Chimbote
Huaraz
Cord. Blanca
Cord. Negra
Esperanza
Rio Branco
Huánuco
Xapuri
Brasiléia
6220
Ambo
Oxapampa
Atalaya
Nevado Yerupajá
6632
Cerro de Pasco
Iñapari
Cobija
Paramonga
4338
Iberia
Huacho
Canta
Tarma
Jauja
La Oroya
Manu
Puerto Maldonado
CALLAO
3271
LIMA
Huancayo
Quillabamba
Miguel
MACHUPICCHU
1594
Urubamba
S. Vicente de Cañete
Huancavelica
Salcantay
6271
Nudo Ausangate
Ayacucho
Abancay
Cusco
3399
6384
Cord. de Carabaya
Chincha Alta
Pisco
Is. de Chincha
Altiplano del Peru
Nevado Palomani
5999
I. San Gallan
Ica
Chalhuanca
Sicuani
Ayaviri
NICARAGUA
Bluefields
San Juan d. Norte
COSTA RICA
Limón
Bocas d. Toro
Cerro Chirripó
3820
Almirante
G. de los Mosquitos
Colón
PANAMÁ
La Chorrera
Penonomé
Puerto Cortés
3478
David
Chitré
Arch. de las Perlas
La Palma
Puerto Armuelles
Santiago
Pen. de Azuero
Las Tablas
Golfo de Chiriquí
Isla de Coiba
Gulf of Panama
Isla de Malpelo (Col.)
PACIFIC OCEAN
80
10
0
A
B
a
b
c
d
© ISTITUTO GEOGRAFICO DE AGOSTINI S. p. A. - NOVARA

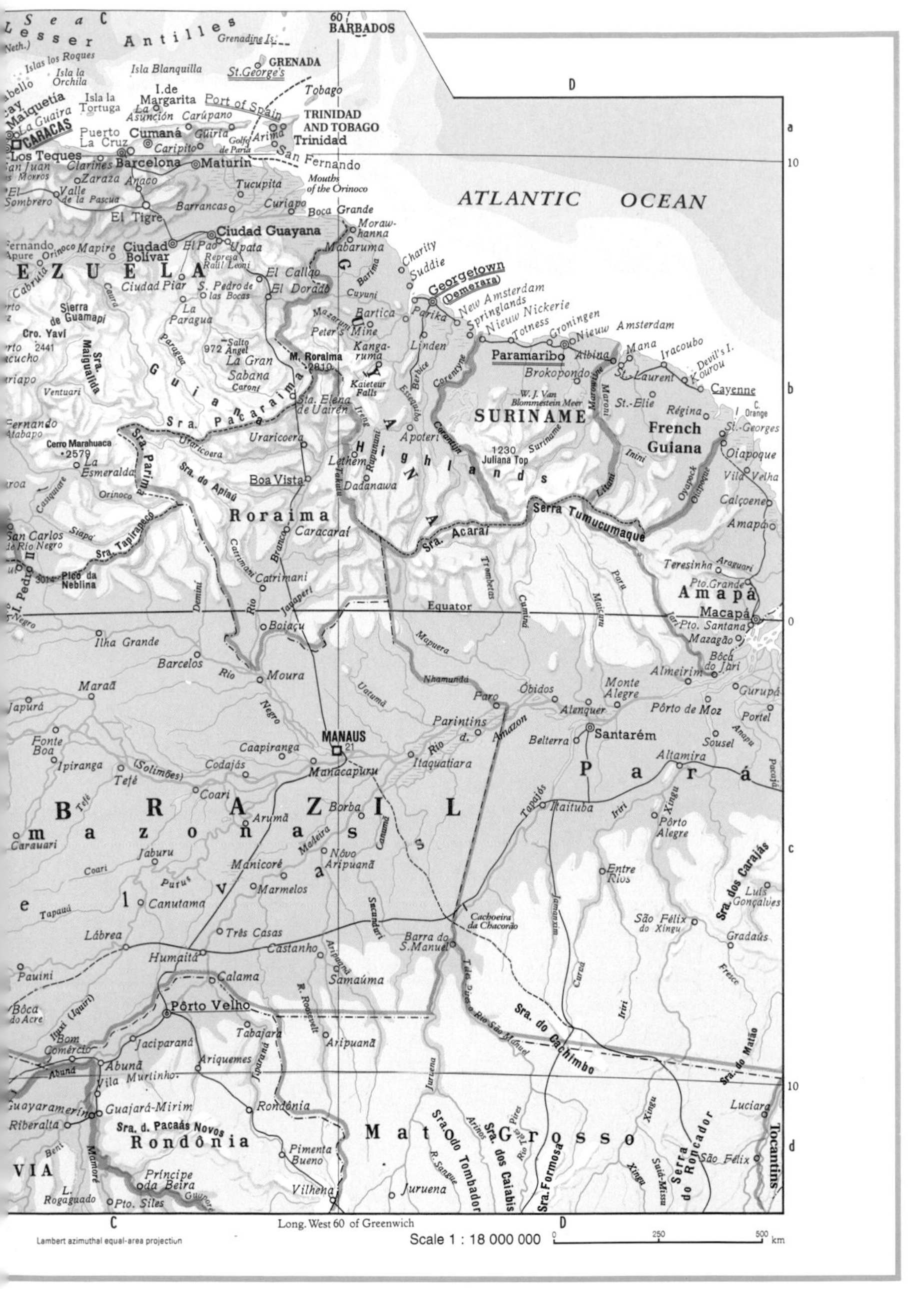
Lesser Antilles
Grenadine Is.
BARBADOS
GRENADA
St.George's
Isla Blanquilla
Islas los Roques
Isla la Orchila
Tobago
I.de Margarita
Isla la Tortuga
Port of Spain
La Asunción
Carúpano
TRINIDAD AND TOBAGO
Trinidad
Maiquetía
La Guaira
CARACAS
Puerto La Cruz
Cumaná
Güiria
Golfo de Paria
Arima
San Fernando
Los Teques
Caripito
Barcelona
Maturín
Clarines
Zaraza
Anaco
Tucupita
Mouths of the Orinoco
Valle de la Pascua
Barrancas
Curiapo
Boca Grande
El Tigre
Ciudad Guayana
Morawhanna
Mapire
Ciudad Bolívar
El Pao
Upata
Represa Raúl Leoni
Mabaruma
Charity
Suddie
Georgetown (Demerara)
El Callao
El Dorado
Cuyuni
Ciudad Piar
S. Pedro de las Bocas
La Paragua
Sierra de Guamapi
Cro. Yavi 2441
Sra. Maigualida
972 Salto Angel
La Gran Sabana
Caroní
M. Roraima 2810
Bartica
Parika
Peter's Mine
Kangaruma
Kaieteur Falls
Linden
New Amsterdam
Springlands
Nieuw Nickerie
Totness
Groningen
Nieuw Amsterdam
Paramaribo
Albina
Mana
Iracoubo
Devil's I.
Kourou
Cayenne
Brokopondo
St. Laurent
ATLANTIC OCEAN
Ventuari
Guiana
Sra. Pacaraima
Sta. Elena de Uairén
W. J. Van Blommestein Meer
SURINAME
St.-Elie
Régina
C. Orange
St.-Georges
French Guiana
Uraricoera
Apoteri
Cerro Marahuaca 2579
La Esmeralda
Sra. Parima
Sra. do Apiaú
Boa Vista
Lethem
Dadanawa
1230 Juliana Top
Oiapoque
Vila Velha
Calçoene
Guiana Highlands
Orinoco
Roraima
Caracaraí
Sra. Acaraí
Serra Tumucumaque
Amapá
San Carlos de Río Negro
Sra. Tapirapecó
3014 Pico da Neblina
Catrimani
Teresinha
Pto. Grande
Amapá
Macapá
Pto. Santana
Mazagão
Equator
Boiaçu
Ilha Grande
Barcelos
Moura
Mapuera
Nhamundá
Bôca do Jari
Almeirim
Gurupá
Marañ
Japurá
Uatumã
Óbidos
Monte Alegre
Alenquer
Pôrto de Moz
Portel
Parintins
Paro
Fonte Boa
Ipiranga
MANAUS
Caapiranga
Codajás
Manacapuru
Itaquatiara
Belterra
Santarém
Sousel
Altamira
Tefé
Coari
BRAZIL
Amazonas
Pará
Arumã
Borba
Itaituba
Pôrto Alegre
Carauari
Jaburu
Manicoré
Nôvo Aripuanã
Entre Rios
Sra. dos Carajás
Canutama
Marmelos
Luís Gonçalves
Lábrea
Três Casas
Cachoeira da Chacorão
São Félix do Xingu
Gradaús
Humaitá
Castanho
Barra do S.Manuel
Pauini
Calama
Samaúma
Bôca do Acre
Pôrto Velho
Sra. do Cachimbo
Tabajara
Bom Comércio
Jaciparaná
Aripuanã
Sra. do Matão
Abunã
Ariquemes
Vila Murtinho
Guayaramerín
Guajará-Mirim
Rondônia
Riberalta
Luciara
Sra. d. Pacaás Novos
Rondônia
Mato Grosso
Sra. do Tombador
Sra. dos Caiabis
Sra. Formosa
Serra do Roncador
São Félix
Tocantins
Pimenta Bueno
Príncipe da Beira
Vilhena
Juruena
L. Rogaguado
Pto. Siles
Long. West 60 of Greenwich
Lambert azimuthal equal-area projection
Scale 1 : 18 000 000
0 250 500 km

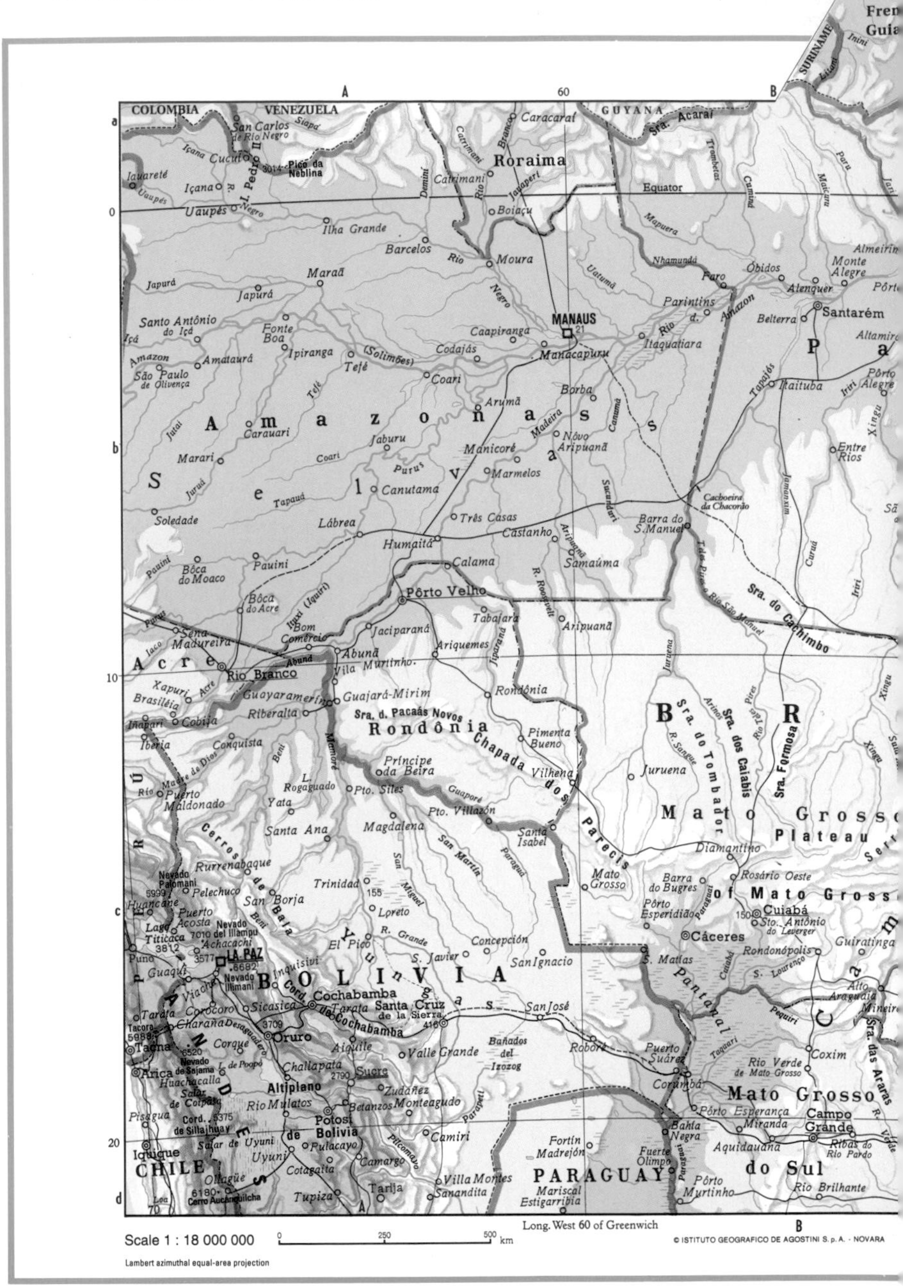

Scale 1 : 18 000 000

Lambert azimuthal equal-area projection

Long. West 60 of Greenwich

© ISTITUTO GEOGRAFICO DE AGOSTINI S. p. A. - NOVARA

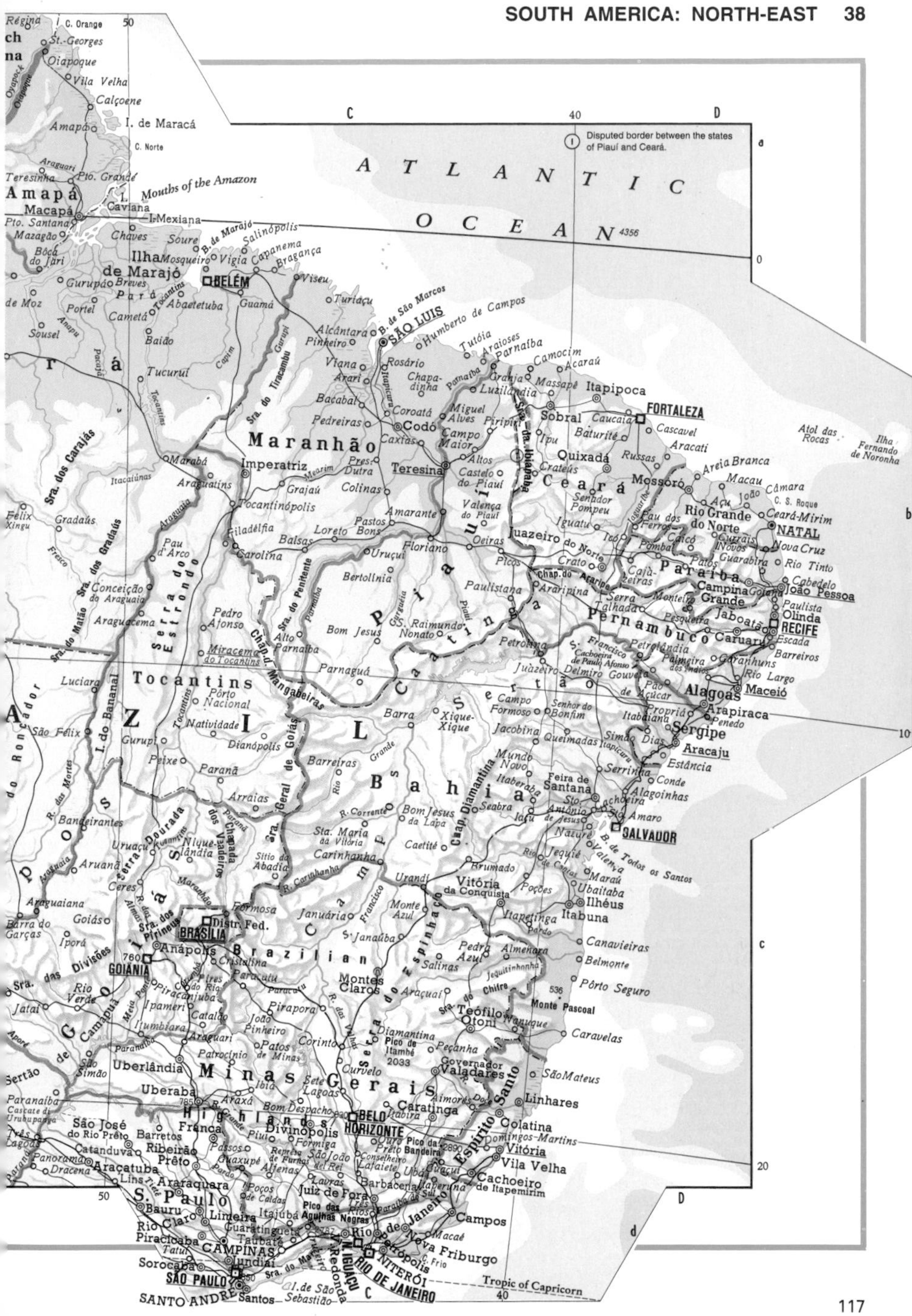

Disputed border between the states of Piauí and Ceará.

ATLANTIC

OCEAN 4356

Régina
C. Orange 50
ch St-Georges
na Oiapoque
Vila Velha
Calçoene
Amapá
I. de Maracá
C. Norte
Pto. Grande
Teresina
Amapá
Mouths of the Amazon
Macapá
I. Caviana
Pto. Santana
I.Mexiana
Mazagão
B. de Marajó
Bôca
do Jari
Chaves
Soure
Salinópolis
Mosqueiro Vigia Capanema
Gurupá
Ilha
Breves
Bragança
de Moz
Portel
de Marajó
Viseu
Pará
BELÉM
Sousel
Gurupá
Abaetetuba
Guamá
Turiaçu
B. de São Marcos
de Moz
Baião
Cametá
Alcântara
SÃO LUÍS
Humberto de Campos
Tucuruí
Pinheiro
Tutóia
Parnaíba
Araioses
Camocim
Viana
Rosário
Chapa-
Acaraú
Itapipoca
Marabá
Imperatriz
Araxi
Pedreiras
Coroatá
Miguel
Sobral
Caucaia
FORTALEZA
Sra. dos Carajás
Itacaiúnas
Grajaú
Caxias
Campo
Altos
Quixadá
Russas
Aracati
Gradaús
Araguatins
Maranhão
Colinas
Teresina
Ceará
Mossoró
Macau
C. S. Roque
Filadélfia
Loreto
Amarante
Valença
do Piauí
Areia Branca
Câmara
Carolina
Balsas
Uruçuí
Floriano
Oeiras
Juazeiro do Norte
Rio Grande
do Norte
NATAL
Conceição
do Araguaia
Bertolínia
Piauí
Crato
Paraíba
João Pessoa
Tocantins
Pôrto
Nacional
Pedro
Afonso
Alto
Parnaíba
Bom Jesus
R. Raimundo
Nonato
Petrolina
Pernambuco
Caruaru
RECIFE
Paulista
Luciara
Miracema
do Tocantins
Parnaguá
Juàzeiro
Delmiro Gouveia
Alagoas
Barreiros
Rio Largo
Maceió
BRAZIL
Natividade
Barra
Xique-
Xique
Jacobina
Arapiraca
Penedo
Dianópolis
Barreiras
Bahia
Feira de
Santana
Alagoinhas
Sergipe
Aracaju
Arraias
Bom Jesus
da Lapa
Seabra
SALVADOR
Sta. Maria
da Vitória
Caetité
B. de Todos os Santos
Aruanã
Sítio do
Abadia
Carinhanha
Urandi
Vitória
da Conquista
Ilhéus
Iporá
Januária
Janaúba
Pedra
Almenara
Canavieiras
Belmonte
GOIANIA
BRASÍLIA
Distr. Fed.
Anápolis
Brazilian
Montes
Claros
Salinas
Pôrto Seguro
Rio
Verde
Ipameri
Pirapora
Teófilo
Monte Pascoal
Jataí
Catalão
Diamantina
Pico do
Itambé
Caravelas
Uberlândia
Minas
Gerais
Governador
Valadares
São Mateus
Uberaba
Araxá
Linhares
São José
do Rio Prêto
Barretos
Franca
BELO
HORIZONTE
Colatina
Vitória
Ribeirão
Prêto
Juiz de Fora
Vila Velha
Araçatuba
Araraquara
Campos
S. Paulo
Bauru
Rio de Janeiro
Piracicaba
Pico das
Agulhas Negras
Niterói
RIO DE JANEIRO
CAMPINAS
SÃO PAULO
NITERÓI
SANTO ANDRÉ
Santos
Tropic of Capricorn

117

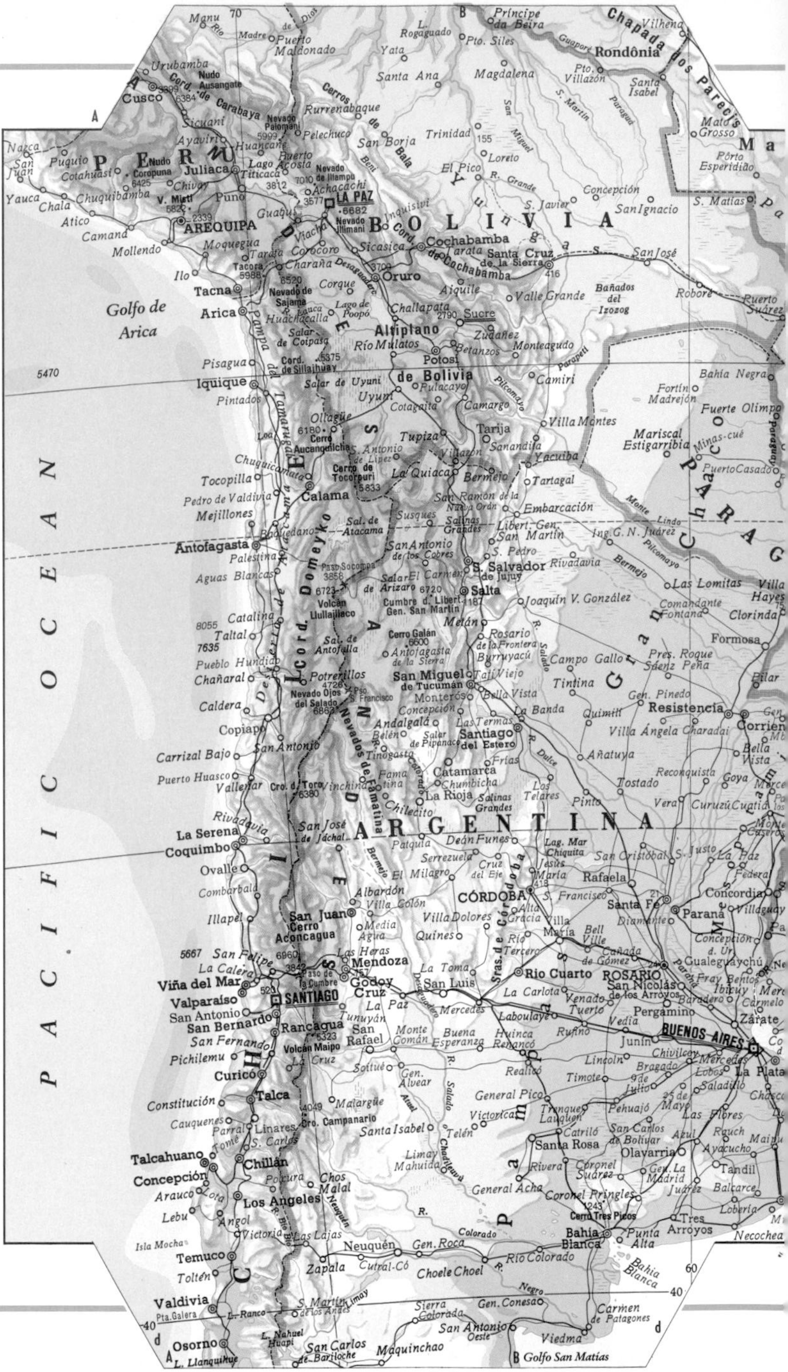

PACIFIC OCEAN

Country labels
PERU
BOLIVIA
PARAGUAY
ARGENTINA
CHILE

Golfo de Arica

Selected place names
Cusco
Urubamba
Nudo Ausangate
Sicuani
Ayaviri
Juliaca
Puno
Lago Titicaca
LA PAZ
AREQUIPA
Moquegua
Tacna
Arica
Iquique
Pisagua
Antofagasta
Mejillones
Tocopilla
Calama
Copiapó
Caldera
Vallenar
La Serena
Coquimbo
Ovalle
Illapel
San Felipe
Valparaíso
Viña del Mar
SANTIAGO
Rancagua
San Fernando
Curicó
Talca
Constitución
Chillán
Talcahuano
Concepción
Los Ángeles
Temuco
Valdivia
Osorno
Oruro
Cochabamba
Santa Cruz
Sucre
Potosí
Uyuni
Tarija
Salta
S. Salvador de Jujuy
San Miguel de Tucumán
Catamarca
La Rioja
Santiago del Estero
CÓRDOBA
San Juan
Mendoza
San Luis
Río Cuarto
ROSARIO
Santa Fe
Paraná
Concordia
Resistencia
Corrientes
Formosa
BUENOS AIRES
La Plata
Bahía Blanca
Neuquén
Viedma

Cerro Aconcagua 6960
Volcán Maipo
Nevado Ojos del Salado

RONDÔNIA
Chapada dos Parecís

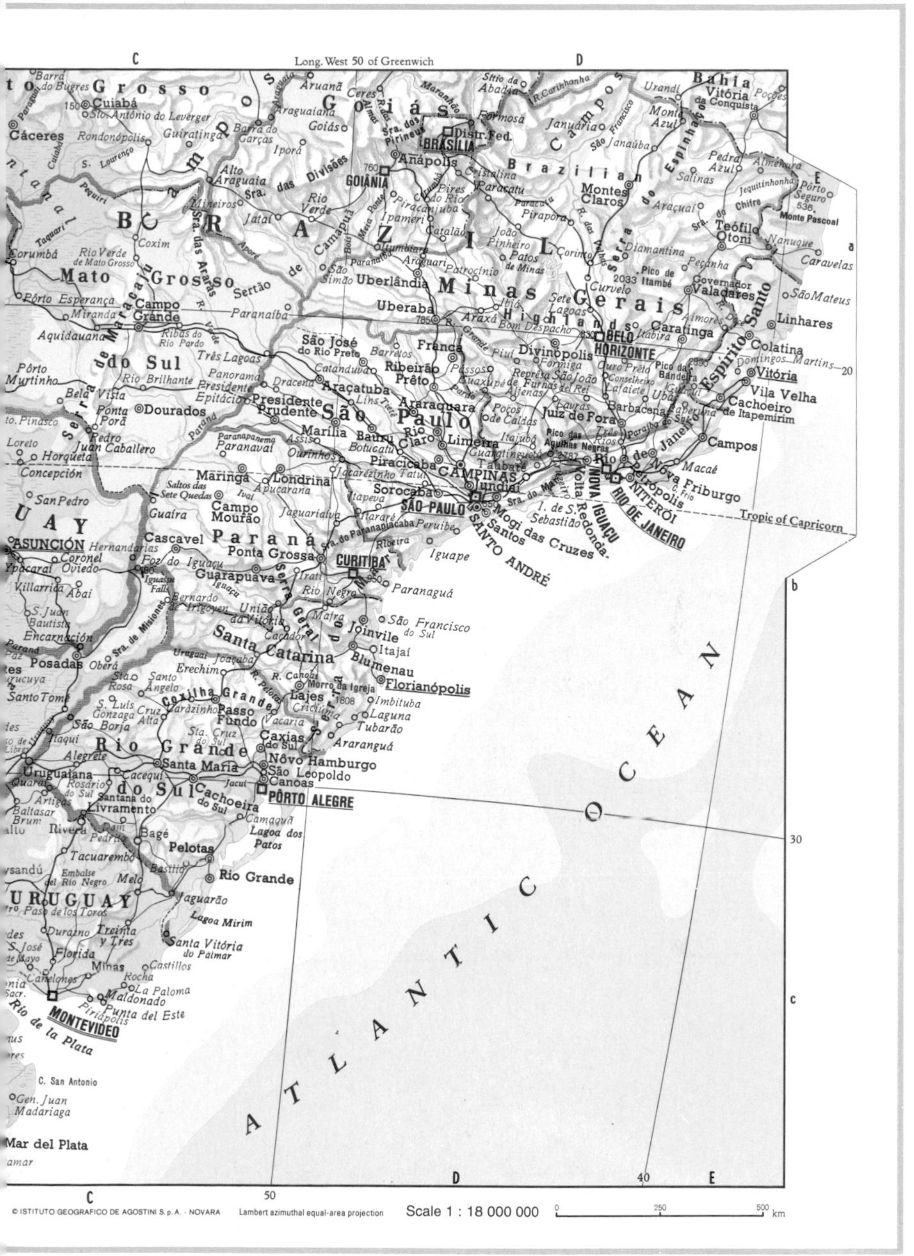

Long. West 50 of Greenwich

to Grosso   Aruanã   Ceres   Sra. dos Abada   R. Carinhana   Urandi   Bahia
Barra do Bugres   Goiás   Goiás   Maranhão   R. Carinhana   Urandi   Vitória
Cuiabá   Araguaiana   Goiás   Formosa   Januária   Monte   Conquista
São Antônio do Leverger   Goiás   Goiás   Formosa   Azul   Monte   Poços
Cáceres   Rondonópolis   Guiratinga   Barra do Garças   Iporá   Distr. Fed.   São Janaúba   Azul
S. Lourenço   BRASÍLIA   B r a z i l i a n   Pedra   Almeira
Alto   Anápolis   Espira   Paracatu   Montes   Salinas   Azul   Pôrto
Araguaia   das Divisões   GOIÂNIA   São do Rio   Paracatu   Claros   Jequitinhonha   Seguro
B   R   Sra.   Jataí   Rio   Piracanjuba   Ipameri   Piraporo   Araçuaí   Chifre   536.
Verde   Monte Pascoal

Corumbá   Coxim   Rio Verde de Mato Grosso   Catalão   João Pinheiro   Diamantina   Teófilo   Nanuque   a
Mato   Grosso   de   São Simão   Uberlândia   Minas   Gerais   Valadares   São Mateus
Pôrto Esperança   Campo   Sertão   Paranaíba   Uberaba   Araxá   Curvelo   Caratinga   Linhares
Aquidauana   Miranda   Grande   Ribas do Rio Pardo   São José   Barretos   França   Divinópolis   BELO   20
Três Lagoas   do Rio Preto   Catanduva   Ribeirão   HORIZONTE   Colatina
Pôrto   Bela   Rio Brilhante   Panorama   Dracena   Prêto   Repr. São João   Vitória
Murtinho   Vista   Presidente   Agraquara   Vila Velha
Loreto   Pedro   Ponte   Dourados   Epitácio   Presidente   São   Juiz de Fora   Cachoeiro
Horqueta   Juan Caballero   Pará   Assis   Marília   Bauru   Limeira   de Itapemirim
Concepción   Paranavaí   Piracicaba   Rio de Janeiro   Campos
San Pedro   Maringá   Londrina   CAMPINAS   Jundiaí   NITERÓI   Friburgo
U A Y   Saltos das Sete Quedas   Campo   Sorocaba   SÃO PAULO   Petrópolis   RIO DE JANEIRO
ASUNCIÓN   Hernandarias   Mourão   Mogi das Cruzes   Tropic of Capricorn
Yporá   Coronel Oviedo   Cascavel   Paraná   Ponta Grossa   Santos   SANTO ANDRÉ
Villarrica   Abaí   Foz do Iguaçu   Guarapuava   Iguape
S. Juan Bautista   Bernardo   União   CURITIBA   Paranaguá
Encarnación   Rio Negro   Joinvile   São Francisco do Sul
Posadas   Oberá   Santa   Itajaí
Santo Tomé   Santa   Catarina   Blumenau
São Luis   Rosa   Angelo   Florianópolis   O C E A N
São Borja   Cruz Alta   Lajes   Morro da Igreja   1808   Laguna
Uruguaiana   Rio   Grande   Passo   Caxias   Tubarão
Alegrete   Fundo   Araranguá
Rosário   do Sul   Santana   Novo Hamburgo   30
Cacequi   Santa Maria   Cachoeira   São Leopoldo
Uruguaiana   Livramento   do Sul   Canoas
Baltasar Brum   Bagé   PÔRTO ALEGRE
Rivera   Tacuarembó   Pelotas   Lagoa dos Patos
sandú   Embalse del Rio Negro   Melo   Rio Grande
Paso del Toros   Durazno   Treinta   Jaguarão   A T L A N T I C
des José   Florida   y Tres   Lagoa Mirim
Mayo   Minas   Santa Vitória do Palmar
nia   Sacr.   Castillos
Maldonado   La Paloma   Rocha
MONTEVIDEO   Punta del Este   c
Rio de la Plata

C. San Antonio
Gen. Juan Madariaga

Mar del Plata
amar

© ISTITUTO GEOGRAFICO DE AGOSTINI S.p.A. - NOVARA   Lambert azimuthal equal-area projection   Scale 1 : 18 000 000   0   250   500 km

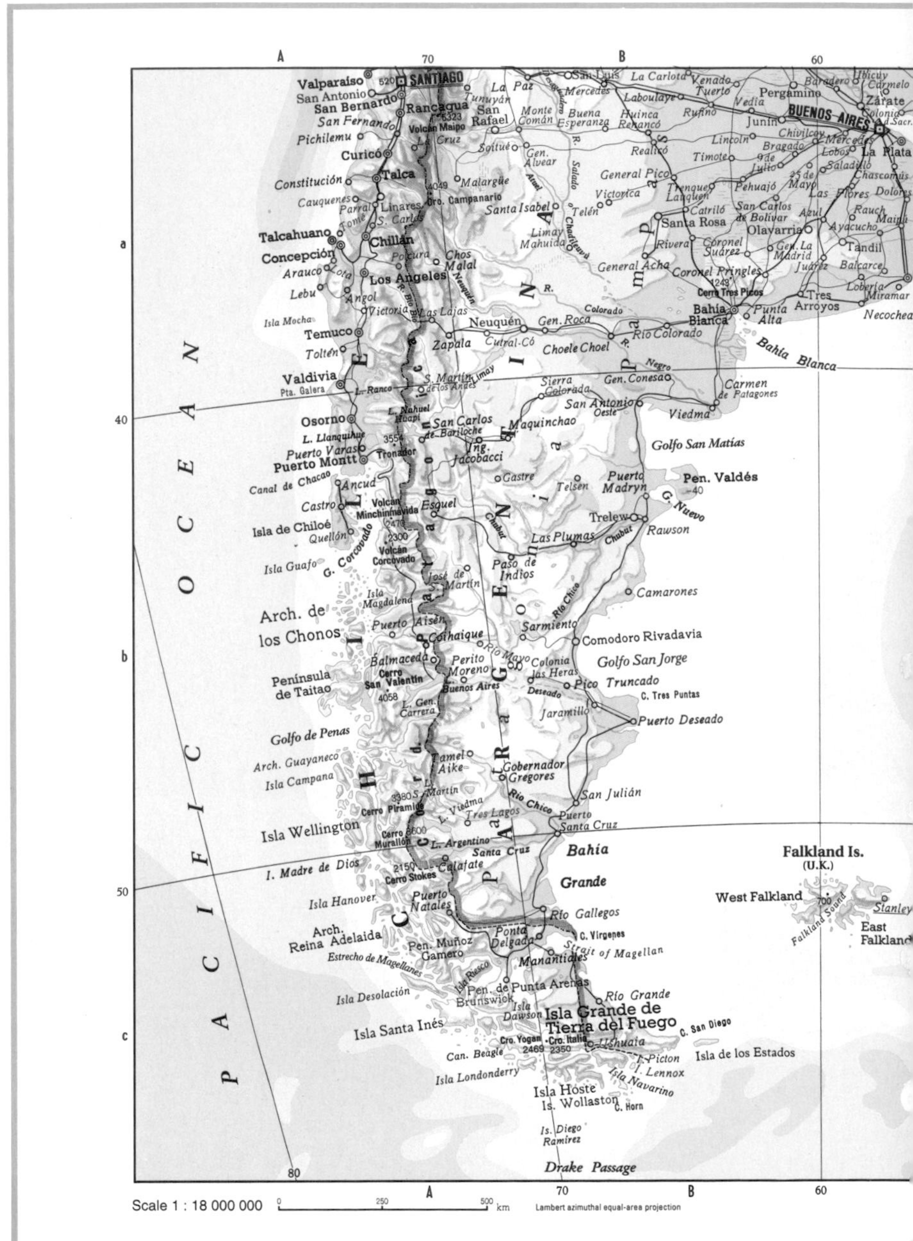
Valparaíso
San Antonio
SANTIAGO
San Bernardo
Rancagua
San Fernando
Pichilemu
Volcán Maipo
Curicó
Talca
Constitución
Cauquenes
Parral
Linares
Talcahuano
Concepción
Chillán
Arauco
Lota
Lebu
Los Angeles
Angol
Isla Mocha
Victoria
Temuco
Toltén
Valdivia
Pta. Galera
L. Ranco
Osorno
L. Llanquihue
Puerto Varas
Puerto Montt
Tronador
Canal de Chacao
Ancud
Castro
Isla de Chiloé
Quellón
Volcán Minchinmávida
Volcán Corcovado
G. Corcovado
Isla Guafo
Isla Magdalena
Arch. de los Chonos
Puerto Aisén
Coihaique
Balmaceda
Cerro San Valentín
Península de Taitao
Golfo de Penas
Arch. Guayaneco
Isla Campana
Cerro Pirámide
Isla Wellington
Cerro Murallón
I. Madre de Dios
Cerro Stokes
Isla Hanover
Puerto Natales
Arch. Reina Adelaida
Pen. Muñoz Gamero
Estrecho de Magallanes
Isla Riesco
Isla Desolación
Pen. de Brunswick
Punta Arenas
Isla Santa Inés
Isla Dawson
Can. Beagle
Cro. Yogan
Cro. Italia
Isla Londonderry
Isla Hoste
Is. Wollaston
C. Horn
Is. Diego Ramírez
Drake Passage
P A C I F I C   O C E A N
CHILE
PATAGONIA
La Paz
Tunuyán
San Rafael
Monte Comán
Soitué
Gen. Alvear
Malargüe
Cro. Campanario
Santa Isabel
Telén
Limay Mahuida
Chos Malal
Las Lajas
Neuquén
Zapala
Cutral-Có
Gen. Roca
Choele Choel
Río Colorado
S. Martín de los Andes
L. Nahuel Huapi
San Carlos de Bariloche
Ing. Jacobacci
Maquinchao
Sierra Colorada
Gastre
Telsen
Esquel
Las Plumas
Paso de Indios
José de San Martín
Sarmiento
Río Mayo
Perito Moreno
Buenos Aires
L. Gen. Carrera
Colonia las Heras
Pico Truncado
Jaramillo
Tamel Aike
Gobernador Gregores
S. Martín
L. Viedma
Tres Lagos
L. Argentino
Calafate
Santa Cruz
Río Chico
San Julián
Puerto Santa Cruz
Bahía Grande
Río Gallegos
Punta Delgada
C. Vírgenes
Strait of Magellan
Manantiales
Río Grande
Isla Grande de Tierra del Fuego
Ushuaia
C. San Diego
I. Picton
I. Lennox
Isla Navarino
Isla de los Estados
San Luis
Mercedes
La Carlota
Venado Tuerto
Buena Esperanza
Laboulaye
Huinca Renancó
Rufino
Pergamino
Zárate
BUENOS AIRES
La Plata
Junín
Realicó
General Pico
Victorica
Trenque Lauquen
Pehuajó
Santa Rosa
Catriló
General Acha
Coronel Suárez
Olavarría
Tandil
Azul
Ayacucho
Balcarce
Coronel Pringles
Cerro Tres Picos
Bahía Blanca
Punta Alta
Tres Arroyos
Necochea
Miramar
Colorado
Negro
Gen. Conesa
Carmen de Patagones
San Antonio Oeste
Viedma
Golfo San Matías
Puerto Madryn
Pen. Valdés
G. Nuevo
Trelew
Rawson
Chubut
Camarones
Comodoro Rivadavia
Golfo San Jorge
C. Tres Puntas
Puerto Deseado
Falkland Is.
(U.K.)
West Falkland
East Falkland
Stanley
Falkland Sound
Scale 1 : 18 000 000
Lambert azimuthal equal-area projection

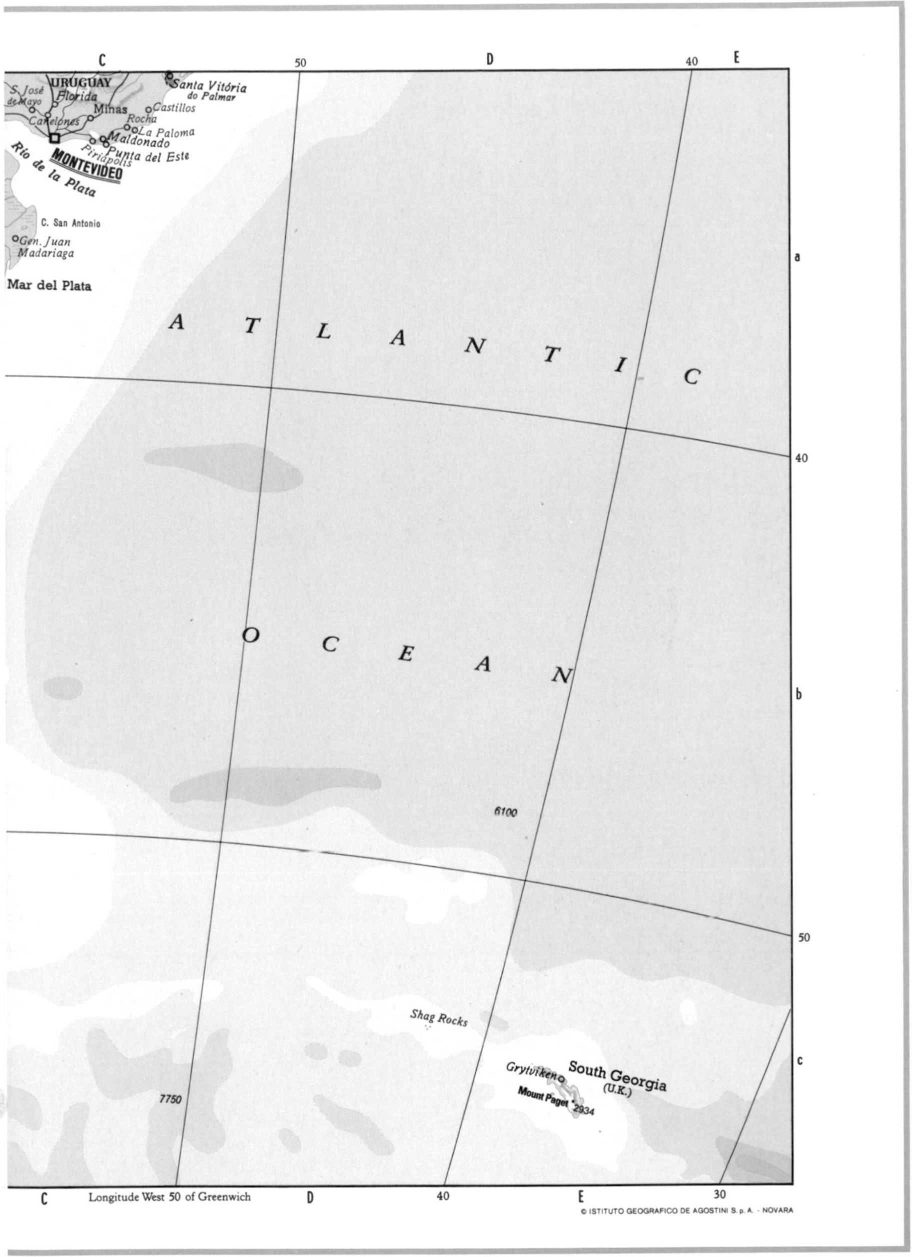

URUGUAY
S. José
de Mayo
Florida
Canelones
Minas
Santa Vitória
do Palmar
Castillos
Rocha
La Paloma
Maldonado
Punta del Este
Piriápolis
MONTEVIDEO
Río de la Plata

C. San Antonio
Gen. Juan
Madariaga

Mar del Plata

A T L A N T I C

O C E A N

6100

Shag Rocks

Grytviken
South Georgia
(U.K.)
Mount Paget 2934

7750

Longitude West 50 of Greenwich

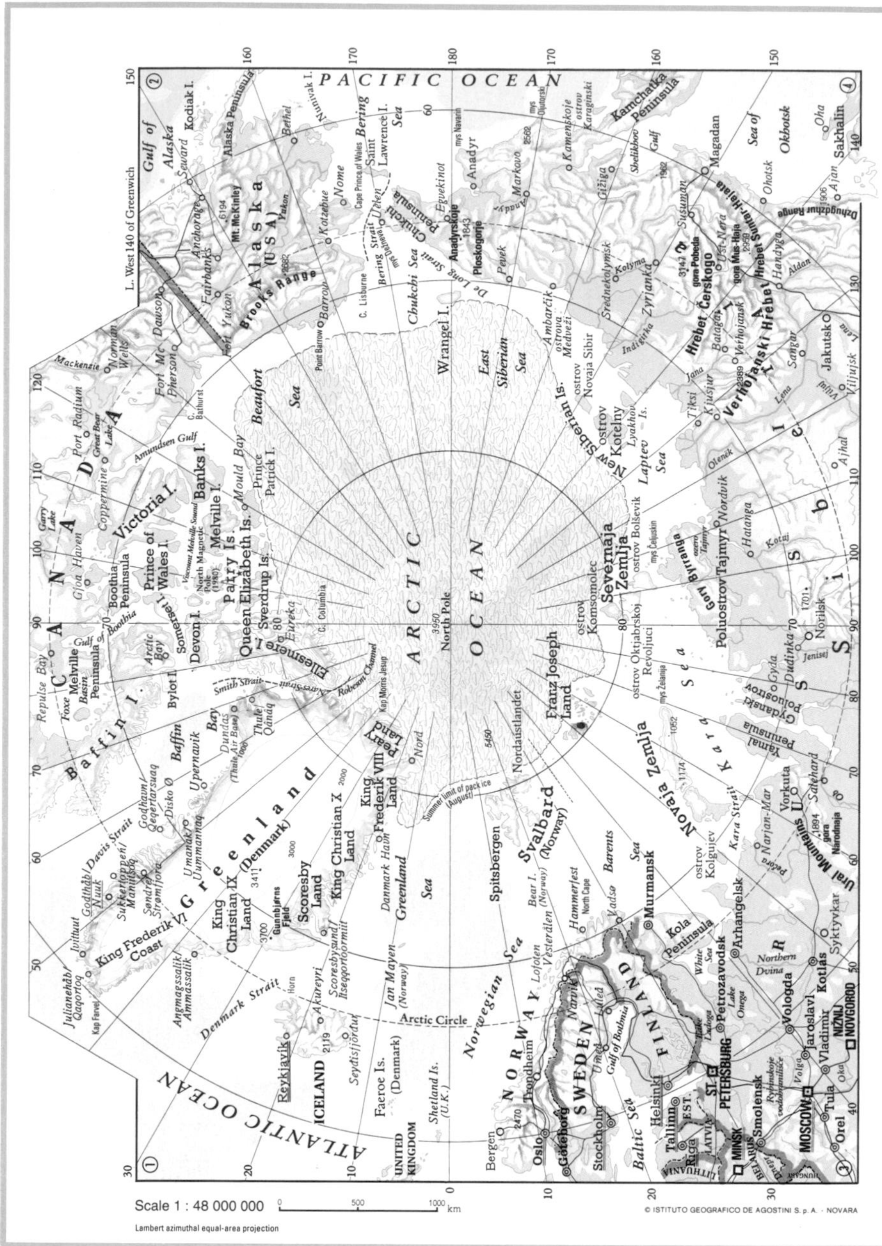

Scale 1 : 48 000 000

Lambert azimuthal equal-area projection

© ISTITUTO GEOGRAFICO DE AGOSTINI S.p.A. · NOVARA

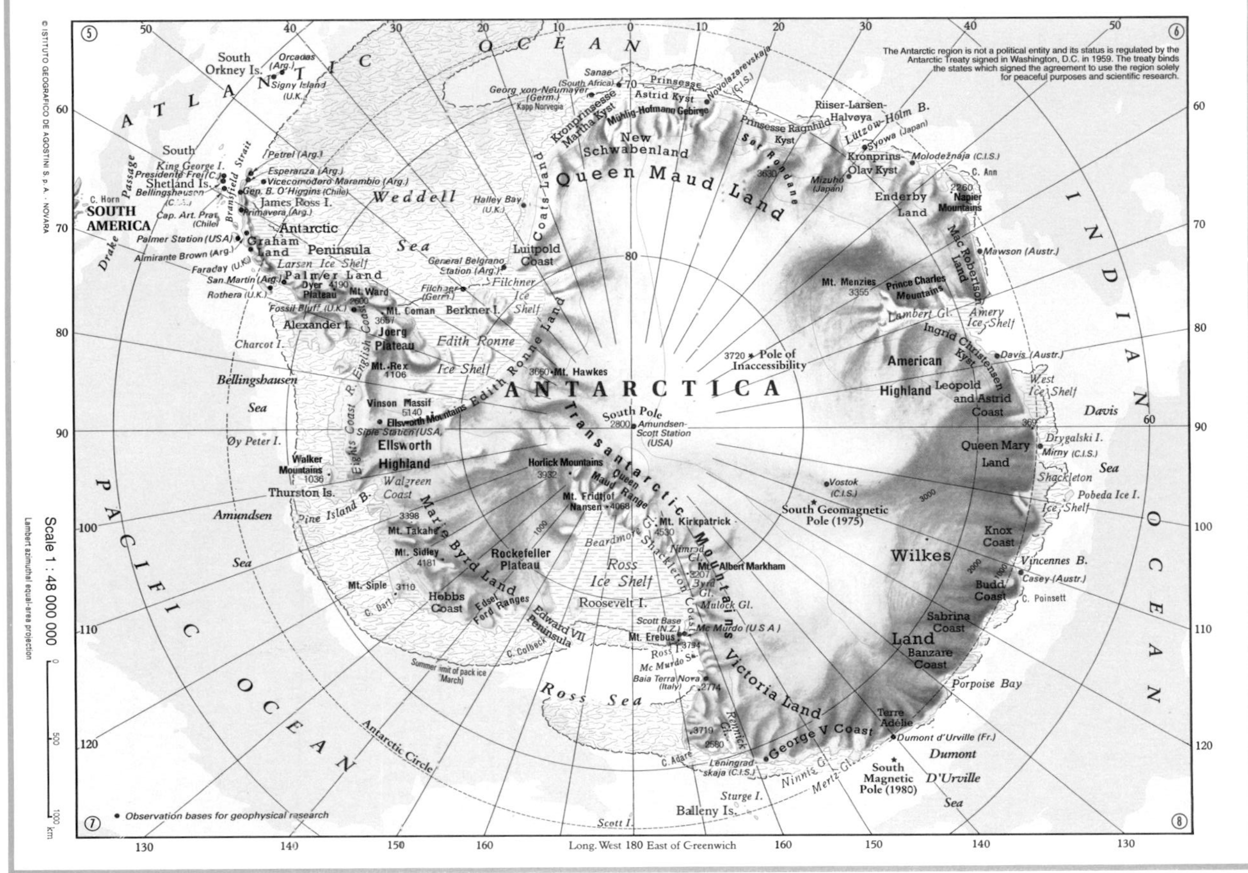

Scale 1 : 48 000 000
Lambert azimuthal equal-area projection

INDEX

All the names shown on the maps are only listed once in the index and normally, the reference given is to the principle map on which they appear.

The individual maps in numerical order are divided by the lines of the meridian and the parallels into grid squares marked from left to right with upper case letters and from top to bottom with lower case letters.

The names which refer to the map inserts are followed by the words "map no."; those refering to the maps of the polar region are followed by the words "grid square no.".

The names referred to on The World Political map are followed only by the number of the map.

In general, names are listed in the index in full even if they are abbreviated on the maps.

All the names are listed in alphabetical order according to their international form, not taking into account any diacritic letter forms (e.g. ā, æ, ö, œ, ū, etc.).

Physical features composed of a proper name and a description are listed alphabetically by the proper name, followed by the description.

To ease understanding for physical features and administrative divisions, an abbreviation of the type of feature is shown in brackets in the index after its name.

In the case of two places with the same name, the political identity is shown in square brackets.

Abbreviations used in the index

at.	atoll
Aut. Reg.	Autonomous Region
Aut. Rep.	Autonomous Republic
b.	bay
c.	cave
can.	canal
cap.	cape
co.	County
Dep.	Dependency, Colony
des.	desert
g.	gulf
gl.	glacier
hist. reg.	historical region
i.	island
Ind. St.	Independent State
is.	islands
l.	lake
lag.	lagoon
mt.	mountain
mts.	mountains
p.	pass
pen.	peninsula
phys. reg.	physical region
plat.	plateau, upland
prov.	Province
r.	ruins
reg.	Region
res.	reservoir
rf.	reef
riv.	river
riv. m.	river mouth
sal. l.	salt lake
sc. stat.	scientific station
s. m.	salt marsh
str.	strait
sw.	swamp, marsh
v.	valley
volc.	volcano
w.	wadi
wf.	waterfall

Abbr.	Place	Abbr.	Place	Abbr.	Place
Ak.-U.S.	Alaska, U.S.	I.C.	Ivory Coast	Nor.	Norway
Al.-U.S.	Alabama, U.S.	Id.-U.S.	Idaho, U.S.	Nv.-U.S.	Nevada, U.S.
Alta.-Can.	Alberta, Canada	Il.-U.S.	Illinois, U.S.	N.Y.-U.S.	New York, U.S.
Ant.	Antarctica	In.-U.S.	Indiana, U.S.	N.Z.	New Zealand
Ar.-U.S.	Arkansas, U.S.	Indon.	Indonesia	Oh.-U.S.	Ohio, U.S.
Arg.	Argentina	Ire.	Ireland	Ont.-Can.	Ontario, Canada
Atg.	Antigua and	It.	Italy	Or.-U.S.	Oregon, U.S.
	Barbuda	Jam.	Jamaica	Pa.-U.S.	Pennsylvania, U.S.
Aus.	Austria	Jap.	Japan	Pak.	Pakistan
Austl.	Australia	Jor.	Jordan	Pan.	Panama
Az.-U.S.	Arizona, U.S.	Kaz.	Kazakhstan	Par.	Paraguay
Bah.	Bahamas	Ky.-U.S.	Kentucky, U.S.	Phil.	Philippines
Bel.	Belgium	Kyrg.	Kyrgyzstan	Pol.	Poland
Bela.	Belarus	La.-U.S.	Louisiana, U.S.	Port.	Portugal
Bngl.	Bangladesh	Lbr.	Liberia	Reu.	Reunion
Bol.	Bolivia	Leb.	Lebanon	Rom.	Romania
Braz.	Brazil	Lib.	Libya	S. Afr.	South Africa
Bul.	Bulgaria	Ma.-U.S.	Massachusetts, U.S.	S. Amer.	South America
Ca.-U.S.	California, U.S.	Mala.	Malaysia	S.C.-U.S.	South Carolina,
Can.	Canada	Me.-U.S.	Maine, U.S.		U.S.
C.A.R.	Central African	Mex.	Mexico	Scot.-U.K.	Scotland, U.K.
	Republic	Mi.-U.S.	Michigan, U.S.	S.D.-U.S.	South Dakota,
Cay. Is.	Cayman Islands	Mn.-U.S.	Minnesota, U.S.		U.S.
Co.-U.S.	Colorado, U.S.	Mo.-U.S.	Missouri, U.S.	Sp.	Spain
Col.	Colombia	Mold.	Moldova	Sud.	Sudan
C.R.	Costa Rica	Moz.	Mozambique	Sur.	Suriname
Cyp.	Cyprus	Ms.-U.S.	Mississippi, U.S.	Swe.	Sweden
Czech Rep.	Czech Republic	Mt.-U.S.	Montana, U.S.	Tn.-U.S.	Tennessee, U.S.
De.-U.S.	Delaware, U.S.	Mtna.	Mauritania	Trin.	Trinidad and
Dom. Rep.	Dominican	Mya.	Myanmar (Burma)		Tobago
	Republic	N. Amer.	North America	Tun.	Tunisia
Ec.	Ecuador	Nb.-U.S.	Nebraska, U.S.	Tur.	Turkey
Eg.	Egypt	N.B.-Can.	New Brunswick,	Tx.-U.S.	Texas, U.S.
El Sal.	El Salvador		Canada	U.K.	United Kingdom
Eng.-U.K.	England, U.K.	N.C.-U.S.	North Carolina,	Ukr.	Ukraine
Eth.	Ethiopia		U.S.	Ur.	Uruguay
Fl.-U.S.	Florida, U.S.	N.D.-U.S.	North Dakota, U.S.	U.S.	United States
Fr.	France	Nep.	Nepal	Va.-U.S.	Virginia, U.S.
Fr. Gui.	French Guiana	Neth.	Netherlands	Ven.	Venezuela
Fr. Poly.	French Polynesia	Newf.-Can.	Newfoundland,	Vt.-U.S.	Vermont, U.S.
Ga.-U.S.	Georgia, U.S.		Canada	Wa.-U.S.	Washington,
Ger.	Germany	N.H.-U.S.	New Hampshire,		U.S.
Grc.	Greece		U.S.	Wi.-U.S.	Wisconsin, U.S.
Guat.	Guatemala	Nic.	Nicaragua	W.V.-U.S.	West Virginia,
Hi.-U.S.	Hawaii, U.S.	Nig.	Nigeria		U.S.
H.K.	Hong Kong	N.Ire.-U.K.	Northern Ireland,	Wy.-U.S.	Wyoming, U.S.
Hond.	Honduras		U.K.	Yugo.	Yugoslavia
Ia.-U.S.	Iowa, U.S.	N.M.-U.S.	New Mexico, U.S.	Zimb.	Zimbabwe

A

Aachen **5** Ac
Aaiún, El– **24** Ab
Aalen **5** Cd
Aalst **8** EFb
Äänekoski **4** Fc
Aansarîyé, Gebel– (mt.) **22** Fe
Aarau **5** Be
Aasiaat / Egedesminde **31** JKb
Aba **24** Cd
Abaco Island **32** Dc
Ābādān **21** Dc
Abādeh **21** Ec
Abaetetuba **38** Cb
Abagnar Qi **16** DEb
Abai **39** Cb
Abakan **14** BCd
Abalakova **14** Cd
Abancay **37** Bd
Abano Terme **10** Cb
Abarqu **21** Ec
Abashiri **16** Jb
Abaya, Lake– **25** Dd
Abaza **14** BCd
Abbeville **8** Db
Abbottabad **20** Db
Abd al Kuri (i.) **21** Eg
Abdulino **12** Hc
Abéché **25** Cc
Abemama Atoll **27** Db
Abengourou **24** Bd
Åbenrå **5** Ba
Abeokuta **24** Cd
Abercorn → Mbala **26** Cb
Aberdeen [S.D.–U.S.] **32** Ba
Aberdeen [U.K.] **7** EFc
Aberdeen [Wa.–U.S.] **33** Ab
Aberystwyth **7** De
Abez **13** Fc
Abha **21** Cf
Abidjan **24** Bd
Abilene **33** CDc
Abitibi Lake **32** Da
Abkhasia (Aut. Rep.) **13** De
Abminga **29** EFd
Abnûb **25** Db
Aboisso **24** Bd
Abomey **24** Cd
Abou Deïa **25** BCc
Abrántes **9** ABc
Abruzzo (reg.) **10** DEcd
Absaroka Range **33** BCb
Abu **20** Dd
Abū 'Alī **21** DEd
Abu Arish **21** Cf
Abu Dhabi **21** Ee
Abu Gharâdiq, Bîr– **22** Bgh
Abū Ḩamad **25** Dc
Abuja **24** Cd
Abū Kamāl **21** Cc
Abū Madd, Ra's– **21** Be
Abu Musa (i.) **21** EFd
Abuná (riv.) **37** Ccd
Abunã **37** Cc
Abū Qīr **22** BCg
Abu Simbel (r.) **25** CDb
Abu Sultân **25** map no.1
Abū Zanīmah **21** Ad
Acajutla **35** ABb
Acámbaro **34** Bbc
Acaponeta **34** Bb
Acapulco de Juárez **30** HIh
Acaraí, Serra– (mts.) **38** Ba
Acaraú **38** CDb
Acarigua **37** Cb
Accra **24** BCd
Achacachi **39** Ba
Achill Island **7** ABe
Acıgöl **22** BCd
Ačinsk **14** Cd
Acireale **10** Ef
Acklins Island **35** Ca
Aconcagua, Cerro– (mt.) **39** ABc
Acqui Terme **10** Bb
Acre **39** Ba
Acre (State) **37** BCc
Acri **10** Fe
Acsu (riv.) **22** Cd
Açu **38** Db
Ada **24** Cd
Adabîya **25** map no.1
Adalar (is.) **11** Hc
Adama **25** DEd
Adamawa **24** Dd
Adamello (mt.) **10** Ca
Adams, Mount– **33** Ab
Adamstown **28** Cd
Adana **22** Ed
Adapazarı **22** Cb
Adare, Cape– **42** grid square no.4
Adavale **29** GHd
Adda (riv.) **10** Bb
Ad Dir'īyah **21** De
Addis Ababa **25** Dd
Adelaide **29** FGef
Adelaide River **29** Ea
Adele Island **29** Cb
Adélie, Terre– **42** grid square no.4
Aden **21** Dg
Aden, Gulf of– **25** EFc
Adige (riv.) **10** Ca
Adigrat **25** DEc
Adīrī **24** Db
Adirnaz (riv.) **22** Bc
Adi Ugri **21** Bg
Adıyaman **22** FGd
Admiralty (i.) **31** Bc
Admiralty Gulf **29** CDa
Admiralty Islands **27** Cc
Adonara, Pulau– (i.) **18** Ff
Adoni **20** Ee
Adour (riv.) **8** Cf
Adra [India] **19** Ik
Adra [Sp.] **9** Dd
Adrar **24** Bb
Adrar (mt.) **24** Cb
Adrar, Dhar– (mts.) **24** Ab
Adré **25** Cc
Adria **10** Db
Adriatic Sea **10** Ec
Adwa **25** Dc
Adzhar (Aut. Rep.) **13** De
Aegean Sea **11** FGde
Aegina (i.) **11** Ee
Ærø **5** Ca
Afghanistan (Ind. St.) **15** Cf
Afgooye **25** Ed
'Afif **21** Ce
Afyonkarahisar **22** Cc
Agadez **24** Cc
Agadir **24** ABab
Agadyr **13** Ge
Agalega Islands **15** BCk
Agaña **27** map no.1
Aga Point (cap.) **27** map no.1
Agartala **19** Bd
Agats **27** Bc
Agboville **24** Bd
Agde **8** Ef
Agen **8** De
Agidyen Atoll **28** map no.3
Aginskoje **14** Ed
Agnew **29** Cd
Agnita **6** Gcd
Agordat **25** Dc
Agout (riv.) **8** DEf
Agra **15** Cg
Agreb, El– **24** Ca
Agrigento **10** Df
Agrinion **11** Dd
Agropoli **10** Ed
Agryz **12** Hb
Aguas Blancas **39** ABb
Aguascalientes **34** Bb
Águilas **9** Ed
Aguja, Punta– (cap.) **37** Ac
Agulhas, Cape– **26** ABe
Agulhas Negras, Pico das– (mt.) **39** Db
Ahaggar (mts.) **24** Cb
Ahar **21** Db
Ahmadabad **15** Cg
Aḩmadī, Al– **21** Dd
Ahmadnagar **20** DEe
Ahmar (hist. reg.) **25** Dc
Ahtopol **11** GHb
Ahtuba (riv.) **13** De
Ahtubinsk **3** Hc
Ahtyrka **12** Ec
Ahuachapán **35** ABb
Ahunui Atoll **28** Bc
Åhus **5** Ea
Ahvāz **21** Dc
Ahvenanmaa / Åland (is.) **4** DEc
Ahwar **21** Dg
Aigoual, Mont– (mt.) **8** Ee
Aigues (riv.) **8** Fe
Aihui **16** Ga
Aim **14** Gd
Aimorés **39** Da
Ain (riv.) **8** Fd
Ainaži **4** EFd
Aïn–Beni Mathar **24** Ba
Aïn–Defla **9** FGd
Aineman Atoll **28** map no.3
Ain–Sefra **24** BCa
Aïn–Témouchent **24** Ba
Aiquile **39** Ba
Aïr (mt.) **24** Cc
Aitutaki Atoll **28** ABc
Aiud **6** Fc
Aix–en–Provence **8** FGf
Aix–les–Bains **8** FGe
Aiyion **11** Ed
Āīzawl **19** Bd
Aizpute **4** Ed
Aizuwakamatsu **16** IJc
Ajaccio **8** map no.1
Ajaccio, Golfe d'– **8** map no.1
Ajaguz **13** GHe
Ajan **14** Gd
Ajanta (r.) **20** Ed
Ajdābiyā **24** DEa
Ajhal **14** Ec
Ajigasawa **17** FGd
Ajka **6** Cc
'Ajlūn **22** EFf
Ajmer **20** Dc
Ajon, ostrov– (i.) **14** Jbc
Ajtos **11** Gb
Akademgorodok, Novosibirsk– **13** GHd
Akan **17** HIc
Akanthoú **22** De
Akapatok Island **31** Ib
Akashi **17** Dg
Akbulak **12** Ic
Akçakoca **22** Cb
Akchar (hist. reg.) **24** Abc
Akdağ [Tur.] (mt.) **22** Bd
Akdağ [Tur.] (mt.) **22** Eb
Akdağ [Tur.] (mt.) **22** Bc
Akdağ [Tur.] (mt.) **22** BCc
Aketi **25** Cd
Akhḑar, Al Jabal al– (mts.) **24** Ea
Akhdar, Gebel al– (mt.) **21** Fe
Akheloos (riv.) **11** Dd
Akhisar **22** ABc
Aki **17** CDh
Akimiski Island **31** GHc
Akita **16** IJc
Akjoujt **24** Abc
Akkajaure (l.) **4** Db
Akkeshi **17** Ic
'Akko **22** Ef
Akköy **11** Ge
Aklavik **31** Bb
Akmol (Temirtau) **13** Gd
Akobo **25** Dd
Akola **20** Ed
Akranes **4** map no.1
Akritas, Ákra– **11** De
Akron **32** Ca
Akrotiri **22** De
Akrotíri, Kersónisos– **11** Ff
Aksaj **12** Hc
Aksaray **22** DEc
Akşehir **22** Cc
Akşehir Gölü **22** CDc
Akseki **22** CDd
Aksenovo–Zilovskoje **14** Ed
Aksoran, gora– (mt.) **13** Ge
Aksu [China] **13** He
Aksu [Kaz.] **13** Gd
Aktaš **13** Hd
Aktau (Ševčenko) **13** Ee
Aktjubinsk **13** Ede
Aktogaj **13** Ge
Akureyri **4** map no.1
Akyab → Sittwe **19** Bde
Alabama (riv.) **32** Cb
Alabama (State) **32** Cb
Alaca **22** Eb
Alacahan **22** FGc
Alacrán, Arrecife– (rf.) **34** CDb
Ala Dağ (mt.) **22** Dcd
Ala dağları (mts.) **22** Ed
Alagoas (State) **38** Db
Alagoinhas **38** Dc
Alagón **9** Eb
Alagón (riv.) **9** Bbc
Alajuela **35** Bbc

Alakol, ozero– (l.) **13** He
Alakurtti **4** Gb
Alamagan Island **27** Cb
Alamein, El– **22** Bg
Alamogordo **33** Cc
Álamos **34** Bb
Alamos, Los– **33** Cc
Alamosa **33** Cc
Åland / Ahvenanmaa (is.) **4** DEc
Ålandshav (g.) **4** Dcd
Alanya **22** CDd
Alaotra, Farihy– **26** map no.1
Alapajevsk **13** Fd
Alaşehir **22** Bc
Alaska (State) **30** CDc
Alaska, Gulf of– **41** grid square no.2
Alaska Peninsula **41** grid square no.2
Alassio **10** Bbc
Alatri **10** Dd
Alatyr **13** Dd
Alavus **4** Ec
Alba **10** Bb
Albacete **9** DEc
Alba Iulia **6** Fcd
Albania (Ind. St.) **3** EFc
Albany (riv.) **31** Db
Albany [Austl.] **29** Bef
Albany [Ga.–U.S.] **32** Cb
Albany [N.Y.–U.S.] **32** Da
Albany [Or.–U.S.] **33** Ab
Albardón **39** Bc
Albarracin, Sierra de– (mts.) **9** Eb
Albatross Bay **29** Ga
Albenga **10** Bb
Alberche (riv.) **9** Cb
Albergaria-a-Velha **9** ABb
Albert, Lake– **25** Dd
Alberta (prov.) **31** Dc
Albert Markham, Mount– **42** grid square no.4
Albert Nile (riv.) **26** Ca
Albertville **8** FGe
Albi **8** Ef
Albina **37** Db
Albino **10** Bb
Ålborg **4** Bd
Albufeira **9** Ad
Albuquerque **33** Cc
Alburquerque **9** Bc
Albury **20** Hf
Alcalá de Chivert **9** EFb
Alcalá de Guadaira **9** Cd
Alcalá de Henares **9** Db
Alcalá la Real **9** Dd
Alcamo **10** Df
Alcañiz **9** EFb
Alcântara **38** Cb
Alcántara **9** Bc
Alcaraz, Sierra de– (mts.) **9** Dc
Alcarria, La– (hist. reg.) **9** Db
Alcázar de San Juan **9** Dc
Alčeusk **12** EFd
Alcira **9** Ec
Alcoy **9** Ec
Alcudia **9** Gc
Aldabra Islands **23** Gf
Aldan **14** Fd
Aldan (riv.) **14** Gc
Alderney (i.) **8** Bc
Aleg **24** Ac
Alegrete **39** Cb
Alejsk **13** Hd
Aleksandrov **12** EFb
Aleksandrov Gaj **13** DEde
Aleksandrovsk-Sahalinsk **14** Hd
Aleksandry, Zemlja– **13** CDa
Aleksin **12** Ec
Aleksinac **6** EFe
Alençon **8** Dc
Alenquer **38** Bb
Alentejo (phys. reg.) **9** ABcd
Alenuihaha Channel **28** map no.1
Aleppo **21** Bb
Aléria **8** map no.1
Alès **8** EFe
Alessandria **10** Bb
Ålesund **4** Ac
Aleutians Islands **30** Bd
Alexander Archipelago **31** Bc
Alexanderbaai **26** Ad
Alexander Island **42** grid square no.1
Alexandria [Austl.] **29** Fb
Alexandria [Eg.] **25** Ca
Alexandria [La.–U.S.] **32** Bb
Alexandria [Rom.] **6** Gde
Alexandria [S. Afr.] **26** Be
Alexandroúpolis **11** Fc
Alfambra **9** Eb
Alfenas **39** Db
Alföld (phys. reg.) **6** DEc
Alga **12** Id
Algarve (phys. reg.) **9** ABd
Algeciras **9** Cd
Algemesí **9** Ec
Algena **25** Dc
Algeria (Ind. St.) **23** Cbc
Alghero **10** Bd
Algiers **24** Ca
Al Harūj-al Aswad (mts.) **24** Db
Aliákmōn (riv.) **11** DEcd
Alibunar **6** Ed
Alicante **9** EFc
Alice **32** Bc
Alice, Punta– (cap.) **10** Fe
Alice Springs **29** EFc
Alicudi (i.) **10** Ee
Aligarh **20** Ec
Aliwal North **26** Be
Aljustrel **9** Ad
Alkmaar **8** Fa
Al Kuwait **21** Dd
Allahabad **15** Cg
Allah-Jun **14** GHc
Allariz **9** ABa
Allegheny Mountains **32** CDab
Allen, Lake– **7** Bd
Allentown **32** Da
Alleppey **20** Eg
Aller (riv.) **5** BCb
Alliance **33** Cb
Allier (riv.) **8** Ee
Alloa **7** DEc
Alluitsup Paa / Sydprøven **31** Kb
Alma-Ata **13** Ge
Almada **9** Ac
Almadén **9** Cc
Almalyk **13** Fe
Almansa **9** Ec
Almanzor, Pico de– (mts.) **9** Cb
Almas, Rio das– (riv.) **39** Da
Almazán **9** Db
Almeirim **38** Bb
Almelo **8** Ga
Almenara **39** DEa
Almendralejo **9** BCc
Almería **9** Dd
Almería, Golfo de– **9** DEd
Almetjevsk **12** Hbc
Älmhult **4** Cd
Almirante **35** Bc
Almirante Brown **42** grid square no.1
Almirós **11** Ed
Almorox **9** Cb
Almuñécar **9** Dd
Alofi **28** Ac
Alonnisos (i.) **11** EFd
Alor, Pulau– (i.) **18** FGf
Álora **9** Cd
Alor Setar **19** CDg
Alpena **32** Ca
Alpes Maritimes **10** Ab
Alpha **29** Hc
Alpi Carniche **10** Da
Alpi Cozie **10** Ab
Alpi Graie **10** Ab
Alpine **33** Cc
Alpi Retiche **10** BCa
Als (i.) **5** Ba
Alsace (hist. reg.) **8** Gcd
Alsasua **9** DEa
Alta **4** Ea
Altafjord (g.) **4** Ea
Alta Gracia **39** Bc
Altagracia **37** Ba
Altaj **14** Ce
Altaj (mts.) **13** Hde
Altamira **38** Bb
Altamura **10** Fd
Altata **34** Bb
Altay **13** He
Altdorf **10** Ba
Altenburg **5** Dc
Altinova **22** Ac
Alto Araguaia **38** Bc
Alton **32** BCb
Altoona **32** Da
Alto Parnaíba **38** Cb
Altos **38** Cb
Altun Shan (mts.) **20** FGb
Altus **33** CDc
Alvand, Kū- e- (mt.) **21** Dc
Alvdalen **4** Cc
Älvkarleby **4** Dc
Älvsbyn **4** Eb
Alwar **20** Ec
Alyangula **29** Fa
Alytus **4** EFe
Alzamaj **14** CDd
Amadeus, Lake– **29** Ecd
Amadi **25** Dd
Amadjuak Lake **31** HIb
Amador, Fort– **35** map no.1
Amagasaki **16** HIcd
Amahai **18** Ge
Amakusa-Nada **17** Ah
Amakusa-Shotō **17** Ah
Åmål **4** Cd
Amaliás **11** De
Amami-Shotō (is.) **16** GHe
Amanave **28** map no.5
Amanus Mountains **22** EFd
Amapá (State) **38** Ba
Amapá **38** Ba
'Amārah, Al– **21** Dc
Amarante **38** Cb
Amarillo **33** Cc
Amasra **22** CDb
Amasya **22** EFb
Amataurá **37** Cc
Amazon (riv.) **38** Bb
Amazon, Mouths of the– **38** Ca
Amazonas (State) **37** CDc
Ambala **15** Cf
Ambalavao **26** map no.1
Ambam **24** Dd
Ambarčik **14** Jc
Ambato **37** Bc
Ambatondrazaka **23** GHg
Ambelau, Pulau– (i.) **18** Ge
Amberg **5** CDd
Ambès **8** Ce
Ambikapur **20** Fd
Ambilobe **26** map no.1
Amble **7** Fd
Ambo **37** Bcd
Ambodifototra **26** map no.1
Ambohimahasoa **26** map no.1
Ambon **18** Ge
Ambositra **26** map no.1
Ambovombe **26** map no.1
Ambre, Cap d'– **23** GHg
Ambriz **26** Ab
Ambrym, Île– (i.) **28** map no.4
Amderma **13** Fbc
American Highland **42** grid square no.2
American Samoa (is.) **28** map no.5
Amersfoort **8** FGa
Amery Ice Shelf **42** grid square no.2
Ames **32** Ba
Amfilokhia **11** Dd
Ámfissa **11** DEd
Amga (riv.) **14** Fd
Amga **14** Gc
Amgu **17** Eb
Amgun (riv.) **14** Gd
Amherst **32** Ea
Amiata, Monte– **10** Cc
Amiens **8** DEc
Amik Gölü **22** Fd
Amīndivi Islands **20** Df
Amirante Islands **15** Bj
'Āmirīyah, Al– **22** Bg
Amlekhganj **19** Ij
'Ammān **22** Fg
Ammassalik / Angmagssalik **30** Oc
Ammersee **5** Cde
Amnok-Kang (riv.) **16** FGb
Amorgós (i.) **11** FGe
Ampanihy **26** map no.1
Amposta **9** Fb
'Amran **21** Cf
Amrāvati **20** Ed
Amritsar **15** Cf

Amroha **20** Ec
Amsterdam **8** Fa
Amsterdam, Île- (i.) **2**
Amstetten **5** Ed
Am Timan **25** Cc
Amuay **37** Ba
Amudarja (riv.) **13** Ff
Amundsen Gulf **31** CDab
Amundsen Scott **42** grid square no.2
Amundsen Sea **42** grid square no.3
Amur (riv.) **14** Fd
Amvrakikós, Kólpos- **11** Dd
Anaa Atoll **28** Bc
Anabar **27** map no.2
Anabar (riv.) **14** Eb
Anaco **37** Cb
Anaconda **33** Bb
Anadolu Dağlari **21** ACa
Anadyr (riv.) **14** Kc
Anadyr **14** Kc
Anadyr Gulf **14** Lc
Anadyrskoje Ploskogorje **14** Kc
Anáfi (i.) **11** FGe
'Ānah **21** Cc
Anai Mudi (mt.) **20** Efg
Analalava **26** map no.1
Anambas, Kepulauan- **18** Cd
Anamur **22** Dd
Anamur Burun **22** Dde
Anantapur **20** Ef
Anantnag **20** DEb
Anapa **12** Ee
Anápolis **39** Da
Anapu (riv.) **38** Bb
Anatahan Island **27** Cb
Anatolia (phys. reg.) **22** BFc
Añatuya **39** Bb
Ancenis **8** Cd
Anchorage **30** CDc
Ancona **10** Dc
Ancud **40** Ab
Anda **16** FGa
Andalgalá **39** Bb
Andalsnes **4** ABc
Andalusia (phys. reg.) **9** CDd
Andaman and Nicobar **19** Bfg
Andaman Islands **19** Bf
Andaman Sea **19** Cfg
Andara **26** Bc
Andelys, Les- **8** Dc
Andermatt **10** Ba
Anderson (riv.) **31** Cb
Anderson **32** Cb
Andes **37** Bcd
Andfjorden (g.) **4** CDa
Andhra Pradesh (State) **20** EFe
Andikíthira (i.) **11** Ef
Andíparos (i.) **11** Fe
Andiria Burun **22** Ee
Andirlangar **20** Fa
Andižan **13** Gef
Andkhoy **20** BCa
Andŏng **16** Gc
Andorra (Ind. St.) **9** FGa
Andøya (i.) **4** CDa
Andria **10** Fd
Androka **26** map no.1
Ándros (i.) **11** Fe
Andros Island **32** Dc
Androth Island **20** Df
Andruševka **6** Iab
Andújar **9** CDc
Anegada Passage (str.) **35** Db
Anécho **24** Cd
Aneto, Pico de- (mt.) **9** Fa
Aney **24** Dc
Aneytioum, Île- (i.) **28** map no.4
Angara (riv.) **14** Dd
Angarsk **14** Dd
Angaur (i.) **27** Bb
Ånge **4** Cc
Angel, Salto- (wf.) **37** Cb
Ángel de la Guarda, Isla- **34** Ab
Ángeles, Los- **39** Ac
Angeles, Los- **33** ABc
Angeles-Hollywood, Los- **33** ABc
Ängelholm **4** BCd
Ångermanälven (riv.) **4** Dbc
Angermünde **5** Db
Angers **8** Cd
Angkor (r.) **19** Df
Anglesey (i.) **7** De
Angmagssalik / Ammassalik **30** Oc
Ango **25** Cd
Angoche **26** CDc
Angol **39** Ac
Angola (Ind. St.) **23** DEg
Angoulême **8** De
Angoumois **8** CDde
Angren **13** Ge
Anguilla (i.) **35** Db
An Hoa **19** Ee
Anhui (prov.) **16** Ed
Anina **6** EFd
Aniva **17** GHa
Aniva, mys- **16** Ja
Aniva, zaliv- **17** Ha
Aniwa, Île- (i.) **28** map no.4
Anjou (hist. reg.) **8** Cd
Anju **16** Gc
Ankang **16** Cd
Ankara **22** Dc
Ankara (riv.) **22** Dbc
Ankaratra **26** map no.1
Ankazoabo **26** map no.1
Anklam **5** Db
Ankober **25** Dcd
An Loc **19** Ef
Ann, Cape- **42** grid square no.2
Anna [Nauru] **27** map no.2
Anna [Russia] **12** EFc
Anna, Pulo- (i.) **27** Bb
Annaba **24** Ca
An Najaf **21** Cc
Annam (phys. reg.) **19** Eef
Anna Point **27** map no.2
Annapolis **32** Db
Annapurna (mt.) **20** Fc
Ann Arbor **32** Ca
An Nāsirīyah **21** Dc
Annecy **8** FGe
Anniston **32** Cb
Annobón (i.) **23** Cf
Annonay **8** Fe
An Nuqub **21** Dfg
Ánō Viánnos **11** Ff
Anpu **16** CDf
Anqing **16** Ed
Anşāb **21** Cd
Ansbach **5** Cd
Anshan **16** Fb
Anshun **16** Ce
Ansongo **24** BCc
Antakya **22** Fd
Antalaha **26** map no.1
Antalya **22** Cd
Antalya Körfezi **22** Cd
Antananarivo (Tananarive) **23** GHgh
Antarctica **42** grid square no.1
Antarctic Peninsula **42** grid square no.1
Antequera **9** Cd
Anti-Atlas (mts.) **24** Bab
Antibes **8** Gf
Antibes, Cap d'- (cap.) **8** Gf
Anticosti, Île d'- (i.) **31** Icd
Antigua (i.) **35** Db
Antigua and Barbuda (Ind. St.) **35** Db
Antigua Guatemala **35** Ab
Antilebanon (mts.) **22** Fef
Antilla **35** Ca
Antioche, Pertuis d'- (str.) **8** Cd
Antipodes Islands **27** DEe
Ántissa **11** Fd
Antofagasta **39** Ab
Antofagasta de la Sierra **39** Bb
Antofalla, Salar de- (s. m.) **39** Bb
Antongil, Baie d'- **26** map no.1
Antsirabe **23** GHgh
Antsiranana **23** GHg
Antsohihy **26** map no.1
Antwerp **8** Fb
An Uaimh / Navan **7** CDe
Anxi **15** Def
Anyang **16** DEc
A'nyêmaqên Shan (mts.) **16** ABcd
Anžero-Sudžensk **13** HId
Anzio **10** Dd
Anžu, ostrova- **14** GHb
Aoba, Île- (i.) **28** map no.4
Aoga-Shima (i.) **17** Fh
Aomori **16** IJb
Aosta **10** Ab
Aoulef **24** Cb
Apalachicola **32** Cc
Apaporis (riv.) **37** Bbc
Apąrri **18** Fa
Apatin **6** Dd
Apatzingán **34** Bc
Api (mt.) **20** Fbc
Apia **28** Ac
Apiaú, Serra do- (mts.) **37** Cb
Apo, Mount- **18** FGc
Apolda **5** Cc
Apollonia **24** Ea
Aporé (riv.) **39** Ca
Apoteri **37** Db
Appalachian Mountains **32** CDab
Appennino Abruzzese **10** Dc
Appennino Calabro **10** Fe
Appennino Ligure **10** Bb
Appennino Lucano **10** EFde
Appennino Tosco-Emiliano **10** Cbc
Appleton **32** BCa
Apucarana **39** Cb
Apure (riv.) **37** Cb
Apurimac (riv.) **37** Bd
Apuseni, Munţii- **6** Fc
'Aqaba **21** Bd
Aqaba, Gulf of- **22** Fh
Aquidauana **39** Cb
Aquila, L'- **10** Dc
'Arab, Baḩr al- (riv.) **25** Ccd
'Arabab, Wādī al- (riv.) **22** Eg
Arabian Sea **20** BCef
Araç **22** Db
Aracaju **38** Dc
Aracati **38** Db
Araçatuba **39** CDb
Aracena, Sierra de- (mts.) **9** Bd
Araçuaí **39** Da
Arad **6** Ec
Arafura Sea **27** Bc
Aragón (phys. reg.) **9** Eab
Aragón (riv.) **9** Ea
Araguacema **38** BCb
Araguaia (riv.) **38** Bc
Araguaiana **39** Ca
Araguari **39** Da
Araguari (riv.) **38** Ba
Araguatins **38** Cb
Araioses **38** Cb
Arak **24** Cb
Arāk **21** DEc
Arakan Yoma **19** Bde
Araks (riv.) **21** Db
Aral Sea **13** EFe
Aralsk **13** Fe
Aramac **29** GHc
Aranda de Duero **9** Db
Aran Island (i.) **7** Bd
Aran Isles **7** ABe
Aranjuez **9** Dbc
Aranyaprathet **19** Df
Araouane **24** Bc
Arapiraca **38** Dbc
Araranguá **39** Db
Araras, Serra das- (mts.) **39** Ca
Ararat **29** Gf
Ararat (Büyük Ağri daği) (mt.) **13** De
Arari **38** Cb
Araripe, Chapada do- (mts.) **38** CDb
Araripina **38** CDb
Aras (riv.) **21** Db
Arauca (riv.) **37** Cb
Arauca **37** Bb
Arauco **39** Ac
Arawalli Range **20** Dcd
Araxá **39** Dab
Arba, L'- **9** Gd
Arbaj-Here **14** De
Arboga **4** Cd
Arbroath **7** EFc
Arcachon **8** Ce
Arcadia (hist. reg.) **11** DEe
Archidona **9** CDd
Arciz **6** Icd
Arco **10** Cb

Bed - Big

Big - Bor

Bighorn Mountains 33 Cb
Big Island 31 Hb
Big River 31 Ec
Big Spring 33 Cc
Bihać 6 Bd
Bihar (State) 20 FGc
Bihar 20 Gcd
Biharamulo 26 Cb
Bihoro 17 Ic
Bija (riv.) 13 Hd
Bijagos Islands 24 Ac
Bijapur 20 Ee
Bijauri 19 Hi
Bijeljina 6 Dd
Bijie 16 Ce
Bijsk 13 Hd
Bikaner 20 Dc
Bikin (riv.) 16 Hla
Bikin 14 Ge
Bikini Atoll 27 Db
Bikljan 12 Hb
Bikoro 26 Ab
Bilaspur 20 Fd
Bilauktaung Range 19 Cf
Bilbao 9 Da
Bilbays 22 Cg
Bileća 11 Cb
Bilecik 22 BCb
Bílé Karpaty (mts.) 5 FGd
Bilin 19 Ce
Billings 33 Cb
Bill of Portland 7 EFf
Bilma 24 Dc
Biloela 29 Hlc
Bilo gora (mts.) 6 Ccd
Biloxi 32 Cb
Biltine 25 Cc
Bina 20 Ed
Binalud, Kuh– e– (mt.) 21 Fb
Binboğa dağ (mts.) 22 Fcd
Bingen 5 ABcd
Binghamton 32 Da
Bingöl 21 Cb
Binhai 16 EFd
Binjai 18 Ad
Binongko, Pulau– (i.) 18 Ff
Bintuhan 18 Be
Bintulu 18 Dd
Bío Bío, Río– (riv.) 39 Ac
Biograd na Moru 6 Bde
Bioko 24 Cd
Biqā', Al– (phys. reg.) 22 EFef
Bi'r, Al– 21 Bd
Birāk 24 Db
Bi'r al Wa'r 24 Db
Birao 25 Ccd
Biratnagar 19 Ij
Bîr Damdûm 22 Ag
Birdsville 29 FGd
Birdum 29 Cb
Birecik 22 Gd
Bireuen 18 Ac
Birganj 20 FGc
Birjand 21 FGc
Birjusa (riv.) 14 Cd
Birk, Al– 21 Cf
Birkenhead 7 Ee
Bîrlad 6 Hlc
Birlad (riv.) 6 Hcd
Birmingham [U.K.] 7 Fe
Birmingham [U.S.] 32 Cb
Birmitrapur 19 Ik

Birnin Kebbi 24 Cc
Birni Nkonni 24 Cc
Birobidžan 14 Ge
Birpur 19 Ij
Birr 7 BCe
Bi'r Safājah 25 Db
Birsk 13 Ed
Bîr Tarfâwi 25 Cb
Biržai 4 Fd
Bisa, Pulau– (i.) 18 Ge
Bisbee 33 BCc
Biscay, Bay of– 8 BCef
Bisceglie 10 Fd
Bischofshofen 5 De
Bîshah, Wādī– 21 Cf
Bishnupur 19 Ik
Biškek (Frunze) 13 Ge
Biskra 24 Ca
Bismarck 33 CDb
Bismarck Archipelago 27 Cc
Bissau 24 Ac
Bissett 31 Fc
Bistrița 6 Gc
Bistrița (riv.) 6 Gc
Bitam 24 Dd
Bitlis 21 Cb
Bitola 11 Dc
Bitonto 10 Fd
Bitterfontein 23 Di
Bitterroot Range 33 Bb
Biu 24 Dc
Biwa–Ko 16 Ic
Biyad, Al– (phys. reg.) 21 De
Bochum 5 Ac
Biyalā 22 Cg
Bizerte 24 CDa
Bjala Slatina 11 Eb
Bjargtangar (cap.) 4 map no.1
Bjelovar 6 Ccd
Bjerkreim 4 Ad
Bjuröklubb (cap.) 4 Eb
Blackall 29 Hc
Blackburn 7 Ee
Black Forest (mts.) 5 ABde
Black Hills 33 Cb
Blackpool 7 Ee
Black River 19 Dd
Black Sea 13 Ce
Black Volta (riv.) 24 Bcd
Blackwater (riv.) 7 Be
Blackwood River 29 Be
Blagodarny 12 Fd
Blagojevgrad 11 Ebc
Blagoveščensk [Russia] 14 FGd
Blagoveščensk [Russia] 12 Hlb
Blair Athol 29 Hc
Blaj 6 FGc
Blanc, Cap– [Mtna.] 24 Ab
Blanc, Cap– [Tun.] 24 CDa
Blanc, Le– 8 Dd
Blanc, Mont– 10 Ab
Blanca, Bahía– (b.) 39 BCcd
Blanca, Cordillera– (mts.) 37 Bc
Blanca, Costa– 9 Ec
Blanca Peak 33 Cc
Blanche, Lake– 29 FGd
Blanco, Cape– 33 Ab
Blanc–Sablon 31 IJc
Blanquilla, Isla– (i.) 35 Db
Blantyre 26 Cc
Blåvands Huk (cap.) 5 ABa

Blaye 8 Ce
Bloemfontein 23 Eh
Blois 8 Dd
Błonie 5 Hb
Bluefield 32 Cb
Bluefields 35 Bb
Blue Mountains 33 Bb
Blue Nile 25 Dc
Blue Ridge 32 Cb
Blumenau 39 Db
Blyth 7 Fd
Blythe 33 Bc
Blytheville 32 BCb
Bo 24 Ad
Boac 18 Fb
Bo'ai 16 Dc
Boano, Pulau– (i.) 18 Ge
Boa Vista 37 Cb
Bobbio 10 Bb
Bobo Dioulasso 24 Bc
Bóbr (riv.) 5 Ec
Bobriki (Novomoskovsk) 13 CDd
Bobrka 6 Gb
Bobrujsk 13 BCd
Bôca do Acre 37 Cc
Bôca do Jari 38 Bb
Bôca do Moaco 37 Cc
Boca Grande (riv. m.) 37 CDb
Bocas del Toro 35 Bc
Bochnia 5 Hd
Bocholt 5 Ac
Bochum 5 Ac
Bocșa 6 Ed
Böda 4 Dd
Bodajbo 14 Ed
Bodélé (phys. reg.) 25 Ac
Boden 4 Eb
Bodmin 7 Df
Bodø 4 Cb
Bodrum 22 ABd
Boende 25 Cde
Boffa 24 Ac
Bogalusa 32 BCb
Bogan River 29 He
Bogatynia 5 Ec
Boğazlıyan 22 Ec
Bogdanović 12 Jb
Bogor 18 Cf
Bogorodick 12 Ec
Bogorodsk 12 Fb
Bogra 19 Jj
Bogué 24 Ac
Bo Hai (b.) 16 EFc
Bohemia (phys. reg.) 5 DEcd
Bohemian Forest (mts.) 5 DEd
Bohol (i.) 18 Fbc
Boiaçu 37 Cc
Bois (i.) 39 CDa
Doise 33 Bb
Bojador, Cabo– 24 Ab
Bojnurd 21 Fb
Boké 24 Ac
Boknafjorden (b.) 4 Ad
Bokspits 26 Bd
Bolama 24 Ac
Bolbec 8 Dc
Bolehov 6 Fb
Bolesławiec 5 Ec
Bolgatanga 24 Bcd
Bolgrad 6 Id
Boli 16 Ha

Boliden 4 DEb
Bolinao 18 Ea
Boliohertu (mt.) 18 Fd
Bolívar, Pico– (mt.) 37 Bb
Bolivia (Ind. St.) 36 De
Bolivia, Altiplano de– 38 Acd
Bolkar dağları (mts.) 22 Ed
Bollnäs 4 Dc
Bollon 29 Hd
Boločanka 14 Cb
Bologna 10 Cb
Bologne 8 Fc
Bologoje 12 Db
Bol'šaja Ussurka (riv.) 16 Hla
Bolsena, Lago di– 10 Cc
Bol'ševik, ostrov– 41 grid square no.4
Bolšój Anjuj (riv.) 14 Jc
Bol'šoj Begičev, ostrov– 14 Eb
Bolsoj Jenisej (riv.) 14 Cd
Bolsoj Ljahovski, ostrov– (i.) 14 Hlb
Bol'šoj Uzen (riv.) 12 Gd
Bolton 7 Ee
Bolu 22 Cb
Bolzano 10 Ca
Boma 26 Ab
Bombala 29 Hlf
Bombay 15 Ch
Bom Comércio 37 Cc
Bom Despacho 39 Da
Bomili 26 Ba
Bom Jesus 38 Cb
Bom Jesus da Lapa 38 Cc
Bon, Cape– 24 Da
Bonaire (i.) 35 Db
Bonaparte Archipelago 29 CDa
Bonavista 31 Jd
Bonda 26 Ab
Bondo 25 Cd
Bondowoso 18 Df
Bone → Watampone 18 EFe
Bone, Teluk– 18 Fef
Bongor 25 Bcd
Bonifacio 8 map no.1
Bonifacio, Strait of– 10 Bd
Bonin Islands 27 Ca
Bonn 5 Ac
Bontoc 18 Fa
Bonyhád 6 Dc
Boosaaso 25 EFc
Boothia Gulf 31 FGab
Boothia Peninsula 31 Fa
Booué 26 Aab
Bophuthatswana (hist. reg.) 26 Bd
Bor [Russia] 12 Fb
Bor [Sud.] 25 Dd
Bor [Tur.] 22 Ed
Bor [Yugo.] 6 Fd
Borah Peak 33 Bb
Borås 4 Cd
Borāzjān 21 DEd
Borba 37 CDc
Borcea, Bratul– (riv.) 6 Hd
Bordeaux 8 Ce
Borden Peninsula 31 Ga
Bordertown 29 FGf
Bordj Omar Driss 24 Cb
Borgå 4 Fc
Borgarnes 4 map no.1
Børgefjell (mt.) 4 Cb

© ISTITUTO GEOGRAFICO DE AGOSTINI - Novara

133

Bor - Bun

Borger 33 Cc
Borgholm 4 Dd
Borgomanero 10 Bb
Borislav 5 Id
Borisoglebsk 13 Dd
Borisov 5 Ka
Borispol 12 Dc
Borja 37 Bc
Borkou (phys. reg.) 25 BCc
Borlänge 4 Cc
Borlu 22 Bc
Borneo (Kalimantan) (i.) 18 DEd
Bornholm (i.) 4 CDe
Bornholmsgatten (str.) 4 Ce
Bornova 22 Ac
Boromo 24 Bc
Boroviči 12 Db
Borroloola 29 EFb
Borşa 6 Gc
Borščovočny, Hrebet– 14 DEde
Borujerd 21 Dc
Borzja 14 Ed
Bosa 10 Bd
Bosanska Gradiška 6 Cd
Bosanska Krupa 6 Cd
Bosanski Novi 6 Cd
Bosanski Petrovac 6 Cd
Bosansko Grahovo 6 Cd
Bose 16 Cf
Boshan 16 Ec
Bosna (riv.) 6 CDd
Bosnia (phys. reg.) 6 CDd
Bosnia–Herzegovina (Ind. St.) 6 CDde
Bosobolo 26 ABa
Bösö–Hantö 17 Gg
Bosphorus (str.) 22 Bb
Bossangoa 25 Bd
Bossembélé 25 Bd
Bossier City 32 Bb
Bostan 20 Cb
Boston [U.K.] 7 FGe
Boston [U.S.] 32 DEa
Botev (mt.) 11 Fb
Bothnia, Gulf of– 4 DEbc
Botletle (riv.) 26 Bd
Botoşani 6 Hc
Botswana (Ind. St.) 23 Eh
Botucatu 39 Db
Bouaké 24 Bd
Bouar 25 Bd
Bouârfa 24 Ba
Bouca 25 Bd
Boudouaou 24 Ca
Boufarik 9 Gd
Bougainville Island 27 Cc
Bougouni 24 Bc
Bouguenais 8 Cd
Boulder 33 Cbc
Boulia 29 FGc
Boulogne–sur–Mer 8 Db
Bouna 24 Bd
Boundiali 24 Bd
Boundji 24 De
Bountiful 33 Bb
Bounty Islands 27 DEe
Bourail 28 map no.4
Bourbonnais (hist. reg.) 8 Ed
Bourem 24 BCc
Bourg–en–Bresse 8 Fd
Bourges 8 Ed

Bourg–lès–Valence 8 Fe
Bourgogne, Canal de– 8 Fd
Bourg–Saint–Maurice 8 Ge
Bourke 29 GHde
Bournemouth 7 Ff
Bou–Saada 24 Ca
Bousso 25 Bc
Boutilimit 24 Ac
Bow (riv.) 33 Ba
Bowen 29 Hbc
Bowling Green 32 Cb
Bowmore 7 Cd
Boxian 16 Ed
Bozburun 11 He
Bozcaada (i.) 22 Ac
Bozdağ (mt.) 22 Bc
Bozeman 33 BCb
Bozhen 16 Ec
Bozkır 22 Dd
Bozoum 25 Bd
Bozüyük 22 Cbc
Bra 10 Ab
Brač (i.) 11 Bb
Bracciano, Lago di– 10 Dc
Bräcke 4 CDc
Brad 6 Fc
Bradford 7 EFe
Braga 9 Ab
Bragado 39 Bc
Bragança [Braz.] 38 Cb
Bragança [Port.] 9 Bb
Brahmani (riv.) 20 FGd
Brahmaputra (Maquan He) (riv.) 20 GHc
Brahmaputra (Yarlung Zangbo Jiang) 20 GHc
Brăila 6 Hd
Brainerd 32 Ba
Brake 5 Bb
Branco, Rio– (riv.) 37 Cbc
Brandberg (mt.) 26 Ad
Brandenburg 5 Db
Brandenburg (hist. reg.) 5 Db
Brandon 31 EFcd
Braniewo 5 GHa
Bransfield Strait 42 grid square no.1
Brasiléia 37 Bd
Brasilia 39 Da
Braşov 6 GHd
Bratislava 5 Fd
Bratsk 14 CDd
Bratskoje vodohranilišče 14 Dd
Braunau am Inn 5 Dd
Braunschweig 5 BCb
Brava, Costa– 9 Db
Bravo, Rio– (riv.) 34 Bb
Bray (hist. reg.) 8 DEc
Brazil (Ind. St.) 36 DFde
Brazilian Highlands 39 Da
Brazos (riv.) 32 Bb
Brazzaville 26 Ab
Brčko 6 Dd
Brdy (mt.) 5 Dd
Breakfast Island 28 map no.3
Breaza 6 Gd
Břeclav 5 Fd
Brecon 7 Ef
Breda 8 Fb
Bredasdorp 23 Ei
Bredy 12 Jc
Bregalnica (riv.) 11 Ec

Bregenz 5 BCe
Breidafjördur (g.) 4 map no.1
Bremen 5 Bb
Bremerhaven 5 Bb
Bremerton 33 Ab
Brenham 32 Bbc
Brenne (phys. reg.) 8 Dd
Brennero (p.) 10 Ca
Breno 10 Cb
Brenta (riv.) 10 Cab
Brescia 10 Cb
Breslav 5 Fc
Bressanone / Brixen 10 Ca
Bressuire 8 CDd
Brest [Bela.] 5 IJb
Brest [Fr.] 8 Ac
Breton, Pertuis– (str.) 8 Cd
Breueh, Pulau– (i.) 18 Ac
Breves 38 BCb
Brewarrina 29 Hde
Bria 25 Cd
Briançon 8 Ge
Briare 8 Ed
Bričany 6 Hb
Bridgeport 32 Da
Bridgetown 29 Be
Bridgwater 7 Ef
Bridlington 7 FGd
Brie (phys. reg.) 8 Ec
Brig 10 ABa
Brighton 7 FGf
Brijuni 6 Ad
Brilon 5 Bc
Brindisi 10 Fd
Brisbane 29 Id
Bristol 7 Ef
Bristol Channel 7 DEf
British Columbia (prov.) 31 Cc
Brittany (phys. reg.) 8 BCcd
Brive–la–Gaillarde 8 De
Briviesca 9 Da
Brixen / Bressanone 10 Ca
Brixlegg 5 CDe
Brjansk 13 Cd
Brno 5 Fd
Broad Sound 29 Hlc
Brocken (mt.) 5 Cc
Brockman, Mount– 29 Bc
Brodeur Peninsula 31 Ga
Brodnica 5 Gb
Brody 12 BCcd
Broken Hill 29 Ge
Broken Hill – Kabwe 26 Bc
Brokopondo 37 Db
Bron 8 Fe
Brønnøysund 4 Cb
Bronte 10 Ef
Brookings 32 Ba
Brooks Range 41 grid square no.2
Brookton 29 Be
Broome 29 Cb
Brothers, The– (i.) 21 Eg
Brownsville 32 Bc
Brownwood 32 Bb
Browse Island 29 Ca
Bruay–en–Artois 8 Eb
Bruce, Mount– 29 Bc
Bruck an der Leitha 5 Fde
Bruck an der Mur 5 Ee
Brugge 8 Eb
Brumado 39 Da
Brunei (Ind. St.) 15 Di

Brunsbüttel 5 Ba
Brunswick 32 CDb
Brunswick, Península de– 40 Ac
Bruny Island 29 map no.1
Brussel / Bruxelles 8 Fb
Bruxelles / Brussel 8 Fb
Bryan 32 Bb
Brza Palanka 6 Fd
Brzeg 5 Fc
Buada Lagoon 27 map no.2
Buala 27 Cc
Bučač 6 Gb
Bucak 22 Cd
Bucaramanga 36 CDc
Buchanan 24 ABd
Buchans 31 Jd
Bucharest 6 Hd
Buckingham Bay 29 Fa
Budapest 6 Dc
Budardalur 4 map no.1
Budaun 20 EFc
Budd Coast 42 grid square no.4
Bude 7 Df
Budennovsk 3 Hc
Búdir 4 map no.1
Budjala 25 BCd
Budogošč 12 Db
Budva 11 Cb
Buea 24 Cd
Buena Esperanza 39 Bc
Buenaventura 36 BCc
Buenos Aires [Arg.] 39 BCc
Buenos Aires [Pan.] 35 map no.1
Buenos Aires, Lago– 40 ABb
Buffalo [N.Y.–U.S.] 32 Da
Buffalo [Tx.–U.S.] 32 Bb
Buffalo [Wy.–U.S.] 33 Cb
Bug (riv.) 5 Jc
Buga 37 Bb
Bugsuk (i.) 18 Ec
Bugulma 12 Hc
Buguruslan 12 Hc
Buhara 13 Ff
Buhayrat al–Assad (l.) 22 Fde
Builth Wells 7 Ee
Buinsk 12 Gbc
Buir–Nur (l.) 16 Ea
Buj 13 Dd
Bujalance 9 CDd
Bujumbura 26 Bb
Bukačača 14 Ed
Bukama 26 Bb
Bukavu 26 Bb
Bukit Mertajam 19 Dgh
Bukittinggi 18 ABde
Bükk 6 Ebc
Bukoba 25 De
Bukovina (hist. reg.) 6 GHbc
Bula 18 He
Bulan 18 Fb
Bulandshahr 19 Gi
Bulawayo 23 Egh
Buldan 22 Bc
Bulgan 14 De
Bulgaria (Ind. St.) 3 Fc
Bullfinch 29 Be
Bulloo River 29 Gd
Bumba 25 Cd
Bumbah, Al– 24 Ea
Buna 26 CDa

Čerlak **13** Gd
Čermoz **12** HIb
Černiahov **6** Ia
Černigov **13** BCd
Černjahovsk **12** Bc
Černogorsk **14** Cd
Černomorskoje **12** Dd
Černovcy **6** GHb
Černyševski **14** Ec
Cerritos **34** BCb
Cerro de Pasco **37** Bd
Čerski **14** Jc
Čerskogo Hrebet **14** GHc
Červen brjag **11** Fb
Cervera **9** Fb
Červonograd **6** FGa
Cesarea (r.) **22** Ef
Cesena **10** Db
Cēsis **4** Fd
České-Budějovice **5** Ed
Ceskomoravská Vrchovina (mts.) **5** EFd
Çeşme **22** Ac
Cessnock **29** Ie
Cettigne **11** Cb
Ceuta **24** Ba
Cévennes (mts.) **8** EFef
Cevizli dağı (mt.) **22** ABc
Ceyhan **22** EFd
Ceyhan (riv.) **22** Ed
Ceylon → Srī Lanka (Ind. St.) **15** Ci
Chacao, Canal de- (str.) **40** Ab
Chachapoyas **37** Bc
Chacorão, Cachoeira- **38** Bb
Chad (Ind. St.) **23** DEd
Chad, Lake- **25** Bc
Chadileuvú (riv.) **39** Bc
Chadron **33** Cb
Chāgai Hills **20** Bc
Chaghcharān **20** BCb
Chagos Archipelago **15** Ci
Chahbahar **21** FGde
Chaibasa **19** Ik
Chake Chake **26** CDb
Chakradharpur **19** Ik
Chala **39** Aa
Chalbi Desert **26** Ca
Chalcidice **11** Ec
Chalhuanca **37** Bd
Challapata **39** Ba
Chalna **19** Jk
Châlons-sur-Marne **8** Fc
Châlon-sur-Saône **8** Fd
Cham **5** Dd
Chamalières **8** Ee
Chaman **20** Cb
Chamba **16** Bd
Chambal (riv.) **20** Ec
Chamberlain **32** Ba
Chambéry **8** Fe
Chambeshi (riv.) **26** Cbc
Champagne (hist. reg.) **8** EFcd
Champagne (phys. reg.) **8** EFcd
Champerico **35** Ab
Champigny-sur-Marne **8** Ec
Champlain, Lake- **32** Da
Champotón **34** Cc
Chan, Ko- (i.) **19** Cg
Chañaral **39** Ab
Chan Chan (r.) **37** Bc
Chanda **20** EFde
Chandigarh **20** Eb
Chandil **19** Ik
Chandpur **20** Hd
Chang, Ko- (i.) **19** Df
Changbai Shan (mts.) **16** Gb
Changchun **16** FGb
Changde **16** De
Changhua **16** EFf
Changjiang **16** Cg
Changli **16** EFc
Changsha **15** Dg
Changzhi **16** Dc
Changzhou **16** EFd
Channel Islands [U.K.] **8** Bc
Channel Islands [U.S.] **33** ABc
Channel-Port-aux-Basques **31** Jd
Channel Tunnel (dam) **7** GHf
Chanthaburi **19** Df
Chanute **32** Bb
Chao'an **16** Ef
Chao Phraya (riv.) **19** Def
Chaor He (riv.) **16** Fa
Chaoyang [China] **16** Ef
Chaoyang [China] **16** EFb
Chapadinha **38** Cb
Chapala, Lago de- **34** Bb
Chapleau **32** Ca
Chapra **20** Fc
Charadai **39** BCb
Charaña **39** Ba
Charcas **34** Bb
Charcot Island **42** grid square no.1
Charente (riv.) **8** CDe
Chari (riv.) **25** Bc
Charikar **20** CDab
Charité-sur-Loire, La- **8** Ed
Chariton **32** Ba
Charity **37** Db
Charleroi **8** Fb
Charleston [S.C.-U.S.] **32** CDb
Charleston [W.V.-U.S.] **32** CDb
Charleville **29** Hd
Charleville-Mézières **8** EFc
Charlotte **32** CDb
Charlottesville **32** Db
Charlottetown **31** Id
Charters Towers **29** GHc
Chartres **8** Dc
Chascomús **39** Cc
Châteaubriant **8** Cd
Château-du-Loir **8** Dd
Châteaudun **8** Dc
Château-Gontier **8** Cd
Château-Renault **8** Dd
Châteauroux **8** DEd
Château-Thierry **8** Ec
Châtellerault **8** CDd
Chatham [N.B.-Can.] **32** Ea
Chatham [Ont.-Can.] **32** Ca
Chatham [U.K.] **7** Gf
Chatham Island (i.) **27** Ee
Chatham Islands **28** Ae
Châtillon-sur-Seine **8** Fd
Châtre, La- **8** DEd
Chattahoochee (riv.) **32** Cb
Chattanooga **32** Cb
Chaumont **8** Fc
Chauny **8** Ec
Chaux-de-Fonds, La- **5** Ae
Chaves [Braz.] **38** BCb
Chaves [Port.] **9** Bb
Cheb **5** Dcd
Checheno-Ingush (Aut. Rep.) **13** De
Cheduba (i.) **19** Be
Cheju **16** Gd
Cheju-Do (i.) **16** FGd
Cheju-Haehyŏp **16** Gd
Cheliff **24** BCa
Chełm **5** Ic
Chełmno **5** Gb
Chelmsford **7** Gf
Chełmża **5** Gb
Cheltenham **7** EFf
Chemnitz **5** Dc
Chemult **33** Ab
Chenab (riv.) **20** Eb
Chengde **16** Eb
Chengdu **16** Bd
Chenxian **16** De
Chepo **35** Cc
Cher (riv.) **8** Ede
Cherbourg **8** Cc
Cherchell **9** FGd
Chesapeake Bay **32** Db
Chester **7** Ee
Chesterfield **7** Fe
Chesterfield, Iles- **27** Cc
Chesterfield Inlet **31** FGb
Chesterfield Inlet (str.) **31** Fb
Chetumal **34** Dc
Chetumal, Bahía de- **34** Dc
Cheviot, The- (mt.) **7** EFd
Cheyenne (riv.) **33** Cb
Cheyenne **33** Cb
Chhatarpur **19** Gj
Chi (riv.) **18** Ba
Chiang Mai **19** Ce
Chiang Rai **19** CDde
Chianje **26** Ac
Chiari **10** Bb
Chiavari **10** Bb
Chiavenna **10** Ba
Chiayi **16** EFf
Chiba **17** Gg
Chibougamau **31** Hcd
Chicago **32** Ca
Chichagof Island **31** Bc
Chichaoua **24** ABa
Chichén Itzá (r.) **34** Db
Chichester **7** Ff
Chichibu **17** Ffg
Chickasha **32** Bb
Chiclayo **36** BCd
Chico **33** Ac
Chico, Río- (riv.) **40** Bb
Chicomo **26** Cd
Chicoutimi **31** HId
Chiemsee **5** Dde
Chieti **10** Ec
Chifeng **16** Eb
Chifre, Serra do- (mts.) **39** Da
Chihuahua **30** Hg
Chilas **20** Da
Childers **29** Id
Chile (Ind. St.) **36** CDfg
Chilecito **39** Bb
Chilia, Bratul- (riv.) **6** Id
Chilibre **35** map no.1
Chilivani **10** Bd
Chillagoe **29** Gb
Chillán **39** Ac
Chiloé, Isla de- **40** Ab
Chilpancingo de los Bravos **34** Cc
Chimanimani **26** Ccd
Chimborazo, Volcán- (mt.) **37** Bc
Chimbote **37** Bc
Chimoio **26** Cc
Chin (State) **19** Bd
China (Ind. St.) **15** Df
Chinandega **35** Bb
Chincha, Islas de- (is.) **37** Bd
Chincha Alta **37** Bd
Chinchilla **29** HId
Chinchilla de Monte Aragón **9** Ec
Chinde **26** Cc
Chindwin (riv.) **19** Bd
Chingola **26** Bc
Chinguetti **24** Ab
Chinhae **17** Ag
Chinhoyi **26** BCc
Chiniot **20** Db
Chinju **16** Gc
Chinmen Quemoy **16** Ef
Chinon **8** CDd
Chinsura **19** IJk
Chioggia **10** Db
Chios (i.) **22** Ac
Chipata **26** Cc
Chiquinquirá **37** Bb
Chira (riv.) **37** Ac
Chiriquí, Golfo de- **35** Bc
Chirripó, Cerro- (mt.) **35** Bc
Chişinău (Kišinev) **13** BCe
Chitato **26** Ab
Chitipa **26** Cb
Chitorgarh **20** DEcd
Chitose **17** GHc
Chitradurga **20** DEf
Chitral **20** Da
Chitré **35** Bc
Chittagong **15** CDg
Chittoor **20** Ef
Chivasso **10** Ab
Chivay **39** Aa
Chivhu **26** Cc
Chivilcoy **39** BCc
Chodzież **5** Fb
Choele Choel **39** Bc
Choix **34** Bb
Chojnice **5** Fb
Chojnów **5** EFc
Chōkai-San (mt.) **17** FGe
Cholet **8** Cd
Choiseul Island **27** Cc
Choluteca **35** Bb
Choma **26** Bc
Chomo Lhari (mt.) **19** Jij
Chomutov **5** DEc
Chone **37** ABc
Ch'ŏngjin **14** FGe
Chŏngju **16** FGc
Ch'ŏngju **16** Gc
Chongqing **15** Dg
Chŏnju **16** Gc
Chonos, Archipiélago de los- (is.) **40** Ab
Chorrera, La- **35** BCc

Chorzów 5 Gc
Chōshi 16 Jc
Chos Malal 39 ABc
Choszczno 5 EFb
Christchurch 27 De
Christmas → Kiritimati 28 Bb
Christmas Island 18 Cg
Chrudim 5 EFd
Chubut (riv.) 40 Bb
Chūgoku–Sanchi 17 BDg
Chukchi Peninsula 14 Lc
Chukchi Sea 14 Lc
Chulucanas 37 ABc
Chumbicha 39 Bb
Chumphon 19 CDf
Ch'unchŏn 16 Gc
Ch'ungmu 17 Ag
Chuŏr Phnum Krävanah 19 Df
Chuquibamba 39 Aa
Chuquicamata 39 ABb
Chur 5 Be
Churchill 31 Fc
Churchill [Alta.–Can.] (riv.) 31 Ec
Churchill [Newf.–Can.] (riv.) 31 Ic
Churchill Peak 31 Cc
Churk 19 Hj
Churu 20 Dc
Churuguara 37 BCa
Chuvash (Aut. Rep.) 13 Dd
Chuxiong 16 Bef
Cianjur 18 Cf
Cide 22 Db
Ciechanów 5 Hb
Ciechanowiec 5 HIb
Ciego de Ávila 35 BCa
Ciénaga 37 Ba
Cienfuegos 35 Ba
Cieszyn 5 Gd
Cieza 9 Ec
Čiganak 13 Ge
Ciguela (riv.) 9 Dc
Cihanbeyli 22 Dc
Cilacap 18 Cf
Cilician Gates (p.) 22 Ed
Cimarron (riv.) 32 Bb
Čimbaj 13 EFe
Čimkent → Šimkent 13 FGe
Cimljansk 12 Fd
Cimljanskoje vodohranilišče 12 Fd
Cimone, Monte– 10 Cb
Cimpia Turzii 6 Fc
Cîmpina 6 GHd
Cîmpulung 6 Gd
Cîmpulung Moldovenesc 6 Gc
Cinca (riv.) 9 Fb
Cincinnati 32 Cb
Cindrelu, Vîrful– (mt.) 6 Fd
Çine 11 GHe
Čingirlau 12 Hc
Cinto, Monte– 8 map no.1
Ciotat, La– 8 Ff
Circeo, Monte– 10 Dd
Čirčik 13 FGe
Circle 31 Ab
Cirebon 18 Cf
Cirò Marina 10 Fe
Čirpan 11 Fb
C.I.S. → Commonwealth of Independent States 15 BDd
Cisa, Passo della– 10 Bb

Cisco 32 Bb
Ciskei (hist. reg.) 26 Be
Cisnădie 6 Gd
Cisne, Islas del– 35 Bb
Čistopol 13 Ed
Čita 14 Ed
Citlaltépetl (mt.) 34 Cc
Citrusdal 26 ABe
Cittanova 10 Fe
Ciucaşu, Vîrful– (mt.) 6 GHd
Ciudad Acuña 34 Bb
Ciudad Altamirano 34 Bc
Ciudad Bolívar 37 Cb
Ciudad Camargo 34 Bb
Ciudad Cuauhtémoc 34 Bb
Ciudad del Carmen 34 Cc
Ciudad Delicias 34 Bb
Ciudad de Río Grande 34 Bb
Ciudadela 9 GHbc
Ciudad Guayana 37 Cb
Ciudad Guerrero 34 Bb
Ciudad Juárez 34 Ba
Ciudad Madero 34 Cb
Ciudad Mante 34 Cb
Ciudad Obregón 34 ABb
Ciudad Piar 37 Cb
Ciudad Real 9 CDc
Ciudad Rodrigo 9 Bb
Ciudad Valles 34 Cb
Ciudad Victoria 34 Cb
Civita Castellana 10 Dc
Civitanova Marche 10 Dc
Civitavecchia 10 Cc
Civray 8 Dd
Çivril 22 Bc
Cizre 21 Cb
Clacton–on–Sea 7 GHf
Claire, Lake– 31 Dc
Clamecy 8 Ed
Claremorris 7 Be
Clarence Strait 29 DEa
Clarines 37 Cb
Clarión (i.) 30 Gh
Clark Fork (riv.) 33 Bb
Clarksville 32 Cb
Clearwater, Lake– 31 Hc
Clermont 29 Hc
Clermont–Ferrand 8 Ee
Cleveland [Oh.–U.S.] 32 CDa
Cleveland [Tn.–U.S.] 32 Cb
Cleveland, Mount– 33 Bb
Cleveland Hills 7 Fd
Clifden 7 ABe
Clipperton, Île– (i.) 30 Hhi
Clisham (mt.) 7 Cb
Clonakilty 7 Bf
Cloncurry 29 FGc
Clonmel 7 Ce
Cloppenburg 5 Bb
Clorinda 39 Cb
Cloud Peak 33 Cb
Clovis 33 Cc
Cluj Napoca 6 Fc
Cluny 8 Fd
Clyde 31 Ia
Clyde (riv.) 7 Ed
Clyde, Firth of– (b.) 7 Dd
Cna (riv.) 12 Fc
Cnossus (r.) 11 Ff
Côa (riv.) 9 Bb
Coari (riv.) 37 Cc
Coari 37 Cc
Coast Mountains 31 BCab

Coast Ranges 33 Abc
Coats Island 30 Jc
Coats Land 42 grid square no.1
Coatzacoalcos (Puerto México) 34 Cc
Cobalt 31 GHd
Cobán 35 ABb
Cobar 29 He
Cobh 7 Bf
Cobija 37 Cd
Cobourg Peninsula 29 Ea
Coburg 5 Cc
Cochabamba (mts.) 39 Ba
Cochabamba, Cordillera de– 39 Ba
Cochem 5 Ac
Cochim 20 DEfg
Cochin China (phys. reg.) 19 Efg
Cochrane 31 GHd
Cocklebiddy 29 De
Coco (riv.) 35 Bb
Coco, Isla del– (i.) 30 Ji
Cocos (i.) 27 map no.1
Cocos Islands [Austl.] 2
Cocos Islands [Mya.] 19 Bf
Cod, Cape– 32 DEa
Codajás 37 Cc
Codlea 6 Gd
Codó 38 Cb
Coen 29 Ga
Coesfeld 5 Abc
Coetivy (i.) 15 Bj
Cœur d'Alene 33 Bb
Coff's Harbour 29 IJe
Cognac 8 Ce
Cogo 26 Aa
Coiba, Isla de– (i.) 35 Bc
Coihaique 40 Ab
Coimbatore 20 Ef
Coímbra 9 Ab
Coín 9 Cd
Coipasa, Salar de– (s. m.) 39 Ba
Čojbalsan 14 Ee
Čokurdah 14 HIb
Colac 29 Gf
Colatina 39 DEab
Colbeck, Cape– 42 grid square no.3
Colchester 7 Gf
Coleraine 7 Cd
Coleroon (riv.) 20 Ef
Colima 34 Bc
Colima, Nevado de– (mt.) 34 Bbc
Colinas 38 Cb
Coll (i.) 7 Cc
Collie 29 Be
Collier Bay 29 Cb
Collinsville 29 Hc
Colmar 8 Gc
Colmenar 9 CDd
Colmenar Viejo 9 Db
Colômbia 39 Bab
Colombia (Ind. St.) 36 CDc
Colombo 15 Ci
Colón [Cuba] 35 Ba
Colón [Pan.] 35 BCc
Colonia del Sacramento 39 Cc
Colonia las Heras 40 Bb
Colonsay (i.) 7 Cc

Colorado (State) 33 Cc
Colorado [Co.–U.S.] (riv.) 33 Bc
Colorado [Tx.–U.S.] (riv.) 33 CDc
Colorado, Río– [Arg.] (riv.) 39 Bb
Colorado, Río– [Arg.] (riv.) 39 Bc
Colorado Plateau 33 BCc
Colorado Springs 33 Cc
Columbia (riv.) 33 ABb
Columbia [S.C.–U.S.] 32 Cb
Columbia [Tn.–U.S.] 32 Cb
Columbia, Cape– 41 grid square no.2
Columbia, District of– (State) 32 Db
Columbretes, Islas– 9 Fbc
Columbus [Ga.–U.S.] 32 Cb
Columbus [In.–U.S.] 32 Cb
Columbus [Nb.–U.S.] 32 Ba
Columbus [Oh.–U.S.] 32 Cb
Colwyn Bay 7 Ee
Comacchio 10 Db
Comacchio, Valli di– (lag.) 10 Db
Coman, Mount– 42 grid square no.1
Comandante Fontana 39 BCb
Comăneşti 6 GHc
Comayagua 35 Bb
Combarbalá 39 Ac
Comilla 20 Hd
Còmiso 10 Ef
Comitán de Dominguez 34 Cc
Commentry 8 Ed
Commercy 8 Fc
Commonwealth of Independent States (C.I.S.) 15 BDd
Como 10 Bb
Como, Lago di– 10 Bab
Comodoro Rivadavia 36 DEh
Comorin, Cape– 20 Eg
Comoros (Ind. St.) 23 Cg
Compiègne 8 Ec
Čona (riv.) 14 Ec
Conakry 24 Ad
Concarneau 8 ABd
Conceição do Araguaia 38 BCb
Concepción [Arg.] 39 Bb
Concepción [Bol.] 39 Ba
Concepción [Chile] 39 Ac
Concepción [Par.] 39 Cb
Concepción del Oro 34 Bb
Concepción del Uruguay 39 BCc
Conchos (riv.) 34 Bb
Concord 32 Da
Concordia 39 Cc
Condamine River 29 HId
Conde 38 Dc
Condobolin 29 Hc
Condom 8 Df
Condor, Cordillera del– (mts.) 37 BC
Congo (Ind. St.) 23 Def
Congo (riv.) 26 Ab
Cong Tum → Kontum 19 Ef
Conn, Lake– 7 Bde
Connaught (prov.) 7 Be

Dewa-Sanchi (mts.) **17** Gde
Dez (riv.) **21** Dc
Dezfūl **21** Dc
Dezhou **16** Ec
Dežneva, mys- **14** LMc
Dhaka **15** CDg
Dhalak Archipelago **25** DEc
Dhalli Rajhara **20** Fde
Dhamar **21** Cg
Dhamtari **20** Fd
Dhanbad **20** Gd
Dhangarhi **19** Hi
Dhankuta **19** Ij
Dharwar **20** DEe
Dhaulagiri (mt.) **20** Fc
Dhidhimótikhon **11** FGc
Dhikti Óros (mt.) **11** Ff
Dhílos (i.) **11** Fe
Dhírfis Óros (mt.) **11** Ed
Dholpur **19** Gj
Dhond **20** DEe
Dhone **20** Ee
Dhonoúsa (i.) **11** FGe
Dhoraji **20** Dd
Dhubri **19** ABc
Dhule **20** DEd
Dhulian **19** IJj
Dhuri **20** Eb
Día (i.) **11** Ff
Diala (riv.) **21** Dbc
Diamante **39** Bc
Diamantina **39** Da
Diamantina, Chapada- (plat.) **38** Cc
Diamantina River **29** Gc
Diamantino **38** Bc
Diamond Harbour **19** Jk
Dianópolis **38** Cc
Dibrugarh **19** BCc
Dibulla **37** Ba
Dickinson **33** Cb
Diefenbaker, Lake- **33** Ca
Diego Garcia (i.) **15** Cj
Diego Ramírez, Islas- **40** ABc
Dien Bien Phu **19** Dd
Diepholz **5** Bb
Dieppe **8** Dc
Digby **31** Id
Digne **8** Ge
Digoin **8** Ed
Digos **18** Gc
Dijon **8** Fd
Dikson **13** Hb
Dikwa **24** Dc
Dilam, Ad- **21** De
Dili **15** Ej
Dillon **33** Bb
Dilolo **23** Efg
Dimboola **29** Gf
Dîmbovița (riv.) **6** Gd
Dimitrovgrad [Bul.] **11** FGb
Dimitrovgrad [Russia] **13** DEd
Dimitrovgrad [Yugo.] **11** Eb
Dimona **22** Eg
Dinagat (i.) **18** Gbc
Dinajpur **19** Jj
Dinan **8** BCc
Dinant **8** Fb
Dinapur **19** Ij
Dinar **22** BCc
Dinard **8** Bc
Dinaric Alps **6** Cde
Dindigul **20** Efg
Dingbian **16** Cc
Dingle Bay **7** Aef
Dingwall **7** Dc
Diourbel **24** Ac
Dipolog **18** Fc
Dir **20** Da
Dire Dawa **25** Ecd
Dirk Hartog Island **29** Ad
Dirkou **24** Dc
Dirranbandi **29** Hd
Disappointment, Lake- **29** Cc
Disko Bugt **31** Jb
Disko Ø (i.) **41** grid square no.1
Dispur **19** Bc
Distrito Federal **39** Da
Diu **20** Dd
Divinópolis **39** Db
Divisões, Serra das- (mts.) **39** Ca
Divisor, Sierra de- (mts.) **37** Bc
Divnoje **12** Fd
Divriği **22** FGc
Dīwānīyah, Ad- **21** CDc
Dixon Entrance **31** Bc
Diyarbakır **21** BCb
Diz (r.) **20** Bc
Dja (riv.) **26** Aa
Djado **24** Db
Djado, Plateau du- (plat.) **24** Db
Djambala **26** Ab
Djanet **24** CDb
Djedeïda **10** Bf
Djelfa **24** Ca
Djénné **24** Bc
Djerba (i.) **24** Da
Djibouti (Ind. St.) **25** Ec
Djibouti **23** Gd
Djolu **26** Ba
Djougou **24** Ccd
Djugu **26** BCa
Dmitrijev-Lgovski **12** DEc
Dmitri Laptev Strait **14** GHb
Dmitrov **12** Eb
Dnepr (riv.) **13** Ce
Dneprodzeržinsk → Kamenskoje **12** Dd
Dnepropetrovsk → Jekaterinoslav **13** Ce
Dnestr (riv.) **13** Be
Dno **12** CDb
Dobbiaco / Toblach **10** Da
Doboj **6** CDd
Dobrič (Tolbuhin) **11** GHb
Dobrjanka **12** HIb
Dobruja (phys. reg.) **6** HIde
Doce, Rio- (riv.) **39** Da
Doda Betta (mt.) **20** Ef
Dodecanese (is.) **11** Gde
Dodge City **33** CDc
Dodoma **23** Ff
Dogai Coring **19** Ab
Döğer **22** Cc
Dōgo (i.) **17** Cf
Dogondoutchi **24** Cc
Doha **21** Ed
Dohad **20** Dd
Dokšicy **4** Fe
Dolak, Pulau- **27** Bc
Dolbeau **31** Hd
Dole **8** Fd
Dolgellau **7** DEe
Dolina **6** FGb
Dolinsk **14** He
Dolinskaja **12** Dd
Dolinskoje **6** Ic
Dolo **25** Ed
Dolomites (mts.) **10** CDa
Dolores **39** Cc
Domaniç **22** BCc
Domažlice **5** Dd
Dombarovski **13** Ed
Dombas **4** Bc
Dombóvár **6** CDc
Domeyko, Cordillera- (mts.) **39** Bb
Domfront **8** Cc
Domingos Martins **39** DEab
Dominica (Ind. St.) **36** DEb
Dominican Republic (Ind. St.) **30** KLgh
Domo **25** Ed
Domodossola **10** Ba
Dom Pedrito **39** Cc
Don [Russia] (riv.) **13** De
Don [U.K.] (riv.) **7** Ec
Donaueschingen **5** Bde
Donauwörth **5** Cd
Don Benito **9** Cc
Doncaster **7** Fe
Dondo **26** Abc
Dondra Head **20** Fg
Donec (riv.) **12** Ed
Doneck → Juzovka **13** Ce
Donegal **7** BCd
Donegal Bay **7** Bd
Dongara **29** ABd
Donggala **18** EFe
Dong Hoi **19** Ee
Dongliao He (riv.) **16** Fb
Dongning **17** Bb
Dong Rak, Phanom- **19** Df
Dongsha Dao (i.) **16** Ef
Dongting Hu (l.) **16** De
Dora, Lake- **29** Cc
Dora Baltea (riv.) **10** Ab
Dorada, La- **37** Bb
Dorado, El- [U.S.] **32** Bb
Dorado, El- [Ven.] **37** Cb
Dorchester **7** Ef
Dordogne (riv.) **8** De
Dordrecht **8** EFb
Dore, Monts- (mts.) **8** Ee
Dorgali **10** Bd
Dori **24** BCc
Dornbirn **5** BCe
Dornoch **7** DEc
Dorohoi **6** Hc
Dorotea **4** Db
Dorset (co.) **7** Ef
Dortmund **5** ABc
Doruma **26** Ba
Dosatuj **16** Ea
Dos Hermanas **9** BCd
Dosso **24** Cc
Dossor **13** Ee
Dothan **32** Cb
Douai **8** Eb
Douala **24** CDd
Douarnenez **8** ABc
Douglas [Ak.-U.S.] **31** Bc
Douglas [Az.-U.S.] **33** Cc
Douglas [S. Afr.] **26** Bd
Douglas [U.K.] **7** Dd
Douglas [Wy.-U.S.] **33** Cb
Dourada, Serra- (mts.) **38** BCc
Dourados **39** Cb
Douro (riv.) **9** Bb
Dovbyš **6** Ha
Dover [U.K.] **7** Gf
Dover [U.S.] **32** Db
Dover, Strait of- **8** Db
Dovrefjell (mts.) **4** Bc
Downpatrick **7** Dd
Dozen (i.) **17** Cf
Drâa **24** Bab
Drâa, Hamada du- (des.) **24** Bb
Dracena **39** Cb
Drăgăşani **6** Gd
Draguignan **8** FGf
Drakensberg **26** DEe
Drake Passage **40** ABc
Dráma **11** Fc
Drammen **4** Bd
Drancy **8** Ec
Drangajökull (mt.) **4** map no.1
Dravograd **6** Bc
Drawsko Pomorskie **5** Eb
Dresden **5** DEc
Dreux **8** Dc
Drevsjø **4** BCc
Drina (riv.) **6** Dd
Drin Gulf **11** Cc
Drini (riv.) **11** Db
Drogheda **7** Ce
Drogobyč **5** Id
Drôme (riv.) **8** Fe
Dronne (riv.) **8** De
Drontes (riv.) **22** Fe
Drumheller **33** Ba
Drummond Range **29** Hc
Drumochter, Pass of- **7** DEc
Druskininkai **5** IJab
Družba (i.) **12** Dc
Družba **13** He
Družina **14** Hc
Drvar **6** Cd
Dryden **31** Fd
Drygalski Island **42** grid square no.4
Drysdale River **29** Dab
Dubai **21** EFde
Dubawnt (riv.) **31** Eb
Dubawnt Lake **31** Eb
Dubbo **29** He
Dubesar **6** Ic
Dublin (Baile Átha Cliath) **7** CDe
Dubna **12** Eb
Dubno **12** Cc
Dubovka **12** FGd
Dubrovnik **11** BCb
Dubuque **32** Ba
Duc de Gloucester, Îles du- **28** Bd
Ducie Island **28** Cd
Dudinka **13** Hc
Dudley **7** Ee
Duero (riv.) **9** Cb
Dugi Otok **6** Bd
Dugo Selo **6** BCd
Duisburg **5** CDc
Dukhan **21** Ede
Dukielska, Przełęcz- **5** HId
Dulawan → Datu Piang **18** Fc
Dulce, Rio- (riv.) **39** Bb

Dulovo **11** Gb
Duluth **32** Ba
Dūmā **22** Ff
Dumaguete **18** Fc
Dumaran (i.) **18** EFb
Dumbarton **7** Dcd
Dumfries **7** Ed
Dumka **19** Ij
Dumond d'Urville **42** grid square no.4
Dumont D'Urville Sea **42** grid square no.4
Dunaföldvár **6** Dc
Dunaharaszti **6** Dc
Dunajevcy **6** Hb
Dunántúl (phys. reg.) **6** CDc
Dunaújváros **6** Dc
Duncansby Head **7** Eb
Dundalk **7** Cde
Dundalk Bay **7** CDe
Dundas, Lake- **29** Ce
Dundas Strait **29** Ea
Dundee **7** Ec
Dunedin **27** De
Dunfermline **7** DEc
Dungarpur **20** Dd
Dungarvan **7** Cef
Dungeness (cap.) **7** Gf
Dunhua **16** Gb
Dunkerque **8** Eb
Dunkwa **24** Bd
Dún Laoghaire / Dunleary **7** CDe
Dunleary / Dún Laoghaire **7** CDe
Dunqulah **25** CDc
Duns **7** Ed
Duolun **16** Eb
Durance (riv.) **8** Ge
Durango **33** Cc
Durazno **39** Cc
Durazzo **11** Cc
Durban **23** Fhi
Durg **20** Fd
Durgapur **19** IJk
Durham [U.K.] **7** EFd
Durham [U.S.] **32** Db
Durmitor (mt.) **11** Cb
Durness **7** Db
Dursunbey **11** Hd
Durūz, Jabal al- (mt.) **22** Ff
Dušanbe **13** Ff
Dushan **16** Ce
Düsseldorf **5** CDc
Dutch Harbor **31** Bc
Duwaym, Ad- **25** Dc
Duyun **16** Ce
Düzce **22** Cb
Dyer Plateau (plat.) **42** grid square no.1
Dymer **6** IJa
Dyrhólaey (cap.) **4** map no.1
Džalal-Abad **13** Ge
Džalinda **14** Fd
Džambul **13** Ge
Dzamyn-Ud **16** Db
Džankoj **12** Dd
Džardžan **14** Fc
Džargalant, Ar- **16** DEa
Dzeržinsk **12** Fb
Džetygara **13** Fd
Džezkazgan → Žezkazgan **13** Fe
Dzhugdzhur Range **14** Gd
Działdowo **5** Hb
Dzierżoniów **5** Fc
Dzun-Bajan **16** CDb
Dzungarian Basin (phys. reg.) **14** Be
Džungarski Alatau, Hrebet- (mts.) **13** GHe
Dzun-Mod **14** De
Džusaly **13** Fe

E

Eagle **31** Ab
Eagle Pass **33** CDd
Eastbourne **7** Gf
East Cape **27** Dd
East China Sea **16** FGde
Easter Island **2**
Eastern Carpathians (mts.) **6** FHbc
Eastern Ghats (mts.) **20** EFef
Eastern Malaysia **18** DEcd
Eastern Prussia (hist. reg.) **5** GIab
East Falkland (i.) **40** Cc
East London **26** Be
Eastmain (riv.) **31** Eb
Eastmain **31** Hc
East Point **32** Cb
East Saint Louis **32** BCb
East Sea / Japan, Sea of- **16** HIbc
East Siberian Sea **41** grid square no.4
Eau Claire **32** BCa
Eau Gallie **32** CDc
Eauripik Atoll **27** Cb
Ebensee **5** DEe
Eber Gölü **22** Cc
Eberswalde **5** Db
Ebla (r.) **21** Bb
Eboli **10** Ed
Ebro (riv.) **9** Da
Eceabat **22** Ab
Echigo-Sanmyaku (mts.) **17** FGef
Echo Bay **30** GHc
Echuca **29** GHf
Écija **9** Cd
Ecuador (Ind. St.) **36** BCd
Ed **25** Ec
Edéa **24** CDd
Edefors **4** Eb
Eden **29** HIf
Edgeøya **13** Bb
Edhessa **11** DEc
Edinburgh **7** Ed
Edirne **11** Gc
Edith Ronne Ice Shelf **42** grid square no.1
Edith Ronne Land **42** grid square no.1
Edjeleh **24** Cb
Edmonton **30** Gd
Edmundston **31** Id
Edremit **22** Ac
Edremit Körfezi **22** Ac
Edsel Ford Ranges **42** grid square no.3
Edward, Lake- **25** Ce
Edwards Creek **29** Ee
Edwards Plateau **33** CDcd
Edward VII Peninsula **42** grid square no.3
Efaté, Île- (i.) **28** map no.4
Effingham **32** Cb
Eforie **6** Id
Egadi, Isole- **10** Df
Egan Range **33** Bbc
Egedesminde / Aasiaat **31** JKb
Eger **6** Ec
Egersund **4** Ad
Eğnar **22** Ed
Eğridir **22** Cd
Eğridir Gölü **22** Ccd
Eğrigöz dağı (mt.) **22** Bc
Egvekinot **14** KLc
Egypt (Ind. St.) **23** EFc
Ehingen **5** Bd
Eiao, Île- (i.) **28** Bc
Eibar **9** Da
Eichstätt **5** Cd
Eifel (mt.) **5** Ac
Eigg (i.) **7** Cc
Eight Degree Channel **20** Dg
Eights **42** grid square no.1
Eights Coast **42** grid square no.1
Eighty Mile Beach **29** Cb
Eindhoven **8** Fb
Eiriksjökull (gl.) **4** map no.1
Eirunepé **37** BCc
Eisenach **5** BCc
Eisenerz **5** Ee
Eisenhüttenstadt **5** Eb
Eisenstadt **5** Fe
Eisleben **5** Cc
Ejin Qi **16** Bb
Ekecek dağı (mt.) **22** DEc
Ekenäs **4** EFcd
Ekibastuz **13** Gd
Ekonda **14** Dc
El Affroun **9** Gd
Elafonísou, Stenón- (str.) **11** Ee
Elassŏn **11** Ed
Elat **22** Eh
Elâzığ **21** BCb
Elba (i.) **10** Cc
Elbasani **11** CDc
El-Bayadh **24** Ca
Elbe (riv.) **5** Cb
Elbert, Mount- **33** Cc
Elbeuf **8** Dc
Elbistan **22** Fc
Elbląg **5** Ga
El Boulaïda **24** Ca
Elbrus (mt.) **21** Ca
Elburz Mountains **21** DEb
Elche **9** Ec
Elda **9** Ec
Eldoret **25** Dde
Elektrostal **12** EFb
Eleusís **11** Ed
Eleuthera Island **32** Dc
Elgin **7** Ec
Elgon (mt.) **25** Dd
Elhovo **11** Gb
Elista **13** De
Elizabeth City **32** Db
Elizabeth Island **28** map no.3
Ełk **5** Ib
Elk City **33** CDc
Elko **33** Bb
Ellesmere Island **41** grid square no.1
Elliston **29** EFe
Ellora (r.) **20** Ed
Ellsworth Highland **42** grid square no.3
Ellsworth Mountains **42** grid square no.1
Elmalı **22** BCd
Elmira **32** Da
Elmshorn **5** BCb
Elne **8** Ef
Elorza **37** BCb
El Salvador (Ind. St.) **30** IJh
Eluru **20** Fe
Elvas **9** Bc
Elverum **4** BCc
Ely **33** Bc
Emaé (i.) **28** map no.4
Emāmshahr **21** Fb
Emba **13** Ee
Emba (riv.) **13** Ee
Embarcación **39** Bb
Embetsu **17** Gb
Embu **26** Cb
Emden **5** Ab
Emerald **29** Hc
Emerson **31** Fd
Emet **22** Bc
Emi Koussi (mt.) **25** Bbc
Emilia-Romagna (reg.) **10** BCb
Emine, Nos- **22** ABa
Emirdağ **22** Cc
Emir dağları (mts.) **22** Cc
Emmen **8** Ga
Emmendingen **5** ABd
Emmet **29** Gc
Empalme **34** ABb
Émpoli **10** Cc
Emporia **32** Bb
Ems (riv.) **5** Ab
Encantada, Cerro de la- (mt.) **34** Aa
Encarnación **39** Cb
Ende **18** Ff
Endeavour Strait **29** Ga
Enderbury Atoll **28** Ac
Enderby Land **42** grid square no.2
Enewetak Atoll **27** Db
Enez **11** Gc
Enez Körfezi **11** Fc
Engaru **17** Hb
Engels **13** Dd
Enggano, Pulau- (i.) **18** Bf
England (reg.) **7** EFde
Englewood **33** Cc
English Channel **8** ACbc
Enid **32** Bb
Enkhuizen **8** Fa
Enköping **4** Dd
Enna **10** Ef
Ennadai **31** Eb
Ennedi (plat.) **25** Cc
Ennis **7** Be
Enniscorthy **7** CDe
Enniskillen **7** Cd
Enns (riv.) **5** DEe
Enontekiö **4** EFa
Enschede **8** Ga

Geraldton [Austl.] **29** Ad
Geraldton [Can.] **31** Gd
Gereshk **20** Bb
Gerlachovský štit (mt.) **5** Hd
Germany (Ind. St.) **3** DEbc
Germiston **26** Bd
Gerona **9** Gab
Gers (riv.) **8** Df
Gerze **22** Eb
Geser **18** He
Getafe **9** CDb
Geteina, El- **25** Dc
Gevgelija **11** Ec
Geyik dağ (mt.) **22** Dd
Geysir **4** map no.1
Ghadāmis **24** CDab
Ghaghara (riv.) **20** Fc
Ghana (Ind. St.) **23** BCe
Ghanzi **26** Bd
Ghardaïa **24** Ca
Ghardimaou **10** Bf
Gharyān **24** Da
Ghāt **24** CDb
Ghatsila **19** Ik
Ghaydah, Al- **21** Ef
Ghazāl, Baḩr al- (riv.) **25** CDd
Ghazālah, Al- **21** Cd
Ghaziabad **19** Gi
Ghazipur **19** Hj
Ghazni **20** Cb
Gheorghe Gheorghiu-Dej **6** Hc
Gheorghieni **6** GHc
Gherla **6** FGc
Ghor, El- **22** Efg
Ghugri (riv.) **19** Ij
Ghurdaqah, Al- **25** Db
Gialoúsa **22** DEe
Giandža (Kirovabad) **13** De
Giant's Causeway **7** Cd
Giarre **10** Ef
Gibara **35** Ca
Gibeon **26** Ad
Gibraltar **9** Cd
Gibraltar, Strait of- **24** Ba
Gibson Desert **29** CDc
Gidole **25** Dd
Gien **8** Ed
Gießen **5** Bc
Gifu **16** Ic
Giglio (i.) **10** Cc
Gijón **9** Ca
Gila (riv.) **33** Bc
Gila Bend **33** Bc
Gilbâna **25** map no.1
Gilbert River **29** Gb
Gilgit **20** Da
Gillingham **7** Gf
Gineifa **25** map no.1
Gingoog (mt.) **18** FGc
Ginir **25** Ed
Gioia del Colle **10** Fd
Gióna Óros (mt.) **11** Ed
Giovi, Passo dei- (p.) **10** Bb
Girardot **37** Bb
Giresun **21** Ba
Giresun dağlari (mts.) **22** FGb
Giridih **19** Ij
Gironde (riv. m.) **8** Ce
Gisborne **27** Dd
Giulianova **10** DEc
Giurgiu **6** Gde
Givet **8** Fb
Givors **8** Fe
Giza **25** CDab
Gižiga **14** IJc
Giżycko **5** Hab
Gjirokastra **11** CDc
Gjoia Haven **31** Fb
Gjøvik **4** Bc
Gjuhës, Kep i- **11** Cc
Glace Bay **32** Fa
Gladstone **29** Ic
Gláma (mt.) **4** map no.1
Glåma (riv.) **4** Bcd
Glasgow [U.K.] **7** DEd
Glasgow [U.S.] **33** Cb
Glauchau **5** Dc
Glazov **13** Ed
Glendale **33** Bc
Glendive **33** Cb
Glenelg River **29** Gf
Glen Innes **29** Id
Glen More (phys. reg.) **7** Dc
Glens Falls **32** Da
Glenwood Springs **33** Cbc
Glina **10** EFb
Glittertind (mt.) **4** Bc
Gliwice (mt.) **5** Gc
Globe **33** BCc
Głogów **5** EFc
Glomfjord **4** Cb
Glommersträsk **4** DEb
Glorieuses, Iles- **26** map no.1
Gloucester **7** EFf
Głuchołazy **5** Fc
Glückstadt **5** Bb
Gluhov **12** Dc
Gmünd **5** Ed
Gmunden **5** DEe
Gniezno **5** Fb
Gnjilane **11** Db
Gnowangerup **29** Be
Goa (State) **20** De
Goalpara **19** Jj
Goba **25** DEd
Gobabis **23** DEh
Gobernador Gregores **40** ABb
Gobi Desert **14** De
Gobijski Altaj **16** ABab
Gobō **17** Dgh
Goce Delčev **11** EFc
Godavari (riv.) **20** Ee
Godhavn / Qeqertarsuaq **30** MNc
Godhra **20** Dd
Godollő **6** Dc
Godoy Cruz **39** Bc
Godthåb / Nuuk **30** MNc
Gō-Gawa (riv.) **17** Cg
Gogland, ostrov- (i.) **4** Fc
Goiana **38** Db
Goiânia **39** CDa
Goiás (State) **38** Cc
Goiás **39** Ca
Gökçeada (i.) **11** Fc
Gökırmak (riv.) **22** Eb
Göksu [Tur.] (riv.) **22** Bb
Göksu [Tur.] (riv.) **22** Dd
Göksu [Tur.] (riv.) **22** EFd
Göksun **22** Fc
Gol **4** Bc
Golburn Islands **29** Ea
Golčiha **13** Hb
Gölcük **22** BCb
Gołdap **5** Ia
Gold Coast (phys. reg.) **24** Bd
Gold Coast **29** IJd
Golden **31** Dc
Goléa, El- **24** Ca
Goleniów **5** Eb
Golfito **35** Bc
Golija (mt.) **11** CDb
Goljam Perelik (mt.) **11** EFc
Golmud **15** Df
Golo (riv.) **8** map no.1
Golpāyegān **21** DEc
Golspie **7** Ebc
Goma **25** Ce
Gomati (riv.) **19** Hj
Gombe **24** Dc
Gomel **13** Cd
Gomera (i.) **24** Ab
Gómez Palacio **34** Bb
Gomo **20** Gb
Gonābād **21** FGc
Gonaïves **35** Cb
Gonâve, Isla de la- (i.) **35** Cb
Gonbad-e-Qabus **21** EFb
Gonda **19** Hj
Gonder **25** Dc
Gondia **20** EFd
Gönen **11** Gc
Gong'an **16** Dde
Gongbo'gyamda **19** Bbc
Gongga Shan (mt.) **16** Be
Gonghe **16** ABc
Good Hope, Cape of- **26** Ae
Goodland **33** Cc
Goomalling **29** Be
Goondiwindi **29** Hld
Goose Bay **31** Jc
Gorakhpur **20** FGc
Gördes **11** Hd
Gordonvale **29** Hb
Gore **27** De
Goré [Chad] **25** Bd
Goré [Eth.] **25** Dd
Gorgān **21** EFb
Gorgogna, Isla- (i.) **37** Bb
Gorgora **25** Dc
Gorizia **10** Dab
Gorki **12** Dc
Gorki → Nižni Novgorod **13** Dd
Gorlice **5** Hd
Görlitz **5** Ec
Gorlovka **13** CDe
Gorna Orjahovica **11** FGb
Gornjacki **13** Fc
Gornji Vakuf **6** Ce
Gorno Altajsk **13** Hd
Gornozavodsk **14** GHe
Gorny **17** CDb
Gorodec **12** Fb
Gorodenka **6** Gb
Gorodišče **12** Dd
Gorodnica **6** Ha
Gorodok [Mold.] **6** Hb
Gorodok [Ukr.] **12** Cd
Gorohov **6** Ga
Gorontalo **18** Fd
Goryn (riv.) **12** Cc
Gorzów Wielkopolski **5** Eb
Goshogawara **17** FGd
Goslar **5** Cc
Gospić **6** Bd
Gosport **7** Ff
Gostivar **11** Dc
Gostyń **5** Fc
Gostynin **5** Gb
Göta älv (riv.) **4** Cd
Göta kanal **4** CDd
Götaland **4** Cd
Göteborg **4** BCd
Gotel Mountains **24** Dd
Gotha **5** Cc
Gotland (i.) **4** Dd
Gotō-Rettō **16** Gd
Gotska Sandön (i.) **4** Dd
Göttingen **5** BCc
Gough (i.) **23** ABj
Gouin, Réservoir- (res.) **31** Hd
Goulburn **29** Hlef
Goulette, La- **10** Cf
Gouménissa **11** Ec
Goundam **24** Bc
Gourdon **8** De
Gouré **24** Dc
Gouro **25** BCc
Goväter **20** Bc
Gove Peninsula **29** Fa
Goverla, gora- (mt.) **6** Gb
Governador Valadares **39** Da
Goya **39** Cb
Göynük **22** Cb
Gozo (i.) **10** Ef
Graaff Reinet **26** Be
Gračac **6** BCd
Gracias a Dios, Cabo- **35** Bb
Gradaús **38** Bb
Gradaús, Serra dos- (mts.) **38** Bb
Grafton **29** Id
Grafton, Cape- **29** Hb
Graham Island **31** Bc
Graham Land **42** grid square no.1
Grahamstown **26** Be
Grain Coast **24** ABd
Grajaú **38** Cb
Grajewo **5** Ib
Grampian Mountains **7** DEc
Granada [Nic.] **35** Bb
Granada [Sp.] **9** Dd
Gran Arber (mt.) **5** Dd
Granby **31** Hd
Gran Canaria (i.) **24** Ab
Gran Chaco (phys. reg.) **39** BCb
Grand Bahama Island **32** Dc
Grand Ballon **8** Gd
Grand-Bassam **24** Bd
Grand Canal **7** Ce
Grand Canyon (v.) **33** Bc
Grand Canyon **33** Bc
Grand Cayman (i.) **35** Bb
Grand'Combe, La- **8** EFe
Grande, Rio- [Bol.] (riv.) **39** Ba
Grande, Rio- [Braz.] (riv.) **39** Dab
Grande, Rio- [Braz.] (riv.) **38** Cc
Grande, Río- [N. Amer.] (riv.) **33** CDd
Grande, Río- [Nic.] (riv.) **35** Bb
Grande Comore (i.) **26** Dc

Grande Prairie **31** CDc
Grand Erg Occidental **24** BCab
Grand Erg Oriental (des.) **24** Cab
Gran Deserto (phys. reg.) **34** Aa
Grand Falls **31** Gc
Grand Forks **32** Ba
Grand Island **32** Ba
Grand Junction **33** Cc
Grand–Lahou **24** Bd
Grand–Lieu, Lac de– (l.) **8** BCd
Grand Rapids **32** Ca
Grange, La– **32** Cb
Granite City **32** BCb
Granites, The– **29** Ec
Granja **38** Cb
Granollers **9** Gb
Gran Paradiso (mt.) **10** Ab
Gran Sabana, La– (mts.) **37** Cb
Gran San Bernardo (p.) **10** Ab
Gran Sasso d'Italia (mt.) **10** Dc
Gran Teton (mt.) **33** Bb
Grants **33** Cc
Grants Pass **33** Ab
Granville **8** Cc
Gras, Lac de– (l.) **31** Db
Grasse **8** Gf
Grassy **29** map no.1
Gravina in Puglia **10** Fd
Gray **8** Fd
Grays Peak **33** Cc
Graz **5** Ee
Grazalema **9** Cd
Grdelica **11** DEb
Great Artesian Basin **29** FGd
Great Australian Bight **29** DEe
Great Barrier Reef **29** GIab
Great Basin (phys. reg.) **33** Bbc
Great Bear Lake **31** Db
Great Bend **32** Bb
Great Bitter Lake **25** map no.1
Great Channel **19** BCg
Great Dividing Range **29** GHbc
Greater Antilles (is.) **30** JLgh
Greater Khingan Range **14** EFde
Great Exuma Island **32** Dc
Great Falls **33** Bb
Great Inagua Island **35** Ca
Great Namaland (hist. reg.) **26** Ad
Great Nicobar (i.) **19** BCg
Great Poland (hist. reg.) **5** EGb
Great Ruaha (riv.) **26** Cb
Great Salt Lake **33** Bb
Great Sandy Desert [Austl.] **29** CDc
Great Sandy Desert [U.S.] **33** ABb
Great Sleave Lake **31** CDb
Great Victoria Desert **27** Bd
Great Yarmouth **7** GHe
Grebenka **12** Dcd
Greco, Akra– **22** Ee
Gredos, Sierra de– (mts.) **9** Cb
Greece (Ind. St.) **3** Fd
Greeley **33** Cb
Greem–Bell, ostrov– **13** FGa
Green Bay **32** Ca
Greenland (co.) **30** Nbc
Greenland Sea **41** grid square no.1
Greenock **7** Dd
Green River **33** BCbc
Greensboro **32** CDb
Greenville [Lbr.] **24** ABd
Greenville [Ms.–U.S.] **32** Bb
Greenville [S.C.–U.S.] **32** Cb
Greenville [Tx.–U.S.] **32** Bb
Greenwich **7** FGf
Greenwood **32** BCb
Gregory, Lake– [Austl.] **29** Fd
Gregory, Lake– [Austl.] **29** BCd
Gregory Lake **29** Dc
Gregory Range **29** Gb
Greifswald **5** Da
Grein **5** Ed
Greiz **5** CDc
Gremiha **13** CDc
Gremjačinsk **12** Ib
Grenå **4** Bd
Grenada (Ind. St.) **30** Lh
Grenadine Islands **35** Db
Grenen (cap.) **4** Bd
Grenoble **8** FGe
Grevená **11** Dc
Grey Range **29** Gd
Gribanovski **12** Fc
Griffith **29** He
Grigoriopol **6** Ic
Grijalva (riv.) **34** Cc
Grimsby **7** Fe
Grimstad **4** Bd
Grintavec (mt.) **6** Bc
Gris–Nez, Cap– **8** Db
Grjazi **12** EFc
Grodno **13** Bd
Groix, Ile de– **8** Bd
Grombalia **10** Cf
Grong **4** Cb
Groningen [Neth.] **8** Ga
Groningen [Sur.] **37** Db
Groote Eylandt **29** Fa
Grootfontein **23** DEgh
Groot Karasberge (mt.) **26** ABd
Grosa, Punta– (cap.) **9** FGc
Grosser Beerberg (mt.) **5** Cc
Grosseto **10** Cc
Großglockner (mt.) **5** De
Grozny **13** De
Grudovo **11** Gb
Grudziądz **5** Gb
Gryfice **5** Eb
Gryfino **5** Eb
Grytviken **40** Ec
Guaçuí **39** Db
Guadalajara [Mex.] **30** Hg
Guadalajara [Sp.] **9** Db
Guadalaviar (Turia) (riv.) **9** Ebc
Guadalcanal Island **27** CDc
Guadalquivir (riv.) **9** Cd
Guadalupe **9** Cc
Guadalupe, Isla de– (i.) **30** FGg
Guadarrama, Sierra de– (mts.) **9** CDb
Guadeloupe (i.) **36** DEb
Guadiana (riv.) **9** Bc
Guadix **9** Dd
Guafo, Isla– (i.) **40** Ab
Guainía (riv.) **37** Cb
Guaíra **39** Cb
Guaira, La– **37** Ca
Guajará–Mirim **37** Cd
Guajira, Península de la– (pen.) **37** Ba
Gualeguaychú **39** BCc
Guam (i.) **27** map no.1
Guamá **38** Cb
Guamapi, Sierra de– **37** Cb
Guamúchil **34** Bb
Guanabacoa **35** Ba
Guanajuato **34** BCb
Guanare **37** Cb
Guane **35** Ba
Guangdong (prov.) **16** DEf
Guanghua **16** Dd
Guangyuan **15** Df
Guangzhou → Canton **16** Df
Guantánamo **35** Ca
Guantánamo Bay Naval Station **35** Cab
Guanxian **16** Bd
Guapí **37** Bb
Guaporé (riv.) **39** Ba
Guaqui **39** Ba
Guarabira **38** Db
Guarapuava **39** Cb
Guaratinguetá **39** Db
Guarda **9** Bb
Guardafui, Cape– **25** Fc
Guasave **34** Bb
Guastalla **10** Cb
Guatemala (Ind. St.) **30** Ih
Guatemala **30** Ih
Guaviare, Río– (riv.) **37** BCb
Guaxupé **39** Db
Guayama **35** Db
Guayaneco, Archipiélago– (is.) **40** Ab
Guayaquil **36** BCd
Guayaquil, Golfo de– **37** Ac
Guayaramerín **37** Cd
Guaymas **34** Ab
Gubaha **12** Ib
Gubān (phys. reg.) **25** Ecd
Gubbio **10** Dc
Guben **5** Ebc
Gubin **5** Ec
Gubkin **12** Ec
Gudbrandsdalen (v.) **4** Bc
Gudivada **20** Fe
Gudiyattam **20** EFf
Gudur **20** EFf
Gudvangen **4** Ac
Guebwiller **8** Gcd
Guelma **24** Ca
Guéret **8** Dd
Guernsey (i.) **8** Bc
Guiana Highlands **37** CDb
Guider **24** Dcd
Guiding **16** Ce
Guijá **26** Cd
Gui Jiang (riv.) **16** Df
Guildford **7** Ff
Guilin **16** De
Guimarães **9** ABb
Guimaras (i.) **18** Fb
Guinea (Ind. St.) **23** ABd
Guinea, Gulf of– **23** BCef
Guinea–Bissau (Ind. St.) **23** Ad
Güines **35** Ba
Guingamp **8** Bc
Guiping **16** Df
Guiratinga **39** Ca
Güiria **37** Ca
Guixian **16** Cf
Guiyang **16** Ce
Guizhou (prov.) **16** Ce
Gujarat (State) **20** Dd
Gujranwala **20** Db
Gujrat **20** Db
Gukovo **12** Fd
Gulbarga **20** Ee
Gulbene **4** Fd
Gulen **4** Ac
Gulfport **32** Cb
Güllük **11** Ge
Gülnar **22** Dd
Gulu **25** Dd
Guna **20** Ed
Gunnbjørns Fjeld (mt.) **41** grid square no.1
Gunnedah **29** HIe
Guntakal **20** Eef
Guntur **20** EFe
Gunungsitoli **18** Ad
Gura Humorului **6** GHc
Gurguéia (riv.) **38** Cb
Gurjev → Aterau **13** DEe
Gurk **10** Ea
Gurkha **19** Ii
Gürün **22** Fc
Gurupá **38** Bb
Gurupi (riv.) **38** Cb
Gurupi **38** Cc
Guru Sikhar (mt.) **20** Dcd
Gusau **24** Cc
Gusev **5** Ia
Gushan **16** Fbc
Gushi **16** Ed
Gus–Hrustalny **12** Fb
Gústrow **5** Db
Gütersloh **5** Bc
Guyana (Ind. St.) **36** Ec
Guyenne (hist. reg.) **8** CEef
Guymon **33** Cc
Gwādar **21** Gde
Gwalior **20** Ec
Gwda (riv.) **5** Fb
Gweru **23** Eg
Gyala Shankou **12** Dde
Gyangzê **19** Ac
Gya Pass **19** Ii
Gyda **13** GHb
Gydanski Poluostrov **13** GHbc
Gyirong **19** Ii
Gympie **29** Id
Gyöngyös **6** DEc
Győr **6** Cc
Gypsumville **31** Fc
Gyula **6** Ec

H

Ha'apai Group **28** Acd
Haapajärvi **4** Fc
Haapsalu **4** EFd
Haarlem **8** EFa
Haasts Bluff **29** Ec
Habarovsk **14** Ge
Ḩabarūt **21** Ef

Kartal **22** Bb
Kartaly **13** Fd
Karumba **29** Gb
Kārun (riv.) **21** Dc
Karviná **5** Gd
Karwar **20** Df
Karymskoje **14** Ed
Kaş **22** Bd
Kasai (riv.) **26** ABb
Kasai Occidental (reg.) **26** Bb
Kasai Oriental (reg.) **26** Bb
Kasama **26** Cbc
Kasane **26** Bc
Kasba Lake **31** Eb
Kasempa **26** Bc
Kasenga **26** Bc
Kasese **25** CDde
Kasganj **19** Gj
Kāshān **21** Ec
Kashi **15** Cf
Kashipur **19** Gi
Kashiwazaki **17** EFf
Kāshmar **21** Fb
Kashmir **20** Eb
Kasimov **12** Fc
Kašira **12** Ec
Kasiruta, Pulau- (i.) **18** Ge
Kaskö **4** Ec
Káson, Stenón- **11** Gf
Kasongo **26** Bb
Kásos (i.) **11** Gf
Kaspijski **12** Gd
Kasr, Ra's- **25** Dc
Kassala **25** Dc
Kassándra (pen.) **11** Ecd
Kassándra, Gulf of- **11** Ecd
Kassel **5** Bc
Kasserine **24** Ca
Kassubia (hist. reg.) **5** FGab
Kastamonu **22** DEb
Kastéllion **11** Ef
Kastoría **11** Dc
Kastornoje **12** Ec
Kasur **20** Db
Katanga (hist. reg.) **26** Bb
Katangli **14** Hd
Katanning **29** Be
Katarnian Ghat **19** Hi
Katav-Ivanovsk **12** Ic
Katchall (i.) **19** Bg
Kateríni **11** Ec
Katha **19** Cd
Katherine **29** Ea
Kathgodam **19** Gi
Kathiawar (phys. reg.) **20** CDd
Kathmandu **15** Cg
Katihar **19** Ij
Katingan (riv.) **18** De
Katiola **24** Bd
Káto Akhaïa **11** Dde
Katoomba **29** Ie
Katowice **5** Gc
Kātrīnā, Jabal- (mt.) **25** Db
Katrineholm **4** CDd
Katsina **24** Cc
Kattakurgan **13** Ff
Kattegat (str.) **4** BCd
Katun (riv.) **13** Hd
Kau **18** Gd
Kauai (i.) **28** Ba
Kauai Channel **28** map no.1
Kaufbeuren **5** Ce
Kauhajoki **4** Ec
Kaula (i.) **28** map no.1
Kaulakahi Channel **28** map no.1
Kauliranta **4** EFb
Kaunas **4** EFe
Kaura Namoda **24** Cc
Kautokeino **4** EFa
Kavacık **22** Bc
Kavaja **11** Cc
Kavála **11** Fc
Kavalerovo **17** Db
Kavaratti (i.) **20** Df
Kavarna **11** Hb
Kawagoe **17** Ffg
Kawaguchi **17** FGfg
Kawaikini (mt.) **28** map no.1
Kawasaki **16** IJc
Kawio, Kepulauan- **18** FGd
Kawm **25** Db
Kawthaung **19** Cfg
Kaya **24** Bc
Kayah (State) **19** Ce
Kayan (riv.) **18** Ed
Kayes **24** Ac
Kayoa, Pulau- (i.) **18** Gde
Kayseri (Cesarea Mazaca) **22** EFc
Kazačje **14** Gb
Kazakhstan (Ind. St.) **13** EGe
Kazalinsk **13** EFe
Kazan **13** Dd
Kazan (riv.) **31** Eb
Kazanlăk **11** Fb
Kazatin **6** Ib
Kaz dağı (mt.) **22** Ac
Kāzerun **21** Ed
Kažim **12** Ha
Kāẓimīyah, Al- **21** Cc
Kazincbarcika **6** Eb
Kéa (i.) **11** Fe
Kearney **33** CDb
Kebir (riv.) **22** Fe
Kebnekaise (mt.) **4** Dab
Kecskemét **6** Dc
Kėdainiai **4** Ee
Kediri **18** Df
Kédougou **24** Ac
Keele Peak **31** Bb
Keelung **16** Fef
Keetmanshoop **23** DEh
Keewatin, District of- **31** Fb
Kefa (phys. reg.) **25** Cd
Keflavík **4** map no.1
Kehl **5** ABd
Keitele (l.) **4** Fc
Keith **29** Gf
Kelang **18** Bd
Kelang, Pulau- (i.) **18** Ge
Kelasa, Selat- **18** Ce
Kelkit (riv.) **22** Fb
Kéllé **26** Ab
Kelloselkä **4** FGb
Kelowna **31** Dcd
Keltepe (mt.) **22** Db
Keluang **18** Bd
Kem **13** Cc
Kemerovo **13** Hd
Kemi **4** Fb
Kemijärvi (l.) **4** Fb
Kemijärvi **4** Fb
Kemijoki (riv.) **4** Gb
Kempsey **29** Ie
Kempten im Allgäu **5** Ce
Ken (riv.) **20** Ed
Kendal **7** Ed
Kendari **18** Fe
Kenema **24** Ad
Kenge **26** Ab
Kengtung **19** Cd
Kenhardt **26** Bd
Kéniéba **24** ABc
Kénitra **24** Ba
Kenmare **7** Bf
Kenmare River **7** ABf
Kennedy, Cape- → Canaveral, Cape- **32** CDc
Keno Hill **31** Bb
Kenora **31** Fcd
Kent (co.) **7** Gf
Kent **24** Ad
Kentau **13** FGe
Kent Peninsula **31** Eb
Kentucky (State) **32** Cb
Kenya (Ind. St.) **23** Fe
Kenya (mt.) **25** De
Keokuk **32** Ba
Keonjhargarh **20** Gd
Kerala (State) **20** Efg
Kerama-Rettō **16** Ge
Kerč **13** Ce
Kerčensky Poluostrov **12** Ed
Kerempe Burun **22** Da
Keren **25** Dc
Kerguelen, Îles- (is.) **2**
Kerinci, Gunung- (mt.) **18** Be
Kerkennah Islands **24** Da
Kerki **13** Ff
Kerkíras, Stenón- (str.) **11** CDd
Kermadec Islands **27** Ed
Kermān **21** Fc
Kermānshāh **21** Dc
Kerme Körfezi **11** GHe
Kérouané **24** ABd
Kerulen (riv.) **14** Ee
Keşan **11** Gc
Keşap **22** Gb
Kesennuma **17** GHe
Keshan **16** FGa
Kestenga **4** Gb
Kestep **22** Bd
Keszthely **6** Cc
Kéta **24** Cd
Ketapang **18** CDe
Ketchikan **31** BCc
Ketoj, ostrov- (i.) **14** Ie
Ketrzyn **5** Ha
Kettering **7** Fe
Keuruu **4** Fc
Keweenaw Peninsula **32** Ca
Key West **32** Cc
Kezel Owzan (riv.) **21** Db
Kežma **14** CDd
Khābūra, Al- **21** Fe
Khairpur **20** Cc
Khalīg el Tīna (g.) **25** map no.1
Khálki (i.) **11** Ge
Khalkís **11** EFd
Khalūf **21** Fe
Khamasin, Al- **21** CDe
Khambhāt **20** Dd
Khambhāt, Gulf of- **20** Dd
Khamir **21** Cf
Khamis Mushayt **21** Cf
Khamsa **25** map no.1
Khanabad **20** CDa
Khanaqin **21** CDc
Khandaq, Al- (str.) **25** CDc
Khandwa **20** Ed
Khanewal **20** Db
Khanh Hung **19** Eg
Khánia **11** EFf
Khaníon, Kólpos- **11** EFf
Khanpur **20** Dc
Khān Yūnus **22** DEg
Kharagpur **15** Cg
Kharga Oasis **25** CDb
Khārijah, Al- **25** CDb
Khārk, Jazireh- ye- (i.) **21** DEd
Khartoum **25** Dc
Khartoum North **25** Dc
Khāsh **21** Gd
Khashm al Qirbah **25** Dc
Khasi-Jaintia Hill **16** Ee
Khawr al Fakkān **21** Fd
Khaybar **21** BCd
Khíos **22** Ac
Kholm **20** Ca
Khong **19** Ef
Khong Sedon **19** Ee
Khon Kaen **19** De
Khorāsān (phys. reg.) **21** Fbc
Khóra Sfakíon **11** Ff
Khorat → Nakhon Ratchasima **19** Def
Khorixas **26** Ad
Khorramābād **21** Dc
Khorramshahr **21** DEc
Khouribga **24** Ba
Khrisí (i.) **11** Ff
Khufrah, Al- **24** Eb
Khulna **20** GHd
Khums, Al- **24** Da
Khurīyā Murīya, Jazā'ir- **21** Ff
Khurmah, Al- **21** Ce
Khuzdar **20** Cc
Khvoy **21** CDb
Khyber Pass **20** Db
Kiantajärvi **4** Gb
Kibombo **26** Bb
Kibondo **26** Cb
Kičevo **11** Dc
Kidal **24** Cc
Kidderminster **7** Ee
Kidira **24** Ac
Kiel **4** Be
Kiel Canal **5** Bab
Kielce **5** Hc
Kieler Bucht **5** Ca
Kieta **27** Cc
Kiev **13** Cd
Kiffa **24** Ac
Kifísiá **11** EFd
Kigali **26** BCb
Kigoma **23** EFf
Kii-Hantō **17** Eh
Kii-Suidō **17** Dh
Kijevskoje vodohranilišče **12** CDc
Kikai-Jima (i.) **16** GHe
Kikinda **6** Ed
Kikonai **17** FGd
Kikori **27** Cc
Kikwit **26** Ab
Kil **4** Cd

Küre dağları (İsfendiyar) (mts.) **22** DEb
Kure Island (Ocean) **27** DEa
Kurejka (riv.) **14** Cc
Kuressaare (Kingissepp) **4** Ed
Kurgan **13** Fd
Kuri Bay **29** Cb
Kuril Islands **14** HIe
Kurilsk **14** He
Kurnool **20** Ee
Kuro-Shima (i.) **17** Ai
Kuršėnai **4** Ede
Kursk **13** Cd
Kurski Zaliv (l.) **4** Ee
Kuršumlija **11** Db
Kuru (riv.) **25** Cd
Kuruman **26** Bd
Kurume **16** Hd
Kurunegala **20** Fg
Kuşada Körfezi **22** Acd
Kuşadası **11** Ge
Kusagaki-Guntō **17** Ai
Kuş Gölü **22** Ab
Kushima **17** Bi
Kushiro **16** Jb
Kushtia **19** Jk
Kuška **15** Cf
Kussaro-Ko **17** HIc
Kustanaj **13** Fd
Kūstī **25** Dc
Kušva **13** EFd
Kūt, Al- **21** Dc
Kut, Ko- (i.) **19** Df
Kütahya **22** Bc
Kutaisi **21** Ca
Kutch (phys. reg.) **20** CDd
Kutch, Gulf of- **20** Cd
Kutch, Rann of- **20** CDd
Kutina **6** Cd
Kutno **5** Gb
Kutu **26** Ab
Kutum **25** Cc
Kuusamo **4** Gb
Kuusankoski **4** Fc
Kuvandyk **12** Ic
Kuwait (Ind. St.) **15** Bfg
Kuzneck **12** Gc
Kvaløy (i.) **4** Da
Kvarner (g.) **6** ABd
Kvarnerić (g.) **6** Bd
Kvikkjokk **4** Db
Kvitøya **13** Ca
Kwa (riv.) **26** Ab
Kwajalein Atoll **27** Db
Kwando (riv.) **26** Bc
Kwangju **16** Gcd
Kwango (riv.) **26** Ab
Kwangsi **15** Dg
Kwekwe **26** Bc
Kwenge (riv.) **26** Ab
Kwidzyn **5** Gb
Kwilu (riv.) **26** Ab
Kyangin **19** BCe
Kyaukpadaung **19** BCd
Kyaukpyu **19** Be
Kyaukse **19** Cd
Kyle of Lochalsh **7** CDc
Kynuna **29** Gc
Kyoga, Lake- **25** Dd
Kyōga-Misaki **17** Dg
Kyŏngju **17** ABg
Kyŏngsŏng **17** ABd
Kyōto **16** Icd
Kyrēnia **22** De
Kyrgyzstan (Ind. St.) **13** Ge
Kyštym **12** Jb
Kyūshū (i.) **16** Hd
Kyushū-Sanchi **17** Bh
Kyzyl **14** Cd
Kyzylkum (phys. reg.) **13** Fe
Kzyl-Orda **13** Fe

L

Labé **24** Ac
Labouheyre **8** Ce
Laboulaye **39** Bc
Labrador **31** HIc
Labrador, Coast of- **31** IJc
Labrador City **31** Ic
Labrador Sea **31** Jc
Lábrea **37** Cc
Labuan, Pulau- **18** Dc
Labuha **18** Ge
Labytnangi **13** Fc
Lacaune, Monts de- (mts.) **8** Ef
Laccadive Islands **20** Df
Lacepede Islands **29** Cb
Lachlan River **29** GHe
Lac la Biche **31** DEc
Laconia, Gulf of- **11** Ee
Lacq **8** Cf
Ladakh Range **20** EFb
Ladoga, Lake- **13** BCc
Ladysmith **26** BCd
Lae **27** Cc
Lærdalsøyri **4** Ac
Læsø (i.) **4** Bd
Lafayette **32** Bbc
Lafia **24** Cd
Laghouat **24** Ca
Lagos [Nig.] **24** Cd
Lagos [Port.] **9** Ad
Lagos de Moreno **34** Bb
Lagrange **29** Cb
Laguna **39** Db
Lahad Datu **18** Ecd
Lahaina **28** map no.1
Lahat **18** Be
Laḩij **21** CDg
Lāhījān **21** Eb
Lahn **5** Bc
Lahn (riv.) **5** ABc
Laholm **4** Cd
Lahore **15** Cf
Lahti **4** Fc
Laï **25** Dd
Lai Chau **19** Dd
Laingsburg **26** ABe
Lainioälven (riv.) **4** Ea
Lairg **7** Dbc
Laixi (Shuiji) **16** Fc
Lajas, Las- **39** ABc
Lajes **39** CDb
Lajkovac **6** DEd
Lake Charles **32** Bb
Lake City **32** Cbc
Lake Constance **5** BCe
Lake Harbour **31** Ib
Lakeland **32** Cc
Lakemba (i.) **28** map no.6
Lake Nash **29** Fc
Lakewood **32** Ca
Lakhimpur **19** Hj
Lak Sao **19** DEe
Laksefjord (b.) **4** Fa
Lakselv **4** Fa
Lakshadweep **20** Dfg
Lalapaşa **22** Ab
Lalín **9** ABa
Lalitpur **19** Gj
Lamar **33** Cc
Lambaréné **24** De
Lambasa **28** map no.6
Lambert Glacier **42** grid square no.2
Lamego **9** Bb
Lamezia Terme **10** Fe
Lamía **11** Ed
Lamon Bay **18** Fb
Lampang **19** Ce
Lampedusa (i.) **10** Dg
Lamphun **19** CDe
Lamu **26** Db
Lanai (i.) **28** map no.1
Lanbi Kyun (i.) **19** Cf
Lancang Jiang (riv.) **19** CDd
Lancaster [Can.] **31** Id
Lancaster [Ca.-U.S.] **33** Bc
Lancaster [Pa.-U.S.] **9** Hd
Lancaster [U.K.] **7** Ed
Lancelin **29** ABe
Lanciano **10** Ec
Lańcut **5** Ic
Landeck **5** Ce
Landenpohja **4** Gc
Landerneau **8** Ac
Lander River **29** Ec
Landes (phys. reg.) **8** Cef
Land's End (cap.) **7** CDf
Landshut **5** Dd
Landskrona **4** Cde
Langeland (i.) **5** Ca
Langjökull (gl.) **4** map no.1
Langkawi, Pulau- (i.) **19** Cg
Langon **8** Ce
Langøya (i.) **4** Ca
Langreo **9** Ca
Langres **8** Fd
Langres, Plateau de- (plat.) **8** Fd
Langsa **10** Ad
Lang Son **19** Ed
Languedoc (phys. reg.) **8** EFef
Lan Hsu (Hungtao Yu) (is.) **16** Ff
Lannion **8** Bc
Lansing **32** Ca
Lanusei **10** Be
Lanzarote (i.) **24** Ab
Lanzhou **16** BCc
Laoag **15** DEh
Laoang **18** FGb
Lao Cai **19** Dd
Laodicea → Latakia **22** Ee
Laoha He (riv.) **16** EFb
Laon **8** Ec
Laos (Ind. St.) **15** Dh
Lapalisse **8** Ed
La Pérouse Strait **16** Ja
Lapland (phys. reg.) **4** EGab
Lappeenranta **4** FGc
Lâpseki **11** Gc
Laptev Sea **41** grid square no.4
Lapua **4** Ec
Łapy **5** Ib
Lār **21** EFd
Larache **24** Ba
Laramie **33** Cb
Larantuka **18** Ff
Larche, Col de- → Maddalena, Colle della- **10** Ab
Laredo [Sp.] **9** Da
Laredo [U.S.] **32** Bc
Lārestān (phys. reg.) **21** EFd
Larino **10** Ed
Lárisa **11** Ed
Larkana **20** Cc
Lárnaca **22** DEe
Larne **7** Dd
Larrimah **29** Eb
Larsen Ice Shelf **42** grid square no.1
Larvik **4** Bd
Lascaux (c.) **8** De
Lashio **15** Dg
Laskargah **20** BCb
Lastovo (i.) **11** Bb
Latacunga **37** Bc
Latakia (Laodicea) **22** Ee
Late Island **28** Ac
Latina **10** Dd
Latvia (Ind. St.) **4** EFd
Lauca, Río- (riv.) **39** Ba
Lauenburg an der Elbe **5** Cb
Lau Group **27** Ec
Launceston **29** map no.1
Laura **29** Gb
Laurel [Ms.-U.S.] **32** BCb
Laurel [Mt.-U.S.] **33** BCb
Lauria **10** Ed
Lausanne **10** Aa
Lausitz (hist. reg.) **5** DEc
Laut, Pulau- (i.) **19** Eh
Laut Kecil, Kepulauan- **18** Ee
Lautoka **28** map no.6
Laval **8** Cc
Lavaur **8** Df
Laverton **29** Cd
Lavras **39** Db
Lávrion **11** EFe
Lavumisa **26** Cd
Lawdar **21** Dg
Lawrence **32** Bb
Lawton **32** Bb
Lawz, Jabal al- (mt.) **21** Bd
Laylá **21** De
Laysan Island **28** Aa
Lazio (reg.) **10** CDcd
Leaf (riv.) **31** Hc
Learmouth **29** Ac
Łeba **5** Fa
Lebanon (mts.) **22** EFef
Lebanon (Ind. St.) **15** Bf
Lebedin **12** DEc
Lębork **5** Fa
Lebrija **9** Bd
Łebsko, Jezioro- **5** Fa
Lebu **39** Ac
Lecce **10** Gd
Lecco **10** Bb
Lech (riv.) **5** Cd
Lectoure **8** Df
Leczyca **5** Gb
Ledesma **9** BCb
Ledjanaja, gora- (mt.) **14** Kc

M

Malolos **27** map no.1
Malosmadulu Atoll **20** Dg
Måløy **4** Ac
Malpelo, Isla de– (i.) **37** Ab
Malta (Ind. St.) **10** Efg
Malta (i.) **10** Efg
Maltahöhe **26** Ad
Malung **4** Cc
Malūţ **25** Dc
Maly Anjuj (riv.) **14** Jc
Maly Jenisej (riv.) **14** Cd
Maly Ljahovski, ostrov– (i.) **14** GHb
Maly Tajmyr, ostrov– **14** DEb
Maly Uzen (riv.) **12** Gd
Mamaia **6** Id
Mamatlar **22** BCd
Mambasa **26** Ba
Mamfe **24** Cd
Mammola **10** Fe
Mamonovo **5** Ha
Mamoré (riv.) **37** Cd
Mamou **24** Acd
Mampong **24** BCd
Mamry, Jezioro– **5** Ha
Mamuju **18** Ee
Mamuno **26** ABd
Man **24** Bd
Man, Isle of– **7** Dd
Mana [Fr. Gui.] **37** Db
Mana [Hi. U.S.] **28** map no.1
Manacapuru **37** CDc
Manacor **9** Gc
Manado **18** Fd
Managua **30** Jh
Managua, Lago de– **34** Bc
Manah **21** Fe
Manakara **23** GHh
Manāmah, Al– **21** Ed
Mananara **26** map no.1
Mananjary **26** map no.1
Manantiales **40** ABc
Manas (riv.) **19** Jj
Manaus **36** DEd
Manavgat **22** CDd
Mancha, La– (phys. reg.) **9** Dc
Manchester [U.K.] **7** EFe
Manchester [U.S.] **32** DEa
Manciuria (hist. reg.) **16** FGa
Mand (riv.) **21** Ed
Manda **26** Cc
Mandal **4** ABd
Mandalay **15** Dg
Mandal–Gobi **14** De
Mandalya Körfezi **22** Ad
Mandan **33** Cb
Mandasor **20** DEd
Mandera **26** Da
Mandla **20** Fd
Mandurah **29** ABe
Manduria **10** Fd
Mandya **20** Ef
Manfredonia **10** Ed
Manfredonia, Golfo di– **10** EFd
Manga (phys. reg.) **24** Dc
Mangabeiras, Chapada del– (plat.) **38** Cbc
Mangaia Island **28** ABd
Mangalia **6** Ie
Mangalore **15** Ch
Mangareva, Île– (i.) **28** Cd
Mangoche **26** Cc
Mangoky (riv.) **26** map no.1
Mangole, Pulau– (i.) **18** FGe
Manhattan **32** Bb
Manica **26** Cc
Manicoré **37** Cc
Manicouagan, Réservoir– **31** Ic
Manihiki Atoll **28** ABc
Maniitsoq / Sukkertoppen **31** Jb
Manikpur **20** Fc
Manila **15** DEh
Manila Bay **18** EFb
Maningrida **29** Ea
Manipur (State) **19** Bcd
Manisa **22** Ac
Manitoba (prov.) **31** EFc
Manitoba, Lake– **31** Fc
Manitoulin (i.) **32** Ca
Manitowoc **32** Ca
Manizales **36** Cc
Manja **26** map no.1
Manjacaze **26** Cd
Manjra (riv.) **20** Ee
Mankato **32** Ba
Manna **18** Be
Mannahill **29** FGe
Mannar **20** EFg
Mannar, Gulf of– **20** Eg
Mannheim **5** Bd
Manokwari **27** Bbc
Manono **26** Bb
Manosque **8** FGf
Manresa **9** FGb
Mans, Le– **8** Dd
Mansa **26** BCc
Mansel Island **31** GHb
Mansfield [U.K.] **7** Fe
Mansfield [U.S.] **32** Ca
Manşūrah, Al– **25** Da
Manta **37** Ac
Mantalingajan, Mount– **18** Ec
Mantaro (riv.) **37** Bd
Mantes–la–Jolie **8** Dc
Mantova **10** Cb
Mänttä **4** EFc
Manturovo **12** FGb
Manu **39** Aa
Manuae Atoll [Cook] **28** ABcd
Manuae Atoll [Fr. Poly.] **28** Bc
Manua Islands **28** map no.5
Manui, Pulau– (i.) **18** Fe
Manuk, Pulau– (i.) **18** GHf
Manus Island **27** Cc
Manyč (riv.) **13** De
Manyč–Gudilo, ozero– **12** Fd
Manzanares **9** Dc
Manzaneda, Cabeza de– (mt.) **9** Ba
Manzanillo [Cuba] **35** Ca
Manzanillo [Mex.] **30** Hh
Manzhouli **14** Ee
Manzilah, Al– **22** CDg
Manzilah, Buḩayrat al– **25** map no.1
Manzil Bū Ruqaybah **10** Bf
Manzil Tamīn **10** Cf
Mao **25** Bc
Maoke, Pegunungan– **27** BCc
Maoming **16** Df
Mapai **26** Cd
Mapi **27** BCc
Mapire **37** Cb
Mapuera (riv.) **38** Bb
Maputo (Lourenço Marques) **26** Cd
Maputo, Baía de– **26** Cd
Maquan He → Brahmaputra (riv.) **20** FGc
Maquela do Zombo **26** Ab
Maquinchao **40** Bb
Mar, Serra do– **39** CDb
Maraã **37** Cc
Marabá **38** Cb
Maracá, Ilha de– (i.) **38** BCa
Maracaibo **36** Cb
Maracaibo, Lago de– **37** Bab
Maracaju, Serra de– (mts.) **39** Cab
Maracay **36** Dbc
Marādah **24** Db
Maradi **24** Cc
Marāgheh **21** Db
Marahuaca, Cerro– (mt.) **37** Cb
Maraió, Ilha de– **38** BCb
Marajó, Baia de– (b.) **38** Cab
Maralal **26** Ca
Maramba (Livingstone) **26** Bc
Marana, La– **10** Bc
Maranhão (State) **38** Cb
Maranhão (riv.) **38** Cc
Marañón (riv.) **37** Bc
Marão **26** Cd
Marari **37** Cc
Mărăşeşti **6** Hd
Marathón **11** EFd
Maratua, Pulau– (i.) **18** Ed
Maraú **38** Dc
Marawī **25** Dc
Marbella **9** Cd
Marble Bar **29** BCc
Marburg an der Lahn **5** Bc
Marca **25** Ed
Marcaria **10** Cb
Marche (reg.) **10** Dc
Marche (hist. reg.) **8** DEde
Marchena **9** Cd
Marchinbar Island **29** Fa
Mar Chiquita, Laguna– **39** Bc
Marcus Island **27** Ca
Mardan **20** Db
Mar del Plata **39** Cc
Mardin **21** Cb
Maré, Île– (i.) **27** Dd
Mareeba **29** GHb
Marettimo (i.) **10** Df
Marganec **12** Dd
Margaret River **29** Db
Margarita, Isla de– (i.) **35** Db
Margate **7** Gf
Margeride, Monts de la– (mts.) **8** Ee
Marghita **6** Fc
Marha (riv.) **14** Ec
Mari (Aut. Rep.) **13** Dd
Maria Atoll **28** Bd
Maria Island **29** Fab
Marianao **35** Ba
Mariánské Lázně **5** Dd
Marías, Islas– **34** Bb
Maria Theresa Reef **28** Bd
Ma'rib **21** Df
Maribo **5** Ca
Maribor **6** BCc
Maricourt **31** Hb
Maridi **25** CDd
Marie Byrd Land **42** grid square no.3
Marie–Galante (i.) **35** DEb
Marienhamn **4** DEc
Mariental **26** Ad
Mariestad **4** Cd
Marignane **8** Ff
Mariinsk **13** HId
Marijampolė (Kapsukas) **5** Ia
Marília **39** CDb
Marinduque (i.) **18** Fb
Marinette **32** Ca
Maringa (riv.) **25** Cde
Maringá **39** Cb
Marinha Grande **9** Ac
Marion Reefs (i.) **29** Ib
Mariscal Estigarribia **39** BCb
Marismas, Las– (phys. reg.) **9** BCd
Mariupol (Ždanov) **13** Ce
Marj, Al– (Barce) **24** DEa
Markovo **14** JKc
Marktredwitz **5** CDcd
Marlborough **29** HIc
Marmande **8** De
Marmara, Sea of– **22** ABb
Marmara Adası (i.) **22** ABb
Marmara ereğlisi **22** ABb
Marmara Gölü **11** GHd
Marmaris **22** ABd
Marmelos **37** Cc
Marmolada (mt.) **10** Ca
Marne (riv.) **8** Fc
Marne au Rhin, Canal de la– **8** Gc
Maro (riv.) **25** Bc
Maroa **37** Cb
Maroantsetra **26** map no.1
Maroni (riv.) **37** Db
Maroua **24** Dc
Marovoay **26** map no.1
Marowijne (riv.) **37** Db
Marqab, Qal'at al– **22** Ee
Marquesas Islands **28** BCc
Marquette **32** Ca
Marrah, Jabal– (mt.) **25** Cc
Marrakech **24** Ba
Marrawah **29** map no.1
Marree **29** Fd
Marromeu **26** Cc
Marrupa **26** Cc
Marsá al Burayqah **24** DEab
Marsabit **25** Dd
Marsala **10** Df
Marseille **8** FGf
Marshall **32** Bb
Marshall Islands (Ind. St.) **27** Db
Martaban **19** Ce
Martaban, Gulf of– **19** Ce
Martapura **18** De
Martigny **10** Aab
Martigues **8** Ff
Martim Vaz, Ilhas– **36** Hef
Martin **5** Gd
Martina Franca **10** Fd
Martinique (i.) **35** DEb
Martos **9** CDd
Martre, Lac la– (l.) **31** CDb
Marutea Atoll **28** Cd

Mar - Mer

Marvdasht 21 Ed
Marx 12 Gc
Mary 13 Ff
Maryborough 29 Id
Maryland (State) 32 Db
Masaka 25 De
Masan 16 Gcd
Masasi 23 Fg
Masaya 35 Bb
Masbate 18 Fb
Masbate (i.) 18 Fb
Mascara 24 Ca
Mascarene Islands 23 map no.1
Masela (i.) 17 Hlg
Maseru 23 Eh
Mashhad 21 FGb
Mashike 17 Gc
Mashkel (riv.) 20 Bc
Mashra'ar Raqq 25 CDd
Masïlah, Wädï al– 21 DEf
Masindi 25 Dd
Maşïrah, Jazïrat– (i.) 21 FGe
Maşïrah, Khalïj– 21 Fef
Masjed–Soleymän 21 DEc
Mask, Lake– 7 Be
Masoala, Cap– 26 map no.1
Mason City 32 Ba
Massa 10 Cbc
Massachusetts (State) 32 Da
Massa Marittima 10 Cc
Massangena 26 Cd
Massapê 38 CDb
Massat 8 Df
Massawa 25 DEc
Massena 32 Da
Massénya 25 Bc
Masset 31 Bc
Massif Central (mts.) 8 EFe
Massinga 26 Cd
Mastouta 10 Bf
Masuda 17 BCg
Masuku 26 Ab
Masvingo 26 Ccd
Maşyäf 22 Fe
Matadi 26 Ab
Matagalpa 35 Bb
Matagorda Bay 32 Bc
Mataiea 28 map no.2
Matak, Pulau– (i.) 18 Cd
Matala 26 Ac
Matam 24 Ac
Matamoros 30 Ig
Matanzas 35 Ba
Matão, Serra do– (mts.) 38 Bbc
Matapán, Cape– 11 Ee
Mataporquera → Valdeolea 9 CDa
Matara 20 EFg
Mataram 18 Ef
Mataranka 29 Eab
Matariya, El– 25 map no.1
Mataró 9 Gb
Matehuala 34 BCb
Matera 10 Fd
Matese (mts.) 10 Ed
Mátészalka 6 Fc
Mathura 20 Ec
Mati 18 Gc
Mätir 20 Bf
Matočkin Šar 13 EFb
Matočkin Šar, proliv– 13 EFb

Mato Grosso (State) 38 Bc
Mato Grosso 39 BCa
Mato Grosso, Plateau of– 38 Bc
Mato Grosso do Sul (State) 39 Cab
Matopo Hills 26 Bcd
Matosinhos 9 Ab
Mátra 6 DEc
Matrah 21 Fe
Maţrüḥ 25 Ca
Matsue 16 Hc
Matsu Liehtao 16 Fe
Matsumae 17 FGd
Matsumoto 16 Ic
Matsusaka 17 Egh
Matsuyama 16 Hd
Matua, ostrov– (i.) 14 Ie
Matuku Island 28 map no.6
Maturin 37 Cb
Mau 19 Hj
Maubeuge 8 EFb
Maui 28 Ba
Maumere 18 Ff
Maun 26 Bc
Mauna Kea (mt.) 28 map no.1
Mauna Loa (mt.) 28 map no.1
Maungdaw 19 Bd
Maupihaa Atoll 28 Bc
Mau Ranipur 19 Gj
Mauriac 8 Ee
Mauritania (Ind. St.) 23 ABcd
Mauritius (Ind. St.) 23 map no.1
Mawchi 19 Ce
Mawlaik 19 BCd
Mawson 42 grid square no.2
Mayaguana Island 32 Dc
Mayagüez 35 Db
Maydh 25 Ec
Maydi 21 Cf
Mayenne 8 Cc
Mayenne (riv.) 8 Cd
Maynas (phys. reg.) 37 Bc
Mayo 31 Bb
Mayor, Puig– (mt.) 9 Gc
Mayotte (i.) 23 Gg
May Pen 35 Cb
Mayumba 26 Ab
Mayum La (p.) 20 Fb
Mazabuka 26 Bc
Mazagão 38 Bb
Mazamet 8 Ef
Mazara del Vallo 10 Df
Mazâr–e Sharïf 15 Cf
Mazarrón 9 Ed
Mazaruni (riv.) 37 CDb
Mazatlán 30 Hg
Mažeikiai 12 Bb
Mazirbe 12 Bb
Mazovia (phys. reg.) 5 GHb
Mbabane 26 Cd
Mbaïki 25 Bd
Mbala (Abercorn) 26 Cb
Mbale 26 Ca
Mbalmayo 24 Dd
Mbandaka 26 Aab
M'banza Congo 26 Ab
Mbanza–Ngungu 26 Ab
Mbeya 23 Ff
Mbinda 26 Ab
Mbini (phys. reg.) 24 CDd
Mbomou (riv.) 26 Ba

Mbout 24 Ac
M'Bridge (riv.) 26 Ab
Mbuji–Mayi 26 Bb
Mbulu 26 Cb
Mburucuya 39 Cb
Mead, Lake– 33 Bc
Meadow Lake 31 DEc
Mealháda 9 ABb
Mearim (riv.) 38 Cb
Meaux 8 Ec
Mecca 21 BCe
Mechelen 8 Fb
Mecklenburg (hist. reg.) 5 CDb
Mecklenburger Bucht 5 Ca
Mecsek (mt.) 6 Dc
Medan 15 Di
Medellín 36 Cc
Mederdra 24 Ac
Medford 33 Ab
Medgidia 6 Id
Media Agua 39 Bc
Mediaş 6 Gc
Medicine Hat 33 BCab
Medina 21 BCe
Medinaceli 9 Db
Medina del Campo 9 Cb
Medina del Ríoseco 9 Cb
Medina–Sidonia 9 Cd
Medinïpur 20 Gd
Mediterranean Sea 23 CEb
Medjerda, Montes de la– 10 ABf
Medjez el–Bab 10 Bf
Mednogorsk 12 Ic
Medny, ostrov– 14 Jd
Médoc (phys. reg.) 8 Ce
Medvedica (riv.) 12 Fc
Medveži, ostrova– 14 Jb
Medvežjegorsk 13 Cc
Medyado Atoll 28 map no.3
Medyai Atoll 28 map no.3
Medžibož 6 Hb
Meekatharra 29 Bd
Meerut 20 Ec
Mega 25 Dd
Mega, Pulau– (i.) 18 Be
Megara 11 Ede
Meghalaya (State) 19 Bc
Meghna (riv.) 19 Jjk
Meia Ponte (riv.) 39 Da
Meiganga 24 Dd
Meiktila 19 Cd
Meiningen 5 Cc
Meissen 5 Dc
Meixian 16 Ef
Mejillones 39 Ab
Mékambo 24 Dd
Mekele 25 DEc
Meknès 24 Ba
Mekong (riv.) 19 Eef
Mekong Delta 19 Efg
Mekongga, Gunung– (mt.) 18 Fe
Melaka (Malacca) 18 Bd
Melalap 18 Ec
Melanesia (is.) 27 BDbc
Melawi (riv.) 18 Dde
Melbourne 29 Gfd
Melchor Ocampo 34 Bc
Melenki 12 Fb
Meleuz 12 Hlc
Melfi [Chad] 25 Bc

Melfi [It.] 10 Ed
Melilla 24 Ba
Mèlito di Porto Salvo 10 Ef
Melitopol 12 DEd
Mělník 5 Ec
Melo 39 Cc
Melrhir, Chott– (l.) 24 Ca
Melun 8 Ec
Melville 33 Ca
Melville, Cape– 29 GHa
Melville Bay 29 Fa
Melville Island [Austl.] 29 Ea
Melville Island [Can.] 41 grid square no.2
Melville Peninsula 31 Gb
Memmingen 5 Cde
Mempawah 18 Cd
Memphis 32 Cb
Menai Strait 7 De
Ménaka 24 Cc
Mende 8 Ee
Mendocino, Cape– 33 Ab
Mendoza 39 Bc
Menemen 22 Ac
Meneng Point 27 map no.2
Mengdingjie 19 CDd
Menggala 18 Ce
Menglian 19 CDd
Mengzi 16 Bf
Menindee 29 Ge
Meningie 29 Ff
Menongue 26 Ac
Menphis (r.) 22 Ch
Mentakab 18 Bd
Mentawai, Selat– 18 ABde
Mentawai Islands 18 Ae
Mentok 18 BCe
Menzies 29 Cde
Menzies, Mount– 42 grid square no.2
Meppel 8 FGa
Meppen 5 Ab
Mequinenza, Embalse de– (l.) 9 EFb
Merabéllou, Kólpos– 11 FGf
Merak 18 Cf
Méralab (i.) 28 map no.4
Merano 10 Ca
Meratus, Pegunungan– 18 Ee
Merauke 27 BCc
Merced 33 ABc
Mercedes [Arg.] 39 Cc
Mercedes [Arg.] 39 Cb
Mercedes [Arg.] 39 Bc
Mercedes [Ur.] 39 Cc
Merceg 25 Ed
Merefa 12 Ed
Mergenevo 12 Hd
Mergui 19 Cf
Mergui Archipelago 19 Cf
Meriç (riv.) 11 Gc
Mérida [Mex.] 30 IJg
Mérida [Sp.] 9 Bc
Mérida [Ven.] 37 Bb
Mérida, Cordillera de– (mts.) 37 BCb
Meridian 32 Cb
Mérignac 8 Ce
Merir (i.) 27 Bb
Merksen 5 Cc
Merredin 29 Be
Merrick (mt.) 7 Dd

© ISTITUTO GEOGRAFICO DE AGOSTINI - Novara

162

Merritt **31** CDc
Merriwa **29** Ie
Mersa Fatma **21** Cg
Merseburg **5** CDc
Mersey (riv.) **7** Ee
Mersin **22** Ed
Merta Road **20** Dc
Merthyr Tydfil **7** Ef
Merzifon **22** Eb
Mesa **33** Bc
Mesagne **10** Fd
Mesola **10** Db
Mesolóngion **11** Dd
Mesopotamia [Arg.] (phys. reg.) **39** Cbc
Mesopotamia [Iraq] (phys. reg.) **21** CDbc
Messalo (riv.) **26** Cc
Messaoud, Hassi- **24** Ca
Messina [It.] **10** Ee
Messina [S. Afr.] **23** EFh
Messina, Gulf of- **11** Ee
Messina, Stretto di- **10** Ee
Messíni **11** DEe
Mesta (Néstos) (riv.) **11** Fc
Mestghanem **24** BCa
Meta (riv.) **37** Bb
Meta, La- (mt.) **10** DEd
Metán **39** Bb
Metauro (riv.) **10** Dc
Metković **11** BCb
Metrz Glacier **42** grid square no.4
Métsovon **11** Dd
Metz **8** Gc
Meulaboh **18** ABd
Meurthe (riv.) **8** Gc
Meuse (riv.) **8** Fc
Mexiana, Ilha- **38** Cab
Mexicali **34** Aa
Mexico (Ind. St.) **30** HIgh
Mexico, Gulf of- **34** CDb
Mexico City **30** Igh
Meyísti (i.) **22** Bd
Meymaneh **20** BCa
Mezdra **11** EFb
Mezen (riv.) **13** Dc
Mezen **13** Dc
Mézenc, Mont- (mt.) **8** Fe
Mezökövesd **6** Ec
Mezötúr **6** Ec
Mhow **20** Ed
Miami **32** Cc
Miandrivazo **26** map no.1
Mīāneh **21** Db
Miangas, Pulau- (is.) **18** Gc
Mianwali **20** Db
Mianyang **16** BCd
Miaodao Qundao **16** EFc
Miarinarivo **26** map no.1
Miass **13** EFd
Miastko **5** Fab
Micenae (r.) **11** Ee
Michalovce **5** HId
Michigan (State) **32** Ca
Michigan, Lake- **32** Ca
Michigan City **32** Ca
Michipicoten **31** Gd
Micronesia (is.) **27** BDbc
Mičurin **11** GHb
Mičurinsk **12** Fc
Midar **24** Ba
Middelburg [S. Afr.] **26** BCd
Middelburg [S. Afr.] **26** Be
Middelfart **5** BCa
Middle Andaman (i.) **19** BCf
Middle Atlas (mts.) **24** Ba
Middlesbrough **7** FGd
Midi, Canal du- **8** DEf
Midi d'Ossau, Pic du- (mt.) **8** Cf
Midland **33** Ca
Midway Islands **28** Aa
Midžor (mt.) **11** Fe
Miechów **5** GHc
Międzyrzec Podlaski **5** Ibc
Międzyrzecz **5** EFb
Mielec **5** Hc
Miercurea Ciuc **6** GHc
Mieres **9** BCa
Miguel Alves **38** Cb
Mihajlovgrad **11** Fe
Mihajlovka **13** Dd
Mikkeli **4** FGc
MíKonos (i.) **11** Fe
Mikun **13** DEc
Mikuni-Sanmyaku (mts.) **17** Ff
Mikura-Jima (i.) **17** FGh
Miladummadulu Atoll **20** DEg
Milagro, El- **39** Bc
Milan **10** Bb
Milâs **22** ABd
Milazzo **10** Ee
Mildura **29** Ge
Miles **29** HId
Miles City **33** Cb
Miletus (r.) **22** Ad
Milfort Haven **7** Df
Miliana **9** FGd
Milikapiti **29** Ea
Miling **29** Bde
Milk (riv.) **33** Cb
Millau **8** Ee
Millerovo **12** Fd
Millevaches, Plateau de- (plat.) **8** DEe
Millicent **29** FGf
Mílos (i.) **11** Fe
Milparinka **29** Gde
Milwaukee **32** Ca
Milwaukee Depth **35** Dab
Mimizan **8** Ce
Mimmaya **17** FGd
Mīnā' al 'Aḥmadī **21** Dd
Minahassa **18** Fd
Minamata **17** ABh
Minami-Daito-Jima (i.) **16** He
Minami-lō-Jima **27** BCa
Minas **39** Cc
Minas-cué **39** Cb
Minas de Ríotinto **9** BCd
Minas de São Domingos **9** ABd
Minas Gerais (State) **39** Da
Minatitlán **34** Cc
Minbu **19** Bde
Minbya **19** Bd
Minchinmávida, Volcán- (mt.) **40** Ab
Mindanao (i.) **15** Ei
Minden **5** Bb
Mindoro (i.) **15** DEh
Mindoro Strait **18** EFb
Mineiros **39** Ca
Mineralnyje Vody **12** Fe
Minervino Murge **10** Fd
Minfeng **20** Fa
Mingan **31** Ic
Minhe **16** Bc
Minho (riv.) **9** Aab
Minho (hist. reg.) **9** Ab
Minicoy Island **20** Dg
Minigwal, Lake- **29** Cd
Minilya **29** Ac
Minjar **12** Ib
Min Jiang (riv.) **16** Ee
Minna **24** Cd
Minneapolis **32** Ba
Minnesota (State) **32** Ba
Minnipa **29** EFe
Miño (riv.) **9** Ba
Minorca (i.) **9** GHc
Minot **33** Cb
Minqin **16** Bc
Min Shan (mts.) **16** Bd
Minsk **13** Bd
Mińsk Mazowiecki **5** HIb
Minto, Lac- **31** Hc
Minusinsk **14** Cd
Minxian **16** Bd
Minyā, Al- **25** CDb
Miquelon (i.) **31** Jd
Mira (riv.) **9** Ad
Miracema do Tocantins **38** Cbc
Miraflores **37** Bb
Miraflores Locks **35** map no.1
Miraj **20** DEe
Miramar **39** Cc
Miranda **39** Cb
Miranda de Ebro **9** Da
Miranda do Douro **9** Bb
Mirande **8** CDf
Mirandela **9** Bb
Mirandola **10** Cb
Mirbat **21** EFf
Mirecourt **8** FGc
Mirgorod **12** Dd
Miri **18** Dd
Mirim, Lagoa- (lag.) **39** Cc
Mírina **11** Fd
Mirny [Ant.] **42** grid square no.4
Mirny [Russia] **14** Ec
Mirpur Khas **20** CDc
Miryang **17** Ag
Mirzapur **20** Fcd
Mishan **16** Ha
Mi-Shima (i.) **17** Bg
Misiones, Sierra de- (mts.) **39** Cb
Miskitos, Cayos- (is.) **35** Bb
Miskolc **6** Eb
Mismār **21** Bf
Mismīyah, Al- **22** Ff
Misool, Pulau- (i.) **18** He
Mississauga **31** GHd
Mississippi (riv.) **32** Bb
Mississippi (State) **32** BCb
Missoula **33** Bb
Missouri (State) **32** Bb
Missouri (riv.) **32** Ba
Mistassini, Lac- **31** Eb
Mistelbach an der Zaya **5** Fd
Misti, Volcán- (volc.) **39** Aa
Misurata **24** Da
Mitchell [Austl.] **29** Hd
Mitchell [U.S.] **32** Ba
Mitchell, Mount- **32** Cb
Mitchell River **29** Gb
Mitchell River (riv.) **29** Gb
Mit Ghamr **22** Cg
Mithimna **11** FGd
Mitiaro Island **28** Bc
Mitilíni **22** Ac
Mitilínis, Stenón- **11** Gd
Mitla Pass **25** map no.2
Mito **17** Gf
Mittellandkanal (can.) **5** ABb
Mitú **37** BCb
Mitumba, Monts- **26** Bbc
Mitwaba **26** Bb
Mitzic **24** Dd
Miyake-Jima (i.) **17** FGg
Miyako **16** Jc
Miyako-Jima (i.) **16** Gef
Miyakonojō **16** Hd
Miyanoura-Dake (mt.) **17** Bi
Miyazaki **16** Hd
Miyun **16** Eb
Mizdah **24** Da
Mizen Head **7** ABf
Mizil **6** Hd
Mizoč **6** GHa
Mizoram (State) **19** Bd
Mizuho **42** grid square no.2
Mizusawa **17** Ge
Mjölby **4** Cd
Mjøsa (l.) **4** Bc
Mkuze **26** Cd
Mladá Boleslav **5** Ec
Mladenovac **6** Ed
Mława **5** GHb
Mljet (i.) **11** Bb
Mo **4** Cb
Moa (riv.) **24** Ad
Moa, Pulau- (i.) **18** Gf
Moala (i.) **28** map no.6
Moanda **26** Ab
Moba **26** Bb
Mobaye **26** Ba
Mobayi-Mbongo **26** Ba
Mobile **32** Cb
Mobridge **33** Cb
Moçambique **23** FGg
Mocha, Isla- (i.) **39** Ac
Mochis, Los- **34** ABb
Mochudi **26** Bd
Mocímboa da Praia **26** Dc
Môco, Serra- (mts.) **26** Ac
Mocoa **37** Bb
Mocuba **23** Fg
Modane **8** Ge
Módena **10** Cb
Modica **10** Ef
Modřany **5** Ecd
Moe **29** Hf
Mogadishu **25** Ed
Mogaung **19** Cc
Mogi das Cruzes **39** Db
Mogilev **13** Cd
Mogilev-Podolski **6** Hb
Mogoča **14** EFd
Mogok **19** Cd
Mogrein **24** ABb
Moguer **9** Bd
Mohács **6** Dd
Mohanganj **19** Jj
Mohenjo Daro (r.) **20** Cc
Moinești **6** Hc
Moissac **8** De

© ISTITUTO GEOGRAFICO DE AGOSTINI - Novara

Mojave 33 Bc
Mojave Desert 33 Bc
Mojynty 13 Ge
Mokolo 24 Dc
Mokp'o 14 Ff
Mola di Bari 10 Fd
Moldav (riv.) 5 Ed
Moldavia (phys. reg.) 6 Hcd
Molde 4 Ac
Moldefjorden (b.) 4 Ac
Moldova (Ind. St.) 6 Ic
Moldova Nouă 6 Ed
Moldoveanu, Vîrful– (mt.) 6 Gd
Molepolole 26 Bd
Molfetta 10 Fd
Molise (reg.) 10 Ed
Mollendo 39 Aa
Mölndal 4 BCd
Molodečno 12 Cc
Molodežnaja 42 grid square
 no.2
Mologa (riv.) 12 Eb
Molokai (i.) 28 Ba
Molopo (w.) 26 Bd
Moluccas (is.) 18 GHde
Molucca Sea 18 Gef
Moma 26 CDc
Mombasa 23 FGf
Mombetsu 16 Jb
Momboyo (riv.) 25 BCe
Momčilgrad 11 Fc
Møn (i.) 5 Da
Mona, Isla– (i.) 35 Db
Monaco (Ind. St.) 10 Ac
Monaghan 7 Cd
Mona Passage (str.) 35 Db
Moncayo, Sierra del– (mts.) 9
 DEb
Mončegorsk 13 Cc
Mönchengladbach 5 CDc
Monclova 34 Bb
Moncton 31 Id
Mondego (riv.) 9 ABb
Mondego, Cape– 9 Ab
Mondello 10 De
Mondovi 10 Ab
Monemvasía 11 Ee
Moneron, ostrov– (i.) 17 Ga
Monfalcone 10 Db
Monforte de Lemos 9 Ba
Monga 26 Ba
Mongalla 25 Dd
Mong Cai 19 Ed
Monger, Lake– 29 Bd
Monghpayak 19 CDd
Mongnai 16 Af
Mongo 25 BCc
Mongolia (Ind. St.) 15 De
Mongolski Altaj (mts.) 14 Ce
Mongororo 25 Cc
Mongu 26 Bc
Monkoto 25 BCe
Monmouth 7 Ef
Monopoli 10 Fd
Monor 6 Dc
Monreale 10 De
Monroe 32 Bb
Monrovia 24 Ad
Mons 8 EFb
Monselice 10 Cb
Montagne Noire (mt.) 8 Ef
Montalbán 9 Eb
Montana (State) 33 BCb

Montaña, La– (phys. reg.) 37
 Bcd
Montánchez 9 Bc
Montargis 8 Ed
Montauban 8 DEef
Montbard 8 Fd
Montbéliard 8 Gd
Montceau–les–Mines 8 EFd
Mont–de–Marsan 8 CDef
Montdidier 8 Ec
Mont Dore 8 Ee
Monteagudo 39 Ba
Monte Albán (r.) 34 Cc
Monte Alegre 38 Bb
Monte Azul 39 Da
Monte Bello Islands 29 ABc
Monte Caseros 39 Cbc
Montecatini Terme 10 Cc
Monte Comán 39 Bc
Montecristo (i.) 10 Cc
Montefiascone 10 Dc
Montego Bay 35 Cb
Monteiro 38 Db
Montélimar 8 Fe
Monte Lindo (riv.) 39 BCb
Monte Lirio 35 map no.1
Montemorelos 34 Cb
Montenegro 11 Cb
Montepuez 26 Cc
Montepulciano 10 Cc
Montereau–Faut–Yonne 8 Ec
Monterey 33 Ac
Montería 37 Bb
Monterós 39 Bb
Monterrey 34 BCb
Monte Sant'Angelo 10 Ed
Montes Claros 39 Da
Montevideo 39 Cc
Montgenèvre (p.) 10 Ab
Montgomery [U.K.] 7 Ee
Montgomery [U.S.] 32 Cb
Montigny–lès–Metz 8 Gc
Montijo [Port.] 9 Ac
Montijo [Sp.] 9 Bc
Montilla 9 Cd
Mont–Joli 32 Ea
Mont–Laurier 32 Da
Montluçon 8 Ed
Montmagny 31 Hd
Montmorillon 8 Dd
Monto 29 Icd
Montoro 9 Ccd
Montpelier 32 Da
Montpellier 8 EFf
Montréal 31 Hd
Montreux 10 Aa
Montrose [U.K.] 7 EFc
Montrose [U.S.] 33 Cc
Mont–Saint–Michel, Le– 8 Cc
Montserrat (i.) 35 Db
Monywa 19 BCd
Monza 10 Bb
Monzón 9 Fb
Moonie 29 Id
Moonta 29 Fe
Moora 29 Be
Moore, Lake– 29 Bde
Moorea (i.) 28 map no.2
Moorhead 32 Ba
Moose (riv.) 32 Ca
Moose Jaw 33 Cab
Moosonee 31 Db
Mopti 24 Bc

Moquegua 39 ABa
Mora [Port.] 9 Ac
Mora [Sp.] 9 CDc
Mora [Swe.] 4 Cc
Moradabad 15 Cg
Mora de Rubielos 9 Eb
Moratalla 9 DEc
Morava 5 Fd
Morava, Južna– 11 DEb
Moravia (phys. reg.) 5 Fd
Morawa 29 Bd
Morawhanna 37 Db
Moray Firth (b.) 7 Ec
Morcenx 8 Cef
Mordvinia (Aut. Rep.) 13 Dd
Morecambe Bay 7 Ede
Moree 29 Hld
Morelia 34 Bc
Morella 9 EFb
Morena 19 Gj
Morena, Sierra– (mts.) 9 BDc
Morenci 33 Cc
Moresby Island 31 Bc
Moreton 29 Ga
Moreton Bay 29 Id
Moreton Island 29 Id
Mórfou 22 De
Morgan 29 FGe
Mori 17 Gc
Morioka 16 Jc
Morlaix 8 ABc
Mornington Island 29 FGb
Morocco (Ind. St.) 23 Bbc
Morogoro 23 Ff
Moro Gulf 18 Fc
Morombe 26 map no.1
Morón 35 Ca
Morondava 23 Gh
Morón de la Frontera 9 Cd
Moroni 26 Dc
Morotai, Pulau– 18 Gd
Morotai, Selat– 18 Gd
Moroto 26 Ca
Morozovsk 12 Fd
Morphou Bay 22 De
Morris Jesup, Kap– 41 grid
 square no.1
Morrumbene 26 Cd
Moršansk 12 Fc
Mortara 10 Bb
Mortes, Rio das– (riv.) 38 Bc
Mortlock Islands 27 Cb
Morvan, Monts du– 8 EFd
Morven (mt.) 7 Eb
Morven 29 Hd
Morvi 20 Dd
Morwell 29 Hf
Moscow 13 Dd
Mosel (riv.) 5 Acd
Moselle (riv.) 5 Acd
Moshi 26 Cb
Mosjøen 4 Cb
Moskenesøya (i.) 4 BCb
Moskva (riv.) 12 Eb
Mosonmagyaróvár 5 Fe
Mosquero 38 Cb
Mosquitia (phys. reg.) 35 Bb
Mosquitos, Costa de– 35 Bb
Mosquitos, Golfo de los– 35
 Bbc
Moss 4 Bd
Mossaka 24 De
Mosselbaai 23 Ei

Mossendjo 26 Ab
Mossman 29 Hb
Mossoró 38 Db
Moss Vale 29 Hle
Most 5 Dc
Mostar 11 BCb
Mostiska 5 Id
Mosty 12 Bc
Mosul 21 Cb
Motagua (riv.) 35 ABb
Motala 4 Cd
Motherwell 7 Ed
Motihari 20 FGc
Motril 9 Dd
Motu One Atoll 28 Bc
Moudjéria 24 Ac
Moúdros 11 Fd
Mouila 26 Ab
Mould Bay 41 grid square
 no.2
Moulins 8 Ed
Moulmein 15 Dh
Moulouya (riv.) 24 Ba
Moultrie 32 Cb
Moundou 25 Bd
Mountain Nile (riv.) 25 Dd
Mount Barker 29 Bef
Mount Douglas 29 Hc
Mount Gambier 29 FGf
Mount Garnet 29 GHb
Mount Isa 29 Fc
Mount Magnet 29 Bd
Mount Morgan 29 Hlc
Mount Vernon 32 Cb
Moura [Austl.] 29 Hc
Moura [Braz.] 37 Cc
Moura [Port.] 9 Bc
Mourne Mountains 7 CDd
Mouscron 8 Eb
Moussoro 25 Bc
Moyale 25 Dd
Moyo, Pulau– (i.) 18 Ef
Moyobamba 37 Bc
Mozambique (Ind. St.) 23 Fgh
Mozambique Channel 26
 CDcd
Možga 12 Hb
Mozyr 12 Cc
Mpanda 26 Cb
Mpika 26 Cc
Mragowo 5 Hb
Mreïti, El– 24 Bb
Mreyyé, El– (phys. reg.) 24 Bc
Mtwara 23 FGfg
Muang Pakxan 19 De
Muang Sing 19 Dd
Muang Xaignabouri 19 De
Muang Xépôn 19 Ee
Muar 18 Bd
Muarasiberut 18 Ae
Muaratebo 18 Be
Muaratewe 18 De
Mubarraz, Al– 21 Dd
Mubi 24 Dc
Muchinga Mountains 26 Cc
Mudan Jiang (riv.) 17 Ab
Mudanjiang 16 GHb
Mudanya 22 Bb
Mudawwarah, Al– 22 Fh
Mueda 26 Cc
Muende 26 Cc
Mufulira 26 Bc
Mugi 17 Dh

Pecos (riv.) **33** Cc
Pecos **33** Cc
Pécs **6** CDc
Pedra Azul **39** Da
Pedreiras **38** Cb
Pedrera, La– **37** BCc
Pedro Afonso **38** Cb
Pedro Cays (is.) **35** Cb
Pedro de Valdivia **39** ABb
Pedro II, Ilha– **37** Cb
Pedro Juan Caballero **39** Cb
Pedro Miguel **35** map no.1
Pedro Miguel Locks **35** map no.1
Peebles **7** Ed
Pee Dee (riv.) **32** CDb
Peel Sound **31** Fa
Peene (riv.) **5** Db
Pegai **11** Dd
Pegu **19** Ce
Pegu Yoma **19** Cde
Pehuajó **39** Bc
Peipus, Lake– **13** Bd
Peixe **38** Cc
Pekalongan **18** CDf
Peking → Beijing **16** Ebc
Pelagie, Isole– **10** Dg
Pélagos (i.) **11** EFd
Pelat, Mont– (mt.) **8** Ge
Peleaga, Vîrful– (mt.) **6** Fd
Pelechuco **39** Ba
Peleduj **14** Ed
Peleng, Pulau– (i.) **18** Fe
Peljesac (pen.) **11** Bb
Pello **4** EFb
Pelly (riv.) **31** Bb
Pelly Bay **31** FGb
Pelopónnisos (phys. reg.) **11** DEe
Peloritani (mts.) **10** Eef
Peloro o Punta del Faro, Capo– (cap.) **10** Ee
Pelotas **39** Cc
Pelotas, Rio– (riv.) **39** Cb
Pelusium (r.) **25** map no.1
Pelvoux, Massif du– (mt.) **8** Ge
Pelym (riv.) **12** Ja
Pematangsiantar **18** ABd
Pemba **26** Dc
Pemba (i.) **26** CDb
Pemberton **29** Be
Pembroke [Can.] **32** Da
Pembroke [U.K.] **7** Df
Pembuang (riv.) **18** De
Penafiel **9** ABb
Peñafiel **9** CDb
Peñalara (mt.) **9** CDb
Penambo Range **18** Ed
Peña Nevada, Cerro– (mt.) **34** BCb
Peña Prieta (mt.) **9** Ca
Peñaranda de Bracamonte **9** Cb
Peñarroya–Pueblonuevo **9** Cc
Peñas, Cabo de– (cap.) **9** Ca
Penas, Golfo de– (b.) **40** Ab
Peña Ubiña (mt.) **9** BCa
Pendembu **24** ABd
Pendleton **33** ABb
Peneda (mt.) **9** Ab
Penedo **38** Dc
Penganga (riv.) **20** Ede

Peniche **9** Ac
Peñíscola **9** Fb
Penitente, Serra do– (mts.) **38** Cb
Penju, Kepulauan– **18** Gf
Penne **10** Dc
Penner (riv.) **20** Ef
Pennine Alps **10** Aab
Pennines **7** EFde
Pennsylvania (State) **32** Da
Peno **12** Db
Penong **29** Ee
Penonomé **35** Bc
Penrhyn Atoll **28** ABc
Penrith **29** Ie
Pensacola **32** Cb
Pentecôte, Île– (i.) **28** map no.4
Penticton **33** ABb
Pentland Firth **7** Eb
Penza **13** Dd
Penzance **7** CDf
Penžina (riv.) **14** Jc
Penžinskaja guba **14** Jc
Peoria **32** Ca
Pequiri (riv.) **39** Ca
Perabumulih **18** BCe
Perche, Col de la– (p.) **8** Ef
Perche, Collines du– (mts.) **8** Dc
Percival Lakes **29** CDc
Perdido, Monte– **9** EFa
Perečin **5** Id
Pereira **37** Bb
Pereslavl–Zalesski **12** Eb
Pergamino **39** BCc
Pergamum → Bergama **22** Ac
Peribonca (riv.) **32** Da
Périgord (phys. reg.) **8** De
Périgueux **8** De
Perija, Sierra de– (mts.) **37** Bab
Peristéri (mt.) **11** Dd
Perito Moreno **40** Ab
Perlas, Archipiélago de las– (is.) **35** Cc
Perm **13** Ed
Përmeti **11** Dc
Pernambuco (State) **38** Db
Pernik **11** Eb
Péronne **8** Ebc
Pérouse Pinnacle, La– (i.) **28** Aa
Perpignan **8** Ef
Perry Island **31** Eb
Persepolis (r.) **21** Ecd
Persian Gulf **21** DEd
Perth [Austl.] **29** ABe
Perth [U.K.] **7** Ec
Perthus, Col de– **9** Ga
Pertusato, Capo– **8** map no.1
Perú (Ind. St.) **36** Cde
Peru, Altiplano del– **37** Bd
Perugia **10** Dc
Peruíbe **39** Db
Pervomajsk [Russia] **12** Fc
Pervomajsk [Ukr.] **12** CDd
Pervouralsk **13** EFd
Pesaro **10** Dc
Pescadores (is.) **16** EFf
Pescara **10** Ec
Peschici **10** Fd

Peshāwar **15** Cf
Peshkopia **11** Dc
Peskovka [Russia] **12** Hb
Peskovka [Ukr.] **6** IJa
Pesqueira **38** Db
Pessac **8** Ce
Peštera **11** Fbc
Pestovo **12** Eb
Petah Tiqwa **22** Ef
Petalioi, Gulf of– **11** Fde
Petauke **26** Cc
Peterborough [Austl.] **29** FGe
Peterborough [Can.] **32** Da
Peterborough [U.K.] **7** FGe
Peterhead **7** Fc
Petermann Ranges **29** DEcd
Petersburg [Ak.–U.S.] **31** Bc
Petersburg [Va.–U.S.] **32** Db
Peter's Mine **37** CDb
Peter the Great Bay **16** Hb
Peto **34** Dbc
Petrel **42** grid square no.1
Petrič **11** Ec
Petrila **6** Fd
Petrolândia **38** Db
Petrolina **38** Cb
Petropavlovsk **13** FGd
Petropavlovsk Kamčatski **14** IJd
Petrópolis **39** Db
Petroşani **6** Fd
Petrovsk **12** Gc
Petrovsk–Zabaikalski **14** Dd
Petrozavodsk **13** BCc
Petuhovo **13** Fd
Peureulak **18** Ad
Pevek **14** Kc
Pforzheim **5** Bd
Phalodi **20** Dc
Phangan, Ko– (i.) **19** CDg
Phang–nga **19** Cg
Phan Rang **18** CDb
Phan Thiet **19** Ef
Phatthalung **19** CDg
Phet Buri **19** CDf
Phetchabun **19** De
Philadelphia **32** Dab
Philippines (Ind. St.) **15** Ehi
Philippine Sea **27** Bb
Phitsanulok **19** De
Phnum Pénh **15** Dh
Phoenix (i.) **28** Ac
Phoenix **33** Bc
Phoenix Islands **28** Ac
Phöngsali **19** Dd
Phrae **19** De
Phu Bia (mt.) **19** De
Phuket **19** Cg
Phu Miang (mt.) **19** De
Phu Qui **19** Ee
Phu Quoc, Dao– (i.) **19** Df
Piacenza **10** Bb
Pianosa (i.) **10** Cc
Piaozero, ozero– **4** Gb
Piaseczno **5** Hbc
Piatra Neamţ **6** Hc
Piauí (riv.) **38** Cb
Piauí (State) **38** Cb
Piave (riv.) **10** Da
Piazza Armerina **10** Ef
Pibor Post **25** Dd
Picardy (hist. reg.) **8** DEbc
Pichilemu **39** Ac

Pickle Crow **31** FGc
Pico, El– **39** Ba
Picos **38** Cb
Pico Truncado **40** Bb
Picton, Isla– **40** Bc
Pidurutalagala (mt.) **20** Fg
Piedras, Río de las– (riv.) **37** BCd
Piedras Negras **34** Bb
Pieksämäki **4** Fc
Pielavesi **4** Fc
Pielinen (l.) **4** Gc
Piemonte (reg.) **10** Ab
Pierre **33** Cb
Piešťany **5** Fd
Pietermaritzburg **26** Cd
Pietersburg **26** BCd
Pietrasanta **10** Cc
Pietrosu, Vîrful– (mt.) **6** Gc
Pigs, Bay of– **35** Ba
Pikalevo **12** DEb
Pikelot Island **27** Cb
Piła **5** Fb
Pilar **39** Cb
Pilcomayo (riv.) **39** Bb
Pilibhit **20** EFc
Pilica (riv.) **5** Hc
Pilion Óros (mt.) **11** Ed
Pilos **11** De
Pimenta Bueno **37** Cd
Piña **35** map no.1
Pinang (i.) **19** CDg
Pınarbaşı **22** Fc
Pinar del Río **35** Ba
Pincota **6** EFc
Pindus Mountains **11** Dd
Pine Bluff **32** Bb
Pine Creek **29** Ea
Pine Island Bay **42** grid square no.3
Pine Point **31** Db
Pinerolo **10** Ab
Ping (riv.) **19** Ce
Pingdingshan **16** Dd
Pingelap Atoll **27** Db
Pinglap Atoll **28** map no.3
Pingle **16** CDf
Pingliang **16** Cc
Pingtung **16** Ff
Pingwu **16** Bd
Pingxiang [China] **16** DEe
Pingxiang [China] **16** Cf
Pingyao **16** Dc
Pinheiro **38** Cb
Pini, Pulau– (i.) **18** Ad
Pinios (riv.) **11** DEd
Pinjarra **29** Be
Pinnaroo **29** Gef
Pinotepa Nacional **34** Cc
Pins, Îles des– **27** Dd
Pinsk **13** Bd
Pintados **39** ABb
Pinto **39** Bb
Piombino **10** Cc
Pioner, ostrov– **14** BCab
Pionki **5** Hc
Piotrków Trybunalski **5** Gc
Pipanaco, Salar de– (s. m.) **39** Bb
Piperi (i.) **11** Fd
Piqua **32** Ca
Piracambu, Serra do– (mts.) **38** Cb

Regina [Can.] **31** Ec
Regina [Fr. Gui.] **38** Ba
Registan (phys. reg.) **20** BCb
Regnitz (riv.) **5** Cd
Reguengos de Monsaraz **9** Bc
Rehoboth **26** Ad
Rehovot **22** Eg
Reigate **7** Ff
Reims **8** Fc
Reina Adelaida, Archipiélago– (is.) **40** Ac
Reindeer Depot **31** Bb
Reindeer Lake **31** Ec
Reinosa **9** Ca
Remanso **38** Cb
Rembang **18** Df
Remiremont **8** Gc
Remscheid **5** Ac
Rendsburg **5** BCa
Rengat **18** Be
Reni **6** Id
Renmark **29** Ge
Rennell Island **27** CDc
Rennes **8** Cc
Rennick Glacier **42** grid square no.4
Reno (riv.) **10** Cb
Reno **33** ABbc
Reno, El– **32** Bb
Réole, La– **8** CDe
Republican River **32** Bab
Repulse Bay **30** IJc
Requena [Peru] **37** Bc
Requena [Sp.] **9** Ec
Reşadiye Yarimadasi **11** Ge
Resia, Passo di– **10** Ca
Resistencia **39** BCb
Reşiţa (mts.) **6** Ed
Resolute **31** Fa
Resolution Island **31** Ib
Rethel **8** Fc
Réthimmon **11** Ff
Reunion (i.) **23** map no.1
Reus **9** Fb
Reuss (riv.) **5** Be
Reutlingen **5** Bd
Revda **12** IJb
Revelstoke **33** Ba
Revermont (mt.) **8** Fd
Revillagigedo, Islas– **30** GHh
Rewa **20** Fd
Rewari **19** Gij
Rex, Mount– **42** grid square no.1
Rey **21** Eb
Reykjanes (cap.) **4** map no.1
Reykjavík **4** map no.1
Reynosa **34** Cb
Rež **12** Jb
Rezé **8** Cd
Rēzekne **4** Fd
Rezina **6** Ic
Rhein (riv.) **5** Be
Rheine **5** Ab
Rheinland-Pfalz (phys. reg.) **5** Acd
Rhir, Cap– **24** ABa
Rhode Island (State) **32** Da
Rhodes **22** Bd
Rhodes (i.) **22** Bde
Rhodope Mountains **11** EFbc
Rhön (mt.) **5** BCc
Rhône (riv.) **10** Aa
Rhum (i.) **7** Cc
Riaño **9** Ca
Riau, Kepulauan– **18** Bd
Ribadeo **9** Ba
Ribas do Rio Pardo **39** Cb
Ribatejo (phys. reg.) **9** Ac
Ribáuè **26** Cc
Ribe **5** Ba
Ribeira (riv.) **39** Db
Ribeira → Santa Eugenia **9** Aa
Ribeirão Prêto **39** Db
Ribérac **8** CDe
Riberalta **37** Cd
Riccione **10** Dc
Richard's Bay **26** Cd
Richardson Mountains **31** Bb
Richard Toll **24** Ac
Richfield **33** Bc
Richland **33** Bb
Richmond [Austl.] **29** Gc
Richmond [In.–U.S.] **32** Cb
Richmond [Ky.–U.S.] **32** Cb
Richmond [Va.–U.S.] **32** Db
Ried im Innkreis **5** Dd
Riesa **5** Dc
Riesco, Isla– (i.) **40** Ac
Riesi **10** Ef
Rieti **10** Dc
Rif (mts.) **24** Ba
Rifstangi (cap.) **4** map no.1
Rift Valley **26** Cab
Rīga **4** Fd
Rīga, Gulf of– **4** EFd
Rihand (riv.) **20** Fd
Rihand Sāgar **20** Fd
Riihimäki **4** EFc
Riiser-Larsen Halvøya **42** grid square no.2
Rijeka **6** Bd
Riksgränsen **4** Da
Rila (mts.) **11** Eb
Rimal, Ar– → Rub' al Khali **21** DEef
Rimatara, Île– (i.) **28** Bd
Rimavská Sobota **5** GHd
Rimini **10** Db
Rîmnicu Sărat **6** Hd
Rîmnicu Vîlcea **6** Gd
Rimouski **31** Id
Ringebu **4** Bc
Ringerike **4** Bc
Ringsted **5** CDa
Ringus **19** Gj
Ringvassøy (i.) **4** Da
Rinjani, Gunung– (mt.) **18** Ef
Riobamba **37** Bc
Rio Branco **37** Ccd
Rio Brilhante **39** Cb
Rio Claro **39** Db
Rio Colorado **39** Bc
Rio Cuarto **39** Bc
Rio de Janeiro (State) **39** Db
Rio de Janeiro **39** Db
Río Gallegos **36** Di
Rio Grande **39** Cc
Río Grande **40** Bc
Rio Grande do Norte (State) **38** Db
Rio Grande do Sul (State) **39** Cbc
Ríohacha **37** Ba
Rioja, La– **39** Bb
Rioja, La– (phys. reg.) **26** DEa
Rio Largo **38** Db
Riom **8** Ee
Río Mayo **40** ABb
Río Mulatos **39** Ba
Rio Negro **39** CDb
Río Negro, Embalse del– (l.) **39** Cc
Río Tercero **39** Bc
Rio Tinto **38** Db
Rio Verde **39** Ca
Rio Verde de Mato Grosso **39** Ca
Rishiri-Tō (i.) **16** Jab
Risle (riv.) **8** Dc
Risør **4** Bd
Ritchie's Archipelago **19** Bf
Ritter, Mount– **33** Bc
Riva → Cayağzi **22** Bb
Rivadavia [Arg.] **39** Bb
Rivadavia [Chile] **39** Ab
Riva del Garda **10** Cb
Rivas **35** Bb
Rive-de-Gier **8** Fe
Rivera [Arg.] **39** Bc
Rivera [Ur.] **39** Cc
River Cess **24** ABd
Riverside **33** Bc
Rivière-du-Loup **32** Ea
Rivoli **10** Ab
Riyadh **21** De
Rize **21** Ca
Rizzuto, Capo– **10** Fe
Rjazan **13** CDd
Rjažsk **12** Fc
Rjukan **4** ABd
Roa **9** CDb
Roanne **8** Fde
Roanoke **32** CDb
Roanoke (riv.) **32** Db
Robert English Coast **42** grid square no.1
Robertsport **24** Ad
Robeson Channel **41** grid square no.1
Robinvale **29** Ge
Robla, La– **9** DCa
Roboré **39** BCa
Robson, Mount **31** CDc
Roca, Cabo da– (cap.) **9** Ac
Roca Partida, Isla– (i.) **34** Ac
Rocas, Atol das– (i.) **38** Db
Rocha **39** Cc
Rochechouart **8** De
Rochefort **8** Ce
Rochelle, La– **8** Cd
Rochester [Mn.–U.S.] **32** Ba
Rochester [N.Y.–U.S.] **32** Da
Roche-sur-Yon, La– **8** Cd
Rockefeller Plateau (plat.) **42** grid square no.3
Rockford **32** Ca
Rockhampton **29** Ic
Rockingham **29** ABe
Rock Island **32** BCa
Rockland **32** Ea
Rock Springs **33** BCb
Rocky Mount **32** Db
Rocky Mountains **31** CDcd
Roda, La– **9** DEc
Rødberg **4** ABc
Rødbyhavn **5** Ca
Rodez **8** Ee
Rodrigues (i.) **23** map no.1
Roebourne **29** Bc
Roebuck Bay **29** Cb
Roermond **8** FGb
Roeselare **8** Eb
Roes Welcome Sound **31** Gb
Rogaguado, Lago– **39** Ba
Rognan **4** Cb
Rohtak **20** Ec
Roi Et **19** De
Roja, La– **36** Dfg
Rojo, Cabo– **34** Cb
Rokan (riv.) **18** Bd
Rolla **32** Bb
Roma **29** Hd
Roman **6** Hc
Romana, La– **35** Db
Romang, Pulau– (i.) **18** Gf
Români **25** map no.1
Romania (Ind. St.) **3** Fc
Romanovka **14** DEd
Romans-sur-Isère **8** Fe
Rome [Ga.–U.S.] **32** Cb
Rome [It.] **10** Dd
Romilly-sur-Seine **8** EFc
Romny **12** Dc
Rømø (i.) **5** Ba
Romorantin-Lanthenay **8** DEd
Ronas Hill **7** Fa
Ronave **27** map no.2
Roncador, Cayos de– (is.) **35** BCb
Roncador, Serra do– (mts.) **38** Bc
Roncesvalles **9** Ea
Ronda **9** Cd
Rondane (mt.) **4** Bc
Rondônia **37** Cd
Rondônia (State) **37** Cd
Rondonópolis **39** Ca
Rong, Kaōh– (i.) **19** Df
Ronge, La– **31** Bb
Rongelap Atoll **27** Db
Rønne **4** Ce
Rooniu (mt.) **28** map no.2
Roosendaal **8** Fb
Roosevelt, Rio– (riv.) **38** Ab
Roosevelt Island **42** grid square no.3
Roosevelt Lake **33** Bb
Roper River **29** Ea
Roper Valley **29** EFa
Roques, Islas los– (is.) **35** Db
Roquetas de Mar **9** Dd
Roraima (State) **37** Cb
Roraima, Monte– **37** CDb
Røros **4** BCc
Rørvik **4** BCb
Ros (riv.) **6** Ib
Rosa, Monte– **10** Ab
Rosário **38** Cb
Rosario [Arg.] **39** Bc
Rosario [Mex.] **34** Bb
Rosario [Mex.] **34** Aab
Rosario de la Frontera **39** Bb
Rosário do Sul **39** Cc
Rosário Oeste **39** Ca
Roseau **35** Db
Rosebery **29** map no.1
Rosebud **29** GHf
Roseburg **33** Ab
Rosenheim **5** CDe
Rosetown **31** Ec

Sarnia **31** Gd
Sarny **13** Bd
Saroako **18** Fe
Saroma-Ko **17** HIb
Saronikos Kólpos **11** Ee
Saros, Gulf of- **22** Ab
Sárospatak **6** Eb
Šar planina (mts.) **11** Dbc
Sarpsborg **4** BCd
Sarrebourg **8** Gc
Sarreguemines **8** Gc
Sarria **9** Ba
Sars, As- **10** Bf
Sartène **8** map no.1
Sarthe (riv.) **8** Cd
Sárvár **6** Cc
Saryč, mys- **12** De
Saryg-Sep **14** Cd
Sary-Šagan **13** Ge
Sarysu (riv.) **13** Fe
Sary-Taš **13** Gef
Saryžaz **13** GHe
Sasaram **19** Ij
Sasebo **16** Gd
Saskatchewan (prov.) **31** Ec
Saskatchewan (riv.) **31** Bb
Saskatoon **33** Ca
Saskylah **14** Eb
Sasovo **12** Fc
Sassandra (riv.) **24** Bd
Sassandra **24** Bd
Sassari **10** Bd
Sassnitz **4** Ce
Sata-Misaki **17** Bi
Satara **20** De
Satawal Island **27** Cb
Säter **4** CDc
Satka **12** Ibc
Satna **20** Fcd
Sátoraljaújhely **6** Eb
Sātpura Range **20** Ed
Satsuma-Hantō **17** ABi
Sattahip **19** CDf
Satu Mare **6** Fc
Satun **19** Cg
Sauda **4** Ad
Saudárkrókur **4** map no.1
Saudi Arabia (Ind. St.) **15** Bgh
Sauldre (riv.) **8** Ed
Sault Sainte Marie [Can.] **31** Gd
Sault Sainte Marie [U.S.] **32** Ca
Saumur **8** Cd
Saurimo **26** Bbc
Sava (riv.) **6** Dd
Savai'i Island **28** Ac
Savannah (riv.) **32** Cb
Savannah **32** CDb
Savannakhet **19** DEe
Savanna-la-Mar **35** Cb
Savaştepe **22** ABc
Savé **24** Cd
Save [Fr.] (riv.) **8** Df
Save [Moz.] (riv.) **26** Cd
Saveh **21** DEb
Savigliano **10** Ab
Savona **10** Bb
Savonlinna **4** Gc
Savoy (hist. reg.) **8** Gde
Savran **6** IJb
Savusavu **28** map no.6
Savu Sea **18** Ffg
Sawahlunto **18** Be
Sawai Madhopur **20** Ec
Sawākin **25** Dc
Sawhāj **25** Db
Sawqirah **21** Ff
Şawqirah, Ghubbat- **21** Ff
Sawu, Pulau- (i.) **18** Fg
Saxony (phys. reg.) **5** DEc
Say **24** Cc
Sayhut **21** Efg
Sazanit, Ishull i- (i.) **11** Cc
Sázava (riv.) **5** Ed
Scapa Flow (g.) **7** Eb
Scarborough **7** FGd
Scarborough Reef (i.) **18** Ea
Ščekino **12** Ec
Schaffhausen **5** Be
Schefferville **30** Ld
Schelde (riv.) **8** EFb
Schenectady **32** Da
Schleswig **5** Ba
Schleswig-Holstein (State) **5** BCab
Schlüchtern **5** Bc
Schmidta, ostrov- **14** BCa
Schouwen (i.) **8** Eb
Schwaben (phys. reg.) **5** BCde
Schwäbische Alb (mts.) **5** BCd
Schwäbisch Hall **5** BCd
Schwandorf in Bayern **5** Dd
Schwaner, Pegunungan- **18** De
Schwarze Elster (riv.) **5** Dc
Schwedt **5** Eb
Schweinfurt **5** Cc
Schwerin **5** Cb
Sciacca **10** Df
Scicli **10** Ef
Ščigry **12** Ec
Scilly, Isles of- **7** Cg
Scoresby Land **41** grid square no.1
Scoresbysund / Itseqqortoormit **30** PQb
Ščors **12** Dc
Scotland (reg.) **7** DEcd
Scott **42** grid square no.4
Scott, Cape- **31** Cb
Scott, Mount- **33** Ab
Scott Island **42** grid square no.3
Scott Reef (i.) **29** Ca
Scottsbluff **33** Cb
Scottsdale [Austl.] **29** map no.1
Scottsdale [U.S.] **33** Bc
Scranton **32** Da
Ščučinsk **13** Gd
Scunthorpe **7** FGe
Scutari, Lake- **11** Cb
Seabra **38** Cc
Seal, Cape- **26** Be
Seattle **33** Ab
Sebastián Vizcaíno, Bahía- (g.) **34** Ab
Šebekino **12** Ec
Seben **22** Cb
Sebeş **6** Fd
Sebuku, Pulau- (i.) **18** Ee
Secchia (riv.) **10** Cb
Sechura, Bahía de- **37** Ac
Sechura, Desierto de- (des.) **37** ABc
Second Cataract **25** CDb
Sedan **8** Fc
Sederot **22** Eg
Sédhiou **24** Ac
Seeheim **26** Ad
Sefidar, Kūh- e- (mt.) **21** Ed
Segeža **13** Cc
Ségou **24** Bc
Segovia **9** Cb
Segré **8** Cd
Segre (riv.) **9** Fb
Seguédine **24** Dbc
Séguéla **24** Bd
Seguin **32** Bc
Segura (riv.) **9** DEc
Segura, Sierra de- (mts.) **9** Dcd
Sehwan **20** Cc
Seinäjoki **4** EFc
Seine (riv.) **8** Dc
Seine, Baie de la- **8** Cc
Sejm (riv.) **12** Dc
Sejmčan **14** Ic
Sekondi-Takoradi **24** Bd
Sekota **25** DEc
Šeksna **12** Eb
Šelagski, mys- **14** Kb
Selajar, Pulau- (i.) **18** EFf
Selajar, Selat- **18** EFf
Selatan, Cape- **18** De
Selçuk **11** Gde
Selemdža (riv.) **14** Gd
Selenga (riv.) **14** De
Sélestat **8** Gc
Sélibabi **24** Ac
Selinunte (r.) **10** Df
Selkirk **7** Ed
Selkirk Mountains **33** Bab
Selma **32** Cb
Selvagens, Ilhas- **24** Aab
Selvas (phys. reg.) **37** CDc
Selwyn **29** Gc
Selwyn Range **29** FGc
Semani (riv.) **11** Cc
Semara **24** ABb
Semarang **15** Dj
Semenovka **12** Dc
Semeru, Gunung- (mt.) **18** Df
Semiluki **12** Ec
Semipalatinsk **13** GHd
Semmering (p.) **5** Ee
Semnān **21** Eb
Šemonaiha **13** GHd
Semur-en-Auxois **8** Fd
Senador Pompeu **38** Db
Sena Madureira **37** Cc
Senanga **26** Bc
Sendai [Jap.] **17** ABhi
Sendai [Jap.] **16** Jc
Senegal (riv.) **24** Ac
Senegal (Ind. St.) **23** Ad
Senftenberg **5** Ec
Sengilej **12** Gc
Senhor do Bonfim **38** CDc
Senigallia **10** Dc
Senj **6** Bd
Senja (i.) **4** Da
Senkaku-Shotō **16** Fe
Šenkursk **12** Fa
Senmonorom **19** Ef
Senneterre **31** Hd
Sens **8** Ec
Senta **6** Ecd
Sento Sé **38** Cbc
Senyavin Islands **27** CDb
Seo de Urgel **9** Fa
Seoni **20** Ed
Seoul (Sŏul) **14** Ff
Sepanjang, Pulau- (i.) **18** Ef
Šepetkovo **14** IJc
Šepetovka **6** Ha
Sept-Iles **31** Ic
Serafimovič **12** Fd
Seraing **8** Fb
Serang **18** Cf
Serbia **6** Ede
Serdobsk **12** FGc
Şereflikochisar **22** Dc
Seremban **18** Bd
Serena, La- **39** Ab
Serengeti Plain **26** Cb
Seret (riv.) **6** Gb
Sergeja Kirova, ostrova- **14** BCb
Sergiev Posad (Zagorsk) **13** Cd
Sergino **13** Fc
Sergipe (State) **38** Dc
Seria **18** Dd
Seribu Kepulauan **18** Cf
Sérifos (i.) **11** Fe
Sernyje Vody **12** Hc
Serov **13** Fd
Serowe **26** Bd
Serpa **9** Bd
Serpentine Lakes **29** DEd
Serpuhov **3** Gb
Sérrai **11** Ec
Serrana, Banco de- (is.) **35** BCb
Serranilla, Banco de- (is.) **35** BCb
Serrat, Cap- **10** Bf
Serra Talhada **38** Db
Serrezuela **39** Bc
Serrinha **38** Dc
Sertão (phys. reg.) **38** CDbc
Serua, Pulau- (i.) **18** Hf
Sesfontein **26** Ac
Sesheke **26** Bc
Sesimbra **9** Ac
Sessa **9** Da
Sestroreck **4** Gc
Setana **17** Fc
Sète **8** Ef
Sete Lagoas **39** Da
Sete Quedas, Saltos das- **39** Cb
Sétif **24** Ca
Settat **24** Ba
Setté Cama **26** Ab
Setúbal **9** Ac
Seul, Lac- **31** Fc
Sevan, Lake- **21** Da
Sevastopol **13** Ce
Ševčenko → Aktau **13** Ee
Severn [Can.] (riv.) **31** FGc
Severn [U.K.] (riv.) **7** Eef
Severnaja Zemlja (i.) **41** grid square no.4
Severnyje Ualy (mts.) **12** GHab

Severodvinsk **13** CDe
Severo-Jenisejski **14** Ccd
Severo Krymski Kanal **12** DEd
Severo-Kurilsk **14** Id
Severomorsk **13** Cc
Severouralsk **13** EFc
Seville **9** Bd
Sevlijevo **11** Fb
Sèvre (riv.) **8** Cd
Seward **30** Dcd
Seychelles (Ind. St.) **15** Bj
Seydişehir **22** Cd
Seyđisfiörđur **4** map no.1
Seyhan (riv.) **22** Ed
Seyhan Barajı **22** Ed
Seyitgazi **22** Cc
Seylac **25** Ec
Seymour **29** Hf
Seyne-sur-Mer, La- **8** Ff
Sézanne **8** EFc
Sezze **10** Dd
Sfîntu Gheorghe **6** GHd
Sha'ab, Al- **21** Cg
Shaanxi (prov.) **16** Cd
Shaba (reg.) **26** Bb
Shabunda **26** Bb
Shache **15** Cf
Shackleton Coast **42** grid square no.4
Shackleton Ice Shelf (gl.) **42** grid square no.4
Shag Rocks **40** Dc
Shahdol **20** Fd
Shahganj **19** Hj
Shahjahanpur **20** EFc
Shakawe **26** Bc
Shakotan-Misaki **17** FGc
Shali **19** Jj
Sha'm, Ash- **21** Fd
Shām, Jabal ash- (mt.) **21** Fe
Shammar, Jabal- (mts.) **21** BCd
Shamva **26** Cc
Shan (State) **19** Cd
Shandan **16** Bc
Shandī **25** Dc
Shandong (phys. reg.) **16** Ec
Shandong Bandao (pen.) **16** Ec
Shanghai **15** Ef
Shangqiu **16** Ed
Shangrao **16** Ee
Shangzhi **16** Gab
Shanhaiguan **16** EFb
Shannon (riv.) **7** Be
Shantar Islands **14** GHd
Shantou **16** Ef
Shanxi (prov.) **16** Dc
Shaoguan **16** DEf
Shaowu **16** Ee
Shaoxing **16** EFde
Shaoyang **16** De
Shaqrā **21** Dg
Shaqrā', Ash- **21** CDd
Shāriqah, Ash- **21** EFd
Shark Bay **29** Acd
Sharm ash Shaykh **21** Ad
Sharqāţ, Ash- **21** Cb
Shashe (riv.) **26** Bd
Shashi **16** Dd
Shasta, Mount- **33** Ab
Shatt-al-Arab (riv.) **21** Dcd
Shawinigan **31** Hd
Shay Gap **29** Cc
Shaykh 'Uthman **21** Dg
Sheberghan **20** Ca
Sheboygan **32** Ca
Sheffield **7** Fe
Shelby **33** Bb
Shelikhov Gulf **14** IJcd
Shenyang **16** Fb
Sheopur **19** Gj
Shepparton **29** GHf
Sherbro Island **24** Ad
Sherbrooke **31** HId
Sheridan **33** Cb
Sheringham **7** Ge
Sherman **32** Bb
Sherman, Fort- **35** map no.1
Sherridon **31** Ec
Shetland Isles **7** FGa
Shibam **21** Df
Shibata **17** Fef
Shibecha **17** Ic
Shibetsu **17** GHb
Shibīn al Kawm **25** CDa
Shidao **16** Fc
Shihr, Ash- **21** DEfg
Shijiazhuang **15** Df
Shikarpur [India] **19** Ij
Shikarpur [Pak.] **20** CDc
Shikoku (i.) **16** Hd
Shilla (mt.) **20** Eb
Shillong **15** Dg
Shimizu **17** EFg
Shimoga **20** DEf
Shimokita-Hantō **17** GHd
Shimonoseki **16** GHd
Shimono-Shima **17** Ag
Shinano-Gawa (riv.) **17** Ff
Shingū **17** DEh
Shinji-Ko **17** Cg
Shinjō **17** FGe
Shinyanga **26** Cb
Shiôgama **17** Ge
Shio-no-Misaki **17** DEh
Shiquan **16** Cd
Shiquanhe **15** Cf
Shiragami-Misaki **17** FGd
Shirampur **19** IJk
Shirane-San (mt.) **17** Ff
Shiranuka **17** HIc
Shirāz **21** Ecd
Shirbīn **22** Cg
Shire (riv.) **26** Cc
Shiretoko-Hantō **17** Ib
Shiretoko-Misaki **17** Ib
Shir-Kuh (mt.) **21** Ec
Shiroishi **17** Gef
Shiwpuri **20** Ec
Shizuishan **16** Cc
Shizukawa **17** GHe
Shizunai **17** GHc
Shizuoka **16** IJcd
Shkodra **11** Cb
Shkumbini (riv.) **11** CDc
Shoshone Mountains **33** Bbc
Shoshong **26** Bd
Shreveport **32** Bb
Shrewsbury **7** Ee
Shuangcheng **16** Gab
Shuangliao **16** Fb
Shuangyashan **16** Ha
Shuiji → Laixi **16** Fc
Shumlul, Ash- **21** Dd
Shuoxian **16** Dc
Shuqayq, Ash- **21** Cf
Shurayk, Ash- **25** Dc
Shushtar **21** Dc
Shwebo **19** Cd
Shweli (riv.) **16** Af
Siahan Range **20** BCc
Sialkot **20** DEb
Siam → Thailand (Ind. St.) **19** De
Siantan, Pulau- (i.) **18** Cd
Siapa (riv.) **37** Cb
Siargao (i.) **18** Gbc
Šiaškotan, ostrov- (i.) **14** Ie
Siau, Pulau- (i.) **18** Gd
Šiauliai **13** Bd
Siazan **21** DEa
Sibaj **13** Ed
Sibenik **6** BCe
Siberia (phys. reg.) **13** GOc
Siberut, Pulau- (i.) **15** Dj
Sibi **20** Cc
Sibillini, Monti- **10** Dc
Sibirjakova, ostrov- **13** Gb
Sibirtsevo **17** Cb
Sibiu **6** FGd
Sibolga **18** Ad
Sibu **18** Dd
Sibut **25** Bd
Sibutu Islands **18** Ed
Sibuyan (i.) **18** Fb
Sicasica **39** Ba
Sichuan (prov.) **16** BCd
Sicily (reg.) **10** DEef
Sicuani **39** Aa
Sideby **4** Ec
Sidērókastron **11** Ec
Sideros, Ákra- **11** Gf
Sidhi **19** Hj
Sîdi Barrâni **25** Ca
Sidi-Bel-Abbès **24** BCa
Sidi Ifni **24** Ab
Sidley, Mount- **42** grid square no.3
Sidon **22** Ef
Sidra, Gulf of- **24** Da
Sidrah, As- **24** Dab
Siedlce **5** Ib
Sieg (riv.) **5** Ac
Siegburg **5** Ac
Siegen **5** ABc
Siemiatycze **5** Ib
Siĕmréab **18** IJe
Siena **10** Cc
Sieradz **5** Gc
Sierpc **5** GHb
Sierra Blanca **33** Cc
Sierra Blanca Peak **33** Cc
Sierra Colorada **40** Bab
Sierra Leone (Ind. St.) **23** Ae
Sierra Mojada **34** Bb
Sífnos (i.) **11** Fe
Sıgaçık **22** Ac
Sighetul Marmației **6** FGc
Sighişoara **6** Gc
Sigli **18** Ac
Siglufjörđur **4** map no.1
Signy Island **42** grid square no.1
Sigüenza **9** Db
Siguiri **24** ABc
Sigulda **4** Fd
Sihote-Alin (mts.) **14** Ge
Siirt **21** Cb
Sikar **20** DEc
Sikaram (mt.) **20** CDb
Sikasso **24** Bc
Síkinos (i.) **11** Fe
Sikkim (State) **19** Ac
Siktjah **14** Fb
Sil (riv.) **9** Ba
Sila, la- (mt.) **10** Fe
Silchar **19** Bd
Şile **22** Bb
Silesia (phys. reg.) **5** EFc
Silgarhi **19** Hi
Silifke **22** DEd
Siliguri **20** Gc
Siling Co (l.) **19** ABb
Silistra **11** Gab
Silivri **11** GHc
Siljan **4** Cc
Šilka (riv.) **14** Ed
Silkeborg **4** Bd
Sillajhuay, Cordillera de- (mts.) **39** Bab
Sillon de Talbert (cap.) **8** Bc
Šilovo **12** Fc
Silvassa **20** Dde
Silver City **33** Cc
Silverton **29** Ge
Silves **9** Ad
Simanggang **18** CDd
Šimanovsk **14** Fd
Simão Dias **38** Dc
Simav **22** Bc
Simav (riv.) **22** Bc
Simbirsk **13** DEd
Simelue, Pulau- (is.) **15** Di
Simeri Crichi **10** Fe
Simferopol **13** Ce
Simhan, Gebel- (mt.) **21** EFf
Sími (i.) **22** Ad
Šimkent (Čimkent) **13** FGe
Simla **20** Eb
Şimleu Silvaniei **6** Fc
Simojärvi **4** Fb
Simonstown **26** Ae
Simplon (p.) **10** Ba
Simpson Desert **29** Fcd
Simrishamn **5** Ea
Simušir (i.) **14** Ie
Sinabang **18** Ad
Sinaia **6** Gd
Sinai Peninsula **25** Db
Sinan **16** Ce
Sincelejo **37** Bb
Sind (riv.) **19** Gj
Sind (phys. reg.) **20** Cc
Sındırgı **11** Hd
Sindri **19** Ik
Sinelnikovo **12** Ed
Sines **9** Ad
Singapore (Ind. St.) **15** Di
Singaraja **18** Ef
Singatoka **28** map no.6
Singen **5** Be
Singida **26** Cb
Singitic Gulf **11** EFcd
Singkang **18** EFe
Singkawang **18** CDd
Singkep, Pulau- (i.) **18** BCe
Sinj **6** Ce
Sinjah **25** Dc
Sinkat **25** Dc
Sinkiang (Aut. Reg.) **15** Cef

Sousse **24** Da
Souterraine, La– **8** DEd
South Africa (Ind. St.) **23** Ehi
Southampton **7** EFf
Southampton Island **31** Gb
South Andaman (i.) **19** Bf
South Australia (State) **29** EFde
South Bend **32** Ca
South Carolina (State) **32** CDb
South China Sea **16** DEf
South Dakota (State) **33** CDb
South East Cape **29** Hg
Southeast Pass **28** map no.3
South East Point **29** Hf
Southend–on–Sea **7** Gf
Southern Alps **27** De
Southern Cross **29** BCe
Southern Indian Lake **31** Fc
Southern Uplands (mts.) **7** DEd
Southern Urals (mts.) **12** Ic
South Geomagnetic Pole (1975) **42** grid square no.4
South Georgia (i.) **40** Ec
South Island **27** De
South Korea (Ind. St.) **15** Ef
South Magnetic Pole (1980) **42** grid square no.4
South Orkney Islands **36** Fj
South Platte (riv.) **33** Cb
South Point **28** map no.3
South Pole **42** grid square no.1
Southport **7** Ee
South Ronaldsay (i.) **7** EFb
South Sandwich Islands **36** HIi
South Saskatchewan (riv.) **33** BCa
South Shetland Islands **36** Dj
South Shields **7** Fd
South Uist (i.) **7** BCc
Southwest Cape **27** De
Southwest Pass (str.) **28** map no.3
Southwold **7** GHe
Sovetsk [Russia] **12** Bbc
Sovetsk [Russia] **12** Gb
Sovetskaja Gavan **14** GHe
Sõya–Misaki **17** GHb
Soyo **26** Ab
Sož (riv.) **12** Dc
Sozopol **11** GHb
Spain (Ind. St.) **3** Ccd
Spalding **7** Fe
Spanish Town **35** Cb
Sparks **33** Bc
Sparta **11** Ee
Spartanburg **32** Cb
Spartha, Cape– **11** Ef
Spartivento, Capo– [It.] **10** Be
Spartivento, Capo– [It.] **10** Ff
Spassk–Dalni **14** Ge
Spencer, Cape– **29** Ff
Spencer Bay **31** Fb
Spencer Gulf **29** Fe
Spey (riv.) **7** Ec
Spezia, La– **10** Bb
Spilimbergo **10** Da
Spišská Nová Ves **5** Hd
Spittal an der Drau **5** De

Spitzbergen (i.) **41** grid square no.3
Split **6** Ce
Spokane **33** Bb
Spoleto **10** Dc
Sporades, Northern– (is.) **11** EFd
Spree (riv.) **5** Dbc
Spremberg **5** Ec
Springbok **26** Ade
Springfield [Il.–U.S.] **32** BCb
Springfield [Ma.–U.S.] **32** Da
Springfield [Mo.–U.S.] **32** Bb
Springfield [Or.–U.S.] **33** Ab
Springfontein **23** Ehi
Springlands **37** Db
Springs **26** BCd
Springsure **29** Hc
Spurn Head **7** Ge
Squamish **33** Ab
Squillace, Golfo di– **10** Fe
Sredinny Hrebet (mts.) **14** IJd
Sredna Gora (mts.) **11** Fb
Srednekolymsk **14** Ic
Srednerusskaja vozvyšennost **13** Cd
Sredni Ural (mts.) **12** IJb
Šrem **5** Fb
Sremska Mitrovica **6** Dd
Srepok (riv.) **19** Ef
Sretensk **14** EFd
Srikakulam **20** FGe
Srī Lanka (Ceylon) (Ind. St.) **15** Ci
Srinagar **20** DEb
Srivardhan **20** De
Środa **5** Fb
Stade **5** Bb
Stadlandet (pen.) **4** Ac
Staffa (i.) **7** Cc
Stafford **7** Ee
Stahanov **12** Ed
Stalowa Wola **5** Ic
Standerton **26** BCd
Stanke Dimitrov **11** Eb
Stanley **36** Eh
Stanovoje Nagorje **14** EFd
Stanovoy Range **14** FGd
Stanthorpe **29** Id
Starachowice **5** Hc
Staraja Russa **12** Db
Stara Pazova **6** DEd
Stara Zagora **11** Fb
Starbuck Island **28** Bc
Stargard Szczecinski **5** Eb
Starica **12** DEb
Starnberg **5** Cde
Starnberger See **5** Cde
Starogard Gdański **5** Gb
Starokonstantinov **6** Hb
Starominskaja **12** Ed
Start Point **7** Ef
Stary Oskol **12** Ec
Stassfurt **5** Cbc
Staunton **32** CDb
Staurós **11** Ec
Stavanger **4** Ad
Stavropol **13** De
Stavropol → Togliatti **13** Dd
Stefanie, Lake– **25** Dd
Stefansson Island **31** Ea
Stege **5** Da
Steinkjer **4** BCbc

Stelvio, Passo dello– **10** Ca
Stendal **5** Cb
Stenhouse Bay **29** Ff
Stepanakert → Harkendi **21** Dab
Stephenville **32** Fa
Sterling **33** Cb
Sterlitamak **13** Ed
Stettin **5** Eb
Stettiner Haff (g.) **5** Eb
Stewart **31** BCc
Stewart Island **27** De
Steyr **5** Ede
Stikine (riv.) **31** BCc
Stikine Ranges **31** BCbc
Stilis **11** Ed
Stilo, Punta– (cap.) **10** Fe
Stintu Gheorghe, Bratul– (riv.) **6** Id
Štip **11** Ec
Stirling **7** DEc
Stirling Range **29** Be
Stjørdal **4** Bc
Stockerau **5** EFd
Stockholm **4** Dd
Stockport **7** Ee
Stockton **33** ABc
Stockton on Tees **7** EFd
Stoěng Trêng **19** Ef
Stojba **14** Gd
Stoke–on–Trent **7** Ee
Stokes, Cerro– **40** Ac
Stolac **11** Bb
Stolbovj, ostrov– (i.) **14** Gb
Ston **11** Bb
Stonehaven **7** EFc
Stonehenge (r.) **7** EFf
Stony Tunguska (riv.) **14** Cc
Stora Lulevatten (l.) **4** DEb
Store Bælt (str.) **4** Be
Storfjord (b.) **4** Ac
Storlien **4** Cc
Storm Bay **29** map no.1
Stornoway **7** CDb
Storsjön (l.) **4** Cc
Storuman **4** Db
Strakonice **5** Dd
Stralsund **5** Da
Strängnäs **4** Dd
Stranraer **7** Dd
Strasbourg **8** Gc
Stratford–upon–Avon **7** Fe
Straubing **5** Dd
Streaky Bay **29** Ee
Strehaia **6** Fd
Stresa **10** Bb
Streževoj **13** GHc
Stříbro **5** Dc
Strimonikós Kólpos **11** EFc
Strofádhes, Nísoi– **11** De
Strómboli (i.) **10** Ee
Strömstad **4** BCd
Strömsund **4** Cc
Stronsay (i.) **7** EFb
Struga **11** Dc
Struma (Strymón) (riv.) **11** Ec
Strumica **11** Ec
Stry **6** FGb
Strymón → Struma (riv.) **11** Ec
Strzelecki Creek **29** FGd
Stubbekøbing **5** Da
Stupino **12** Ebc

Stura (riv.) **10** Ab
Stura di Demonte (riv.) **10** Ab
Sturge Island **42** grid square no.4
Sturt Desert **29** map no.1
Stuttgart **5** BCd
Styria (phys. reg.) **5** Ee
Suao **16** Ff
Šubarkuduk **13** Ee
Subotica **6** Dcd
Suceava **6** Hc
Sucre **39** Ba
Sucunduri (riv.) **37** Dc
Sudak **12** DEe
Sudan (phys. reg.) **24** CDc
Sudan (Ind. St.) **23** EFd
Sudbury **31** GHd
Sudd (phys. reg.) **25** CDd
Suddie **37** Db
Sudety (mts.) **5** EFc
Sueca **9** Ec
Sueco, El– **34** Bab
Suez **25** Dab
Suez, Gulf of– **25** Db
Suez Canal **25** map no.2
Suffolk (co.) **7** Ge
Suffolk **32** Db
Suğla Gölü **22** Dd
Suhar **21** Fe
Suhe–Bator **14** Dde
Suhiniči **12** DEc
Suhl **5** Cc
Suhona (riv.) **13** Dc
Suhumi **13** CDe
Suiá–Missu (riv.) **38** Bc
Suide **16** CDc
Suifenhe **16** Hb
Suihua **16** Ga
Suining **16** BCd
Suir (riv.) **7** Ce
Suita **17** Dg
Šuja **12** Fb
Sujfun (riv.) **17** Bbc
Sukabumi **18** Cf
Sukadana **18** CDe
Şukhayrah, Aş– **24** CDa
Sukhothai **19** CDe
Sukkertoppen / Maniitsoq **31** Jb
Sukkur **15** Cg
Sukumo **17** Ch
Sula, Kepulauan– **18** FGe
Sulaimâniya **21** CDb
Sulaimân Range **20** CDbc
Sula Sgeir (i.) **7** Cb
Sulawesi (Celebes) (is.) **18** EFe
Sulayyil, As– **21** De
Sulina **6** IJd
Sulina, Bratul– (riv.) **6** Id
Sulitjelma **4** Db
Sulitjelma (mt.) **4** Db
Sullana **37** ABc
Sulmona **10** Dc
Sultan dağları (mts.) **22** Ccd
Sultanpur **19** Hj
Sulu Archipelago **18** EFcd
Sulûq **24** DEa
Sulu Sea **18** EFd
Šumadija (phys. reg.) **6** Ed
Sumatra (i.) **15** Dij
Sumba, Pulau– (i.) **15** DEjk
Sumba Strait **18** EFf

Sumbawa, Pulau- (i.) **15** DEj
Sumbawa Besar **18** Ef
Sumbawanga **26** Cb
Sumbe **26** Ac
Sumburgh Head **7** Fb
Šumen **11** Gb
Šumerlja **12** Gb
Sumgait **13** DEe
Sumisu-Jima (i.) **17** FGi
Summerside **32** Ea
Summit **35** map no.1
Šumperk **5** Fcd
Sumprabum **19** Cc
Sumter **32** CDb
Sumy **13** Cd
Sundarbans (phys. reg.) **20** GHd
Sunda Strait **18** Cf
Sunderland **7** Fd
Sundiken dağı (mt.) **22** Cbc
Sundsvall **4** Dc
Sungai Petani **19** Dg
Sungari (Songhua Jiang) (riv.) **16** Gb
Sungurlu **22** Eb
Sun Kosi (riv.) **19** Ij
Sunndalsöra **4** Bc
Sunne **4** Cd
Suntar **14** Ec
Suntar-Hajata, Hrebet- **14** GHc
Sunyani **24** Bd
Suojarvi **12** Da
Suolahti **4** Fc
Suomenselkä (mts.) **4** EGc
Suomussalmi **4** Gb
Suonenjoki **4** Fc
Superior **32** Ba
Superior, Lake- **32** Ca
Süphan dağ (mt.) **21** Cb
Suqian **16** Ed
Sur **21** Fe
Sur, Submeseta (phys. reg.) **9** CDbc
Sura (riv.) **12** Gbc
Surabaya **15** Djk
Surakarta (Solo) **18** Df
Surat [Austl.] **29** Hd
Surat [India] **15** Cg
Surat Thani **15** Di
Surgut **13** Gc
Suri **19** Ijk
Surigao **18** Gc
Surin **19** Def
Suriname (Ind. St.) **36** Ec
Suriname (riv.) **37** Db
Surkhab (riv.) **20** Ca
Surprise, Île- (i.) **28** map no.4
Surrey (co.) **7** Ff
Surt **24** Da
Surtsey (i.) **4** map no.1
Suruga-Wan **17** Fg
Surulangun **18** Be
Susa **10** Ab
Susa (r.) **21** Dc
Susaki **17** Ch
Suşehri **22** Gb
Susong **16** Ed
Susques **39** Bb
Sussex (co.) **7** FGf
Susuman **14** Hc
Susurluk **22** ABc
Sutlej (riv.) **20** Eb
Suttor River **29** Hc
Suva **28** map no.6
Suvorovo **6** Id
Suwałki **5** Ia
Suwarrow Atoll **28** Ac
Suwaydā, As- **22** Ff
Suwŏn **16** Gc
Suxian [China] **16** Dd
Suxian [China] **16** Ed
Suzhou **16** Fd
Suzu **17** Ef
Suzu-Misaki **17** Ef
Svålbard **41** grid square no.3
Svartisen (mt.) **4** Cb
Svealand (phys. reg.) **4** CDd
Svedala **5** Da
Sveg **4** Cc
Švenčionėlia **12** Cbc
Svendborg **4** Be
Sverdlovsk → Jekaterinburg **13** EFd
Sverdrup, ostrov- **13** Gb
Sverdrup Islands **41** grid square no.2
Svetlaja **14** Ge
Svetlogorsk **12** Cc
Svetlograd **12** Fd
Svetlovodsk **12** Dd
Svetly **13** Fd
Svetogorsk **4** Gc
Svetozarevo **6** Ede
Svilengrad **11** FGc
Svir (riv.) **12** Da
Svištov **11** Fb
Svitavy **5** Fd
Svobodny **14** FGd
Svolvær **4** Ca
Swain Reefs (is.) **29** Ic
Swains Atoll **28** Ac
Swakop (riv.) **26** Ad
Swakopmund **23** Dh
Swale (riv.) **7** Fd
Swan Hill **29** Gf
Swan River **33** Ca
Swansea **7** DEf
Swarzędz **5** Fb
Swaziland (Ind. St.) **23** Fh
Sweden (Ind. St.) **3** Ea
Sweetwater **33** Cc
Swellendam **26** Be
Świdnica **5** Fc
Świdnik **5** Ic
Świdwin **5** EFb
Świebodzin **5** Eb
Świecie **5** FGb
Swift Current **33** Cab
Swindon **7** Ff
Swinoujšcie **5** Eab
Switzerland (Ind. St.) **3** Dc
Syčevka **12** DEb
Sydney [Austl.] **29** Ie
Sydney [Can.] **31** IJd
Sydprøven / Alluitsup Paa **31** Kb
Syktyvkar **13** Ec
Sylarna (mt.) **4** BCc
Sylhet **20** Hcd
Sylt **5** Ba
Syowa **42** grid square no.2
Syracuse **32** Da
Syrdarja (riv.) **13** Fe
Syria (Ind. St.) **15** Bf
Syriam **19** Ce
Syrian Desert **21** BCc
Sysert **12** Jb
Sysmä **4** Fc
Syvulja (mt.) **5** IJd
Syzran **13** Dd
Szamos (riv.) **5** Ide
Szamotuły **5** Fb
Szczecinek **5** Fb
Szczytno **5** Hb
Szeged **6** DEc
Székesfehérvár **6** Dc
Szekszárd **6** Dc
Szentes **6** Ec
Szolnok **6** Ec
Szombathely **6** Cc

T

Tabajara **37** Cc
Ţabarqah **10** Bf
Ţabas **21** Fc
Tabašino **12** Gb
Tabelbala **24** Bb
Taberg (mt.) **5** DEa
Tabernas **9** DEd
Tablas (i.) **18** Fb
Tablas, Las- **35** BCc
Tábor **5** Ed
Tabor **14** HIb
Tabora **26** Cb
Tabory **12** Jb
Tabou **24** Bd
Tabrīz **21** Db
Tabuaeran (Fanning) **28** Bb
Tabuk **21** Bd
Tacazzè (riv.) **25** Dc
Tacheng **13** He
Tacloban **18** FGb
Tacna **39** Aa
Tacoma **33** Ab
Tacora (mt.) **39** ABa
Tacuarembó **39** Cc
Tacutu (riv.) **37** CDb
Tademaït, Plateau du- **24** Cb
Taegu **14** FGf
Taejŏn **14** Ff
Tafalla **9** Ea
Ţafīlah, Aţ- **22** Eg
Tafí Viejo **39** Bb
Taftān, Kuh- e- (mt.) **21** Gd
Taga **28** map no.5
Taga Dzong **20** GHc
Taganrog **13** CDe
Taganrogski zaliv **12** Ed
Tagaytay City **18** EFb
Tagbilaran **18** Fc
Tagula Island **27** Cc
Tahan, Gunong- (mt.) **19** Dgh
Tahat (mt.) **24** Cb
Tahiti, Île- **28** Bc
Tahlab (riv.) **21** Gd
Tahoua **24** Cc
Tahtalı dağ (mt.) **22** Fc
Tahulandang, Pulau- (i.) **18** FGd
Tai'an **16** Ec
Taiarapu, Presqu'île de- **28** map no.2
Taichung **16** Ff
Tā'if, Aţ- **21** BCe
Tai Hu (l.) **16** Fd
Tailai **16** Fa
Tain **7** DEc
Tainan **16** EFf
Taipei **15** Eg
Taiping **19** CDgh
Taisetsu-Zan (mt.) **16** Jb
Taitao, Península de- **40** Ab
Taitao, Peninsula de- **36** Ch
Taitung **16** Ff
Taivalkoski **4** FGb
Taiwan (Formosa) (Ind. St.) **15** Eg
Taiwan Strait **15** DEg
Taíyetos Óros (mts.) **11** Ee
Taiyuan **15** Df
Taizhou **16** EFd
Ta'izz **21** Cg
Tajga **13** Hd
Tajgonos, Poluostrov- **14** Jc
Tajikistan (Ind. St.) **13** FGf
Tajimi **17** Eg
Tajmyr, Ozero- **14** Db
Tajmyr, Poluostrov- **14** CDb
Tajmyra (riv.) **14** Cb
Tajo (riv.) **9** Db
Tajrish **21** Eb
Tajšet **14** Cd
Tajumulco, Volcán- (mt.) **34** Cc
Tajuña (riv.) **9** Db
Tak **19** Ce
Takada **17** EFf
Takahe, Mount- **42** grid square no.3
Takamatsu **16** HId
Takaoka **17** Ef
Takaroa Atoll **28** Bc
Takasaki **17** Ff
Takayama **17** Ef
Takefu **17** DEfg
Takengon **18** Ad
Take-Shima / Tok-Do (i.) **17** Bf
Takikawa **17** Gc
Tako-Bana **17** Cg
Talak (phys. reg.) **24** Cc
Talara **37** Ac
Talas **13** Ge
Talâta **25** map no.1
Talaud, Kepulauan- **18** Gd
Talavera de la Reina **9** Cbc
Talca **39** Ac
Talcahuano **39** Ac
Talcher **20** Gd
Taldy-Kurgan **13** Ge
Talence **8** Ce
Talgar **18** Bb
Taliabu, Pulau- (i.) **18** FGe
Talica **12** Jb
Tall 'Afar **21** Cb
Tallahassee **32** Cbc
Tallinn **4** Fd
Tall Kalakh **22** Fe
Tāloqān **20** CDa
Talsi **4** Ed
Taltal **39** Ab
Tamale **24** BCd
Tamanrasset **24** Cb
Tamar River **29** map no.1
Tamarugal, Pampa del- **39** Bab
Tamazunchale **34** Cb
Tambacounda **24** Ac

Tambao **24** BCc
Tambej **13** FGb
Tambelan Islands **18** Cd
Tambo **29** Hcd
Tambo (riv.) **37** Bd
Tambov **13** Dd
Tambura **25** Cd
Tamchaket **24** ABc
Tamdybulak **13** Fe
Tâmega (riv.) **9** Bb
Tamel Aike **40** Ab
Tamil Nadu (State) **20** Efg
Tamīyah, Jabal- (mt.) **21** Cde
Tampa **32** Cc
Tampere **4** EFc
Tampico **30** Ig
Tamsag-Bulak **14** Ee
Tamsweg **5** De
Tamworth **29** Ie
Tana [Kenya] (riv.) **25** De
Tana [Nor.] (riv.) **4** Fa
Tana, Lake- **25** Dc
Tanabe **17** Dh
Tanacross **31** Ab
Tanafjorden **4** Ga
Tanágra **11** Ed
Tanahbala, Pulau- (i.) **18** Ae
Tanahgrogot **18** Ee
Tanahjampea, Pulau- (i.) **18** Ff
Tanahmasa, Pulau- (i.) **18** Ade
Tanakpur **19** Hi
Tanami **29** DEbc
Tanami Desert **29** Eb
Tanana (riv.) **31** Ab
Tananarive → Antananarivo **23** GHgh
Tanaro (riv.) **10** Bb
Tanch'ŏn **17** Ad
Tanda **19** Hj
Tandag **18** Gc
Tandaltī **25** Dc
Tandil **39** Cc
Tandjungkarang **18** Cef
Tandjungpinang **18** CDd
Tane-ga-Shima (i.) **16** Hd
Tanew (riv.) **5** Ic
Tanezrouft (phys. reg.) **24** BCb
Tanga **23** FGf
Tanganyika, Lake- **26** BCb
Tanggu **16** Ec
Tangier **24** Ba
Tang La (cap.) **20** Gc
Tangra Yumco (l.) **20** Gb
Tangshan **16** EFc
Tanimbar, Kepulauan- **27** Bc
Tanjung **18** Ee
Tanjungbalai **18** ABd
Tanjung Cina **18** Bf
Tanjungkarang **18** BCef
Tanjungpandan **18** Ce
Tanjungredeb **18** Ed
Tanjungselor **18** Ed
Tanna, Île- (i.) **28** map no.4
Tannu-Ola (mts.) **14** Cd
Tanout **24** Cc
Tansing **19** Hij
Ṭanṭā **25** Da
Tanzania (Ind. St.) **23** Ff
Tao'an **16** Fa
Tao'er He (riv.) **16** EFa
Taongi Atoll **27** Db
Taormina **10** Ef
Taoudenni **24** Bb
Taouz **24** Ba
Tapa **4** Fd
Tapachula **34** Cc
Tapajós (riv.) **38** Bb
Tapaktuan **18** Ad
Tapauá (riv.) **37** Cc
Tapirapeco, Sierra- (mts.) **37** Cb
Tapti (riv.) **20** Dd
Tapul Group **18** EFc
Taquari Novo (riv.) **38** Bc
Tara **13** Gd
Tara (riv.) **11** Cb
Tarakan **18** Ed
Taraklı **22** Cb
Taraklija **6** Id
Tarama-Jima (i.) **16** FGf
Tarancón **9** Dbc
Taranto **10** Fd
Taranto, Gulf of- **10** Fd
Tarapacá **37** BCc
Tarapoto **37** Bc
Tarare **8** Fe
Tarascon **8** Ff
Tarata **39** ABa
Tarauacá **37** Bc
Tarauacá (riv.) **37** Bc
Taravao **28** map no.2
Taravao, Isthmus of- **28** map no.2
Tarazona **9** DEb
Tarbagataj, Hrebet- (mts.) **13** He
Tarbela **20** Db
Tarbert **7** Cc
Tarbes **8** Df
Tarcoola **29** Ee
Taree **29** Ie
Tareja **14** BCb
Tarfaya **24** Ab
Tărgovište **11** Gb
Tarhankut, mys- **12** Dd
Tarhūnah **24** Da
Tarif **21** Ee
Tarifa **9** Cd
Tarifa, Punta de- (cap.) **9** BCd
Tarija **39** Bb
Tarim (riv.) **22** Ce
Tarim **21** Df
Tarīn Kowt **20** Cb
Tarko-Sale **13** Gc
Tarlac **18** Fa
Tarma **37** Bd
Tarn (riv.) **8** Df
Tärnaby **4** CDb
Tarnobrzeg **5** HIc
Tarnów **5** Hcd
Taroom **29** HId
Tarquinia **10** Cc
Tarragona **9** Fb
Tarraleah **29** map no.1
Tarrasa **9** FGb
Tarso Emisu (mt.) **25** BCb
Tarsus **22** Ed
Tartagal **39** Bb
Tartu **4** Fd
Ṭarṭūs **22** Ee
Tarutau, Ko- (i.) **19** Cg
Tarutung **18** Ad
Tašauz → Dašhovuz **13** Ee
Tasejeva (riv.) **14** Cd
Tasikmalaya **18** Cf
Taškent **13** Fe
Taşköprü **22** DEb
Taşköy **22** EFb
Taš-Kumyr **13** Ge
Tasman (State) **29** map no.1
Tasman Peninsula **29** map no.1
Tasman Sea **27** CDde
Tăsnad **6** Fc
Tassili-n-Ajjer (mt.) **24** Cb
Tassili Oua-n-Ahaggar (plat.) **24** Cbc
Taštagol **13** Hd
Tata **6** CDc
Tatabánya **6** Dc
Tatakoto Atoll **28** Cc
Tatar Autonomous Republic (Aut. Rep.) **13** DEd
Tatarbunary **6** IJd
Tatarsk **13** Gd
Tatar Strait **16** Jab
Tateyama **17** FGg
Tathlīth **21** Cf
Tatta **20** Cd
Tatuí **39** Db
Tau **28** map no.5
Taubaté **39** Db
Taujsk **14** Hcd
Taukum (phys. reg.) **13** Ge
Taunggyi **19** Cd
Taungup **19** Be
Taunton **7** Ef
Taunus (mt.) **5** ABc
Tauragė **12** Bb
Taurus Mountains **22** CEd
Tautira **28** map no.2
Tavas **22** Bd
Tavda (riv.) **13** Fd
Tavda **13** Fd
Taveuni Island **28** map no.6
Tavira **9** Bd
Tavričanka **17** Bc
Tavşanli **22** Bc
Tavua **28** map no.6
Tawau **18** Ed
Tawitawi Group (is.) **18** EFcd
Ṭawkar **25** Dc
Tawzar **24** Ca
Taxila (r.) **20** Db
Tay (riv.) **7** Ec
Taymā **21** Bd
Tay Ninh **19** Ef
Taytay **18** EFb
Taz (riv.) **13** Hc
Taza **24** Ba
Tāzirbū, Wāḩāt al- **24** Eb
Tazovski **13** Gc
Tbilisi **13** De
Tchibanga **26** Ab
Tchien **24** Bd
Tczew **5** Ga
Teano **10** Ed
Tébessa **24** Ca
Tecer dağları (mts.) **22** FGc
Tecuci **6** Hd
Tedžen **13** Ff
Tedžen (riv.) **13** Ff
Tees (riv.) **7** EFd
Tefé **37** Cc
Tefé (riv.) **37** Cc
Tefenni **22** Bd
Tegal **18** Cf
Tegucigalpa **30** Jh
Tehauntepec, Golfo de- **34** Cc
Tehauntepec, Istmo de- **34** Cc
Tehaupoo **28** map no.2
Tehrān **21** DEb
Tehuacán **34** Cc
Tehuantepec **34** Cc
Teifi (riv.) **7** Def
Tejkovo **12** EFb
Tejo (riv.) **9** Bc
Tekeli **13** Ge
Tekirdağ **22** Ab
Tektjur **14** Gc
Tel (riv.) **20** Fd
Tela **35** Bb
Telares, Los- **39** Bb
Telavi **21** Da
Tel Aviv-Yafo **22** DEfg
Telegraph Creek **31** BCc
Telemark (phys. reg.) **4** ABd
Telen (riv.) **18** Ede
Telén **39** Bc
Teleno (mt.) **9** Ba
Teles Pires, Rio- (riv.) **38** Bc
Teles Pires o São Manuel, Rio- (riv.) **38** Bb
Tell Atlas (mts.) **24** BCa
Telok Anson **19** Dh
Telposiz, gora- (mt.) **13** EFc
Telsen **40** Bb
Telšiai **12** Bb
Téma **24** BCd
Tematangi Atoll **28** Bd
Tembilahan **18** Be
Temerloh **19** Dh
Temirtau → Akmol **13** Gd
Temnikov **12** Fc
Tempio Pausania **10** Bd
Temple **32** Bb
Temrjuk **12** Ed
Temuco **39** Ac
Tena **37** Bc
Tenali **20** Fe
Tenasserim (phys. reg.) **19** Cef
Tenasserim (riv.) **19** Cf
Tenda, Col di- (p.) **10** Ab
Ten Degree Channel **19** Bfg
Ténéré (phys. reg.) **24** Dbc
Tenerife (i.) **24** Ab
Ténès **24** Ca
Tengchong **19** Ccd
Tengiz, ozero- **13** Fd
Tengréla **24** Bcd
Tengxian **16** Ec
Teniente Matienzo **42** grid square no.1
Tenke **26** Bc
Tenkodogo **24** BCc
Tennant Creek **29** Eb
Tennessee (State) **32** Cb
Tennessee (riv.) **32** Cb
Tenojoki (riv.) **4** Fa
Tenosique **34** Cc
Ṭenryū **17** EFg
Tenryū-Gawa (riv.) **17** EFg
Tenterfield **29** Id
Teófilo Otoni **39** Da
Teotihuacán **34** Cbc

Tol - Tub

Tolitoli **18** EFd
Tolmezzo **10** Da
Tolo, Gulf of– **18** Fe
Tolosa **9** DEa
Tolstoje **6** Gb
Toltén **39** Ac
Tolú **37** Bb
Toluca de Lerdo **34** BCc
Tom (riv.) **13** Hd
Toma, La– **39** Bc
Tomakomai **17** GHc
Tomari **14** He
Tomaševka **5** lJc
Tomašpol **6** lb
Tomaszów Lubelski **5** lJc
Tomaszów Mazowiecki **5** Hc
Tombador, Serra do– (mts.)
  38 Bc
Tomb–e Bozorg **21** EFd
Tombôco **26** Ab
Tombouctou **24** Bc
Tombua **26** Ac
Tomé **39** Ac
Tomelilla **5** Ea
Tomelloso **9** Dc
Tomini **18** Fd
Tomini, Teluk– **18** Fde
Tommot **14** Fd
Tomorit (mt.) **11** Dc
Tom Price **29** Bc
Tomsk **13** Hd
Tomtabacken (mt.) **4** Cd
Tonalá **34** Cc
Tondano **18** FGd
Tønder **5** Ba
Tone (riv.) **17** Gg
Tonekâbon **21** Eb
Tonga Islands (Ind. St.) **28**
  Acd
Tongatapu Group **28** Ad
Tongchuan **16** CDc
Tonghe **16** Ga
Tonghua **16** FGb
Tongjiang **16** Ha
Tongliao **16** Fb
Tongoa (i.) **28** map no.4
Tongsa Dzong **19** Jj
Tongzi **16** Ce
Tónichi **34** Bb
Tonk **20** Ec
Tonkin (phys. reg.) **19** DEd
Tonkin, Gulf of– **19** Ede
Tonle Sap (l.) **19** Df
Tonneins **8** CDe
Tonopah **33** Bc
Tonota **26** Bd
Tons (riv.) **19** Hj
Tønsberg **4** Bd
Toora–Hem **14** Cd
Toowoomba **29** Id
Topaklı **22** Ec
Topeka **32** Bb
Topki **13** Hd
Topliţa **6** Gc
Topol'čany **5** FGd
Topolovgrad **11** Gbc
Topozero, ozero– **4** Gb
Torat–e–Heydariyeh **21** FGbc
Torbalı **11** Gd
Torbay **7** Ef
Toréz **12** Ed
Torgau **5** Dc
Tori–Shima (i.) **17** Gi

Tormes (riv.) **9** Bb
Torneälven (riv.) **4** EFb
Torneträsk (l.) **4** DEa
Torngat Mountains **31** Ic
Tornio **4** Fb
Tornionjoki (riv.) **4** EFb
Toro **9** Cb
Toro, Cerro del– (mt.) **39** ABb
Toro, Punta– (cap.) **35** map
  no.1
Törökszentmiklós **6** Ec
Toronto **31** GHd
Toropec **12** Db
Tororo **25** Dd
Torre del Greco **10** Ed
Torrelavega **9** CDa
Torremolinos **9** Cd
Torrens, Lake– **29** Fe
Torrens Creek **29** GHc
Torrente **9** Ec
Torreón **30** Hg
Torrés, Îles– **28** map no.4
Torres Strait **27** Cc
Torrijos **9** Cc
Torrington **33** Cb
Torsby **4** Cc
Tortona **10** Bb
Tortosa **9** Fb
Tortosa, Cabo de– (cap.) **9**
  Fb
Tortue, Ile de la– (i.) **35** Cab
Tortuga, Isla la– (i.) **37** Ca
Toruń **5** Gb
Torżok **12** DEb
Tosashimizu **17** Ch
Tosa–Wan **17** Ch
Toscana (reg.) **10** BCbc
Toscano, Arcipelago– **10** BCc
Tossa **9** Gb
Tostado **39** Bb
Tosya **22** Eb
Totana **9** Ed
Totma **12** Fab
Totness **37** Db
Totoya (i.) **28** map no.6
Tottori **16** Hc
Toubkal, Jebel– (mt.) **24** Ba
Touggourt **24** Ca
Touho **28** map no.4
Toul **8** FGc
Toulon **8** FGf
Toulouse **8** DEf
Toungoo **19** Ce
Touraine (phys. reg.) **8** Dd
Tourcoing **8** Eb
Touriñan, Cabo– (cap.) **9** Aa
Tournon **8** Fe
Tours **8** Dd
Towada **17** Gd
Townshend, Cape– **29** Ic
Townsville **29** Hb
Towuti, Danau– **18** Fe
Toyama **16** Ic
Toyama–Wan **17** Ef
Toyohashi **16** Id
Toyooka **17** Dg
Toyota **17** Eg
Tozanlı (riv.) **22** Fb
Trabzon **21** BCa
Trafalgar, Cabo– (cap.)
  9 Bd
Trail **33** Bb
Trajan's wall **6** Hld

Tralee **7** ABe
Tranås **4** Cd
Trang **19** Cg
Trani **10** Fd
Transantarctic Mountains **42**
  grid square no.4
Transcona **33** Da
Transkei (hist. reg.) **26** Be
Transvaal (prov.) **26** BCd
Transylvania (phys. reg.) **6**
  FGc
Transylvanian Alps (Southern
  Carpathians) **6** FGd
Trapani **10** Df
Trasimeno, Lago– **10** Dc
Tras–os–Montes (phys. reg.)
  9 Bb
Trat **19** Df
Traunstein **5** Dde
Traverse City **32** Ca
Travnik **6** Cd
Trbovlje **6** Bc
Trebbia (riv.) **10** Bb
Třebíč **5** Ed
Trebinje **11** Cb
Trebišov **5** Hd
Třebová **5** Fd
Tree Pagodas Pass
  19 Cef
Treinta y Tres **39** Cc
Trélazé **8** Cd
Trelew **40** Bb
Trelleborg **4** Ce
Tremiti, Isole– **10** Ec
Tremp **9** Fa
Trenčín **5** Gd
Trenque Lauquen **39** Bc
Trent (riv.) **7** Fe
Trentino–Alto Adige (reg.) **10**
  Ca
Trento **10** Ca
Trenton **32** Dab
Tréport, Le– **8** Dbc
Tres Arroyos **39** BCc
Três Casas **37** Cc
Tres Esquinas **37** Bb
Três Lagoas **39** Cb
Tres Lagos **40** ABb
Tres Picos, Cerro– (mt.) **39**
  Bc
Tres Puntas, Cabo– **40** Bb
Três Rios **39** Db
Tres Virgenes, Las– (mt.) **34**
  Ab
Treungen **4** ABd
Treviso **10** Db
Tricase **10** Ge
Trichur **20** Ef
Tridentine Alps **10** Ca
Trier **5** Ad
Trieste **10** Db
Trikala **11** Dd
Trikhonís, Límni– **11** Dd
Trincomalee **15** Ci
Trindade, Ilha da– (i.) **36** Gef
Třinec **5** Gd
Trinidad (i.) **37** CDa
Trinidad [Bol.] **39** Ba
Trinidad [U.S.] **33** Cc
Trinidad, Río– (riv.) **35** map
  no.1
Trinidad and Tobago (Ind. St.)
  36 DEbc

Trinity (riv.) **32** Bb
Tripoli [Leb.] **22** Ee
Tripoli [Lib.] **24** Da
Trípolis **11** Ee
Tripura (State) **19** Bd
Tristan da Cunha (is.) **23** ABi
Trivandrum **15** Ci
Trnava **5** FGd
Trogir **10** Fc
Troglav (mt.) **6** Ce
Troia **10** Ed
Troick **13** Fd
Troicko–Pečorsk **13** EFc
Trois–Rivières **31** Hld
Trojan **11** Fb
Trojansky prohod **11** Fb
Trollhättan **4** BCd
Trollheimen (mt.) **4** Bc
Trombetas (riv.) **38** Ba
Tromelin (i.) **23** map no.1
Tromsø **4** DEa
Tronador (mt.) **40** Ab
Trondheim **4** Bc
Trondheimsfjorden (b.) **4** Bc
Troódos, Mount– (Olympus)
  22 De
Trotus (riv.) **6** Hc
Trouville–sur–Mer **8** CDc
Trowbridge **7** EFf
Troy (r.) **22** Ac
Troy [Al.–U.S.] **32** Cb
Troy [N.Y.–U.S.] **32** Da
Troyes **8** Fc
Trucial Coast **21** EFe
Trudovoje [Kaz.] **13** Fd
Trudovoje [Russia] **17** Cc
Trujillo [Hond.] **35** Bb
Trujillo [Peru] **36** BCd
Trujillo [Sp.] **9** BCc
Trujillo [Ven.] **37** BCb
Truk Islands **27** Cb
Truro [Can.] **31** Id
Truro [U.K.] **7** Df
Truskavec **6** FGd
Trutnov **5** Ec
Trysil (riv.) **4** Cc
Trzcianka **5** EFb
Tsaratanana (mt.) **26** map
  no.1
Tsau **26** Bcd
Tshabong **26** Bd
Tshela **26** Ab
Tshikapa **26** Bb
Tshuapa (riv.) **26** Bb
Tsinan (Jinan) **15** Df
Tsingtao (Qingdao) **16** Fc
Tsu **16** Id
Tsugaro–Kaikyô **16** lJb
Tsumeb **23** Dg
Tsuruga **16** Ic
Tsuruoka **17** Fe
Tsushima **17** Ag
Tsushima (is.) **16** Gd
Tsushima–Kaikyô **17** Agh
Tsuyama **16** Hcd
Tual **18** Hf
Tuamoto Archipelago **28**
  BCcd
Tuapse **13** Ce
Tuban **18** Df
Tubarão **39** Db
Tübingen **5** Bd
Ţubruq **24** Ea

Vetlanda **4** Cd
Vetluga (riv.) **12** Gb
Vetta d'Italia (mt.) **10** CDa
Vézère (riv.) **8** De
Viacha **39** Ba
Viana **38** Cb
Viana do Castelo **9** Ab
Viareggio **10** Cc
Viborg **4** Bd
Vibo Valentia **10** Fe
Vic **9** Gb
Vicecomodoro Morambio **42** grid square no.1
Vicenza **10** Cb
Vichada (riv.) **37** BCb
Vichy **8** Ed
Vicksburg **32** BCb
Victor Harbour **29** Ff
Victoria (State) **29** Gf
Victoria [Can.] **33** Ab
Victoria [Chile] **39** Ac
Victoria [H.K.] **15** Dg
Victoria [Mala.] **18** Ecd
Victoria [Malta] **10** Ef
Victoria [U.S.] **32** Bc
Victoria, Lake– **26** Cb
Victoria, Mount– **19** Bd
Victoria de Durango **34** Bb
Victoria de las Tunas **35** Ca
Victoria Falls **26** Bc
Victoria Falls (wf.) **26** Bc
Victoria Island **31** DEa
Victoria Land **42** grid square no.4
Victoria River **29** Eb
Victoria River Downs **29** DEb
Victoria West **26** Be
Victorica **39** Bc
Vičuga **12** Fb
Videle **6** Gd
Vidim **14** Dd
Vidin **11** Eab
Vidisha **20** Ed
Vidzy **4** Fe
Viedma **40** Bb
Viedma, Lago– **40** Ab
Vienna **5** Fd
Vienne (riv.) **8** Dd
Vienne **8** Fe
Vientiane **15** Dh
Vieques, Isla de– (i.) **35** Db
Vierwaldstätter See **5** Be
Vierzon **8** Ed
Vieste **10** Fd
Vietnam (Ind. St.) **15** Dh
Vigan **18** EFa
Vigan, Le– **8** Ef
Vigia **38** Cb
Vigía Chico **34** Dc
Vignemale, Pic de– (mt.) **8** CDf
Vigo **9** Aa
Vihren (mt.) **11** Ec
Viitasaari **4** Fc
Vijayawada **15** Ch
Vijkitski Strait **14** CDb
Vikna (i.) **4** Bb
Viktorija, ostrov– **13** CDab
Vila Franca de Xira **9** Ac
Vilaine (riv.) **8** Cd
Vila Murtinho **37** Cd
Vilanculos **26** Cd
Vila Nova de Gaia **9** Ab
Vilanova i la Geltrú **9** FGb
Vila Real **9** Bb
Vila Real de Santo Antonio **9** ABd
Vila Velha [Braz.] **38** Ba
Vila Velha [Braz.] **38** CDd
Vila Viçosa **9** Bc
Vilejka **12** Cc
Vilhelmina **4** CDb
Vilhena **39** BCa
Viljandi **12** Cb
Viljuj (riv.) **14** Fc
Viljujsk **14** Fc
Villa Angela **39** Bb
Villablino **9** Ba
Villacañas **9** Dc
Villacarrillo **9** Dc
Villacidro **10** Be
Villaco **5** De
Villa Colón **39** Bc
Villa Dolores **39** Bc
Villafranca del Bierzo **9** Ba
Villafranca de los Barros **9** BCc
Villafranca del Panadés **9** Fb
Villagarcía de Arosa **9** ABa
Villaguay **39** Cc
Villa Hayes **39** Cb
Villahermosa **34** Cc
Villajoyosa **9** EFc
Villalba **9** Ba
Villa Maria **39** Bc
Villa Montes **39** Bb
Villanueva de la Serena **9** Cc
Villanueva de los Infantes **9** Dc
Villarreal de los Infantes **9** Ec
Villarrica **39** Cb
Villarrobledo **9** DEc
Villaverde, Madrid– **9** Db
Villavicencio **37** Bb
Villaviciosa **9** Ca
Villazón **39** Bb
Villefranche-de-Rouergue **8** DEe
Villefranche-sur-Saône **8** Fde
Villena **9** Ec
Villeneuve-sur-Lot **8** De
Villeurbanne **8** Fe
Vilnius **4** Fe
Viña del Mar **39** Ac
Vinaroz **9** Fb
Vincennes **32** Cb
Vincennes Bay **42** grid square no.4
Vinchina **39** Bb
Vindelälven (riv.) **4** Db
Vindhya Range **20** DFd
Vinh **15** Dh
Vinh Loi **19** Eg
Vinita **32** Bb
Vinkovci **6** Dd
Vinnica **13** Be
Vinogradov **5** Id
Vinogradovka **17** Cc
Vinson Massif (mt.) **42** grid square no.1
Vir **10** Eb
Virac **18** Fb
Virden **33** Cab
Vire **8** Cc
Virgenes, Cabo– **40** Bc
Virginia **32** Ba
Virginia (State) **32** Db
Virgin Islands **36** Db
Virovitica **6** Cd
Virrat **4** Ec
Virtsu **12** Bb
Vis (i.) **11** ABb
Visalia **33** Bc
Visby **4** Dd
Viscount Melville Sound **31** DEa
Višegrad **6** De
Višera (riv.) **12** Ia
Viseu [Braz.] **38** Cb
Viseu [Port.] **9** ABb
Vişeu de Sus **6** Gc
Vishakhapatnam **15** Ch
Viso, Mont– (mt.) **10** Ab
Vistula (riv.) **5** Gb
Vit (riv.) **11** Fb
Vitebsk **13** Cd
Viterbo **10** Dc
Viti Levu (i.) **27** Dc
Vitim (riv.) **14** Ed
Vitória **39** DEb
Vitoria **9** Da
Vitória da Conquista **39** Da
Vitoša (mt.) **11** Eb
Vitré **8** Cc
Vitry-le-François **8** EFc
Vittel **8** FGc
Vittorio Veneto **10** Dab
Vityaz I Depth **27** Cb
Vityaz II Depth **28** Ad
Vityaz III Depth **28** Ad
Vivero **9** Ba
Vize **11** GHc
Vizianagaram **20** FGe
Vižnica **6** Gb
Vjatka (Kirov) **13** Dd
Vjatskije Poljany **12** GHb
Vjazemski **14** Ge
Vjazma **12** Db
Vjazniki **12** Fb
Vjedinenija, ostrov– **13** GHb
Vjosa (riv.) **11** CDc
Vladikavkaz (Ordžonikidze) **13** De
Vladimir **13** CDd
Vladimirski Tupik **12** Db
Vladimir-Volynski **5** Jc
Vladivostok **14** Ge
Vlašić (mt.) **6** Cd
Vlissingen **5** Bc
Vltava → Moldau (riv.) **5** Ed
Vogelsberg (mt.) **5** Bc
Voghera **10** Bb
Voi **26** Cb
Voinijama **24** ABd
Vóïon (mts.) **11** Dc
Voiron **8** Fe
Vóïviís, Limni– **11** Ed
Vojvodina (phys. reg.) **6** DEd
Volcano Islands **27** Ca
Volčansk **12** IJab
Volda **4** Ac
Volga (riv.) **13** Dd
Volgo-Baltijski vodny put imeni V.I. Lenina **12** Eab
Volgodonsk **12** Fd
Volgo-Donskoj sudohodny kanal imeni V.I. Lenin **12** Fd
Volgograd **3** Hc
Volgogradskoje vodohranilišče **12** Gcd
Volhov (riv.) **12** Db
Volhov **13** Gd
Volinskaja vozvyšennost (phys. reg.) **6** GHa
Volissós **11** Fd
Völkermarkt **10** Ea
Völklingen **5** Ad
Volkovysk **12** Bc
Volnovaha **12** Ed
Vologda **13** CDd
Vólos **11** Ed
Volsk **13** Dd
Volta, Lake– **24** Bd
Volta Redonda **39** Db
Volterra **10** Cc
Volturino, Monte– **10** Ed
Volturno (riv.) **10** Ed
Vólvi, Limni– **11** Ec
Volžsk **12** Gb
Volžski **13** De
Vopnafjördur **4** map no.1
Vorarlberg (reg.) **5** BCe
Vordingborg **5** Ca
Vórios Evvoïkós, Kólpos– **11** Ed
Vorkuta **13** EFc
Vorogovo **14** BCc
Voronež **13** CDd
Vorošilovgrad → Lugansk **13** CDe
Vörts järv **4** Fd
Võru **4** Fd
Vosges (mts.) **8** Gcd
Voss **4** Ac
Vostok **42** grid square no.4
Vostok Island **28** Bc
Votkinsk **13** Ed
Voúxa, Ákra– **11** Ef
Vouziers **8** Fc
Voznesensk **12** Dd
Vraca **11** Eb
Vranica (mt.) **6** CDde
Vranje **11** Db
Vrbas **6** DEd
Vrbas (riv.) **6** Cd
Vršac **6** Ed
Vryburg **26** Bd
Vsetín **5** FGd
Vukovar **6** Dd
Vulcan **6** Fd
Vulcano (i.) **10** Ee
Vúlture, Monte– **10** Ed
Vung Tau **19** Ef
Vuotso **4** FGa
Vyborg **13** BCc
Vyčegda (riv.) **13** Ec
Vyksa **12** Fb
Vyšni Voloček **13** Cd
Vysokogorny **14** GHde
Vysokoje **5** Ib
Vytegra **3** Ga

W

Wāāt Salīmah **25** Db
Wabe Shebele (riv.) **25** Ed
Wabowden **31** Fc
Wąbrzeżno **5** Gb
Wachussett Seamount **28** Bd

Yushan (mt.) **16** Ff
Yutian **20** Fa
Yuyao **16** Fde
Yvetot **8** Dc
Yzeure **8** Ed

Z

Zabajkalsk **14** Ede
Zabib **21** Cg
Zābol **21** Gc
Zabrze **5** Gc
Zacapa **35** Bb
Zacatecas **34** Bb
Zadar **6** Bd
Zafir, Az- **21** Cef
Zafra **9** Bc
Żagań **5** Ec
Zagora **24** Ba
Zagorsk → Sergiev Posad **13** Cd
Zagreb **6** Bd
Zagros Mountains **21** DEc
Zagyva (riv.) **6** Dc
Zāhedān **21** FGd
Zaḩlah **22** EFef
Ẓahrān, Aẓ- **21** DEd
Zaïre (riv.) **26** Ab
Zaire (Ind. St.) **23** DEf
Zaïre → Lualaba (riv.) **26** Bb
Zaječar **6** EFe
Zajsan **13** He
Zajsan, ozero- **13** He
Zakopane **5** Gd
Zalaegerszeg **6** Cc
Zalău **6** Fc
Zaleščiki **6** GHb
Zalṭan **24** DEb
Zambezi (riv.) **26** Cc
Zambezi **26** Bc
Zambia (Ind. St.) **23** EFfg
Zamboanga **18** Fc
Zambrów **5** Ib
Zamora **9** BCb
Zamora de Hidalgo **34** Bbc
Zamosč **5** Ic
Žanatas **13** FGe
Záncara (riv.) **9** Dc
Zanjān **21** Db
Žannetty, ostrov- **14** IJb
Zante (i.) **11** De
Zante **11** De
Zanthus **29** Ce
Zanzibar **23** FGf
Zaoqing **16** Df
Zapadna Morava **6** Ee
Zapala **39** ABc
Zaporožje **13** Ce
Zaqāzīq, Az- **25** Dab
Zara **22** Fc
Zarasai **4** Fe
Zárate **39** Cc
Zaraza **37** Cb
Zard Kūh (mt.) **21** DEc
Zarghunshahr **20** Cb
Zaria **24** Cc
Zarkovski **12** Db
Zarqā, Az- **22** Ff
Zarqa, El- **22** CDg
Żary **5** Ec
Zarzaïtine **24** CDb
Zaskar Mountains **20** EFb
Žaškov **6** IJb
Žatec **5** Dc
Zavidovići **6** Dd
Zavitinsk **14** FGd
Zavolžje **12** Fb
Zavolžsk **12** Fb
Zawi **23** EFg
Zawīlah **24** Db
Zbaraž **6** GHb
Zbąszyń **5** EFb
Zborov **6** Gb
Zbruč (riv.) **6** Hb
Ždanov → Mariupol **12** DEd
Žd'ar nad Sázavou **5** EFd
Zdolbunov **6** Ha
Zduńska Wola **5** Gc
Zeehan **29** map no.1
Zefat **22** Ef
Zeitz **5** Dc
Zeja **14** Fd
Zeja (riv.) **14** Fd
Zélaf **22** Ff
Želanija, mys- **13** FGb
Zelenoborski **4** GHb
Zelenodolsk **12** GHb
Zelenogorsk **4** Gc
Želenogorsk-Ilimski **14** Dd
Zelenogradsk **4** Ee
Zelenyi (i.) **17** Jc
Železnogorsk **12** DEc
Želtyje Vody **12** Dd
Zémio **25** Cd
Zemun, Belgrade- **6** Ed
Zenica **6** CDd
Zeravšan (riv.) **13** Ff
Zernograd **12** Fd
Zézere (riv.) **9** Ac
Žezkazgan (Džezkazgan) **13** Fe
Zgierz **5** Gc
Zgorzelec **5** Ec
Zhangguangcai Ling (mts.) **17** IJbc
Zhangjiakou **16** DEb
Zhangye **16** Bc
Zhangzhou **16** Ef
Zhanjiang **15** Dgh
Zhaodong **16** FGa
Zhaotong **16** Be
Zhejiang (prov.) **16** EFe
Zhengzhou **15** Df
Zhenhai **16** Fde
Zhenjiang **16** EFd
Zhenyuan **16** Ce
Zhijiang **16** Ce
Zhob (riv.) **20** Cb
Zhongba **15** Cfg
Zhongwei **16** BCc
Zhongxian **16** Cd
Zhoushan Qundao **16** Fde
Zhucheng **16** EFc
Zhumadian **16** Dd
Zhuolu **16** DEb
Zhuzhou **16** De
Žiar-nad Hronom **5** Gd
Ẓibā' **21** Bd
Zibo **16** Ec
Ziel, Mount- **29** Ec
Zielona Góra **5** Ebc
Ziftá **22** Cg
Žigansk **14** EFc
Zigong **16** Be
Ziguinchor **24** Ac
Žigulevsk **12** Gc
Zihuatanejo **34** Bc
Zile **22** Eb
Zilfi, Az- **21** CDd
Žilina **5** Gd
Zillah **24** Db
Zima **14** Dd
Zimbabwe (r.) **26** Cd
Zimbabwe (Ind. St.) **23** EFgh
Zimnicea **6** Ge
Zinder **24** Cc
Zipaquirá **37** Bb
Žirje (i.) **6** Be
Žirnovsk **12** FGc
Ziro **19** Bc
Žitny Ostrov (phys. reg.) **5** Fde
Žitomir **13** Bd
Zittau **5** Ec
Zlatica **11** EFb
Zlatograd **11** Fc
Zlatoust **13** Ed
Zlatoustovsk **14** Gd
Zlín **5** Fd
Žlobin **12** CDc
Złocieniec **5** Fb
Złotoryja **5** EFc
Złotów **5** Fb
Zmeiny, ostrov- **12** Dd
Žmerinka **6** HIb
Znamenka **12** Dd
Znojmo **5** EFd
Žohova, ostrov- **14** Ib
Zoločev **6** Gb
Zolotonoša **12** Dd
Zomba **26** Cc
Zonguldak **22** Cb
Zorritos **37** Ac
Zouar **25** Bbc
Zouîrât **24** Ab
Zrenjanin **6** Ed
Zudañez **39** Ba
Ẓufār (phys. reg.) **21** EFf
Zug **5** Be
Zugspitze (mt.) **5** Ce
Zújar (riv.) **9** Cc
Zujevka **12** Hb
Žukovka **12** Dc
Zumba **37** Bc
Zumbo **26** Cc
Zunyi **16** Ce
Županja **6** Dd
Zürich **5** Be
Zürichsee **5** Be
Zuwārah **24** Da
Zvishavane **26** BCd
Zvolen **5** Gd
Zvornik **6** Dd
Zwickau **5** Dc
Zwiesel **5** Dd
Zwolle **8** Ga
Żyradów **5** Hbc
Zyrjanka **14** HIc
Zyrjanovsk **13** He
Żywiec **5** Gd